Imperial Characters

The Bucknell Studies in Eighteenth-Century Literature and Culture

General Editor: Greg Clingham, *Bucknell University*

Advisory Board: Paul K. Alkon, *University of Southern California*
Chloe Chard, *Independent Scholar*
Clement Hawes, *The Pennsylvania State University*
Robert Markley, *University of Illinois at Urbana-Champaign*
Jessica Munns, *University of Denver*
Cedric D. Reverand II, *University of Wyoming*
Janet Todd, *University of Aberdeen*

The Bucknell Studies in Eighteenth-Century Literature and Culture aims to publish challenging, new eighteenth-century scholarship. Of particular interest is critical, historical, and interdisciplinary work that is interestingly and intelligently theorized, and that broadens and refines the conception of the field. At the same time, the series remains open to all theoretical perspectives and different kinds of scholarship. While the focus of the series is the literature, history, arts, and culture (including art, architecture, music, travel, and history of science, medicine, and law) of the long eighteenth century in Britain and Europe, the series is also interested in scholarship that establishes relationships with other geographies, literature, and cultures for the period 1660–1830.

Recent Titles in This Series

Chris Mounsey and Caroline Gonda, eds., *Queer People:*
Negotiations and Expressions of Homosexuality, 1700–1800
Susan Manning and Peter France, *Enlightenment and Emancipation*
Evan Gottlieb, *Feeling British: Sympathy and National Identity in*
Scottish and English Writing, 1707–1832
Roland Racevskis, *Tragic Passages: Jean Racine's Art of the Threshold*
Lesley H. Walker, *A Mother's Love: Crafting Feminine Virtue in Enlightenment France*
Rori Bloom, *Man of Quality, Man of Letters: The Abbé Prévost between Novel and Newspaper*
Barton Swaim, *Scottish Men of Letters and the New Public Sphere, 1802–1854*
Anthony Krupp, *Reason's Children: Childhood in Early Modern Philosophy*
David Collings, *Monstrous Society: Reciprocity, Discipline,*
and the Political Uncanny, c. 1780–1848
Stephen Bygrave, *Uses of Education: Readings in Enlightenment in England*
Adrienne Ward, *Pagodas in Play: China on the Eighteenth-Century Italian Opera Stage*
Miriam Wallace, *Revolutionary Subjects in the English "Jacobin" Novel*
Chantel M. Lavoie, *Collecting Women: Poetry and Lives, 1700–1780*
Raymond F. Hilliard, *Ritual Violence and the Maternal in the British Novel, 1740–1820*
Tara Ghoshal Wallace, *Imperial Characters: Home and*
Periphery in Eighteenth-Century Literature

http://www.bucknell.edu/universitypress/

Imperial Characters

Home and Periphery
in Eighteenth-Century Literature

Tara Ghoshal Wallace

Lewisburg
Bucknell University Press

Associated University Presses
2010 Eastpark Boulevard
Cranbury, NJ 08512

The paper used in this publication meets the requirements of the American National Standard for Permanence of Paper for Printed Library Materials Z39.48-1984.

Library of Congress Cataloging-in-Publication Data

Wallace, Tara Ghoshal, 1952–
   Imperial characters : home and periphery in eighteenth-century literature / Tara Ghoshal Wallace.
       p.   cm.
   Includes bibliographical references and index.
   ISBN 978-0-8387-5740-6 (alk. paper)
   1. English literature—18th century—History and criticism.   2. Imperialism in literature.   3. National characteristics, British, in literature.   4. Great Britain—In literature.   5. Colonies in literature.   I. Title
   PR448.I52W36   2010
   820.9′3581—dc22   2009039929

To Astra, who embodies the best of the two empires

Contents

Preface

SOMETIME AROUND 1960, A BRAND-NEW PUBLIC LIBRARY OPENED IN
the Alipore district of Calcutta. Its cleanliness, brightness, and silence
provided a welcome respite from the noise and dirt that surrounded
even those of us who lived in the "good" parts of town, and it became a
favorite destination for my family. Having gone through the Enid Bly-
ton books housed in the children's section of that library, I wandered
over to the adult shelves, where I came upon the novels of Jane Austen.
It is not too much of an exaggeration to say that my early exposure to
those illustrated Victorian editions of Austen decided the course of my
professional life. When, more than three decades later, I wrote my book
on Austen, it was a labor of love as well as the fulfillment of a childhood
ambition. And it was decidedly the product of a postcolonial education.

This book too arises from those early years of reading Austen in Calcutta. Although professional training and practice have produced the
particular version of eighteenth-century studies worked out here, the
project also represents the culmination of a personal narrative that
could be described as postcolonial hybridity, one that has taken me
from Calcutta to Washington D.C., with a formative stopover in Toronto—all former possessions of imperial Britain, occupying very different but significantly overlapping positions in a postcolonial world. I
think it would be fair to say that this book, more than my earlier work,
articulates a global vision that has always been part of my life. It is a
vision that prevents me from inhabiting resentful or victimized postco-
loniality while it accommodates and assimilates postcolonial critiques of
imperial practices. As the daughter of an Oxford-educated ICS officer
who served the British Raj before joining the government of independent India, I am inevitably the (privileged) product of a colonial culture; as the granddaughter of the historian U. N. Ghoshal, author of
many books on ancient Indian culture and government, I am equally
aware of the value of the world that colonial culture superseded.

Thomas Babington Macaulay's 1835 "Minute" on Indian education
has frequently been a target for postcolonial scorn. The idea of educating the colonized to admire and assimilate the language and values of

the colonizer is, on the face of it, oppressive. And certainly, the much-quoted plan "to form . . . a class of persons, Indian in blood and colour, but English in taste, in opinions, in morals, and in intellect" evinces an arrogant will to power offensive to modern sensibilities. But Macaulay's pragmatic imperialism emerges in part from an earnest belief that the English language "abounds with works of imagination not inferior to the noblest which Greece has bequeathed to us . . . with just and lively representations of human life and human nature." Such chauvinism may be both narrow-minded and insulting, but in its echo of Austen's celebration of novels "in which the greatest powers of the mind are displayed, in which the most thorough knowledge of human nature, the happiest delineation of its varieties, the liveliest effusions of wit and humour are conveyed to the world in the best chosen language," Macaulay's "Minute" also articulates a sincere desire to disseminate what he considers the highest achievements in textual production. We who have committed a lifetime to teaching and writing about these very texts cannot entirely dismiss his pride in British literature.

This book on imperial characters and contradictions completes, to some extent, my long trajectory from Alipore to academic life in Washington D.C. In it, I hope to demonstrate that the British education that Macaulay and Governor General Bentnick imposed on Indian subjects not only produced careful readers of British literature, but also a cohort of global citizens who belie the dichotomy between home and periphery.

Acknowledgments

A BOOK SO LONG IN THE MAKING ACCRUES TO ITSELF DEBTS THAT would constitute a chapter if properly narrated. I beg the forgiveness and indulgence of those who turn up in a list rather than in the fully articulated thanks they really deserve. Two people, however, require special acknowledgment. Jane Millgate has always served as my (unattainable) model for authentic scholarship, inspired teaching, and committed mentorship; her unerring intellectual and professional guidance have been truly formative, from the first course I took with her as a new graduate student to her careful reading of every word of this manuscript. The other essential maker of this book is my brother Animesh Ghoshal, who may be an economics professor by day but clearly leads a double life as a literary scholar. His wide and deep reading manifested itself not only in his helpful commentary on my chapters and many hours of productive discussion about imperial culture, but also in the range of materials to which he directed me. His intellectual range never ceases to amaze.

Bucknell University Press is a writer's dream because Greg Clingham is the kind of editor whose enthusiasm matches his scholarly acumen. The anonymous readers he chose read closely and suggested wisely—I am deeply grateful for their help in revising the manuscript. Christine Retz at Associated University Presses responded to every query patiently and warmly, and Loretta Carlson provided the kind of meticulous copy-editing that makes an author both grateful and humble. The work of getting the manuscript ready was much lightened by the help of the team at the press.

Portions of this book appeared in earlier forms, and I want to thank the publishers for permission to reprint versions of articles. The section on Smollett first appeared as " 'About savages and the awfulness of America': Colonial Corruptions in *Humphry Clinker*" in *Eighteenth-Century Fiction* 18.2; a piece of chapter 3 was published in *Enlightening Romanticism, Romancing the Enlightenment* (Ashgate 2009) as "Reading the Metropole: Elizabeth Hamilton's *Translations of the Letters of a Hindoo Rajah*"; an early version of the Scott chapter was published in *European*

Romantic Review 13.3 (see http://www.informaworld.com). I am grateful to Jacqueline Langille, Ann Donahue, and Regina Hewitt for their responsiveness to permission requests.

I have benefited from extraordinarily acute readers and interlocutors: Paula Backsheider, Margaret Ann Doody, Ian Duncan, Jonathan Lamb, Jim Maddox, Carla Peterson, John Richetti, and Claire Sponsler have all generously contributed their time and scholarly knowledge to improve my work, whether by reading chapters or by responding to conference papers. I thank my colleagues at George Washington University, especially Marshall Alcorn, who has spent patient years educating me on psychoanalytic criticism, and Jonathan Gil Harris, whose intellectual and personal friendship I cherish. Maria Frawley, David Grier, Tony Lopez, Michael Moses, Judith Plotz, Ann Romines, and Margaret Soltan have listened carefully and contributed significantly to my thinking about imperial Britain. My chairs Jeffrey Jerome Cohen and Faye Moskowitz and my deans William Frawley and Marguerite Barratt gave me the gift of time at crucial junctures. I thank them for their consideration and their faith in this project.

My students contribute more than they know. Magali Amalis-Tesereia, Taylor Asen, Lisa Francavilla, Samuel Munford, Kathy Rooney, Katie Sagal, and Sarah Whittemore are only the most recent undergraduates who helped me think more clearly about the issues I raised in class. Among my wonderfully stimulating graduate students, I especially thank Sara Davis, Julie Donovan, Nedda Mehdizadeh, Pat Ortmayer, and Lauren Shababb; engaging with their projects sharpened my own thinking about the long eighteenth century. Jen Butts and Marilena Zackheos were efficient and careful research assistants; I could not have produced this book without their help.

When this book came to fruition, it was welcomed with what I now know to be characteristic warmth by my new decanal colleagues: Peg Barratt, Dan Cronin, Paul Duff, Roy Guenther, Katherine Keller, Randy Packer, and Geralyn Schulz constitute a group of committed scholars who happen to be talented administrators. The staff I work with enables me to retain my scholarly life, and I am particularly grateful to the hyper-efficiency and exemplary work ethic of Iva Beatty, Jeanne Fiander, and Jamie Palumbo.

I am fortunate in claiming as personal friends some of the smartest people on the planet. My Mawrter friends keep me afloat with their acute intelligence and loving support: D'Vera Cohn, Emie Diener, Judy Kimball, and Tina Potter remain my anchors and my playmates, as do my old pals Annette and Esther Kronstadt. I count on Kate Chisolm,

Lucy Maddox, Madhavi Menon, and Bridget Orr for their affection and astute literary insights. Gail Paster simply defines loyal friendship as well as stellar scholarship. My cousin Deborah Douglas knows that she has been my rock and my wings, both as a writer and as a constant friend. The Washington Douglases, the Philadelphia Flemings, and the Florida Wallaces have taught me that family ties go far beyond blood. My sisters, Raka Gutzeit and Barbara Ghoshal, keep me steady. Gordon Turnbull has lived with this book as long as I have and believed in it through my crises of confidence. Although he wisely evaded the dangers of being my reader, his brilliant insights and deep knowledge of eighteenth-century culture seeped into all my thinking about this project; it is so much richer for his pervasive influence. My daughter Astra remains the one person in whose presence I can write diligently and the one person who unfailingly provides rollicking distraction when I don't want to work. To her wisdom and her mirth I owe more than I can say . . . except in loving dedication.

Imperial Characters

Introduction. Roaming the Globe: Aphra Behn's *Oroonoko* and Robert Louis Stevenson's *Master of Ballantrae*

THE MASTER OF BALLANTRAE ENDS WITH A SCENE BOTH CLIMACTICALLY and climatologically chilling. In the frozen expanses of northern New York, a party consisting of the Scottish Lord Henry Durie and his steward MacKellar, the English diplomat Sir William Johnson, the colonial rogue Mountain, and their Mohawk guides come upon the Hindu Secundra Dass frantically digging up the body of his master James Durie. There, in the "dreadful solitude" of "this savage country,"[1] this ill-assorted and mutually suspicious band witnesses the heart-stopping resurrection of the Master—literally heart-stopping in the case of Henry, who falls dead as his brother comes to momentary life. Stevenson himself expressed abashed dissatisfaction with his melodramatic ending; in January 1888, he wrote to Henry James that "the devil and Saranac suggested this *dénouement*. . . . the third supposed death and the manner of the third reappearance is steep; steep, sir. It is even very steep, and I fear it shames the honest stuff so far."[2] In fact, this shamefully over-the-top climax remains one of the most memorable scenes Stevenson wrote, and I fully concur with J. R. Hammond's admiring assessment: "A further instance of Stevenson's descriptive powers is the unforgettable (almost ghoulish) scene at the final denouement in which it is revealed that the Master of Ballantrae has been buried alive. . . . Such a passage, once read, cannot be erased from the memory."[3] Not only does the scene powerfully evoke the ominous desolation of landscape and lives, but it also telescopes and freezes the kinetic movements of a restless text; as Stevenson put it, "the scene of that romance is Scotland—the States— Scotland—India—Scotland—and the States again; so it jumps like a flea."[4]

The multiple sites represent, of course, the two principal peripheries and one internally colonized site of the British empire in the 1760s, and Stevenson's text enacts, however belatedly, the opportunities, disruptions, and dangers of imperial adventurism during the eighteenth century.[5] In the final scene, the disparate elements of Britain's imperial reach come together, not to point to potential union but to point up irreconcilable incongruities. In this vivid (and lurid) picture of the South Asian feverishly working to reanimate the Scottish body endangered by the icy climate of North America, in Secundra's final articulation of failure—"good way in India, no good here" (218)—we note the belated recognition of difference that cannot be resolved by military, political, or ideological manipulations.[6]

My project, too, traces the effects of British adventuring in "the States—Scotland—India," and my inclusion of texts about both America and India expresses tacit agreement with David Armitage's contention that "the differences between the maritime, commercial colonies of settlement in North America and the military, territorial colonies of conquest in India have been crudely overdrawn."[7] This book investigates a range of literary responses to both sets of imperial excursions, highlighting how consistently English and Scottish writers of the period articulate the potential dangers of imperial ambition. The texts I consider occupy diverse and sometimes discordant political positions, but they all rehearse the risks incurred in the course of imperial expansion, which endangers not only the lives of those on the front lines, but also cherished national traditions and the best in national character. They anticipate what Lawrence James sees as British discomfort with imperial power in the wake of a mid-nineteenth-century slave rebellion in Jamaica: "There existed in Liberal, Nonconformist and free trade circles a fear that the empire engendered belligerent nationalism and militarism, which undermined what they saw as Britain's real national virtues, thrift and industriousness."[8] These texts provide a corrective to the kind of postcolonial criticism that posits collusion between literary text and imperial agenda and complicate Edward Said's assertion that "if there was collateral resistance to the notion of an imperial mission, there was not much support for that resistance in the main departments of cultural thought."[9] In fact, I argue, popular and authoritative British writers from Alexander Pope to Walter Scott warn that imperial power poses grave social and moral dangers for the metropole. If at times these warnings come in the shape of fear of contagion from colonial possessions (savagery from America, lethargy and disease from Asia), such xenophobia coexists with a recognition that European imperial values and practices taint both colonizer and colonized.

This introductory chapter looks at two texts on the chronological peripheries of my project: Aphra Behn's *Oroonoko* (1688), so often hailed

as a "first"—first abolitionist text, first feminist text—also serves here
as a first novelistic articulation of many of the imperial paradoxes that
will vex later writers, while Stevenson's *Master of Ballantrae* (1888–89)
provides a kind of analeptic vision of Britain's imperial reach in the
eighteenth century, a reach that includes four continents and multiple
cultures.[10] We see in Behn's narrative the interpenetration of cultures
that exercises later writers like Smollett and Scott. Oroonoko may be a
romanticized and Europeanized African—Laura Brown calls him "an
absurdity generated by the desire for an intimate identification with the
'royal slave'"[11]—but Behn gestures toward a more complex sociohistor-
ical analysis when she attributes his refinement to a French tutor and
his cosmopolitanism to the European presence in Africa: "He lov'd . . .
to see all the *English* Gentlemen that traded thither; and did not only
learn their Language, but that of the *Spaniards* also, with whom he
traded afterwards for Slaves."[12] In Behn's text, slave traders constitute
a kind of traveling professariat, so knowledgeable and cultured that
even the perfidious English Captain who kidnaps Oroonoko "seem'd
rather never to have been bred out of a Court, than almost all his Life
at Sea" (62). Oroonoko's own multilingualism marks him as a superior
being, and, interestingly, aligns him with successful colonists like Defoe's Colonel Jack, whose fluent Spanish (and fluid allegiances) saves
him from being sent to the Peruvian mines: "I got better Quarter among
them . . . much of it owing to my speaking *Spanish,* and to my telling
them how I had fought on so many Occasions in the Quarrel of his
Catholic Majesty, in *Italy..*" Similarly, when the British consolidate their
power in India, it becomes the colonizer's duty to learn native languages. Elizabeth Hamilton bemoans the personal circumstances (the
death of her brother Charles) that prevented her from acquiring "a
competent knowledge of the language" of Oriental texts and constructs
the idealized Englishman Percy, who is a *"perfect master"* of Persian, Ar-
abic, "and the different dialects of Hindostan." And Adam Hartley, in
Scott's *Surgeon's Daughter,* makes "the Oriental languages his study, in
order to hold communication with his patients," a study that eventually
enables him to rescue Menie Grey.[13]

On the other hand, linguistic and other forms of transculturation
have a dark side too. While the Fisherman in *Oroonoko* provides useful
mediation because he has "by long Living there, become a perfect *Indian*
in Colour" (81) as well as language, Lismahago's transculturation produces acute anxiety in *Humphry Clinker,* and Robert Bage's hero, although he admires the sturdy energy of the native Americans among
whom he has lived, makes a point of privileging his European literary

tastes. By the time Stevenson writes about nativized Europeans, they have become—like the trader Chew, "needy, dissolute, and . . . in some disgrace with his family" (54) or the murderous Mountain, who "had not only lived and hunted, but fought and earned some reputation, with the savages" (195)—the dregs of European society. Captain Teach's campy performance as satanic pirate (which anticipates Johnny Depp's antic Jack Sparrow) elicits from Colonel Burke a distasteful dismissal that aligns Teach with Amerindian practices: "Presently he comes on deck, a perfect figure of fun . . . chewing bits of glass so that the blood ran down his chin, and brandishing a dirk. I do not know if he had taken these manners from the Indians of America, where he was a native" (40). Benign assimilation, in other words, has given way to the taint of the savage; unlike Hermsprong, who profits both physically and morally from having spent his youth with Amerindians "whose very sports are athletic; and calculated to render man robust, and inure him to labour and fatigue,"[14] Stevenson's nativized characters exhibit only the repulsive traits of the "primitive," At the other end of the empire, too, transculturation proves to be double-edged, since Hartley's admirable acquisition of native customs is juxtaposed with the criminal duplicities of the nativized Richard Middlemas. Linguistic adaptation may allow Hartley to serve Indian patients, but it also enables Richard Middlemas and Adela Montreville to conspire against British *and* Indian rulers. James Durie's acquisition of Hindi and Secundra Dass's hidden knowledge of English help them outmaneuver both those who would escape their clutches and those who plot kill them, and in Stevenson's text, multilingualism is linked to conspiracy, surveillance, and murder. As the Master and his would-be killers pass into the wilderness of America, the languages of the Eastern empire become part of their mutual homicidal plotting as well as a sign of a shady past: "If Secundra Dass knew and concealed his knowledge of English, Harris was a proficient in several of the tongues of India, and as his career in that part of the world had been a great deal worse than profligate, he had not thought proper to remark upon the circumstance" (196). The linguistic proficiency that had signified aristocratic cosmopolitanism in Oroonoko and conscientious colonial education in Percy and Hartley has degenerated into becoming a tool for "the dregs of colonial rascality" (197). Both Scott and Stevenson complicate, intensify, and invert Homi Bhabha's famous formulation that "mimicry is, thus the sign of double articulation; a complex strategy of reform, regulation and discipline, which 'appropriates' the Other as it visualizes power."[15] While Dass depends on his secret appropriation of the colonists' language to exert covert power over the Master's enemies, Middlemas and Harris deploy their linguistic mimicry to serve their criminal agendas.

Degeneracy of character coexists with imperial power even in Behn's early text. The little colony of British settlers in Suriname exhibits all the corrupt traits made hyperbolically manifest in Stevenson's band of criminals. As Laura Rosenthal says of Behn's colonials, "While ostensibly still under the authority of their king, in this remote location a group of ambitious, dishonourable, and violent men run the colony."[16] Like the English slave-trader, they deceive and conspire against the noble hero, and even the sympathetic narrator participates in the system of surveillance designed to contain him: "I neither thought it convenient to trust him much of our View, nor did the country who fear'd him; but with one accord it was advis'd to treat him Fairly, and oblige him to remain within such a compass, and that he shou'd be permitted, as seldom as cou'd be, to go up to the Plantations of the Negroes; or, if he did, to be accompany'd by some that shou'd be rather in appearance Attendants than Spys." Oroonoko, temporarily lulled by seeming marks of respect from this nation of spies, soon takes their moral measure. Exhorting his fellow Africans to rebellion, he characterizes the slaveowners as *"Rogues, Runagades, that have abandon'd their own Countries, for Rapin, Murders, Thefts and Villainies . . . such a degenerate Race, who have no one Humane Vertue left, to distinguish 'em from the vilest Creatures"* (86). He invokes, of course, those transported felons who, in Defoe's novels, achieve prosperous respectability in the colonies: as Moll Flanders's mother says, "many a *Newgate* Bird becomes a Great Man."[17] I will argue in chapter 2 that Defoe himself manifests a far more complex attitude toward colonial settlers than this quotation would imply, but Behn's narrator is unequivocal in her contempt, asserting that the Governor's Council "consisted of such notorious Villains as *Newgate* never transported; and possibly originally were such, who understood neither the Laws of *God* or *Man*" (93). Drunken, cowardly, perfidious, and violent, these imperial rulers prefigure the kind of moral coarseness connected to imperial power even in such seemingly celebratory poems as Pope's *Windsor Forest* and Thomson's *Seasons*, and they certainly alert readers to the consequences of delegating colonial authority to those who embody the very worst British characters. Edmund Burke's diatribes against rapacious colonists on the Indian subcontinent (see chapter 4) are anticipated in Behn's description of Governor William Byam, "whose Character is not fit to be mention'd with the worst of the Slaves" (88–89).

When Mackellar expresses his reluctant pity for James Durie's abject position in Albany, the Master scorns his sympathy with a speech that neatly combines the seemingly contradictory theories of imperial psychology as put forward by Diane Simmons and John Kucich. Simmons, in *The Narcissism of Empire*, argues that "subject peoples . . . could be compelled in a variety of ways to reflect back to the imperialist a grandiose self-image," while Kucich, in *Imperial Masochism*, points out that "British imperialism also generated a remarkable preoccupation with suffering" and that "ideologically driven glorifications of suffering share an affinity with masochistic fantasy and offer possibilities for transforming painful experience into omnipotent delusion."[18] For the Master, all past failures can be projected on to external events so that he can retain his sense of self as infinitely potent:

> My life has been a series of unmerited cast-backs. That fool, Prince Charlie, mismanaged a most promising affair: there fell my first fortune. In Paris I had my foot once more high up on the ladder . . . a letter came to the wrong hand, and I was bare again. A third time I found my opportunity; I built up a place for myself in India with an infinite patience; and then Clive came, my rajah was swallowed up, and I escaped out of the convulsion, like another Æneas, with Secundra Dass upon my back. Three times I have had my hand upon the highest station: and I am not yet three-and-forty. I know the world as few men know it when they come to die — Court and camp, the East and the West; I know where to go, I see a thousand openings. I am now at the height of my resources. (180)

James's account of his own history not only preserves his grandiose delusions, but also conveniently elides the bad character he so clearly manifests in his early years in Scotland. His financial and sexual excesses, his cruel contempt for Henry, and his systematic manipulation of a doting father all serve as auguries for his conduct in the wider world. Nevertheless, the global reach of eighteenth-century Europe offers particular opportunities for the kind of criminal double-dealing at which he excels. Indeed, James's fantasies of a powerful self are linguistically figured through images of imperial control: "Had I been the least petty chieftain in the Highlands, had I been the least king of naked negroes in the African desert, my people would have adored me. . . . I was born for a good tyrant! Ask Secundra Dass; he will tell you that I treat him like a son. . . . I have a kingly nature: there is my loss!" (167). Robert Kiely attributes James's warped "heroism" to the diminished world he inhabits, one in which "all the old heroic virtues dwindle into cowardice and vice. . . . the protagonist seems a throwback from an older, more heroic time, who by an accident of birth has been cast into a tribe of pygmies. . . . its little members taint and corrupt his ancient virility with their own meanness."[19] It seems to me, however, that the Master participates fully in the imperial psychology of his time, one that enables him to imagine himself as infinitely potent and entitled to all the spoils that imperial adventures make available.

G. K. Chesterton puts the Duries' domestic tragedy in a global context when he compares them to Oedipus and Orestes but adds that these classical heroes "did not wash their bloody linen in public; least of all did they wash it in all the seven seas of the British Empire. But the appearance of the Master first in India and then in America has almost the suggestion of the Prince of Wales on an imperial tour."[20] Indeed, James's peripatetic ambition, like Henry's quest for refuge, depends entirely on the new geography of imperial Britain: European settlements allow James and Captain Burke to survive their first sojourn in America, and European presence in India offers a haven for James when he must flee both Scotland and France. In other words, imperial expansion provides to James the world to bustle in.

In *Oroonoko*, we see the effects of conferring power on those who, like James Durie, "understood neither the Laws of *God* or *Man;* and had no sort of Principles" (*MB* 93). So appalling are Byam and his henchman Banister—a wild Irishman, "a Fellow of absolute Barbarity, and fit to execute any Villainy" (99)—that good colonists like John Trefry and Colonel Martin will have nothing to do with them. Moreover, as these despicable imperial masters accrue power in the New World, they constitute a challenge to both traditional colonists and metropolitan authority. Indeed, as Joanna Lipking points out, "the colonists [in Suriname] are divided, an aggressive new civil administration in conflict with recalcitrant gentleman landholders."[21] Trefry attempts to protect Oroonoko by insisting that Byam has no authority on his lord's plantation, "and that *Parham* was as much exempt from the Law as *White-hall*" because the lord "represented the King's Person . . . and though his Lord were absent in Person, his Power was still in Being there" (94). Trefry asserts, in other words, royal power over the colonial power of the lieutenant governor. Byam, however, not only finds a way to trick the representative of central authority, but also dares to invade and raid "royal" property: Banister "came up to *Parham,* and forcibly took *Caesar*" (99). Trefry and the narrator may resist the (mis)rule of "rude and wild . . . Rabble" and "inhumane Justices" (99), but they cannot effectively counter this new colonial power.

The unstable, even contingent, nature of colonial loyalties to the home government occupies a number of texts considered in this book.

As I will argue in chapter 2, Defoe's two American novels articulate acute anxiety about stirrings of independence on the part of transplanted Britons. The glorified status of plantation owners in America— Colonel Jack expresses awe of his master's great hall, "where he sat in a Seat like a Lord Judge upon the Bench, or a Petty King upon his Throne" (122)—posited a degree of wealth and autonomy that constituted a danger to central authority. J. H. Elliott cites the Earl of Sandwich, who "prophesied in 1671 that within twenty years New Englanders would be 'mighty rich and powerful and not at all careful of their dependence upon old England,'" and adds that "By the 1750s there was a growing belief in Whitehall that, unless discipline were soon applied, colonies that had grown so rich and populous would choose the path of separation." Nicholas B. Dirks, too, notes the danger of colonial success: "One of the many lessons of America for England was the need to control the circulation of its own people. Otherwise they would first claim to be more English than the English . . . then they would siphon off the potential profits of empire, and finally they would declare independence."[22] Where Behn and Defoe gesture toward a potential danger, Smollett, writing in the gap between the Seven Years' War and American independence, wants both to stem the tide of emigration and to castigate the arrogance of nouveau riche imperialists, thus implicitly advising disengagement from imperial activities. At the end of the eighteenth century, the new Republic elicits contradictory responses from two authors who would otherwise be perceived as politically aligned: Wollstonecraft's Darnford is appalled by the vulgarity prevalent in the newly independent colonies, and longs for the civilized political and social life of England. Bage's Hermsprong, on the other hand, exalts the libertarian principles of the United States.[23] In all these texts, the financial power of American colonists enables an autonomy feared by some and applauded by others. At the other end of the social scale from wealthy planters, the illicit traders in Stevenson's Albany also pose a threat to British authority. Throughout the Seven Years' War, these criminals engage in "contraband trade across the desert with the Indians and the French. This, as it was highly illegal, relaxed their loyalty, and . . . divided even their sympathies" (53). Distance and decentralization enable unregulated commercial activity, which in turn loosens colonial ties to the home country. To read imperial history in the texts I consider is to trace a literary articulation of the multiple paths that led to American resistance to metropolitan authority.

And yet, the specter of home haunts the periphery. When the Durie brothers meet in Albany, their confrontation highlights, in unexpected ways, the difference between home and colony. Inverting formulations about the opportunity to remake selves in the New World, Stevenson's text emphasizes the circulation of information and the persistence of the past in America. Henry warns James that "reputation has preceded you": "At home, where you were so little known, it was still possible to keep appearances; that would be quite vain in this province. . . . Your crimes escape the law; but my friend the Governor has promised protection to my family. Have a care, sir! . . . if you are observed to utter two words to my innocent household, the law shall be stretched to make you smart for it" (171). On the one hand, James's criminal connections mark him in the colonies; on the other, Henry and Alison are liberated from the need to protect the family name. The dynastic obligation that impels Alison to burn evidence of James's political double-dealing so that she can "save the reputation of that family" (114) simply does not obtain in the colonies. Whereas James's own indifference to reputation empowers him in Scotland because "he knows how high we prize it" (115), in America, Henry can use James's shady past against him and relish the public disgrace he worked so hard to avert in Durrisdeer. At the same time, Henry himself profits from a new beginning, settling the land inherited by his wife, becoming "immersed in farming" (175), and making political alliances unavailable to him in Scotland. Indeed, Henry deliberately performs power and dignity when he meets his brother "with the Governor upon one hand and various notables upon the other" (171). Like Hermsprong bringing a rival entourage to counter Lord Grondale, Henry makes visible the altered power relations with which his enemy must contend. Just as James looks East and West for new sites to exercise his lust for power and wealth, Henry turns to the New World to escape the prison of home while his wife "daily blessed Heaven her father should have left her such a paradise" (175).

In the end, however, the long arm of the center reaches out to destroy all that Henry has built in the periphery; just as Colonel Jack fears that news of his Jacobite exploits in Scotland will ruin his prosperous colonial life, just as Hermsprong's father discovers that French power can be murderous in Pennsylvania as well as in Paris, the Duries feel the shattering effects of news from home. As Mackellar tells it, "it was reserved for some poor devil in Grub Street, scribbling for his dinner, and not caring what he scribbled, to cast a spell across four thousand miles of the salt sea, and send forth both these brothers into savage and wintry deserts, there to die" (181). The "idle, lying words of a Whig pamphleteer" (184) engaging in the party politics of London, have the power to unleash a chain of events that leads ultimately to that final moment when so many imperial subjects come together in the frozen wilderness of America.

In the texts I consider, the center that exerts such fitful and problematic influence on the peripheries is itself subject to political, economic, and moral decay. In *Oroonoko,* the metropole is an absent presence, but Behn's critique of England is evident, not only in her depiction of corrupt colonials sent out by the home country but also in the censure implied by comparison with more "primitive" cultures. Of the natives of Suriname, she writes: "These People represented to me an absolute *Idea* of the first State of Innocence, before Man knew how to sin . . . Religion wou'd here but destroy that Tranquillity, they possess by Ignorance" (40). The narrator opposes Amerindians' meticulous integrity to Europeans' casual relationship to vows when she recounts that "they once made Mourning and Fasting for the Death of the *English* Governor, who had given his Hand to come on such a Day to 'em, and neither came, nor sent" (40). Justifying polygamy as practiced in Africa, she contends that "the only Crime and Sin with Woman is, to turn her off, to abandon her to Want, Shame and Misery: Such ill Morals are only practis'd in *Christian* Countries, where they prefer the bare Name of Religion; and, without Vertue or Morality, think that's sufficient" (46).[24] These early passages against Christian cant reverberate when, in response to the narrator's somewhat mechanical attempts to convert Imoinda with "Stories of Nuns," Oroonoko mocks "our Notions of the Trinity . . . it was a Riddle, he said, wou'd turn his Brain to conceive" (74); his tone changes from satire to contempt when he excoriates the slaves who so quickly surrender to Byam's forces: "they wanted only but to be whipt into the knowledge of the *Christian Gods* to be the vilest of all creeping things; to learn to Worship such Deities as had not Power to make 'em Just, Brave, or Honest" (90). *Oroonoko* anticipates the harsher and more sustained attacks on European Christianity (and missionary zeal) leveled in *Humphry Clinker* and *Hermsprong,* texts in which sophisticated Amerindians dismantle Christian mythology, and in *Hindoo Rajah,* in which the devout Hindu encounters and exposes the hypocrisy of Christians.

More subtly, the Royalist Behn encodes criticism of imperial policy under the Stuarts. Although the editors of the Bedford edition rightly point to Behn's sympathetic association of Oroonoko's suffering with that of the Stuarts (20),[25] we must note also her nuanced description of

Charles II's complicity in the fate that befalls both hero and colony. Duping Oroonoko a second time, the perfidious English Captain ascribes his reluctance to unchain the hero to his fear that an unfettered Oroonoko "might commit some Outrage fatal to himself and the *King* his Master, to whom his Vessel did belong" (64). Charles, thus identified as a stockholder in the slave trade (the Company of Royal Adventurers into Africa was chartered in 1660), stands indirectly accused of enabling the despicable practices of the trader, who, we remember, seems to have been bred at court. The king, therefore, is at least passively complicit in the illegal practice of kidnapping Africans, which, as Lipking points out, "went on, since the perpetual shortage of slaves in the colonies created a market of buyers who were . . . not sticklers for procedure."[26] Moreover, Behn aims a dart at the king's imperial carelessness. Her lament that "had his late Majesty, of sacred Memory, but seen and known what a vast and charming World he had been Master of in that Continent, he would never have parted so Easily with it to the *Dutch*" (76) may sound like mere imperial covetousness, but the language suggests poor stewardship, and its implications intensify when read in conjunction with the consequences of the change. Although (despite the narrator's early contention that Indians and colonists "live in perfect amity" [38]) the natives certainly constitute a threat even under supposedly benign English rule, they become monstrously violent against "the *Dutch*, who us'd 'em not so civilly as the *English;* so that they cut in pieces all they cou'd take, getting into Houses, and hanging up the Mother, and all her Children about her" (81). Even as the maintenance of empire requires the cooperation of contemptible characters like the slave-trading captain and Byam, it fosters, at the center of imperial power, a kind of casual indifference to forces unleashed by European wars and treaties. Suriname and its inhabitants, perceived by both English and Dutch occupiers as mere commodities to be traded, can never regain the paradise where "all things by Nature . . . are Rare, Delightful and Wonderful" (77).

In *Master of Ballantrae,* both England and Scotland are deeply compromised by political, economic, and moral disarray. In the aftermath of the 1745 Jacobite rebellion, a combination of paranoia and poor intelligence allows James Durie to serve as a spy for the English even as he enjoys, as his fellow exile Burke resentfully points out, "the largest pension on the Scots Fund of any refugee in Paris" (64). Moreover, for Scottish gentry on the eve of the uprising, self-protective expediency has triumphed over romantic idealism; like "many considerable families," the Duries opt "to steer a middle course, one son going forth to strike a blow for King James, my lord and the other staying at home to keep in favour with King George" (11). Not for the Duries the kind of loyalty that sends the Baron Bradwardine, despite the risk to life and property and "In spite of all my [his daughter Rose's] tears and entreaties," to serve the Stuart cause.[27] In comparison with the attenuated chivalric code of Stevenson's Scotland, even Fergus Mac-Ivor's brand of personal ambition looks noble, especially when contrasted with Lord Durrisdeer's craven double-dealing and James's "hope of paying off his private liabilities" (11) in the event of a Stuart victory. The center that claims authority over the homelands of both Eastern and Western Indians thus is always already corrupted by conflict, disloyalty, and selfish ambition.

It is, of course, a truism in postcolonial studies that the psychology of imperialism depends on Othering and objectifying those whose lands and lives are being appropriated. As Dirks points out in the "Prologue" to his study of British India, "Built on fabrication, colonial history mirrors the general distortions and displacements of imperial self-representation—the use of imputed barbarism to justify, and even ennoble, imperial ambition."[28] Tzvetan Todorov's monumental history of colonized America opens with the premise that the constitutive European gaze deliberately denies autonomous subjectivity to those it wants to enslave. Columbus begins this process in his "failure to recognize the Indians, and the refusal to admit them as a subject having the same rights as oneself, but different. . . . he does not perceive alterity . . . and he imposes his own values upon it."[29] Stephen Greenblatt, taking issue with Todorov's contention "that the crucial cultural difference between European and American peoples was the presence or absence of writing," locates instead a crux in the multiple registers of "wonder," which "precedes, even escapes, moral categories," but which can modulate toward a discourse of appropriation through Othering, so that Amerindians become "people who live on the margins . . . apart from settled human community and hence from the very condition of human life."[30] The radical alterity of the New World cannot be applied to European encounters with the East (see Markley's perceptive analysis of early European texts that have to deploy "compensatory strategies to deal with Europe's marginalization in a global economy dominated by the empires of the Far East)"[31]. However, we note of course a similar strategy of Othering those marked for subaltern status: Homi Bhabha points to "the *productive* ambivalence of the object of colonial discourse—that 'otherness' which is at once an object of desire and derision. . . . By 'knowing' the native population in these terms, discriminatory and authoritarian forms of political control are considered appropriate."[32]

The texts I consider inevitably engage in and with these forms of construing colonized populations: Thomson, for example, attributes the barbarity of darker races to the brutal heat of their homelands; Smollett depicts sadistic practices of Amerindians; even Hamilton and Scott, at pains to debunk European fictions about Oriental cultures, re–present stereotypes of arrogant and wily Brahmins. At the same time, however, these texts insist on authentic difference, in part by narrating, often comically, an inverted gaze that exoticizes Europeans. In Behn's novella, the English self-consciously offer themselves up as objects of wonder even as they set out to satisfy their touristlike curiosity about Indians in Suriname; the narrator and her retinue "resolv'd to surprize 'em, by making 'em see something they never had seen (that is, White people)" (81). Behn's witty double-voiced discourse in this episode exposes some of the strategies seized on by Europeans who want to display their superiority to natives, but which instead make them figures of fun. The narrator's bland non sequitur—"we were Dress'd, so as is most comode for the hot countries, very glitering and Rich" (81)— becomes irresistibly comical when we learn that "comode" for them in the tropics consists of silk caps and woolen suits, multiple petticoats, and shoes and stockings. Basking in the Indians' admiration, condescendingly bestowing on them silver lace since "they much Esteem any shining things" (82), the English party fail to note they are being objectified, even when the Indians welcome the translator Tiguamy because "*we shall now know whether those things can speak*" and ask him "if we had Sense, and Wit? if we cou'd talk of Affairs of Life, and War, as they cou'd do?" (82). Suvir Kaul rightly reads this scene "as reverse ethnography, as the narrator and her party become the subjects of examination. . . . Critics have argued that such a reversal of viewpoint is crucial to eighteenth-century satire; here, we might notice its place in texts that subject Englishness (or Britain) to a comparative historical or ethnographic examination."[33] I would merely add that reverse ethnography here works to point up risible European complacency about how colonizers are viewed by indigenous populations.

Reversing the usual trajectory of imperial travel only serves to emphasize the divide between colonizer and colonized. In *Windsor-Forest*, Pope brings to the metropole the wondering gaze of the outsider and adds a cautionary note about problematic incursions from the peripheries. Hamilton and Bage (following Montesquieu and Goldsmith) make the inverted gaze the central motif of their novels, using the outsider to lay bare the degenerate culture of the center. Extending the comical self-satisfaction exposed by Behn's narrator as well as Oroonoko's passionate indictment of *"such a degenerate Race"* (86), Hamilton and Bage build devastating critiques of a society that has imagined itself fit to rule other worlds. Writing almost a hundred years later (and two decades after the violent reprisals in the wake of the Sepoy Mutiny), Stevenson need only gesture at the outsider's view of British character when Secundra Dass's first query to Sir William is "You no murderer?" (216).[34]

In a recent interview with the *New York Times*, the comedian Craig Ferguson alludes to Scottish pessimism: "I come from a very critical culture. You know the Scots. They're always saying: 'Oh no. It will never work. You'll never amount to anything. You've got to know your place in the world.'"[35] The Scots' place during the construction and administration of Britain's empire was everywhere in the world, and the first three chapters of my book, like this introduction, pair an English writer with a Scottish one, not to point up contrasts, but rather to emphasize that these texts address the *British* nature of empire. The special contribution of Scots to imperial endeavors has been amply documented in recent scholarship ranging from T. M. Devine's encyclopedic *Scotland's Empire, 1600–1815* to Douglas J. Hamilton's focused consideration of Scottish presence in the Caribbean.[36] Scotland's swift and successful assimilation into imperial projects initiated in London has been the subject of much careful analysis and has been attributed to Scots' recognition that empire provided opportunity for advancement. Eric Richards, for example, finds that "Scotland seemed to use America (and the later empire) for the release and exercise of its revealed talents and capital. . . . On the other hand the very fear of provincialization, the danger of cultural assimilation, may have been the goad that generated Scotland's extraordinarily vigorous response." Kenneth McNeil, too, locates Scottish imperial energy in a perception of asymmetry in other areas: "imperialism was a prominent element in the acceptance of the British union from its inception. . . . as empire seemed a field of play upon which Scots and English were equally skilled, cultivating this field would therefore ensure Scottish-English parity within Great Britain." According to Bruce P. Lenman, "By the 1720s Scottish writers of a Whig-Unionist disposition were actively promoting the creation and popularization of a new imperial British identity designed to supersede the narrower confines of English or Scottish nationality." Indeed, as

Evan Gottlieb notes, Scots provided both theoretical and practical templates for conducting imperialism: "Adam Smith's *Theory of Moral Sentiments* (1790) consistently appeared on required curricula in British government and missionary institutions in India throughout the nineteenth century; its recurring presence on reading lists designed to help enforce British hegemony suggests that the text's colonizing imperatives did not go unappreciated by the British Empire's (often Scottish) colonial administrators."[37]

Of course, some ideological gymnastics were required to construct and perpetuate this notion of a unified imperial identity. Mark Netzloff opens his fascinating investigation into the formation of such an identity with an explanation of why James I found it necessary to censure the authors of *Eastward Ho!* in 1605. Their offense, he argues, lay not in a comic portrayal of Scots but rather in unveiling the government's tactic of "positioning Scots as the instruments who will enable an extension of the English authority into new colonial spaces. The intercultural relations of the colonial environment serve to dissipate Anglo-Scottish tensions and rivalries, securely rendering Scots as industrious, friendly, and decidedly subordinate partners in cooperative 'British' colonial ventures"; the play offers "insight into the Jacobean state's manipulation of Union rhetoric and use of colonial migration as strategies to consolidate social control over the margins of James' British dominions." Robert J. C. Young is even more explicit about the intersection of political and lexical power: "The dutiful use of the term 'British' rather than 'English' . . . misses the point that in terms of power relations there is no difference between them: 'British' is the name imposed by the English on the non-English."[38] This kind of manipulation seems to have a long history. In 1792, William Robertson writes that, in the sixteenth century, English policy toward Scotland shifted from conquest to covert infiltration: "The leading men of greatest power and popularity were gained; the ministers and favourites of the crown were corrupted; and such absolute direction of the Scottish councils was acquired, as rendered the operation of the one kingdom dependent . . . on the sovereign of the other." And in 1993, Conrad Russell wryly attributes Scottish acceptance of Union to exasperated recognition of English highhanded practices:

In 1649, in a fit of absence of mind, they cut off the head of the King of Scots with the Crown upon it. In 1660, they restored his son to the throne without even bothering to tell the Scots they had done so. In 1688, as in 1649, the English, in removing the King, saw no need even to let his other kingdom know what they had done. In 1701, once again, they changed the line of succession without telling the Scots. The Scots' decision in 1707 that "if you can't beat 'em, join 'em" is in part a response to that action.[39]

However unsavory or underhanded the process of hegemony, by the eighteenth century, the empire, if not the homeland, was definitively British, as are the imperial characters considered in this project.[40]

There were, of course, nationalist contestations within British imperial discourse, whether explicit as in the debate between Lismahago and Bramble in *Humphry Clinker* or coded, as in the assertion of superior Scottish culture in *Hindoo Rajah*. Scottish intellectual thought and culture were proposed as especially conducive to the proper administration of empire. Andrew Hook's study of affinities between America and Scotland points to the congruence of religious and intellectual life, although he also notes that "the Scots, indeed, far from being the original opponents of the oppressive policy of the British government, the proclaimers and the successful defenders of American liberty, the framers of the Constitution, and the most powerful influence for everything good in the American way of life, were certainly the most unpopular national group in the colonies." Martha McLaren's book on the careers of Thomas Munro (1761–1827), John Malcolm (1769–1833), and Mountstuart Elphinstone (1779–1859) explores a specific reciprocal relationship between products of the Scottish Enlightenment and the British empire in India. On the one hand, Enlightenment ideology "provided conceptual tools they could use as a framework for their analyses of Asian cultures and theories of Progress they could apply to the problems of Indian government," perhaps particularly drawing on the stadial theory of progress. On the other hand, due to Enlightenment ideals, "The existence of a dichotomy between the rational and material West and the emotional and spiritual essence of Hinduism is entirely absent from Munro, Malcolm, and Elphinstone's representations of India."[41] So although the disproportionate numbers of Scottish imperial workers can be attributed to Lord Bute's desire to promote Scots in public service, it is also the case that the Scots were particularly adept, through both education and political/economic exigencies, to conduct imperial business.

Interestingly, although Douglas Hamilton's research indicates that "perhaps 4,500 Scots went to the Caribbean in the second half of the seventeenth century, that is, before the Act of Union," and despite the fact the 23,000 prisoners sent to the colonies between 1607 and 1699 "included many Scots banished by Oliver Cromwell for their activities during the English Civil War, the Scottish Covenanters who resisted English rule, and criminals,"[42] *Oroonoko* makes no reference to Scottish presence in the colonies. The omission is curious, particularly since Lord Willoughby, an important (by absence) figure in the novel, requested "the free transfer of Scots to that island," an infusion that would "prevent any accesse of Irish in the future,"[43] — perhaps undesirables like the "wild *Irish*" Banister, whom the narrator excoriates as "a Fellow of absolute Barbarity, and fit to execute any Villany" (99).[44] Despite the omission, however, in her dedication to Lord Maitland, Behn makes a point of extolling the land that can claim such a noble public servant: *"And to the Glory of your Nation be it spoken, it produces more considerable Men . . . than all other Nations can Boast; and the Fruitfulness of your Virtues sufficiently make amends for the Barrenness of your Soil"* (36). Already, in 1688, Behn acknowledges talents that outstrip the geographic limitations imposed on Scottish nationals.

In Stevenson's text, Scotland remains central, always part of the narrative landscape no matter where the Durie brothers travel. J. R. Hammond finds that "for all its wanderings in time and distance, it remains essentially a novel of Scotland, imbued with the atmosphere of Scottish history and landscape."[45] Scottish history itself, of course, precipitates James's travels to imperial sites, and Stevenson's Scottish sensibility inflects his view of British global power. As Manfred Malzah puts it, "a Scottish author's look at Empire was likely to combine an inside with an outside perspective: a duality rooted in the more than proportional participation of Scots in British imperial ventures on the one hand, and the abortiveness of previous Scottish attempts at colonization on the other."[46] Moreover, as Penny Fielding's sensitive reading suggests, Stevenson's writing on empire encodes the peculiar rootlessness of European imperial identity: "Scots, Irish, English, British, French, and Americans form temporary alliances which are dependent on contingent circumstances."[47] In *Master of Ballantrae*, however, multiple loyalties signal betrayal, just as inhabiting multiple identities, especially at the margins of the British empire, constitutes criminality. At a time when, according to Ann Colley, Stevenson "was in the midst of trying to sort out his reactions to . . . the business of war and imperialism in South Africa and India,"[48] he produced a text in which imperial adventuring originates in shoddy motives and results in death.

My principle of selection of texts has been, of course, somewhat arbitrary and personal, given that consideration of the imperial project enters almost all writing in the long eighteenth century. I have, on the whole, wanted to consider authors so well known in their own time that their commentary on imperialism carries a kind of popular weight. According to this criterion, no explanation is needed for the inclusion of Pope, Thomson, Defoe, Smollett and Scott. *Letters of a Hindoo Rajah* may have fallen into obscurity, but it had a large readership and was reviewed by all the major journals; after its publication, "Hamilton established herself at the center of the Edinburgh literary world."[49] Robert Bage did not achieve fame either in his own time or ours, but *Hermsprong* did go into a third edition and elicited positive commentary from Mary Wollstonecraft in the *Analytic Review* and from Sir Walter Scott in *Lives of the Novelists*. Wollstonecraft herself, cited admiringly in *Hermsprong*, was certainly an important literary figure during her lifetime and has achieved iconic status since the mid-twentieth century. In their different ways, these authors both formed and reflected back public opinion on social and cultural issues; their ruminations on the role of empire in British life provide an important archive for any discussion of empire in the long eighteenth century.

1

Global Nationalisms: Alexander Pope's *Windsor-Forest* and James Thomson's *Seasons*

> But it were endless to give an Account of all the divers Wonderfull
> and Strange things that Country affords, and which we took a very
> great Delight to go in search of; though those adventures are often-
> times Fatal and at least Dangerous.
>
> *—Oroonoko*

> "Cast in your lot with me to-morrow, become my slave, my chattel,
> a thing I can command as I command the powers of my own limbs
> and spirit—you will see no more that dark side that I turn upon the
> world in anger."
>
> *—Master of Ballantrae*

WINDSOR-FOREST (1713) AND *THE SEASONS* (1730–46) HAVE ELICITED
remarkably similar trajectories of commentary, especially regarding
their internal discrepancies and their overt or covert role in advancing
Britain's imperial agenda. Influential voices in the eighteenth century
complained about their formal disorder: John Dennis disparaged *Windsor-Forest* because "there is no manner of Design, nor any Artful and
Beautiful Disposition of Parts," and Samuel Johnson noted that "the
great defect of The Seasons is want of method."[1] Some twentieth-century critics have sought transcendental patterns to make sense of seeming disarray. Martin Battestin's reading of *Windsor-Forest* finds that "the
panoramic cataloguing of contrasted elements in Nature . . . conduces
to the impression of the unity of the Whole, a vision redounding to the
glory of the Creator," and Maynard Mack locates a geographical center
for the whole: "Like Eden, like the world, England contains all things,
with an order in variety, an equilibrium of opposites, that the older
poets recognized as a mark of the Creator's hand wherever seen." Janis
A. Tomlinson discovers in *The Seasons* a kind of unity articulated as a
"primary causal connection of human depravity," while Frans De

35

Bruyn situates it in Thomson's poetic voice: 'It is the perceiver and his gentlemanly ethos that unite the disparate elements of the poem.'[2] Much recent scholarship, cited below, has moved toward thematizing the ambivalences and inconsistencies in the poems within the context of British imperialism, thus reanimating their importance as cultural and political documents. This chapter addresses the imperial contradictions in the poems, arguing that both texts manifest misgivings about the deleterious effect of empire on both occupier and occupied, and that Pope and Thomson register the violence inherent to imperial expansion even as they extol the glories of *Pax Britannia.*

Britannia itself is construed somewhat differently by Pope and Thomson. Robert Crawford has pointed out that "When Pope in 'Windsor Forest' . . . hymns 'British Blood' . . . and 'BRITISH QUEEN' . . . there is no hint that the word 'British' means anything other than 'English,'" whereas "Thomson asserts a Britishness which is not . . . the equivalent of Englishness. . . . Thomson is aware of being a Scottish poet who sees Britain as a cultural amalgam comprising more than just England."[3] Indeed, Thomson substitutes Pope's somewhat casual and mechanical reference to Britishness with explicit celebration of the Act of Union that has enabled national and imperial greatness. He contrasts "ancient barbarous times,/When disunited Britain ever bled" to "this deep-laid indissoluble state/Where wealth and commerce lift the golden head/And o'er our labours liberty and law/Impartial watch, the wonder of a world!" (*Spring,* 842–48). Although Thomson differentiates Scotland from England—in his description of romantic Caledonia, in his praise of Scottish energy, in his grateful appreciation of the Duke of Argyll and Duncan Forbes—his commitment to a united Britain is charged with an urgency missing in Pope's poem. In part, Thomson's emphasis on Britishness has to do with being what James Sambrook calls "a child of the Union and perhaps the first important poet to write with a British, as distinct from a Scottish or English, outlook," but Britishness also gives him scope to participate in the imperial adventure denied to independent Scotland. As Crawford says, "Thomson sees an imperial role for Britain, and wants Scotland to be able to take advantage of it by being fully part of Britain."[4] Thomson's allegiance to a united and vibrant Britain connects to the argument of this chapter: that while *Windsor-Forest*'s dystopic vision remains a constant in the poem, *The Seasons* devises a strategy of reassurance by constructing equivalences between imperial practices and domestic ideologies.

POPE'S ECO-HISTORICAL VISION

Alexander Pope's famous *concordia discors*, celebrated as a triumph of nature in *Windsor-Forest*, has elicited a less-than-univocal response when critics consider its attitude toward England's imperial ambitions. Laura Brown detects in its variety of effects an artful and dishonest obfuscation, aimed at screening an imperial ideology of conquest and subjugation of both nature and people: "the poem's elaborate attempts to rationalize imperial violence in the name of peace result in a circular and obsessive return to the theme of violence even in its most pastoral scenes." Christopher Hitt charges that "The harmony that Pope has in mind is less ecological than imperialistic." Sympathetic readings of the poem have uncovered freighted nuances in the ambiguities critiqued by Brown and Hitt, but even these readings articulate a degree of discomfort with the discontinuities of *Windsor-Forest*. Leopold Damrosch, for example, in a carefully historicized reading of the poem, speculates that "its harmonies are an act of faith, or perhaps of wish fulfillment, rather than a fully elaborated picture of the world as Pope perceives it," and Dustin Griffin, addressing the "poem's bifurcation," says "the drift toward lofty song checked by an impulse to retirement may help to account for the ambiguity." in its lines. Wallace Jackson suggests that "*Windsor-Forest* initiates Pope's engagement with ambivalence," while Briraj Singh believes the problem of interpretation lies with critics who look for unity where there is tension.[5] These readings address both the formal properties and the ideological positions of *Windsor-Forest*, recognizing, as Susan J. Wolfson puts it, that "actions of form are enmeshed in . . . networks of social and historical conditions."[6] Defending Pope against the charge of complicit complacency about imperial adventures, Richard Bevis sees the poet maturing beyond his early patriotism, while Robin Grove sees a similar growth in Pope's understanding of the flexible potential of his couplet form. Both these readings place *Windsor-Forest* in Pope's more naïve (or less-skilled) period, and Christine Gerrard sums up this aspect of the critical conversation when she points out that Pope was "inherently suspicious of political myth-making. . . . There could be no more *Windsor-Forests*."[7]

My reading of *Windsor-Forest* joins those that resist seeing the poem's discontinuities as evidence of Pope's covert endorsement of the imperial project, an endorsement muffled in disingenuous hymns to pastoral pleasures; but I argue that, far from falling into troubled, albeit rich, ambiguities, this poem articulates its contradictions strategically. I believe that in *Windsor-Forest*, Pope consciously represents the cultural and moral difficulties inherent to successful empire building. The poem lays out Pope's apprehensions not only about the future of a nation contaminated by those it has conquered, but also by the dangers within: the will to power that leads to violence, coarsening of respect for the homeland, and communal amnesia about history. Pope deploys multiple figures —from hunting to classical mythology to royal chronology—to sound his warnings about the potential damage attendant on imperial expansion. At the same time, the poem is unequivocal about the value of peace itself and equally sincere about celebrating the monarch who has negotiated it. For Pope in *Windsor-Forest,* the Peace of Utrecht is not about the *Asiento,* and not primarily about expanding Britain's political and commercial empire; it is about curtailing wasteful military expenditures and conserving English resources, both material and moral. *Windsor-Forest* argues that while peace is always worth pursuing, imperial adventuring is always worth interrogating.[8]

Pope is fully aware of how empire encroaches into English domestic space, and quite deliberately articulates the congruence of the two realms. Look, for example, at one of the changes he makes between the 1712 manuscript and the 1713 published version. In the latter, Pope lists groves, lawns, glades, trees, plains, hills, and heath, and then goes on to describe how "midst the Desert fruitful Fields arise,/That crown'd with tufted Trees and springing Corn,/Like verdant Isles the sable Waste adorn" (26–28).[9] In case the reader fails to note the odd notion of desert wastes surrounding Windsor, Pope takes us instantly to a distant part of the globe where such incongruities may be imagined: "Let *India* boast her Plants" (29). The juxtaposition of quintessentially English space and alien outlands reminds us that the empire is always with us, even here in this other Eden. The cancelled lines in the 1712 holograph point up his intention: there, he follows his praise of "blueish Hills" (23) with "How am I pleas'd t'imbibe th'untainted Air" before turning to the reference to India,[10] demarcating home from colony through a boundary marking health, so that England remains firmly separate from the tainted Indies. The draft thus articulates what Alan Bewell has called "a *relational* or *differential* model of disease. . . . British 'healthiness' was thus fundamentally structured in relation and often in opposition to colonial disease environments."[11] The published revision erases that line, both in the poem and in the world, moving us swiftly and without remark from the clean, green world of Windsor to the presumably diseased expanses of the tropics, which are, of course, "commanded" (32) by the inhabitants of the verdant isle. Even the succeeding lines elevating England's hills above "proud *Olympus*" (33) hint at a kind of interpenetration, as the "humble Mountains" become overrun by Pan's flocks, Pomona's fruits, Flora's blooms, and Ceres's harvests (35–39), so that the blessings of the gods seem to constitute a kind of invading force.[12]

Pope's double-voiced articulation of expansion and invasion can be detected in the lines that triumphantly prophesy a future when London is the destiny as well as cynosure of all the world, lines so energetic with images of movement that they seem to press through time and space:

> The Time shall come, when free as Seas or Wind
> Unbounded *Thames* shall flow for all Mankind,
> Whole Nations enter with each swelling Tyde,
> And Seas but join the Regions they divide;
> Earth's distant Ends our Glory shall behold,
> And the new World launch forth to seek the Old.
>
> (397–402)

Global movement goes in two directions, as Defoe too proclaims, triumphantly, in *A Tour Thro' the whole Island of Great Britain;* for Defoe, the Thames should be celebrated not in songs and poetry, but "as it really is *made glorious* . . . by its invincible Navies and by the innumerable Fleets of Ships sailing upon it, to and from all Parts of the World."[13] But Pope's articulation is less celebratory than Defoe's: yes, the Thames (and the oceans with which it connects) breaks narrow national boundaries and strides the world, but it also allows the world to enter English space, not always for the nation's profit. When Pope was composing *Windsor-Forest*, the memory of Dutch ships sailing up the Thames in June 1667 would have been very much alive as an episode that exposed England's vulnerability to foreign invasion, and it remained a frightening and mortifying mark of military failure. One Dutch account describes how easily its fleet broke through the chains and fireships deployed to protect London, emphasizing the chaos and humiliation visited on the English: "Then the other four ships were left by their comrades; the crews in confusion sprang overboard; and our people took the ship *Royal Charles* . . . [which] must have cost almost 100,000 in the gilding alone. . . . The chain was burst into pieces, and all within it destroyed and annihilated, so that the English lost the admirals of the red and white flag, besides others of their largest ships."[14] The Thames may "serve as a symbol of England's commercial and political glory," and as "a waterway to empire, an avenue towards the great oceans of the world,"[15] but it also potentially opens up the homeland to penetration by foreign powers. (I use the sexualized figure deliberately, because "Seas but join the Regions they divide" evokes the rape of Belinda's lock—"The Peer now spreads the glitt'ring *Forfex* wide,/T'inclose the Lock; now joins it, to divide" [147–48]).

The final couplet quoted above not only reiterates the dual trajectory of imperial travel, but also points to the doubleness of the imperial gaze, invoking a kind of reverse chronospatial movement. When the new world sets out to find the old, the homeland itself becomes alien; Suvir Kaul has noted that, just as Aphra Behn's Indians exoticize the appearance and dress of European colonizers in Surinam (see introduction, p. 29), Pope's Indian visitors wonder at the outlandish islanders they find in London: "naked Youths and painted Chiefs admire/Our Speech, our Colour, and our strange Attire!" (405–6). The inversion here, however, is even more forceful than in *Oroonoko*, for Englishmen are "orientalized" in their own country by travelers from the west whose wonder carries the potential to turn to representation and appropriation.[16] Moreover, these visitors, arriving in "Ships of uncouth Form," actually change the course of English nature ("stem the Tyde") and demographics—these "Feather'd People crowd my wealthy Side" (403–4), a formulation that sounds like an eighteenth-century version of fear of immigrants. The cumulative effect of these lines is xenophobic: grotesque others, naked, painted, feathered, and uncouth, swarm into England, battening on English wealth and jeopardizing the English right to be normative, unmarked subjects. When G. Wilson Knight characterizes *Windsor-Forest* as a "teeming world" that paints "imperial expansion as creatively interlocking one's own country with a great human whole, to the 'naked youths' . . . of America,"[17] he reads celebration where I find dire warning. These lines of *Windsor-Forest* seem to me to articulate a first alert about the consequences of imperial expansion and about the problem of bringing the empire home.

Journeys to and from the center depend, of course, on the mighty British fleet, invoked in the poem by the figure of the oaks that not only bring imperial loot ("precious Loads" [31]) back to England, but also go forth to conquer the world:

> Thy Trees, fair *Windsor!* Now shall leave their Woods,
> And half thy Forests rush into my Floods,
> Bear *Britain*'s Thunder, and her Cross display,
> To the bright Regions of the rising Day;

Tempt Icy Seas, where scarce the Waters roll,
Where clearer Flames glow round the frozen Pole;
Or under Southern Skies exalt their Sails,
Led by new Stars, and born by spicy Gales!

(385–92)

This image of oaks turning into ships that carry British power to the corners of the globe has elicited congruent readings from critics who disagree about Pope's motives. Earl Wasserman's reading posits a benign agenda—"Britain's fleets will bear her thunder and her Union Jack over the seas, not to create foreign conflict, but to assure the *Concordia discors* of the world"—that is inverted by Christopher Hitt: "The trees are to be cut down and made into warships, which will extend Britain's influence to all corners of the world." Laura Brown and Helen Deutsch point to Pope's strategy of concealing brute imperialism through use of synecdoche, and David Morris finds that "the language of the poem . . . conveys the poet's individual sense that the achievements of civilization often require disheartening sacrifices of natural beauty."[18] I take a slightly different view of what Brown has called the "fantasy of power" inherent in these lines, a fantasy echoed in Thomson's articulation of commercial and military power amassing on the Thames, "whence, ribbed with oak/To bear the British thunder, black, and bold,/The roaring vessel rushed into the main" (*Autumn*, 131–33). The fantasy, I suggest, has to do with imaginary resources: the oaks that are to rush into the Thames and then on to oceans of the world have, by 1713, been so seriously depleted that they can no longer supply the navy's needs; indeed Defoe remarks on the surprising extent of wooded land in Hampshire "notwithstanding the very great consumption of timber in King William's reign, by building or rebuilding almost the whole navy."[19] Pope, I argue, refuses to participate in what Robert Markley identifies as an imperial dream about riches from the Far East, which "serves as a fantasy space for mercantile capitalism because it allows for the rigorous externalization of costs . . . without calculating . . . either the value of lost lives, ships, and cargoes, or the value, in devastated local ecologies, of the deforestation necessary to build ships for the British navy and East India (EIC) fleets."[20]

Robert Greenhalgh Albion's detailed and useful study of the economics of naval timber lists a number of reasons for the dangerous scarcity of English oak in the eighteenth century. These range from the "inefficiency and neglect which permeated the administration of the royal forests," to private owners who either refused to cut ornamental trees or cut them prematurely, to competing demands for limited supply of oak — not only to rebuild London after the fire of 1666 but also to stoke the forges of the growing iron industry.[21] These problems coexisted with urgent and constant needs; Jeremy Black points out that "at a time when warships were made of wood and enjoyed a useful life ranging from eight to fifteen years . . . a constant commitment was required to ensure that an ageing fleet was replenished sufficiently." Diminishing domestic stores required a dependence on imported timber, but in a triumph of circularity, naval power was necessary to ensure adequate naval supplies. According to Oliver Warner, England's seventeenth-century wars with the Dutch were precisely connected with the need for timber: in 1652, "There was . . . fear in London that the Dutch . . . might appropriate the Sound Dues which were exacted at Elsinore. . . . England was sensitive to anything which might interfere with her traffic with the Baltic countries, from which she got timber and naval stores. Owing to the huge inroads made in her oak forests, she was already experiencing a timber problem, and this was to grow ever more acute."[22]

When Pope congratulates Father Thames on the woods "Where Tow'ring Oaks their growing Honours rear,/And future Navies on thy Shores appear" (222–23), he refers to an uncertain future resource, evoked again in his "Epistle to Burlington," "Whose rising Forests, not for pride or show,/But future Buildings, future Navies grow:/Let his plantations stretch from down to down,/First shade a Country, and then raise a Town" (187–90). Pope knows, even as he praises planting for "Use alone" (179), that trees put to the service of nation can no longer provide shade to country. Given the depletion of native woodlands, the cutting down of "half thy Forests" in *Windsor-Forest* seems cautionary rather than celebratory, and the early description of Windsor's groves — "Thin Trees arise that shun each others Shades" (22) — seems to sound an alarm about the visible consequences of shipbuilding. Similarly, the "absent Trees that tremble in the Floods" and the "floating Forests" (214–16; see the allusion to "prodigious forest of masts" in *Humphry Clinker* 123) take on a double meaning: both an actual reflection seen by the shepherd and an illusion that alludes to what has befallen the woods of Windsor. Moreover, Britain's urgent dependence on wood from abroad, and her readiness to go to war to protect access to the imports, profoundly alters the notion of imperial ease, changing the tone of "Realms commanded which those Trees adorn" (32) from triumphant to mordant. Dustin Griffin says that "by describing the Thames as a river that flows from the heart of the country out into the mighty oceans, and linking its ancient oak forests (such as Windsor) with Britain's oak-built navy, Pope amplifies the eighteenth-century British georgic tradition."[23] By inverting or problematizing both figures in *Windsor-Forest*, Pope turns tradition into interrogation; far from hymning the transformation of forests into fleets, the poem points out the internal depredations required to maintain the imperial navy.[24]

The glorious navy itself becomes problematic when read through the lens of historical fact and Pope's representation of it. The British navy's record during the war of the Spanish Succession was decidedly mixed. Although "all English politicians were committed to the myths of English sea power, according to which a truly naval war, against a Catholic enemy, could not fail to succeed," and although "the fleet had held the allied war effort together, transporting dispatches, money, troops and supplies,"[25] Britain's naval engagements during the war were far from triumphant. David Howarth writes that "there were not many full-scale battles at sea, and all that were fought were indecisive."[26] For example, Sir George Rooke's attempt to capture Cadiz in 1701–1702 fell victim to dissension among commanders, to Rooke's own illness, and to the undisciplined behavior of the seamen: Rodger says that Rooke "put the troops ashore at Puerto Santa Maria, some distance from Cadiz, where their officers soon lost control and they fell to drinking, looting and desecrating churches."[27] The expedition was saved from disaster and humiliation only by the victory at Vigo, when Rooke's fleet defeated French and Spanish ships protecting a cargo of treasure from the New World. Even the acquisition of Gibraltar in 1704, possibly the subject of some triumphant lines in *Windsor-Forest* — 'Sudden they seize th'amaz'd, defenceless Prize,/And high in Air *Britannia*'s Standard flies' (109–10) — was as much a result of negotiation as battle and brought no immediate benefit to the war effort.[28] Meanwhile, other calamities overtook the navy, such as the loss of Sir Cloudesley Shovell's ten thousand seamen caught by a storm in the English Channel and a further disaster in 1707, when four British ships were dashed against rocks. As Howarth succinctly puts it, "All in all, it was not a brilliant naval war."[29] Perhaps Pope's uneasiness with the national myth of naval power caused him to omit from the published version of the poem the manuscript lines about Venice: "Let Venice boast her Tow'rs amidst the Main,/Where the rough Adrian swells and roars in vain;/Here, not a Town, but spacious Realm may have/A sure Foundation on the rolling Wave." Schmitz attributes the erasure to improved imagery, but we remember that Venice was also an empire based on naval primacy, a foundation that proved less secure than Venetians had believed, and Pope may have wanted to avoid having his poem "haunted by a sense of historical transience."[30]

Naval power depends, of course, on manpower, and here, too, Britain's resources were strained. The passage purportedly boasting the capture of Gibraltar begins "When *Albion* sends her eager Sons to War" (106). These eager sons, in fact, were generally recruited by pressing them into service, because "volunteers supplied only a modest proportion, so unpopular was the Navy with those who sailed in merchantmen, and so harsh the discipline." Indeed, even before the need for troops increased because of the war, naval administrators bemoaned the difficulties of manning the ships, difficulties caused in part by the government's practice of delaying or omitting payment to its sailors. Samuel Pepys in 1667 narrates a story of "two men [who] leapt overboard, among others, into the Thames out of the vessel into which they were pressed, and were shot by the soldiers placed there to keep them . . . so much people do avoid the King's service." In 1694, a pressmaster, Arthur Todd, complained that 'My trouble has increased mightily every day for want of places to secure my men. . . . The main guard is next door, and the soldiers made a lane and encouraged the seamen to come down and break from us"—that is, even the soldiers hired to guard the pressed sailors helped them to escape. The problem continued well beyond the War of the Spanish Succession, as we see in the accounts of pressing in Wollstonecraft's *Maria* and Hamilton's *Hindoo Rajah;* Howarth recounts the story of five hundred Chelsea pensioners drafted in 1740 to man the *Centurion:* "all those who had limbs and strength to walk out of Portsmouth deserted, leaving behind them only such as were literally invalids, most of them being sixty years of age, and some of them upwards of seventy."[31] Neither eager, nor perhaps the sons of living fathers, the seamen described in historical documents are a far cry from the notional ones who swiftly capture the "thoughtless Town" of line 107. Significantly, the passage comes just after the paean to "Fair *Liberty, Britannia*'s Goddess' (91–92), a liberty emphatically not extended to those pressed to serve on Britannia's ships. The contiguity points up the contrast between a naval conscript and a free peasant: "Ye vig'rous Swains! While Youth ferments your Blood . . . Now range the Hills" (93–95). England's young peasants, who could be ranging through the fields and forests of home, are themselves caught in "the swelling Net" (104) of government conscription when imperial wars require manpower. The juxtaposition here of the free swain at home and the unspoken but implicit chains of military service, once again reminds us of the costs of military/commercial ambitions.[32] When Pat Rogers says that "the culmination of *Windsor-Forest* occurs as the British navy plies the great oceans of the world, its ships ceremonially decked out like floats in a pageant or ritualized naumachia,"[33] he is exactly right: it is a performance, a simulacrum that serves only to point up the chaos and bloodshed that has preceded the ceremony, whether in Spain or at Blenheim.[34]

Bloodshed can be found at home as well, since the domestic activities of British swains include the exuberant yet problematized scenes of hunting that have elicited much helpful critical analysis. There is general agreement that Pope represents the hunt as a legitimate sublimation—like going to war for the country's good—for violent impulses. The hunting scenes, for Heather Jurgens, "have a formalized, almost a ritualistic character that contains, and sets bearable limits to, the vigour of the swains"; the parallel can then be deployed to justify and screen the violence of imperial war, so that, "Pope's contemporary reader can compare the successful hunt to a patriotically pleasing military victory."[35] It is, however, impossible to read the descriptions of these hunts without coming to grips with their mournful and even horrified tone, which anticipates Thomson's unequivocal revulsion from "this falsely cheerful barbarous game of death,/This rage of pleasure" (*Autumn*, 384–85). As Damrosch says, "Surely Pope cannot mean that the high spirits of hunters, which themselves produce such grim results, are a justification for the horrors of warfare."[36] Indeed, the images of these vigorous swains' victims consistently evoke pathos, from the trustful partridge in "th'unfaithful Field" (103) to the pheasant who "Flutters in Blood, and panting beats the Ground" (114) to lapwings and larks who "feel the Leaden Death" and "leave their little Lives in Air" (132–34) to the gorgeous but doomed fish in "Our plenteous Streams" (141).[37]

As part of my argument that Pope articulates misgivings about the winners in imperial contests, I want to turn my attention to the hunters rather than the hunted. The swains so sympathetically portrayed when victimized by William I's tyranny become, in the hunting scenes, not only violent, but also wily, cold-hearted, destructive, and corruptive. The youth with "purer Spirits" quickly moves from ranging the hills to besetting the woods and spreading nets (95–96), language that evokes not a free-spirited hunter but a careful stalker; he carries "slaught'ring Guns" (125) and carelessly tramples through landscapes so lovingly described in the poem's opening lines: these hunters "Swarm o'er the Lawns, the Forest Walks surround" and "Rush thro' the Thickets,

down the Vallies sweep" (149, 156). Most tellingly, they become utterly
indifferent to the vitality and beauty they kill: note the despairing words
that introduce the dazzling pheasant—"Ah! What avail" (115). These
conquerors are no more moved by the multicolored gorgeousness of the
bird they destroy than are the triumphant imperial traders who expro-
priate from the Indies boatloads of "weeping Amber or the balmy Tree"
(30). Nor does the hunter's inexorable focus on slaughter change with
the seasons: "th'unweary'd Fowler roves,/When Frosts have whiten'd
all the naked Groves" (125–26), while "In genial Spring . . . /The patient Fisher takes his silent Stand/Intent" (135–38). Implacable in his
pursuit of prey, the youthful hunter seems utterly alienated from the
natural world within which he ranges.[38] Like Pan single-mindedly chas-
ing Lodona, like the troops who seize the pacific town, these swains
have their eyes firmly on the prize—one that they will capture and destroy.[39] Even more tellingly, human hunters have corrupted their animal companions. The beagles that flush out hares for their masters have
learned unnatural ferocity—"Beasts, urg'd by us, their Fellow Beasts
pursue,/And learn of Man each other to undo" (123–24).[40] So complete
is man's power over beast that "Before his Lord the ready Spaniel
bounds,/Panting with Hope" (99–100) of prey. By analogy, the eager
sons of Albion manifest canine obedience to a murderous master, a parallel clearly visible in the 1712 version of the poem. There, soldiers are
"Pleas'd, in the Gen'ral's Sight" to attack the "unsuspecting Town,"
thus replicating the behavior of submissive dogs. Successful imperial
power, whether exercised over subject peoples or over helpless animals,
leads to degeneration of character manifested by bloodlust and indifference to nature.[41]

When Pope turns to his history of British monarchy, he once again
connects conquest with cruelty and power with abuse, coding within
his chronicle of misrule and destruction a way of reading the effects of
imperial power. Even the hymn to Edward III (299–310), while celebrating the monarch's long triumphs in resplendent language ("shining
Page . . . *Cressi*'s glorious Field . . . Lillies blazing") contains within it
the discordant image of "Monarchs chain'd" and foes doomed to "bleed
for ever" in boastful song. Ballads about the victories of Edward and
the Black Prince evoke pride in mighty *"Britain*'s Spear" at the same
time that they remind us of the humiliation of the kings of Scotland and
France and of the resentment of the nations they lead. As Wasserman
has noted, "It is hardly likely that the English would fail to recognize

the contemporary relevance of Edward's triumphs as a kind of immutable pattern of Anglo-French military relations. . . . But Pope's ultimate purpose is not to celebrate a military triumph. . . . his purpose is to celebrate an arbitrative peace treaty made possible by a partial triumph."[42] Moreover, Pope's mixed language of triumph and loss in these lines acknowledges the historical fact that "English rule in France was doomed," that "Inch by inch the French lands were lost" until "the French capture of Calais, the last remnant of Edward III's conquests, was the final blow."[43] For Pope in *Windsor-Forest*, the Treaty of Utrecht provides an end to the cycle of conflict over disputed territories and brings the boys home. As Father Thames proclaims, "No more my Sons shall dye with *British* Blood/Red *Iber*'s Sands, or *Ister*'s foaming Flood;/ Safe on my Shore each unmolested Swain/Shall tend the Flocks, or reap the bearded Grain' (367–70). But, as the hunting scenes have reminded us, traces of bloodshed remain: the unmolested swains do more than herd and farm; their years of training in violent conflict have taught them the joys of pursuing and undoing their fellow beasts, and they have brought their skills and their bloodlust back from Saragossa and Blenheim, so that the "shady Empire" indeed retains traces of "War and Blood" (371–72).[44]

The Englishman's schooling in oppressor/oppressed relations, however, long pre-dates the lessons of Blenheim. Conquest, as Pope reminds us in his history of the Norman invasion, turns kings into despots and subjects into desperate slaves. William I and his sons are more savage than the laws they impose to protect their game, depopulating and devastating lands until they rule as "lonely Lords of empty Wilds and Woods" (197). Moreover, they are cowards and bullies: "Aw'd by his Nobles, by his Commons curst,/Th'Oppressor rul'd Tyrannick where he *durst*/Stretch'd o'er the Poor, and Church, his Iron Rod,/And serv'd alike his Vassals and his God" (73–76). Pope's hyperbolic, even hysterical language describing the devastation caused by Norman tyranny cannot be entirely bracketed off from the rest of the poem, including more ecologically correct hunting and new imperial practices. As Ruben Quintero astutely notes, "The iconic description of domestic conquest ripple outward, synchronically with associations of imperial conquest and diachronically across mythic time."[45] The destruction visited on the New Forest by William I includes the leveling of towns and temples—the obliteration, in other words, of a native culture, leaving "naked Temples . . . broken Columns . . . Heaps of Ruin" (68–70). Ruined civilizations and enslaved populations, the inevitable consequence

of imperial conquest, are precisely what Pope hopes to see ameliorated
when such oppression ends:

> Oh stretch thy Reign, fair *Peace!* From Shore to Shore,
> Till Conquest cease, and Slav'ry be no more:
> Till the freed *Indians* in their native Groves
> Reap their own Fruits, and woo their Sable Loves,
> *Peru* once more a Race of Kings behold,
> And other *Mexico's* be roof'd with Gold.
>
> (406–12)

The parallels to English swains and English landscapes cannot be
missed. Of course, Pope refers here only to those parts of America colonized by Spain, thus participating in the familiar strategy of projecting
onto another European power the ambitions and practices of all imperial adventurers, but there is no avoiding the connection between conquest and slavery, between colonizing and destroying the occupied
land.[46] Pope's notion of slavery here embraces more than the African
slave trade: he refers to all native populations oppressed by victorious
invaders, whether in the Indies or the British Isles. From this vantage
point, the earlier passage describing the seizure of the "defenceless
Prize" (109) can be reread as yet another example of invasion and oppression.

If we are tempted to read into Pope's narrative a triumphal teleol-
ogy—from Spain's military empire to Britain's peaceful commercial
one—we need only look again to his history of the monarchy, which,
unlike Thomson's brief and celebratory invocation of "thy Edwards and
thy Henrys . . . /Names dear to fame" (*Summer,* 1484–85), dwells on
dark episodes. The death of the first Norman kings brings a period of
peace and prosperity, as "Succeeding Monarchs heard the Subjects
Cries" so that "Fair *Liberty*" rises again (85, 91). The language implies
the Anglicization of the Norman conquerors, so that "subject" becomes
redefined as beloved dependent rather than slave. Once the invaders
have achieved a kind of transculturalization, they can begin to rule
properly—conserving rather than ravaging land and people. But British colonizers do not, at least with official sanction, become Native
American or East Indian; they remain firmly rooted in their own national and imperial identity, always differentiated from those "Feather'd
People" (404) whom they conquer and rule.

Moreover, even acculturation cannot stop the cycle of violence im-
manent to the lust for power, as attested to in Pope's chronicle of civil

wars. Indeed, rather than follow a progression from Edward III's triumphs to those of Henry V, Pope turns immediately to the "Ill-fated *Henry* [VI]," the "Martyr-King" murdered by the forces of Edward IV, "Whom not th'extended *Albion* could contain" (311–15). Similarly, rather than sing the triumphs of Tudor reigns, Pope's genealogy passes on to another martyred king, "sacred" Charles I, whose murder unleashes multiple horrors:

> What Tears has *Albion* shed,
> Heav'ns! What new Wounds, and how her old have bled?
> She saw her Sons with purple Deaths expire,
> Her sacred Domes involv'd in rolling Fire,
> A dreadful Series of Intestine Wars,
> Inglorious Triumphs and dishonest Scars.
>
> (321–25)

The mortification of Scotland's King David, alluded to a few lines earlier, is reenacted here in the regicide of yet another Scottish royal, followed by civil war, plague, fire, and general disintegration of civic order. The 1712 manuscript makes clear that these disasters are a product of English bloodlust: before the passage quoted above, it makes reference to the "sacrilegious Brood/Sworn to Rebellion, principl'd in Blood!"[47] In language reminiscent of Dryden's *Absalom and Achitophel*, Pope seems to be ascribing the death of Charles to the "headstrong, moody, murmuring race" of Englishmen.[48] If, as Pope's history implies, British kings have historically oppressed their subjects and usurped thrones, and if British subjects have in turn killed each other and their rulers, what damage will they inflict when free to roam the globe? Speaking of the British cross referred to in line 387, Pat Rogers says that "the use of this image cements the poetic symbolism, in that British endeavor is traced back to the home of chivalry in Windsor; at a subliminal level we are perhaps invited to conceive of the new empire-builders as crusaders and defenders of the faith."[49] In my reading, the Windsor in this poem's historical narrative is home to ambitious and cruel kings or martyred ones, serving as cautionary rather than inspirational figures for the new race of conquerors.

But Rogers quite rightly points out that "*Windsor-Forest* is a strongly royalist poem." Echoing him, Virginia C. Kenny calls it Pope's "public panegyric to the queen. It is an exquisitely balanced compliment to her as lord of the estate of Windsor Forest, mistress of the realm and most powerful monarch in the world."[50] Indeed, the two parts of Pope's dark rendition of royal history are framed by encomiums to the reigning queen. Before taking us to the "dreary Desart" and "gloomy Waste" (44) of Norman England, Pope rejoices that "Peace and Plenty tell, a STUART reigns" (42), and after enumerating the woes of civil war, he proclaims the peace established by Anne. Queen Anne is almost *sui generis* in this poem, untouched by the violent ambitions and the miserable fates of her predecessors. Pope goes to some lengths to represent Queen Anne as very different from the murderers and martyrs who make up the royal line in *Windsor-Forest*, separating her from other monarchs to show that her decision to press for peace shines like a good deed in a naughty world. The Whig opposition to the Treaty of Utrecht, he implies, links them with those who have waged war for ambition, ruled by oppression, and sacrificed others to their own pride. In particular, of course, he attacks William III, whose global military adventurism has caused the depletion of resources besetting the kingdom. Anne's ill will toward her brother-in-law no doubt informs some of the hyperbolic language deployed to describe William I, and Windsor itself may have been chosen because "William III sometimes hunted in the park, but he had little interest in the castle and rarely resided there, preferring instead Cardinal Wolsey's great palace at Hampton Court. . . . Windsor was to remain Princess Anne's great love throughout her life."[51] Anne, like Diana, "protects the Sylvan Reign" in the parks surrounding Windsor, though the graceful allusion to the queen's love of hunting becomes inevitably complicated by the earlier double-voiced discourse. Indeed, Pope's identification of William I with proud and bloody Nimrod (61–62), brings to mind Swift's description of Anne hunting at Windsor: "she hunts in a chaise with one horse . . . which she drives herself . . . and is a mighty hunter like Nimrod."[52] Despite this momentary complication, Queen Anne is indisputably the teleological heroine of Pope's royal line, not only in the passage connecting her to Peace and Plenty but also in the ringing celebration of her rhetorical power: "At length great ANNA said—Let Discord cease!/She said, the World obey'd, and all was *Peace*" (327–28).[53]

The Peace of Utrecht, in this poem, rises fully formed from Anne's will, a testament to her unwavering care for the country so damaged by the ambitions or misfortunes of previous monarchs. Moreover, the treaty allowed the queen and her government to turn their attention to problems at home; as Gregg points out, the 1713 session of Parliament confronted threats to the union with Scotland as well as the succession crisis: "many observers suspected that Oxford covertly supported the malt tax as the opening step towards the dissolution of the union and a revision of the succession," and the House of Lords' proposal to dissolve the Union "was defeated by a mere four votes."[54] Having abused and murdered Scottish royalty in the past, English imperial ambition could now endanger a fragile domestic union. The queen's determination to end the costly and distracting war with France and Spain wins Pope's unequivocal support, and the treaty, which many Whigs saw as a betrayal of both principle and potential profit,[55] is extolled as a prophecy fulfilled: "Hail Sacred *Peace!* Hail long-expected Days" (355). The accomplishment of this prophecy then leads to a kind of second coming, when Anne's palace and Anne's realm become "The World's great Oracle in Times to come;/There Kings shall sue, and suppliant States be seen/Once more to bend before a *British* QUEEN" (382–84).

The identification with Elizabeth serves, of course, to enhance Anne's stature in what Pat Rogers repeatedly characterizes as "a strongly royalist poem."[56] I suggest that Pope means to be quite specific about the parallel: both are monarchs who courageously insisted upon peace when the country clamored to be at war. The Elizabeth to whom Pope compares Anne is not so much the one constructed in the famous "two bodies" speech at Tilbury, but the one who, in a speech to Parliament in 1593, proudly proclaims her feminine repudiation of imperial ambition: "It may be thought simplicity in me that all this time of my reign I have not sought to advance my territories and enlarge my dominions, for both opportunity hath served me to do it, and my strength was able to have done it. I acknowledge my womanhood and weakness in that respect. . . . my mind was never to invade my neighbors, or to usurp upon any, only contented to reign over mine own and to rule as a just prince."[57] This is the Elizabeth invoked by another eighteenth-century proponent of peace. In George Lillo's *The London Merchant,* Trueman celebrates the avoidance of war with Spain: "What an expense of blood and treasure is here saved! Excellent queen! Oh, how unlike to former princes who made the danger of foreign enemies a pretense to oppress their subjects by taxes great and grievous to be borne."[58] Anne, like Elizabeth, is to eschew the dangers and costs of imperial contests, content instead to see "Temples rise, the beauteous Works of Peace" in contrast to "naked Temples" and "Heaps of Ruin" that followed the territorial ambitions of the Norman invaders or the dangerous triumphs of Edward III. Like Elizabeth, who endured the criticisms of her own courtiers for the sake of peace, Anne has the foresight to repudiate the bellicose position of Marlborough's faction and to opt for peace and its attendant prosperity.[59]

In *Windsor-Forest,* expansionist ideology and its attendant militarism exposes the home country to a multiplicity of perils: as Britain's ships travel outward in search of conquest and markets, other vessels carrying potentially dangerous strangers find their way to her own shores, and the navy itself requires deforestation of the sylvan retreats of home, dependence on foreign products, and the trepanning of British men. British people imbibe, during their service in imperial forces, a kind of arrogant indifference to other life-forms and forget how to contemplate nature for its beauties rather than its potential products, developing the crude narcissism articulated in Father Thames's speech:

> For me the Balm shall bleed, and Amber flow,
> The Coral redden, and the Ruby glow,
> The Pearly Shell its lucid Globe infold,
> And *Phoebus* warm the ripening Ore to Gold.
>
> (393–96)

How different from the humble harmoniousness of retirement, which allows one "T'observe a Mean, be to himself a Friend,/To follow Nature, and regard his End" (251–52). Moreover, engaging in the imperial adventure induces amnesia about the nation's bloody past; unlike the man who "Consults the Dead, and lives past Ages o'er," (248), the imperial citizen forgets the consequences of invasion and conquest—at least until a poet provides a reminder.

THOMSON'S STRATEGIES OF CONTAINMENT

Even more than *Windsor-Forest*, and in part as a consequence of its length and multiple versions, *The Seasons* invites notice of its internal inconsistencies. John Barrell and Harriet Guest, who observe that "nobody in the [eighteenth] century seems to comment upon the contradictions," are among several twentieth-century scholars who take up Thomson's seeming muddles and find cogent meaning in them. Patricia Meyer Spacks observes that "the inconsistencies in Thomson's attitude toward progress and civilization . . . correspond exactly to the inconsistencies in his attitude toward the state of natural man . . . they suggest a complete ambiguity in his position about the relative virtue of natural and civilized man." Ralph Cohen argues that Thomson deliberately shunned organic unity, that "what he presented in *The Seasons* was experimental and exploratory."[60] These comments respond to the multiple discrepancies in the poem, which range from the trivial to the central, from localized shifts of perspective to thematized confusion of effects. In *Autumn,* for example, wine, "the life-refining soul of decent wit" and the "cup of joy" in lines 89 and 702, is also "mutual swill" that causes "feeble tongues" and "maudlin eyes" in line 538. Similarly, the admired "glossy silk, and flowing lawn" that clothe man civilized by industry at the beginning of *Autumn* degenerate into "the glittering robe . . . /The pride and gaze of fools" toward the end (87, 1242–45). Most of the inconsistencies stem, of course, from the kind of contradictory responses to industrial and commercial progress that Spacks identifies, and perhaps no stable viewpoint should be asked of a poem that so often has to praise one season at the expense of another, which in turn becomes the best of all seasons.

Here, I want to focus on Thomson's strategies for dealing with his contradictory impulses in response to the culture and discourse of British imperialism. In doing so, I am indebted, of course, to Suvir Kaul's compelling reading of the contradictions in Thomson's patriotic poetry, and his conclusion that "If Thomson's poem tacks back and forth across an inconsistent variety of intellectual currents, it does so in order to find the best way of charting an uncertain, but nevertheless very attractive, imperial future."[61] But where Kaul's analysis moves toward understanding the formal qualities of the poem in the context of Thomson's desire "to articulate very different, even opposed ideas and positions into a series of arguments for a particular ordering of British power,"[62] I want to focus on a particular strategy of resolution and reassurance. While *The Seasons* articulates the poet's discomfort with the practices of the imperial project—its enslavement or oppression of other races, its use of brute military force, its crude accumulation of wealth and political power—the poem tames these brutalities within domestic space. Caught between his desire to participate in the great imperial adventure and his horror at its effects on human relations, Thomson needs to find a way to re-write the story of British conquest and rule to make it palatable to Britons themselves. As Lennard J. Davis says, "The project of colonizing cannot exist without the help of ideological and linguistic structures. . . . To win hearts and minds, one must occupy hearts and minds—in the dominant as well as the occupied countries."[63] The strategy Thomson selects comes as no surprise to those familiar with the work of Todorov and Said: Thomson casts the colonized as the Other, deploying familiar eighteenth-century ideologies about race, class, and gender to distance and dehumanize those being oppressed and to justify and celebrate colonizers. At the same time, however, he paradoxically erases the *real* otherness of non-European peoples, reconfiguring them

into more familiar modes that facilitate comprehension and appropriation. Like Behn importing elements of Restoration comedy to the Coramantien court, Thomson domesticates the exotic Other. In effect, he
figures colonized people as less-evolved versions of ruling-class British
males, similar to women and working classes, and, like them, subju-
gated for their own and society's good.[64]

When Thomson celebrates the power of Britain, he casts it in terms
of global conquest based on moral righteousness and liberational
agenda, which perhaps explains the text's popularity in Revolutionary
America.[65] He describes Britain's might in Burkean language of the
sublime: "At once the wonder, terror, and delight,/Of distant nations,
whose remotest shore can soon be shaken by the naval arm" (*Summer*,
1597–99). Imperial soldiers are agents of "thoughtful sires" at home,
who are "sincere, plain-hearted, hospitable, kind,/Yet like the mustering
thunder when provoked,/The dread of tyrants, and the sole resource/
Of those that under grim oppression groan" (*Summer*, 1472–78). In ar-
ticulating Britain's imperial mission this way, Thomson merely replicates the nationalist discourse articulated in the work of many
contemporaries.[66] The explicit overlapping of poetry and politics, so
common in the eighteenth century, is particularly evident in considerations of imperial and commercial expansion. At a time when anti-Wal-
pole forces could count on the support of a broad range of commercial
interests by attacking his Eurocentric policy, politics inevitably meant
a discussion of empire. Indeed, as Kathleen Wilson argues, "The energetic insertion of [the] mercantilist imperial vision in opposition politics
in the late 1730s and early 1740s increased the latter's resonances
among the broader political nation, where numbers of citizens were increasingly convinced that imperial ascendancy and a populist, virtuous
polity must go hand-in-hand."[67] In aligning himself with the anti-Wal-
pole and pro-expansionist party, Thomson not only obliged his Tory
and opposition Whig friends, but also joined a national movement co-
hering around the national hero Admiral Vernon, a movement that "em-
anated from elite and middling as well as plebeian quarters, acted out
in theater productions, tavern celebrations, and gentry-sponsored fêtes
as well as effigy-burnings."[68]

But Thomson, like Pope, saw the contradictions inherent in morally
righteous imperialism as clearly as he saw the problematics of industrial
and commercial progress; again and again, *The Seasons* grimly describes
the savagery of imperial forces and the dangers of global adventurism.

At times, the brutality of empire is projected on to other nations, as when he contrasts his peaceful traveling Muse with thuggish Catholics:

> Thou art no ruffian, who beneath the mask
> Of social commerce com'st to rob their wealth;
> No holy fury thou, blaspheming Heaven,
> With consecrated steel to stab their peace,
> And through the land, yet red from civil wounds,
> To spread the purple tyranny of Rome.
>
> (*Summer*, 753–8)

Of course, Thomson here taps into a traditional view of British, Protestant imperialists as the saviors of those under Spanish or French rule (or, as we shall see in *Hindoo Rajah*, under Mughal rule in India). Robert Bliss, for example, traces the longevity of this tactic when he discusses the Elizabethan belief that Spanish exploitation of native Americans could itself be exploited to bring America under English rule.[69] But some of the language in Thomson's passage—"rob their wealth," "stab their peace"—suggests discomfort with any imperial intervention, especially when it conceals an agenda of exploitation under the veneer of mercantile or missionary aims, both standard British practices. Despite his praise of Vernon, Thomson seems aware that the imperial naval force was no place for the morally squeamish, because, in Henry Gray Graham's words, "Never was the naval service more coarse, more brutal than at that period. Manned by the scum of the people—gaol-birds, smugglers, insolvent debtors, rascals of all shades, scoundrels of all degrees."[70] One passage of the poem, in particular, constitutes a comprehensive condemnation of imperial adventuring, when, in the course of extolling the virtues of private life, Thomson paints a horrifying portrait of imperial conduct and character:

> Let others brave the flood in quest of gain,
> And beat for joyless months the gloomy wave.
> Let such as deem it glory to destroy
> Rush into blood, the sack of cities seek—
> Unpierced, exulting in the widow's wail,
> The virgin's shriek, and infant's trembling cry.
> Let some, far distant from their native soil,
> Urged or by want or hardened avarice,
> Find other lands beneath another sun.
>
> (*Autumn*, 1278–86)

In language far more intense than Pope's lines on seizing a defenseless town, Thomson here portrays the sordid and inhumane aspect of imperial ambition, which originates in greed and culminates in looting, murder, and rape. And, like Behn in *Oroonoko,* Thomson too alludes to an edenic pagan world containing "many a happy isle,/The seat of blameless Pan, yet undisturbed/By Christian crimes and Europe's cruel sons" (*Summer,* 854–55). That these lines precede a long lament about "the waste of wealth" (860) in lands untouched by European Enlightenment values—"Progressive truth, the patient force of thought,/Investigation calm" (*Summer,* 878–79)—testifies to the deep contradictions in the poem's view of the "civilizing" mission of imperialism.[71]

Furthermore, even as he joins the national celebration of Britain's naval power, particularly as exercised by Vernon, Thomson points to the cost of such adventuring, even implying that some deaths might be deserved, or at least just. When a slave ship sinks, the shark, "Lured by the scent/Of steaming crowds, of rank disease, and death,/ . . . /Demands his share of prey—demands themselves./The stormy fates descend: one death involves/Tyrants and slaves." (*Summer,* 1015–23).[72] Collapsing distinctions that the poem insists on elsewhere, these lines invoke natural equality of races even as they explicitly condemn the brutalities consequent on trading in human flesh. One can even detect a degree of relish in the savage irony that puts the slavers in the power of a predator who does not value racial difference. Thomson's depiction of the plague that claims the heroes of Porto Bello does not contain punitive connotations, but it provides a terrifying corrective to the kind of abstract glorification of naval power sketched in Wilson's discussion of Vernon and articulated by John More in 1777. To More, navigation "is the most astonishing instance of human ingenuity . . . the greatest miracle of art . . . a *science* by which we subdue the most boisterous elements."[73] Although Thomson too alludes to "the heaven-conducted prow/Of Navigation bold" (Summer, 1767–68), he eschews More's kind of bland complacency. In *The Seasons,* winter winds "Burst into chaos with tremendous roar,/And anchored navies from their stations drive" (*Winter,* 163–64), and summer storms leave sailors helpless: "Art is too slow. By rapid fate oppressed,/His broad-winged vessel drinks the whelming tide,/Hid in the bosom of the black abyss" (*Summer,* 998–1000). Thomson's representation of sailors' bodies as they succumb to disease articulates yet another aspect of the dangers of imperial adventures. After the ill-fated siege of Cartagena in May 1741, thousands die of pestilential fever:

> You, gallant Vernon, saw
> The miserable scene; you, pitying, saw
> To infant-weakness sunk the warrior's arm;
> Saw the deep-racking pang, the ghastly form,
> The lip pale-quivering, and the beamless eye
> No more with ardour bright; you heard the groans
> Of agonizing ships from shore to shore,
> Heard, nightly plunged amid the sullen waves,
> The frequent corse, while, on each other fixed
> In sad presage, the blank assistants seemed
> Silent to ask whom fate would next demand.
>
> (*Summer*, 1041–51)

Like the mariners in Coleridge's poem, these sailors face death "With throats unslacked, with black lips baked"[74]; the dead albatross around their necks is the blue-water policy of imperial expansion.

If imperial conquerors cloak oppression with guile, if imperial servants are motivated by desperate greed (see Gulliver's description of sailors in book 4, chapter 4), and if they become subject to horrible deaths, their mission and methods must be carefully justified. In *The Seasons*, such vindication resides in configuring alien races as victims of savage nature and savage character, in dire need of European intervention. Thus, the harrowing description of sailors succumbing to the plague is followed by othering the disease itself, which originates in dark and alien places, "From Ethiopia's poisoned woods,/From stifled Cairo's filth" (*Summer*, 1055–56) — note that both unpopulated and urban sites in Africa contain unwholesome vapors. Recasting Pope's implied homology between England and tropical spaces, Thomson constructs a binary which argues that imperial intervention in these tainted spaces, far from being destructive to Eden, can be construed as medicinal. *Summer* consistently represents the tropics as exotic and primitive, "with dreadful beauty crowned/And barbarous wealth" (643–44), producing strange vegetation and monstrous beasts.[75] And of course, the very plenitude is arid, since in these lands "the sun smiles and seasons teem in vain/ . . . /wondrous waste of wealth" (849).

Moreover, this unproductively luxurious land is peopled by unhappy barbarians who stand in need of Europe's, or rather Britain's, civilizing hand. In *Winter*, the poet imagines a cozy fireside conversation, part of which consists of speculations about why some nations "pine beneath the brightest skies/In nature's richest lap" (592–93). There is no need to rehearse here eighteenth-century theories of race, which have been amply analyzed and applied to literary texts by critics such as Laura Brown and Felicity Nussbaum. Brown, in a consideration of *Gulliver's Travels*, lays out some specific ideas current in eighteenth-century travel and scientific discourse: that Negroes are close to apes, that they are known to be filthy and ill smelling, that they eat rotten meat, that they "are incapable of civil government," and that their flattened features come from "being carried against their mother's chests." Nussbaum looks at both monogenetic and polygenetic theories of racial difference and finds that "the barbarity of black Africans was often attributed to environmental causes."[76] Thomson, as he engages with contemporary speculation about the nature of the darker races, connects both features and character to climate. After pitying Africans' lack of rational government and liberty, he adds:

> The parent Sun himself
> Seems o'er this world of slaves to tyrannize,
> And with oppressive ray the roseate bloom
> Of beauty blasting, gives the gloomy hue
> And feature gross—or worse, to ruthless deeds,
> Mad jealousy, blind rage, and fell revenge
> Their fervid spirit fires.
>
> (*Summer*, 884–90)

Subscribing, therefore, to the monogenetic theory of race (apparently these grotesque people originally possessed "the roseate bloom of beauty"), Thomson construes Africans as damaged versions of white Europeans, their color, features, and behavior distorted by their climate. As monstrously mutated versions of their conquerors, these no-longer-so-alien races can more easily be understood as inferior beings in need of subjugation and protection, perhaps capable of being brought back to reason and beauty by the careful ministrations of their betters.

When it comes to subjugating and protecting a weaker yet dangerous creature, no one is so confident and able as the ruling-class British male. After all, he has had years of experience reining in that other troublesome inferior being: woman. With varying degrees of success, this important task has been undertaken by many of Thomson's literary precursors, including Jenkins in Chaucer's *Wife of Bath's Tale*, Petruchio in Shakespeare's *Taming of the Shrew*, and even Pinchwife in Wycherley's *Country Wife*. Thomson, by constructing a series of parallels between woman and barbarian, enables his British reader to understand the need to control other races through constraint and surveillance. As Anne McClintock puts it, "Imperialism cannot be fully understood without a theory of gender power. . . . gender dynamics were, from the outset, fundamental to the securing and maintenance of the imperial enterprise."[77]

The "Argument" in *Spring* promises that the poem will conclude "with a dissuasive from the wild and irregular passion of Love, opposed to that of a pure and happy kind," and the poem itself traces the dangers of irregular love in a distinctly gendered manner. Although he warns both men and women against succumbing to seduction, Thomson allots 129 lines to ill effects on "the aspiring youth" (983) and only 10 lines to "ye fair" (973). While no specific consequences are spelled out regarding the fate of the seduced woman, the man is warned about losing money, education, friends, speech, sleep, and reason, so that he is utterly undone: "His brightest aims extinguished all, and all/His lively moments running down to waste" (1111–12). Moreover, though the woman is cautioned against "meek submission" to the "fervent tongue" of "betraying man" (976–82), the man must contend with a far more dangerous Duessa figure:

> the kindling grace,
> The enticing smile, the modest-seeming eye,
> Beneath whose beauteous beams, belying Heaven,
> Lurk searchless cunning, cruelty, and death:
> And still, false-warbling in his cheated ear,
> Her siren voice enchanting draws him on
> To guileful shores and meads of fatal joy.
>
> (989–95)

Woman is construed like the torrid zone, a site of "luxurious bliss" and "fatal treasures," which must be tamed by the "godlike wisdom of the tempered breast" (*Summer*, 861, 869, 877) granted to Adam and other Englishmen. Indeed, Thomson echoes Milton's articulation of gender hierarchy: his Caledon and Amelia are "a matchless pair,/With equal virtue formed and equal grace/The same, distinguished by their sex alone:/Hers the mild luster of the blooming morn,/And his the radiance of the risen day" (*Summer*, 1172–76). Like the native of non-European continents, woman is less evolved, further back along the chain of being, morning rather than full day.[78]

Such arrested development can lead to inappropriate or excessive sexual desire. Although Thomson earlier chastely draws back from describing the "fierce desire" and "horrid loves" of animals (*Spring*, 792,

830), at least in part out of consideration for the sensibilities of his feminine audience, he has, as we have seen, no compunctions about representing the sexually predatory woman. And when, after delineating the
ill effects of succumbing to women's wiles, he turns to a description of
ideal conjugal love, he contrasts it to the practices of "barbarous nations, whose inhuman love/Is wild desire, fierce as the suns they feel"
(*Spring* 1130–31). The juxtaposition of feminine and barbaric carnality
makes it possible, even imperative, that the same powerful force that
was able to subdue illicit female desire and behavior take up the burden
of regulating the lawless passions of lesser races.

A brief moment of explicit conjunction of race and gender comes in
Summer, when Thomson alludes to the Niger River "and all the floods/
In which the full-formed maids of Afric lave/Their jetty limbs" (823–
24). But Thomson, unlike Behn, chooses not to dwell on the black female body, and turns away from the kind of salaciousness evoked by
Imoinda entering the "very rich Bath" under the leering surveillance of
the King (*Oroonoko,* 47). For the reader, however, these well-endowed
and presumably naked African women constitute a silent background
in the subsequent narrative about Damon and Musidora, a narrative
that begins in pornographic mode and ends with a celebration of sexual
innocence and chivalry. Damon, by "lucky chance" (1286) places himself where Musidora has come "to bathe/Her fervent limbs in the refreshing stream" (1291–92). Like Matthew Lewis's lascivious
Ambrosio greedily watching Antonia bathe, Damon, despite some "du-
bious flutterings" (72), relishes the slow striptease of the woman he desires, and the poet's titillating description takes on a more intense erotic
charge from the presence of a fascinated voyeur:

> as from the snowy leg
> And slender foot the inverted silk she drew;
> As the soft touch dissolved the virgin zone;
> And, through the parting robe, the alternate breast,
> With youth wild-throbbing, on thy lawless gaze
> In full luxuriousness rose. But, desperate youth,
> How durst thou risk the soul-distracting view
> As from her naked limbs of glowing white,
> Harmonious swelled by nature's finest hand,
> In folds loose-floating fell the fainter lawn,
> And fair exposed she stood, shrunk from herself,
> With fancy blushing.
>
> (1308–19)

Unlike the terse reference to "jetty limbs," the detail here attests to the poet's delight in Musidora's body, and we note, of course, the multiple emphases on whiteness. The same link between color and feminine beauty recurs in the poem's praise of British women, a description that dwells on "live crimson," and "native white" cheeks and "red rosebud" lips (*Summer*, 1584–88). Like Southerne rewriting Imoinda as a white woman, Thomson turns to whiteness as a sign of desirable femininity.[79]

Ultimately, however, the difference between black and white female bodies becomes subsumed into a metanarrative about benign subjugation. The episode, which begins by objectifying the female body and making it vulnerable to the male gaze, proceeds to reify patriarchal power by demonstrating man's laudable self-restraint. Damon indeed risks losing control as he momentarily allows himself to be ensnared by the sight of her wanton nakedness, imbibing "Such maddening draughts of beauty to the soul/As for a while o'erwhelmed his raptured thought/With luxury too daring" (1332–34; recall the effects of maddening draughts of wine in *Autumn*, 552–55: "feeble tongues" and "maudlin eyes"). But Damon rapidly regains his self-possession and transforms his own illicit peeping into protective surveillance, while his unregulated physical response morphs into the symbolic order of language: his "ready pencil" gives her permission to "Bathe on," secure in the knowledge that "I go to guard thy haunt;/To keep from thy recess each vagrant foot/And each licentious eye" (1339–43). Damon, like British imperialists protecting natives from Spanish or French depredators, reconfigures himself from transgressor to guardian. His selfless vigilance, moreover, results in the very submission he had yearned for: Musidora, who had been coyly distant, confesses her passion and promises that "the time may come you need not fly" (74) from her naked body. Indeed, she even cedes to him absolute power to interpret her words (and her desires), identifying him as "sole judge of what these verses mean" (1367). Musidora's eager acceptance of Damon's authority is markedly different from the fate of the "mere lifeless, violated form" that characterizes the enslaved concubines of "eastern tyrants" (*Summer*, 1132–33), and of Imoinda in the Coramantien court. The story of Damon and Musidora enacts precisely the fantasy of British imperialism: the danger of inappropriate or excessive passion has been contained by regulating both the desire and its target, and the result has been a voluntary, loving submission offered by the object being controlled.[80]

Construing other nations as less evolved and in need of protection certainly clarifies and rationalizes imperial appropriation. In fact,

Thomson unites history and geography when, in praise of industry, he contrasts the current state of civilization with an earlier, unhappy world in which "the sad barbarian roving mixed/With beasts of prey" (*Autumn*, 57–58). In this passage, Thomson situates in the past what he has elsewhere represented as a synchronic condition in non-European spaces, where man cowers in the face of "brute creation" such as serpents, tigers, leopards, hyenas, and lions (*Summer*, 898–927). Conflating the contemporary state of uncivilized space with the former wilderness of industrialized European nations allows him to naturalize imperial interventions that merely accelerate the kind of progress desirable in all parts of the globe and for which residents of these uncouth places will be grateful. Indeed, so frightening is the primitive world teeming with natural enemies that "the wretch" who has recently escaped from pirate or tyrant "half wishes for his bonds again" (*Summer*, 937). Clearly, given a choice among enslavement to tyrants, destruction by beasts, or dependence on British protection, the wise barbarian will do as Musidora does: accept the enlightened guardianship of a superior race.

The surveillance and governance of a far-flung empire requires the work of many bodies, and it is the responsibility of the ruling classes (and their poets) to develop an ideology that produces concord among factions. Thomson, Ralph Cohen points out, "assumed that harmony among groups involves a commerce that can be financed only by wealth and carried out only by authority . . . the functioning of this ideal . . . requires ships, merchants, labourers, and the resources of many enterprises."[81] To achieve this harmony, *The Seasons* aims to enlist the compliance of the working class while simultaneously instilling in the ruling elite a proper sense of patriarchal responsibility. The poem's representation of the rural working class privileges British workers and offers them as models for natives of other lands. In the opening lines of *Spring*, Thomson reminds "generous Britons" not only of the spoils of empire, which "from a thousand shores/Wafts all the pomp of life into your ports" (72–73), but also of their contribution to the global economy, for they "the naked nations clothe" and serve as "the exhaustless granary of a world" (76–77). Furthermore, by invoking the revered Cincinnatus, who "held the scale of empire" and "then, with victorious hand,/ Disdaining little delicacies, seized/The plough" (62–65), Thomson collapses the distinction between ruling-class conqueror and peasant. In *Summer*, he writes a pastoral paean to sheepshearing, during which "gentle tribes" of sheep give themselves up to "the tender swain's well-guided shears" (417–19), thereby replicating the gendered hierarchy articulated in the Damon/Musidora narrative. This rustic activity, however, signifies much more than the shepherd knows:

> A simple scene! Yet hence Britannia sees
> Her solid grandeur rise: hence she commands
> The exalted stores of every brighter clime;
> The treasures of the sun without his rage:
> Hence, fervent all with culture, toil, and arts,
> Wide glows her land: her dreadful thunder hence
> Rides o'er the waves sublime, and now, even now,
> Impending hangs o'er Gallia's humbled coast;
> Hence rules the circling deep, and awes the world.
>
> (423–31)

British power, whether exploiting the wealth of conquered territories or triumphing over imperial rivals, emanates from the simplest activities of its working citizens, who will toil all the more cheerfully once they learn the importance of their lowly tasks.

And workers in *The Seasons* are indeed cheerful. Happy rural workers appear everywhere in the poem.[82] Farmers reap "While through their cheerful band the rural talk,/The rural scandal, and the rural jest/ Fly harmless" (*Autumn*, 158–60). In their glad assumption of laborious tasks, these workers resemble the "lusty steers" that "unrefusing, to the harnessed yoke/ . . . lend their shoulder, and begin their toil,/Cheered by the simple song and soaring lark" (*Spring*, 35–41; contrast this to the insensate "dull Ox" in Pope's *Essay on Man*, Epistle I, 63). Haymakers, including "stooping age" and "infant hands," so enjoy their task that through the countryside "resounds the blended voice/of happy labour, love, and social glee" (*Summer*, 357–70). Villagers in Thomson's Britain dance and flirt, "nor think/That with to-morrow's sun their annual toil/ Begins again the never-ceasing round" (*Autumn*, 1232–34); their childish natures lead them to take pleasure in "Rustic mirth . . . /The simple joke that takes the shepherd's heart,/Easily pleased" (*Winter*, 622–24). Far from resenting or even questioning their station in life or their endless toil, these rural workers live for the moment, enjoying simple pleasures; they are eager to work for their masters, perfectly content to depend on and obey their betters. They subscribe, in other words, to the notion put forward in *Summer*'s hymn to Britannia that the most burdensome work can be glorified—"even Drudgery himself,/As at the car he sweats, or, dusty, hews/The Palace stone, looks gay" (1459–61). Being part of the British workforce is its own reward, and if freeborn Britons enthusiastically embrace their subjugation, it cannot be but right that ignorant natives of other places should benefit from the same paternalistic rule.

Thomson's poem sets out a careful system of ethics for proper paternalistic domination. The progress of civilization, delineated at the beginning of *Autumn,* culminates with the formation of a just and generous government established by enlightened men who, "with joint force Oppression chaining, set/Imperial Justice at the helm, yet still/To them accountable: nor slavish dreamed/That toiling millions must resign their weal/And all the honey of their search to such/As for themselves alone themselves have raised" (103–8). In this ideal community, landlords forgo rent during bad harvests (*Autumn,* 350–59), shepherds lovingly shield their flocks from the elements (*Winter,* 265–68), and men respond to the "winning softness" and "silent adulation" of women by protecting them. Such sterling public and private qualities can only help less fortunate or less enlightened peoples who put themselves in British hands. As Robin W. Winks says, "Idealists and realists alike sought to spread what they felt in their hearts was superior, to spread their institutions *because* they were superior and therefore not only easy to spread but a positive good for those to whom they were applied."[83] Thomson even provides an example from recent history to demonstrate the ameliorative effects of European culture on barbarian races; praising Peter the Great's determination to civilize "A people savage from remotest time," the poem extols his success when "Charged with the stores of Europe home he goes!/Then cities rise amid the illumined waste;/O'er joyless deserts smiles the rural reign" (*Winter* 952, 972–74). The benign authority of the British ruling class has brought happiness through submission to women and workers and has served as a paradigm for Baltic savages; it now holds out the same happy prospect to the sad barbarians of Africa, America, and Asia.

Windsor-Forest and *The Seasons* are often paired as prospect poems that evoke "a reflective flight through time, as well as a visual one through space: the historical and political associations of the landscape carry the mind's eye into the past and future, as though events in time are laid out spatially before the surveyor."[84] Indeed, both poems roam the globe and traverse time even as they return, again and again, to the privileged *and* vexed status of Britain at particular historical time. Both poems articulate dismay at some of the effects of British adventurism and both consider the unique position of power that allows Britain to exert its influence across the globe. For Pope, however, the discontents

of Britain's own civilization are rooted in a violent history and exacerbated by imperial ambition. Marking a controversial treaty at the end
of an indecisive and costly war, Pope registers both the urgent need for
peace and "a plea to return man to nature, above all to his own best
nature. . . . At the bottom of *Windsor-Forest* lies a rejection, probably not
fully conscious, of the old heroic ideal."[85] For Thomson, the heroic ideal
remains a possibility, if not for individual man (Griffin points out that
Thomson's poem does not address the "heroic victory of Admiral Vernon at Porto Bello in 1739"),[86] then for a nation that has already assimilated its Celtic fringes and shows every sign of replicating that success
further afield. Moreover, the political and historical context of *The Seasons* demonstrates the fragility of the peace extolled in *Windsor-Forest*.
As Sambrook notes, "Because of very severe limitations placed upon
concessions secured by British merchants under the Treaty of Utrecht
in 1713, a thriving illicit traffic grew up, which Spanish coastguards
sought to check by the seizure of British ships."[87] Spanish reaction to
British smuggling evoked outrage among politicians and populace,
while the press cast "the conflict in the stark and dramatic terms of a
struggle between liberty and slavery, national honour and disgrace."[88]
The very treaty that Pope hopes will end the damaging effects of imperial conflict proved to be the catalyst for hostilities Thomson seeks to
justify in his troubled but ultimately reassuring portrait of a world in
which Britannia rules.

2

Familial Identifications: Daniel Defoe's *Colonel Jack* and *Moll Flanders* and Tobias Smollett's *Humphry Clinker*

> 'Tis a Continent whose vast Extent was never yet known, and may contain more Noble Earth than all the Universe besides . . . It affords all things both for Beauty and Use.
>
> —*Oroonoko*

> I think it was the third day that we found the body of a Christian, scalped and abominably mangled, and lying in a pudder of his blood. . . . I cannot describe how dreadfully this sight affected us; but it robbed me of all strength and all hope for this world.
>
> —*Master of Ballantrae*

DANIEL DEFOE AND TOBIAS SMOLLETT DIVIDE THE HONORS REGARDing quantity and range of output; as Lewis M. Knapp puts it in his introduction to Smollett's *Letters*, "The hundreds of sheets of handwriting which [Smollett] sent to his publishers must have exceeded in number those of any other eighteenth-century writer except Defoe."[1] Their writings range over many of the same topics (the Union of Scotland and England, the state of the nation, and the role of commerce and empire in British life) and genres (novels, journals, and pamphlets), but unlike Pope and Thomson, Daniel Defoe and Tobias Smollett seem to come from different ideological worlds regarding Britain's imperial ambitions. Defoe's work, both fictional and journalistic, consistently and optimistically urges expanding the commercial and imperial horizons of the newly formed Britain, in part to exercise innate English abilities. As he proclaims in a letter to Harley in 1711, "England is quallifyed to Grow Rich Even where The Spanish Settlement would Perish and Starv."[2] Smollett, on the other hand, frequently writes scathingly of both imperial adventures and the center that generates them. In *Roderick*

Random, he attributes British failures in the Indies, variously, to petty pride on the part of General Wentworth and Admiral Vernon; to the incompetence of the navy, and to ignorance among the ruling elite at home. "Or else," as he sarcastically writes, "the admiral would not have found it such an easy matter, at his return to England, to justify his conduct to a ministry at once so upright and discerning" (188). Where Defoe frequently serves as propagandist for British worth and power, Smollett searches out and exposes the disease within the realm. They come together in this chapter, however, in their discomfort with the implications of a growing British settlement in America. If Defoe's uneasiness with the potential disloyalty of colonists has to be teased out of the text, it corresponds with Smollett's desire to stem the tide not just of luxury at home, but of emigration to America.

Smollett, of course, speaks most eloquently in *Humphry Clinker* about the loss to Scotland of so many able citizens, but Defoe, too, understands that Scottish exodus to other places originates in poverty at home. In September 1710, he writes to Harley of improved conditions in Scotland, and adds that "it is the great Interest of England to Study & Promote the Prosperity and Encrease of Scotland. . . . The People of Scotland do not fly abroad and help to People all Europe because this Country is not Equally Fruitfull and Habitable with other Places, but because want of employment at home for the People makes it more difficult for them to Subsist."[3] Defoe's knowledge of Scotland (much of it as Harley's agent, charged with gauging Scottish attitudes to Union), although often partial and prejudiced, allows him to assert in *A Tour Thro' the whole Island of Great Britain* that he aims to counteract prevailing hyperbolic accounts that portray Scotland as "contemptible" or "Paradise," and even to catch himself "talking like an *Englishman,* rather than like a *Briton.*"[4] Smollett's deeper and more personal knowledge of the other half of the Union gives rise to occasional exasperation with the culture that he needs to tolerate in order to make a living: "I am heartily tired of this Land of Indifference and Phlegm where the finer Sensations of the Soul are not felt, and Felicity is held to consist in stupifying [*sic*] Port and overgrown Buttocks of Beef, where Genius is lost, Learning undervalued, and Taste altogether extinguished."[5] Each, however, is deeply conscious of inhabiting a Britain made up of distinct and often adversarial traditions, and each finds a tenuous kind of national union and identity by firmly characterizing colonial America as definitively foreign.

DEFOE AND THE RETURN NARRATIVE

Perhaps more than any other writer in the eighteenth century, Daniel Defoe is identified with the push to settle the American colonies, thereby making them indisputably part of England's empire, especially in the face of French incursions on the continent. In the June 20, 1704, issue of his *Review*, Defoe castigates those who fail to realize the urgency of the colonial mission: "Those People who think 'tis not our Interest to increase our Plantations on the Continent of *America*, would do well to reflect on the Consequences of this, in future Ages, and for which Posterity may have Reason to blame us. . . . it nearly concerns *England;* to Encourage by all possible Methods, the increase of our Colonies in *America*, that the growing *French* Power may never be able to dispose us there."[6] To those who worry that an overpopulated America might compete with England's commercial interests, he offers unequivocal assurance that more settlers in the cold climates of New England will require even more clothing manufactured in the home country: "For this reason it is doubtless the Interest of *Great Britain* to encourage as much as possible the peopling the Northern Colonies."[7] Defoe's fiction, too, endorses the colonial enterprise, whether allegorically, as in *Robinson Crusoe*, or more explicitly in the pair of colonial novels published in 1722. Indeed, *Colonel Jack* and *Moll Flanders* can serve not only as propaganda but also as manuals for attaining prosperity in and through the American colonies. Moll's mother and Jack extol opportunities for advancement in the New World, even (especially) for those with disadvantaged or criminal pasts. Speaking of transported felons, Moll's mother stresses the egalitarian practices obtaining in the colonies: "When they come here, *says she*, we make no difference. . . . Hence Child, *says she*, many a *Newgate* Bird becomes a Great Man" (133–34). Jack, too, assures readers, "THAT in *Virginia*, the meanest, and most despicable Creature after his time of Servitude is expir'd, if he will but apply himself with Diligence and Industry to the Business of the Country, is sure . . . both of living Well and growing Rich" (173). Yet despite achieving financial and social security in America, both Moll and Jack return to England, enacting a version of the absenteeism that Defoe deplores in Scottish nobles who spend the proceeds of their estates in England rather than at home.[8]

This inconsistency regarding emigration and return has, of course, elicited critical attention, although Firdous Azim oddly asserts that "it is in Virginia that the narrator of *Moll Flanders* finds a final resting place." Lucette Desvignes and Rita DiGiuseppe merely register the irony in Moll's return, while Tony Dunn ascribes it to her restless desire for movement. Brett C. McInelly provides one explanation when he argues that Defoe narrates "a kind of counter colonization. Degenerate individuals are, in a paradoxical reversal, sent to and are eventually reclaimed in the colonies and then readmitted to the ranks of civil society, having acquired through their experience a heightened sense of moral consciousness and the monetary means to become law-abiding citizens."[9] In this chapter, I argue that *Colonel Jack* and *Moll Flanders* make a conscious case for repatriating successful colonists by suggesting that true gentility can reside only in Britain. Defoe wants, I suggest, to insist that although the colonies can rehabilitate those marginalized and criminalized by the home countries, exiles must return in order to establish the kind of citizenry needed to protect the British empire's ideology of domestic stability, both familial and national. By pairing their colonial experiences, I do not mean to elide crucial differences between Moll and Jack. Certainly, Jack's far greater fortune and his easy access to higher social classes are in part an effect of gender: education, military service, and early financial security distinguish him from his more marginalized and vulnerable female counterpart. My argument, however, considers the ways in which both careers serve to construct a clear hierarchy of home and colony.

It would perhaps be useful here to provide a brief chronology of Moll's and Jack's transatlantic voyages, and to note that they are carefully differentiated. Moll makes her first crossing in the 1650s, following her bigamous and incestuous marriage to Humphry. She spends eight years in America and returns to London toward the end of the Civil War. Her second eight years in the colonies come after the Restoration, and she dates her final resettlement in England as 1683, in the middle of the Succession Crisis. David Leon Higdon, who has traced the chronology of Moll's life, points out that Moll seems remarkably removed from the stirring public events around her. She resides in America during the Civil War, and even when she is present "during the significant events such as the Restoration, the Plague, and the Great Fire, egocentricity keeps her unaware of their magnitude."[10] Although Higdon refers to Moll's indifference to British public events, we should note also that Moll makes no reference to upheavals in colonial politics. For example, although she resides in Virginia at the time, she omits any mention of Bacon's Rebellion of 1675, which convulsed the colony, provoked an English military occupation, and scuttled Virginia's chances of gaining a Charter which would have granted relative autonomy from the Crown. Unlike Moll, Jack participates directly, although sometimes involuntarily, in many of the political and military convulsions besetting Europe. Indeed, after fifteen years in the colonies, he develops "an unquenchable Thirst . . . after seeing something that was doing in the World, and the more because the World was at that time engag'd more or less, in the great War wherein the *French* King might be said to be engag'd with, and against all the Powers of *Europe*" (172; Jack refers to the War of the League of Augsburg, 1688–97). Although he acts as a mere tourist at Ghent in 1697 — and in fact escapes being taken by the French because he had "stroll'd away that Day to see the Country about . . . and observe the Beauty of their Fortifications" (183–84) — by 1701, he takes an active role in the War of the Spanish Succession (the end of which Pope celebrates in *Windsor-Forest*) and later engages briefly in the 1715 Jacobite uprising, the failure of which precipitates his return to America. His second sojourn in Virginia is brief, as he almost immediately sets out on a series of trading voyages to Spanish America, from which he finds passage back to London, which represents for him, as for Moll, home and center.

The center that Moll and Jack inhabit before their first journeys to America, however, offers little to bind their loyalty. Both are abandoned children, set adrift in a society that provides no institutional support: Moll contrasts French state orphanages with the English policy of neglect that leaves her "a poor desolate Girl without Friends, without Cloaths, without Help or Helper in the World" (44); and the "Editor" of *Colonel Jack* deplores the lack of "publick Schools, and Charities" that could "prevent the Destruction of so many unhappy Children, as, in this Town, are every Year Bred up for the Gallows" (1). Defoe's compelling portraits of forsaken children have led Lincoln B. Faller to call *Colonel Jack* "a vivid, sympathetic picture of social and economic deprivation practically unmatched by anything else in eighteenth-century literature" and have elicited from Amit Yahav-Brown the conclusion that "Within the logic laid out by *An Essay upon Projects*, England's failure to provide material sustenance for the infant Moll amounts to a positive infringement of this child's rights."[11] If our sympathy erodes as the children mature, if we disapprove of their predatory practices, we yet understand that Moll's dwindling resources as friendless widow and young Jack's vulnerability as thief and deserter make the British Isles seem deeply inhospitable to marginalized citizens. Yet both require an external impetus to embark on their first trans-atlantic voyage: Moll, from the urging of her brother/husband, and Jack, from the unanswerable pressure of being "trappan'd" (112).[12] Moll's subsequent exhortation to Jemy (first when they discover their mutual deception and collective poverty and later when they are in Newgate) and Jack's retreat to Virginia after the 1715 uprising only underscore the point that emigration to America is a last resort for those who face destitution or death in England.

But of course that *is* Defoe's point: the American colonies provide a refuge and an opportunity to those who fail at home. As the experience of Moll and her mother posits, transported felons can begin anew and flourish in the colonies. Jack, enumerating the processes whereby the meanest exile can achieve prosperity, ends with a ringing endorsement of rebirth in America: "In a Word, every *Newgate* Wretch, every Desperate forlorn Creature; the most Despicable ruin'd Man in the World, has here a fair opportunity put into his Hands to begin the World again, and that upon a Foot of certain Gain, and in a Method exactly Honest; with a Reputation, that nothing past will have any Effect upon; and innumerable People have thus rais'd themselves from the worst Circumstance in the World; Namely, from the Condemn'd-Hole in *Newgate*" (153). Jack's glowing account is congruent with Moll's trajectory as articulated by Lou Caton: "Her secular and spiritual transformations merge in the figure of transportation, which offers the optimism of spiritual salvation while simultaneously introducing the material riches of a rising mercantile class."[13] Defoe's rosy portrait, however, is fictional: as historians have pointed out, transportation was hardly a guarantee of a better life; convicts were frequently ill treated or cheated by ships' captains, and once in America, they were barely differentiated from slaves. A. Roger Ekirch describes how the hard life of transported felons was inscribed on their bodies: "Burnt backs, ugly burns, and crooked limbs. . . . Scars criss-crossed entire bodies. Many of these injuries were sustained during times of hard manual labour. . . . Often, however, the worst mutilations stemmed from human violence. Knife and sword wounds were common over all parts of the body."[14] Unlike the ornamental inscriptions on Imoinda's black body or the self-inflicted mutilations on the "red" bodies of the Indians in *Oroonoko*, these marks on white English bodies attest to the brutal treatment accorded to convicts and indentured servants in the new world where they are supposed to be "sure (Life and Health suppos'd) both of living Well and growing Rich" (*CJ* 173). That parenthetical conditional hints at the harsh conditions the exiles must endure; indeed, Jack's convict-tutor, while exalting the punishment that brings redemption, describes the concomitant physical hardships: "Naked and Hungry, weary and Faint, oppress'd with Cold in one Season, and Heat in the other . . . here, I struggl'd with hard fare . . . here, I labour'd till Nature sometimes was just sinking under the Load." (166). Although the tutor praises God for the penance that leads to his moral regeneration, his language betrays his revulsion; deliverance from sin, he asserts, can "make any Man be thankful for *Virginia*, or a worse Place, *if that can be*" (167; italics mine). No wonder then that Jemy expresses "horror . . . at his being sent over to the Plantations as *Romans* sent condemn'd Slaves to Work in the Mines" (*MF* 380).

As propaganda for settling in the colonies, these passages seem singularly inept, unlikely to attract any but the most pathologically guilt-ridden sinner. But of course Defoe's characters are not voluntary exiles, and populating the colonies is really about serving the interests of the home country rather than the colonists themselves. As early as 1582, Richard Hakluyt articulates the rationale behind transportation: "Yea, if wee woulde beholde with the eye of pitie howe al our Prisons are pestered and filled with able men to serve their Countrie, which for small robberies are dayly hanged up in great numbers euen twentie at a clappe . . . wee woulde hasten and further euery man to his power the deducting of some Colonies of our superfluous people into those temperate and fertile parts of America, which . . . seeme to offer themselues vnto vs, stretching neere vnto her Majesties Dominions, then to any other part of Europe."[15] As Ekirch points out, transportation was necessary not for the moral rehabilitation of criminals but for the practical and ideological benefits to England. Removing felons not only checked increasingly counterproductive punishments—"Criminals did not always behave penitently, and even public executions were becoming known for their festive, carnival atmosphere"—but also had an added benefit in that it "did not place traditional British freedoms in jeopardy. . . . By virtue of transportation, Britain was able to avoid a massive corrections system and the creation of a coercive force to staff it."[16] The 1718 Transportation Act makes clear that transportation serves to replace sentences that "have not proved effectual to deter wicked and evil-disposed persons" and to supply "a great want of servants who . . . might be the means of improving and making the said Colonies and plantations more useful to this Nation.'[17]

Given that Defoe could not have been unaware of the rather unsavory "reasons of state" behind the Transportation Act or of the wretched treatment of convicts, it might be argued that he deliberately misrepresents conditions in America, either because he himself had profited from the privatization of the convict trade, or because the truth was less important than extending British colonial power. In fact, I suggest, his two American novels articulate mixed feelings about the colonial enterprise: although Defoe undoubtedly urges settlement to advance British political and commercial power, he also encodes in these two novels deep (and realistic) reservations about life in the colonies. In the tutor's description of his physical miseries, in Jemy's repugnance, and in Jack's own account of his life as servant—"we work'd Hard, lodg'd Hard, and far'd Hard" (119)—we see that Defoe is neither ignorant of nor entirely disingenuous about the real situation of the laboring classes in America. *Colonel Jack* rhetorically (and accurately) conflates Jack's service as servant with that of convicts and slaves when Jack ruefully reflects "that I was brought into this miserable Condition of a Slave by some strange Directing Power . . . as a Punishment for the wickedness of my younger Years" (119) and when the warehouse keeper who fits him out for his new job as overseer decrees, "go in there a slave, and come out a Gentleman" (127).

The conditions of indentured servitude remained dismal into midcentury. In 1756, Elizabeth Sprigs describes her miserable life in Maryland:

> What we unfortunat English People suffer here is beyond the probability of you in England to conceive . . . am toiling almost Day and Night, and very often in the Horses druggery, with only this comfort that Bitch you do not half enough, and then tied up and whipp'd to that Degree that you'd not serve an Animal . . . nay, many Negroes' are better used, almost naked no shoes or stocking to wear, and the comfort after slaving during Masters pleasure, what rest we can get is to rap ourselves in a Blanket and ly upon the Ground.[18]

Clearly, identities and treatments of servant, slave, and convict were fungible and fluid in the early eighteenth century. Abbot Emerson Smith points out that an indentured servant could be bought and sold, "could be alienated temporarily by his master so that his services might pay off a debt . . . He might be won or lost in a card game."[19] It is part of Moll's and Jack's triumph that they are able to overcome the difficulties of colonial life just as they were able to survive the disadvantages of their years in England. Defoe is at some pains to emphasize how atypical his hero and heroine are, whether in their early skill in negotiating an underprivileged life, their ability to impress and manipulate those who exert power over them, or their lifelong ambition to achieve gentility. These extraordinary personal qualities allow Moll and Jack to navigate the difficult terrain of the New World. They do so despite the odds against them and in contrast to those who share their fate: Moll and Jemy buy their freedom for the price of "6000 weight of Tobacco" plus "a present of 20 guineas" (402), a happy ending enabled by Moll's carefully hoarded proceeds of crime and one not available to the vast majority of convicted felons.[20] Jack rises quickly from servant to overseer not only by impressing his master with his hard work (and hard-luck story), but also by demonstrating his respectability in the shape of his bill for £94, also a product of criminal activity. Unlike his friend Captain Jack, who escapes from his master and returns to be hanged in England, Colonel Jack, like Moll, distinguishes himself from his peers in America. A look at average incomes demonstrates the difference between Defoe's protagonists and less-fortunate colonists. Moll's property in America yields £300 a year after a mere eight years of cultivation (426), and Jack lives in London on the proceeds of his Virginia plantation, which "generally return'd me from 400 to 600l. A Year" (233). Contrast these figures to those worked out by David S. Lovejoy. In 1667, the average production in Virginia was 1200 pounds of tobacco; sold at half a penny per pound, the yield for one man's labor was two and a half pounds a year, "out of which came taxes and other necessities. . . . It is revealing to learn what the cost of Empire was to those in Virginia who did the work."[21] Moll and Jack, no longer among those who do the work on plantations, own slaves and servants who toil under harsh conditions to produce the income they so proudly announce to readers. Defoe's careful differentiation of his protagonists from the general class of emigrants belies, I believe, McInelly's argument "that Defoe depicts the colonies as sites of financial and moral regeneration, thereby advocating transportation as a way to reclaim lives and livelihoods . . . [he] recasts the experience of forced migration and servitude as desirable, as banishment refigured as opportunity."[22] Indeed, the very specialness of Defoe's protagonists' experience in America justifies narratives of their lives; by the same token, their unique stories point up the more common (and less uplifting) lives of colonial laborers.

Despite achieving financial security in the course of their initial sojourn in the colonies, both Moll and Jack return to England, impelled by very different but equally urgent motives. I shall take up the issue of Moll's incestuous marriage below; here, I want only to point out that long before any suspicion of such a disaster, Moll had arranged an escape clause: "I claim'd a promise of him which he entered willingly into with me, when I consented to come from *England* with him (*viz.*) That if I found the Country not to agree with me, or that I did not like to live there, I should come away to *England* again when I pleas'd" (138). We never learn what Moll may have feared, but certainly Moll's (and Defoe's) metrocentric outlook could imagine colonial exile itself as a penance. Such is Jack's view, as his increasing literacy returns his longing gaze to Europe: "Now, I look'd upon my self as one Buried alive, in a remote Part of the World, where I could see nothing at all, and hear but a little of what was seen, and that little, not till at least half a Year after it was done, and sometimes a Year or more" (172).[23]

Jack's urgent desire to go back to Europe seems contrarian, given the contrast between his prosperity in the colonies and his poverty in Britain. Indeed, he assures his American master that "I have no mind to go to *England*, for I know not how to get my Bread there" (125), and his faith in colonial opportunity is amply justified when he finds himself, at age thirty, the owner of three plantations, some two hundred slaves and servants, and a flourishing tobacco business. He ascribes his desire for repatriation to his conviction that life in the colonies, no matter how comfortable or gentrified, "was not yet, the Life of a Gentleman" (172). But it is difficult to detect much gentility in the life Jack takes up in London: he lives "in a private Condition" (186) until manipulated into marriage, a disastrous attempt at domesticity that drains him of funds, makes him a cuckold, and exposes him to the violence of hired ruffians. Despite all this, the pull of home is such that Jack remains in London until forced to leave England "to be out of the way of Villains, and Assassinations; for every time I stirr'd out here, I thought I went in danger of my Life" (204). Although he briefly considers retreating to America, Jack crosses the Channel instead and quickly becomes an officer in an Irish regiment: "exceeding pleas'd with my new Circumstances . . . I us'd to say to myself, I was come to what I was Born to, and that I had never till now liv'd the Life of a Gentleman" (207). So it seems Jack has achieved the goal that brought him to Europe, but what he does not tell himself is that the circumstances that please him so much are treasonous; the Irish regiment he has joined fights on the side of France against England's allies, and the commission he wins as recognition for his bravery comes from Louis XIV.[24]

Both Benedick Anderson and E. J. Hobsbawm locate the rise of nations in the period following the American and French Revolutions; despite their disagreements about what constitutes national community, both find that nations, as we understand them, are phenomena of the late eighteenth century.[25] In their formulation, therefore, national identification and patriotism would not operate in Defoe's texts the way they would, say, in Jane Austen's. Nevertheless, there is no doubt that the young Jack identifies himself as English, especially when he finds himself friendless "in a Strange Place," that is, pre-Union Scotland (103); indeed, he consistently distinguishes between the nationalities of the three Englishmen and the two Scotsmen who are collectively tricked into servitude in the colonies, dwelling particularly on the penury of the Scotsmen who "begg'd their way, all along the Road" (108). But by the time he returns to Europe, after fifteen years in Virginia, Jack's Englishness has begun to waver. When his Atlantic crossing is intercepted by French privateers, he first expresses "mortification" at "seeing the Ship I was in Mann'd with Frenchmen" (177), but only a page later, as his French captors engage with an English ship, Jack's personal pronouns align him with the French: "we should not have ventured upon them, but we came up with them"; "as we (the *French*) bore down upon them again, the *English* run boldly on Board us" (178). Jack's cavalier sense of national identity and loyalty becomes more pronounced at Ghent, where he seems to have shed his earlier desire for participation in European affairs. Although he arrives in the character of an exchanged English prisoner and takes up quarters with an English officer, he remains politically disengaged from the conflict he witnesses: "as to the Merit of the Cause on either side, I knew nothing of it, nor had I suffer'd any of the Disputes about it, to enter into my Thought" (183). In fact, he makes use of his French passport to leave occupied Ghent and establishes himself in London as "Colonel Jacques," speaking French, going to the French Church, and acquiring a French servant (185–86). From here it is no great step to take his cuckolded and humiliated self back to the Continent and to join the forces of the French king.

Jack rediscovers his Englishness only when it puts him in serious jeopardy. Eager to abandon military life, he volunteers as a recruiter during the Old Pretender's aborted mission, prompted by the Act of Union, to land in Scotland in 1708, "tho' at the same time I had no particular attachment to his Person, or to his Cause" (223).[26] As the Jacobites flee from a pursuing English fleet, Jack suddenly wakes to the consequences of his casual treason, "for all the while we were thus flying for our Lives, I was under the greatest Terror immaginable, and nothing but Halters and Gibbets run in my Head, concluding, that if I had been taken, I should certainly have been hang'd" (224). The indeterminate nationality that he has chosen to inhabit assumes a dangerous fixity at the very moment Jack becomes vulnerable to the laws of his native country. Nor does his peril pass. Once he resettles in England, leaving behind another unfaithful wife who had maneuvered him into marriage, he is "oblig'd to be very retir'd, and change my Name, letting no Body in the Nation know who I was" (282–83). Yet again, despite the fears that imprison him in solitude, he rejects the idea of returning to Virginia "to be bury'd a-live," choosing to reside in Canterbury, where, like Addison and Steele's Mr. Spectator, he "might know every Body, and no Body know me" (233). Indeed, in Canterbury, Jack finds his ideal home, for he can now alternate between two national identities, calling himself "an *English* Man among the *French;* and a *French* Man among the *English* . . . going by the Name of Monsieur *Charnot,* with the *French* . . . Mr. *Charnock* among the *English*" (234). Tracing the vacillations in Jack's national identifications, we find that the young thief whose Englishness had been most visible as well as most strongly internalized during his brief stay in Scotland has acquired, after his residence in the colonies, a cosmopolitan fluidity that allows him to shift allegiances and self-representations at will. In an ironic inversion of Defoe's exhortations to settle America with Englishmen so as to diminish French influence there, Jack's time in America has provided him with the tools to become French in a way that the London street urchin could never have mastered.

Moll, of course, can never attain the multinational incorporation available to her male equivalent, and the narrative of her first return to England follows a very different trajectory. Moll's impetus for leaving Virginia—her simultaneous discovery of family and incest—has elicited much critical attention, from Ellen Pollak's reading of the incest as "a figure for the freedom of individual desire from the social imperatives of class" to Carl R. Lovitt's gloss on it as an illustration of Defoe's visible textual manipulations.[27] In whatever matrix we decode this episode—patriarchal, financial, spiritual, self-referential—we end with Moll's simultaneous discovery of family and guilt, and her consequent desire to escape from the site of knowledge; as John Richetti puts it, "The net effect of this incestuous melodrama is to propel Moll back to England and further experiences in illegal variations of the family."[28] Moll finds in America a fragile and temporary haven, a material and domestic security built on a catastrophic error. More significantly for my own discussion, Moll learns that the "do-over" promise of colonial life has its limits and slippages; one can hardly make a new life when haunted by the terrible consequences of old family ties.[29] Moreover, she discovers that rebirth in the New World has its dark side: unlike Jack's tutor, who connects Transportation with repentance and virtue—"I was deliver'd from the horrid Temptation of Sinning, to support my Luxury, and making one Vice Necessary to another" (*CJ* 167) — Moll's mother continues to seek immoral (and illegal) solutions to Moll's appalling dilemma. First, she tries to remake history, "willing to forget the Story she had told me of herself . . . to suppose that I had forgot some of the Particulars . . . to tell them with Alterations and Omissions" (145). When the strategy of selective amnesia and editing fails, Moll's mother counsels suppression of the truth, "for my Mother's Opinion was that I should bury the whole thing entirely . . . that we might lie as we us'd to do together, and so let the whole matter remain as close as Death" (146). The mother means, of course, that Moll and Humphry should continue incestuous sexual relations, odd advice from a parent to children; additionally, however, she counsels that she and Moll also "lie" together, colluding in a communal deception that would preserve the hyper-endogamous family unit. If, as Michael Suarez argues, Moll's repentance is suspect, her mother's regeneration is entirely spurious, never reaching beyond the expedient and belying Moll's characterization of her as "a very Pious sober and religious Woman" (137).[30]

Moll, unlike Jack, ends her first sojourn in the colonies on a dystopic note—"all my seeming Prosperity wore off, and ended in Misery and Destruction" (138)—and her return to Europe continues the downward spiral as she plays out increasingly egregious transgressions against the laws of family and country. The worst of her domestic misdemeanors follow her return. The sexual liaison with the Bath gentleman (she freely concedes that "the first Breach was not on his part" [168]); the mutually deceptive marriage with Jemy; the manipulation of the citizen ("I play'd with this Lover as an Angler does with a Trout" [195]); the abandonment of multiple children: all these sins against normative family life occur within the context of the absolute breach of domesticity she experienced in America. She herself characteristically ascribes her descent into domestic and social criminality to material rather than psychic trauma—to what America has *failed* to provide. She blames her actions on the poverty caused by the loss of colonial cargo that, "had it come safe" would have helped her to another stable (albeit bigamous) marriage.[31] Also unlike Jack, Moll falls into the power of the state, which penetrates her disguises and legislates her right to life. The multiple identities she has assumed since her return from the colonies— widow with a prosperous family in Virginia, poor friendless widow, "a Widow Lady of great Fortune" (197), even the protean thief Moll Flanders, which "was no more Affinity with my real Name . . . than black is of Kin to white" (280)—all fall away in Newgate, leaving "a meer *New-*

gate-Bird, as Wicked and as Outrageous as any of them" (355).[32] When Moll escapes the gallows by being granted Transportation, she returns to the site of her earlier (perhaps first) moment of absolute despair, now transformed by the fear of hanging (we remember Jack's tutor's invocation of "*Virginia*, or a worse Place, if that can be"), to a land of opportunity.

Of course, by the time Moll embraces her colonial exile, she has already begun to construe America as a gift to the wretched. Eager to hold on to the marriage with Jemy, she proposes emigration, assuring him "that in a very few Years . . . we should be as certain of being Rich, as we were now certain of being Poor" (215). In Newgate, she urgently presses him to plead for Transportation, emphasizing the prospect of jettisoning their past identities: "Our mutual Misfortunes had been such, as were sufficient to Reconcile us both to quitting this part of the World, and living where no Body could upbraid us with what was past, or we be in any dread of a Prison, and without the Agonies of a condemn'd Hole to drive us to it, where we should look back on all our past Distastes with infinite Satisfaction, when we should consider that our Enemies should entirely forget us, and that we should live as new People in a New World" (383). With Jemy by her side and financial resources in her grasp, Moll feels confident that America will produce both freedom and felicity; it is worth noting, however, that at no point during her earlier panic-stricken reflections on destitution does Moll consider emigrating as an indentured servant. She has, after all, witnessed firsthand the miserable condition of women laborers in the colonies; like Jack, she may have found herself "seriously reflecting on the Misery of human Life, when I saw some of those poor Wretches" (*CJ* 252).[33]

Jack himself returns to America in a much stronger position than Moll, having (passively) accumulated even more wealth than when he left, and considering Virginia to be "the only Place I had been bless'd at, or had met with any thing that deserv'd the Name of Success in" (250). But he too thinks of his departure from Britain as a reprieve rather than a free choice, not only from the domestic sorrows caused by the deaths of his fourth wife and his children, but also from the risk of being executed as a Jacobite rebel. For it transpires that Jack, who seems to have eschewed political entanglements for a decade, suddenly discovers his passionate attachment to the Stuart cause, feeling "all on Fire on that Side" (250). Dissuaded by his wife Moggy from openly enlisting with the Earl of Derwenter, he nevertheless joins the Jacobite forces to advise them on defending the bridge at Preston and abandons the cause only when they reject his counsel: "from that Moment I gave them all up as lost, and meditated nothing but how to escape from them" (265). Metaphorically, the Stuart cause has foundered much earlier in the text, not only during the Old Pretender's abortive invasion of 1708, but in the reference to the wreck in 1682 of the *Gloucester*, also on its way to Scotland with a Stuart on board (8), a wreck that coincides with Jack losing the only adults who had been responsible for him. The Stuart cause to which Jack commits fitfully in the text has been "sunk" from the beginning of the narrative; Jack merely needs to read the fate of the Stuarts as astutely as Defoe's readers do.[34] Anticipating the trajectory of Thackeray's Henry Esmond after the failure of *his* scheme to restore the Stuarts (and, like him, having been urged into Jacobite activity by a Catholic priest), Jack retreats to his American plantations for safety and ease.[35] To his horror, he discovers that "the Danger was come Home to me, even to my Door," in the shape of transported Jacobites who might recognize and betray him.[36] Terrified by this new danger, he thinks of "nothing, but to be inform'd against every Day, be taken up, and sent to *England* in Irons, and have all my Plantations seiz'd on, as a forfeited Estate to the Crown" (267). America, that refuge from the past, that opportunity to remake a compromised identity, proves to be a highly problematized haven in Defoe's texts: Moll's English family origins put her in an intolerable domestic situation; Jack's treasonous politics follow him across the Atlantic to his own plantations. Defoe thus complicates his own polemics about escape and rebirth, putting his colonial protagonists inside their worst nightmares.

Having far greater resources than Moll, Jack eludes the exposure he fears. Under the direction of his rediscovered and penitent first wife, he sails off in his own sloop to the West Indies, characteristically bringing with him goods to trade for profit while he evades justice. At this point in his adventures, Colonel Jack undergoes the kind of epiphany Moll attributes to her incarceration in Newgate. He receives word that George I has issued a general pardon to those who had participated in the Jacobite uprising of 1715. The king's clemency precipitates in Jack not a moral regeneration like that of Moll, but a political one. Suddenly, the boy who had preyed on fellow Londoners, the youth who had deserted from his regiment, the man who had fought on the French side and later galloped off to join the Jacobites at Preston becomes an ardent subject of the Hanoverian monarchy. The king's mercy, Jack proclaims,

> made a generous Convert of me, and I became sincerely given in to the Interest of King GEORGE; and this from a Principle of Gratitude, and a Sense of my Obligation to his Majesty for my Life, and will certainly remain with me as long as any Sense of Honour, and of the Debt of Gratitude remains with me. . . . I must lay it down as a Rule of Honour, that a Man having once forfeited his Life to the Justice of his Prince, and to the Laws of his Country, and receiving it back as a Bounty from the Grace of his Soveraign [*sic*]; such a Man can never lift up his Hand again against that Prince, without a forfeiture of his Vertue, and an irreparable Breach of his Honour and Duty (276–77)

Jack's conversion to the king and the laws of England is passionate and comprehensive. As William H. McBurney puts it, "Defoe . . . decided to purge Jacque of his one dishonorable trait—the political indifference and thoughtless toying with treason which had characterized his entire sporadic military career . . . [the pardon] transforms him at last not only into a complete gentleman, but a complete *English* gentleman."[37] It comes as something of a surprise, then, that his very next order of business constitutes an illicit trade with Spaniards in Havana. Captured by the Spanish and held for ransom, Jack soon reaches a quiet understanding with local merchants to "have an occasion to Trade privately, for the Cargo which I had on Board" (286). Always alert to opportunities to make money, Jack then decides to make a second trading voyage to the Spanish colonies, cut out the middlemen, and deal directly with merchants in Vera Cruz. He anticipates a 400 percent profit on his Anglo-American goods, but, as it transpires, his estimate is low; he returns from his clandestine voyage with a tenfold return on his investment, clearing twenty-five thousand pounds within three months.

Like so much else in Defoe's work, the issue of Jack's illegal trading and Defoe's attitude toward it is by no means straightforward. We know that, beginning in 1660, Parliament had passed a series of Navigation Acts, which "had as one purpose the reestablishment of England's control of its colonial trade," a control that had eroded during the "breakdown of the English Government during the Civil War."[38] When William III established the Board of Trade in 1696, his charge to the commissioners (John Locke among them) included an explicit direction to examine "what trades are taken up and exercised there [in the American colonies] which are or may prove prejudicial to England . . . and to find out proper means of diverting them from such trades,

and whatsoever else may turn to the hurt of our kingdom of England."[39]
Although historians differ on how much American traders suffered
from or resisted the new restrictions, there certainly exists evidence of
British anxieties about compliance. Merrill Jensen says, "The vast bulk
of colonial commerce was carried on within legal channels. Nevertheless, whenever a colonial merchant was accused of breaking a law . . . a
great deal of heat was generated." Smollett castigates "base and treach-
erous" Britons for trading with the French even during the Seven
Years' War: "The temptation of extraordinary profit excited the merchants not only to assist the enemies of their country, but also to run all
risques in eluding the vigilance of the legislature."[40] Jensen's edition
of early colonial documents includes a 1743 letter from Massachusetts
Governor William Shirley to the Board of Trade, in which he complains
of American noncompliance: "The illicit trade which appears to have
been carried on in this province and some of the neighbouring colonies
. . . is such as without the speedy interposition of the Parliament to stop
it, must be highly destructive of the interest of Great Britain . . . weak-
ening the dependence which northern colonies ought to have upon their
mother country."[41] Apparently, colonial trade had to be carefully controlled and infractions severely punished. As the always irascible James
Abercromby explains, "Such are the Principles of the Act, which there-
upon Enacts, under Penalty of Treason for disobedience thereto, and in
Order the more effectually to enforce their Obedience in Government
and Commerce. . . . the Preamble setting forth, that for maintaining
their Subordination, and rendering them more beneficial to the Mother
Country. All Trade with Foreigners, except under certain Regulations
therein mentioned, is prohibited to the Colonys."[42]

Even if we assume that Jack, as an English colonial, does not break
English laws governing foreign trade and shipping, and even if he
brings back to the colonies coveted Spanish gold, we can certainly also
assume that he neglects to pay the duties that were the point of the Navigation Acts. Moreover, Colonel Jack, the born-again patriot, not only
flouts the letter and intent of English law, but does so by once again
inhabiting a non-English identity. Run to ground by Spanish ships during his second voyage, he smoothly adjusts to his new circumstances.
Just as he had become Colonel Jacques the Frenchman during his time
in Europe, he now takes on the character of "a Merchant come from
old *Spain . . . Don Ferdinand de Villa Moresa*" (301), and puts to good use
the fact that he "spoke *Spanish* very well, having serv'd under the King
of *Spain* in *Italy*" (278). In other words, lucky Jack deploys skills acquired during his traitorous past to serve his present subversion of Brit-

ish law. Habited "like a Spaniard of the better sort, [with] three Negroes to attend me," he thoroughly enjoys his months of exile in Vera Cruz: "Here I had nothing to do but walk about, and ride out into the Woods, and come home again to enjoy the pleasantest and most agreeable Retirement in the World" (301). But Jack is being too modest in proclaiming his idleness; even in hiding and in some danger from Spanish authorities, he manages to sell the goods he had smuggled ashore, making "8570 Pieces of Eight . . . so that I was indeed, still very Rich, all things consider'd" (303).

Becoming very rich has, of course, been Jack's lifelong ambition, and the material possession of coins has evoked his most intense passions, more dramatically even than Moll's erotic thrill when she handles gold (*MF* 64, 163). We recall his tumultuous joy when, as a young boy, he recovers the five pounds he thought he had lost in the hollow of a tree: "I was but a Child, and I rejoyced like a Child, for I hollow'd quite out aloud, when I saw it; then I run to it, and snatch'd it up, hug'd and kiss'd the dirty Ragg a hundred Times; then danc'd and jump'd about, run from one End of the Field to the other. . . . It would tire the Reader should I dwell on all the little Boyish Tricks that I play'd in the in the Extacy of my Joy, and Satisfaction, when I had found my Money" (26). Jack may have learned to curb his hysterical raptures, but he retains his delight in accruing money as well as his indifference to legal or ethical impediments. Although his career as a planter seems to be free of criminal activity, he reverts to his larcenous ways during his military service, of which he says, "I gain'd the Reputation of a good Officer, but . . . I got somewhat that I lik'd much better, and that was a good deal of Money" (209), acquired by plundering occupied towns. Of course, Jack has never scrupled to put his own interests ahead of any ideological conviction, but never before his Caribbean adventure has Jack articulated such fervent commitment to a nation and a king.[43] Lincoln Faller dismisses the criminality of Jack's Caribbean trade, because it does little damage to England: "What, after all, is a little 'corporate crime' here and there (especially 'there') to muggings on the way home or at one's very door?" and Hans H. Andersen contends that "Defoe could look at economic activities strictly with reference to economic ends, which were entirely distinct from both religious and political ends."[44] I suggest that in fact Jack's illicit commerce with Spanish colonies is highly significant, not only for the way it exposes the uses of patriotism but also for the light it sheds on a new kind of colonial psychology.

There can be no doubt that Jack opts to incur the risks inherent in his illegal trading because he, like Moll, obsesses about accumulating more wealth. After his second voyage, against the urging of his wife and his own rational knowledge that it is time to "sit down satisfy'd, and push the Affair no farther," his avarice prompts him to pursue his fantasy of amassing untold riches: "I that had a Door open, as I thought to immense Treasure, that had found a way to have a Stream of Golden Rivers of *Mexico* flow into my Plantation of *Virginia*, and saw no hazards . . . I dream'd of nothing but Millions and Hundred of Thousands; so contrary to all moderate Measures, I push'd on for another Voyage" (296–97). Reaching far beyond Moll's dream of "restoring our Fortunes" (*MF* 383) in America, or his own earlier gratitude "that I cou'd live by my own Endeavours" (156), Jack seems to forget or deliberately ignore the laws of the nation to which he has pledged such passionate devotion. In fact, however, it is patriotism, that last refuge of scoundrels, that provides Jack with a justification for his new activities; his sentimental loyalty to the Hanoverian regime becomes yet another useful stratagem in his long performative career, one he can deploy as a screen for pursuing his own ambitions. Consistently suppressing his transgression against British laws, Jack focuses on how cleverly he deceives and exploits the Spanish. To manipulate his gullible Spanish hosts, he enthusiastically fabricates tales of the "Gallantry and personal Bravery of his Catholic Majesty [Philip II] . . . particularly in many Battles where by the Way, his Majesty had never been at all," and revels in fooling "People who knew nothing of the Matter, and so any thing went down with them" (279); he relishes the opportunity to "make my self full amends of *Jack Spaniard*, for all the injuries he had done me" (287); and he gloats over tricking the Spanish fleet by carrying Spanish colors on his American boat (296).[45] Moreover, Jack makes a point of reminding his British readers of the irrational rigidity of Spanish regulations as well as the notorious brutality of Spanish practices against foreigners. He points out that his ship, illegally seized in international waters, is "plundred, as any one that knows the *Spaniards*, especially in that Country, will easily guess" (278), and he expresses his fear "that they would detain me, and keep me as a Prisoner for Life, and perhaps send me to their Mines in Peru, as they have done many, and pretended to do all that come on Shore in their Dominions, how great soever the Distresses may have been which have brought them thither" (279). How fitting, then, that rather than labor in those Peruvian mines, Jack finds a way to siphon off the profits of Spanish tyranny.

Jack dwells on the convoluted illogic of rules governing Spanish colonies. When he protests that the strict injunctions against foreign vessels preclude him from arranging delivery of ransom for himself and his ship, the Corregidore merely shrugs and repeats that "they could not dispense with the least Tittle of them, without a particular Assiento . . . from the Consulado, or Chamber of Commerce at *Sevelle;* or a command under the Hand and Seal of the Viceroy of *Mexico*" (281). Despite the contrary opinion of the military governor, the Corregidore insists upon "adhering with a true *Spanish* stiffness to the Letter of the Law" (282–83), forcing Jack and the governor to contrive a scheme to circumvent Spanish intransigency. Such cumbersome rigidity posits a despotism that begs for subversive activity; and such recalcitrance puts Spain outside the "Customs of Nations," customs practiced even, as Jack points out, by heathen Algerians (280).[46] Jack's interdicted trade with Spanish merchants, carried out in defiance of authorities in Mexico and Seville, constitutes resistance to Spanish power in the New World. In the context of imperial rivalries in the eighteenth century, such covert operations can be construed as patriotic warfare even as they serve to build private fortunes.[47] Replicating the exploits of the great nationalist privateers of the past, conferring on himself the legacy of Drake and Raleigh, Defoe's hero can see himself as a literal "soldier of fortune." Moreover, like those earlier patriotic pirates, Jack moves toward a new social identity, becoming at last in reality the "great Merchant" (185) he had merely impersonated during his earlier visit to London. As we follow the trajectory of Jack's career in Virginia, Europe, and the Caribbean, we see the mutual exploitation by subject and government and the connection between nationalism and individual ambition.[48]

Jack's journey ends, like Moll's and Jemy's, back in the home country where they had all endured privation and isolation; all three abandon the colonies that had granted them safety and prosperity. Moll, although she has "perform'd much more than the limited Terms of my Transportation" (427), remains so vulnerable to English law that she dare not reveal her identity in her memoirs: "there are some things of such Consequence still depending there [Newgate and Old Bailey], relating to my particular Conduct, that it is not to be expected I should set my Name, or the Account of my Family to this Work" (43). Jemy faces even greater peril, being "under Bonds and Security not to return to *England* any more, as long as he liv'd" (391). Defoe carefully prepares us for what at first seems like an inexplicable and dangerous choice on the part of the emigrants. For one thing, he emphasizes their yearning for the life of English gentry, a status available only in the homeland. We note Moll's class-based exasperation when Jemy proves unhelpful during her efforts to cultivate their newly acquired lands in America:

"He was bred a Gentleman, and by Consequence was not only unac-
quainted, but indolent, and when we did Settle, would much rather go
out into the Woods with his Gun, which they call here Hunting, and
which is the ordinary Work of the *Indians*, and which they do as Servants; I say he would much rather do that, than attend the natural Business of his Plantation" (411). Eventually, Moll decides to enable Jemy's
gentlemanly aversion to work, but although she outfits Jemy with the
appropriate accoutrements—"two good long Wigs, two silver hilted
Swords, three or four fine Fowling pieces, a fine Saddle with Holsters
and Pistoles very Handsome, with a Scarlet cloak . . . to make him appear, as he really was, a very fine Gentleman" (424)—appearance and
reality cannot entirely merge in the new world. Even the acquisition of
wigs and saddles and scarlet cloak cannot quite purchase the life that
Jemy covets; what he wants is *English* squiredom, which can be
achieved only in England. As Michael J. Rozbicki points out, colonial
planters suffered from a sense of social inferiority: "their pursuit of gentility amounted to a paradox: the criteria of refinement were prescribed
by British arbiters of culture, but these same arbiters refused to acknowledge the legitimacy of colonial gentry."[49] Moll's telltale phrase,
"work of the *Indians*, and . . . Servants" marks the gap between plantation life in America and country life in England. James Axtell notes that
the Amerindian habit of hunting for food was distressing to the English
because "in England the only people who hunted were members of the
upper classes . . . or poachers. . . . Forests were not public property but
belonged to the nobility who regarded them as private game preserves.
Guns were expensive and their ownership was generally forbidden by
law."[50] One can imagine that the class-obsessed Jemy, no matter how
gorgeously dressed and equipped, might be troubled by sharing his rec-
reational pursuit with half-naked savages hunting for sustenance. No
wonder then that he instructs Moll that he will join her in England,
"where we resolve to spend the Remainder of our Years in sincere Penitence" (427).

Jack has already expressed his repugnance to being buried alive in
Virginia, so perhaps we should not be astonished when he ends his narrative with a list of the grim aspects of colonial settlement. He asks his
readers to "Remember with how much Advantage they may make their
penitent reflections at Home, under the merciful Dispositions of Providence in Peace, Plenty, and Ease, rather than Abroad under the Discipline of a Transported Criminal as my Wife and my Tutor, or under the
Miseries and Distresses of a Shipwreck'd wanderer, as my Skipper . . .
or in Exile, however favourably circumstantiated as mine" (309). It also

comes as no surprise that although Jack, like Moll, frequently characterizes his memoirs as a cautionary tale and a model for repentant sinners, he also lets us know that this literary project (like his mercantile ones) finds a profitable market: "Perhaps, when I wrote these things down, I did not foresee that the Writings of our own Stories would be so much the Fashion in *England*, or so agreeable to others to read" (307). A penitent life can perhaps be lived as productively in the colonies as in the home country; a penitent narrative finds readers and buyers only in the center.

We see, then, that Defoe has carefully constructed a rationale for his protagonists' return to the mother country, but we still need to address the underlying politics of this strategy. I suggest that Defoe anticipates the problems for British imperial ambitions if American colonists become too comfortable, too settled, and too independent in the new world. As early as December 30, 1707, Defoe feels the need to reassure readers of his *Review* that New England colonies will not, *cannot* abandon England because "if you make them rich . . . their Riches springing from you, and depending upon you, they are got with Child by you, and you need not be in Pain about their leaving you, they must marry you, or be undone" (IV.551). But when his heroine literalizes the rather unseemly metaphor, we see that being made rich and pregnant does not prevent a woman from leaving. Moll's desertion of Humphry enacts, in reverse, English fears about colonies siphoning off English trade and manufacture, and posits, as does her ultimate return to England, that America can never exert enough sentimental force to dislodge an affinity for home. Moll may grow prosperous in Virginia, may recount with emotion her reunion with "the kindest and tenderest Child that ever Woman had" (423), but domestic ties in America, incestuously engendered, can never supersede ties to Mother England. In 1709, Defoe responds again to anxieties that an increase in the number of settlers might produce surplus labor in the colonies, "And so invade that noble *Branch* of our Trade to *America*, I mean our Exportation of Woollen Goods" (6.182). To allay these anxieties, Defoe points to Scotland's attempt to rival the southern partner in the manufacture of cloth, an attempt thwarted by England's superior access to materials and experienced workers (6.183).[51] But when Colonel Jack collects goods for his contraband trade with New Spain, he buys from New England merchants rather than await the arrival of English ships to Virginia. He finds in Boston and New York "fine *English* Broad Cloath, Serges, Drugets, *Norwich* Stuffs, Bays, Says, and all kinds of Woollen Manufactures . . . Linnen of all Sorts . . . and near a thousand Pounds in fine

Silks" (293). Jack participates, in other words, in a fledgling Western Hemisphere trading nexus, one that could easily become (and of course does become) independent of European regulation.[52] He belongs, therefore, to a group of colonial scofflaws who incur the wrath of Abercromby: "the Laws of this Kingdom are there most openly Violated, to the great Contempt of the Legislature of this Kingdom." Defoe himself sharpens his rhetoric against American colonists who chafe at metropolitan control; in 1728, anticipating by two centuries a rationale for keeping control of the British Commonwealth (see chapter 1, note 77), he moves from economic to political rationalizations for keeping America dependent: "But with all the Wealth of its Product, *America* is yet in its State of Tutelage, or of Bondage rather, being at present a Dependent upon, and the Property of the People of *Europe* . . . in a word, *America* is a chain'd Slave to *Europe*."[53] The shift in metaphor from pregnant wife to enslaved property argues a degree of desperation.

Jack, for one, has carefully noted the loosening of these political chains and signs of the colonists' growing autonomy. As soon as he arrives in Virginia, he is struck by the power of his master, who addresses his servants "in a large Hall, where he sat in a Seat like a Lord Judge upon the Bench, or a Petty King upon his Throne" (122). Much later, during his exile in Vera Cruz, he marvels that "no Men in the World live in such splendor and wallow in such immense Treasures, as the Merchants of this Place" (301–12). Surely commercial wealth unhampered by the political constraints endured by Spanish colonials represents an ideal existence and one available to so shrewd an entrepreneur as Colonel Jack. Indeed, we see how energetically he practices benevolent despotism toward his African slaves and his indentured servants. He so wins "the Affections of my Negroes, that they serv'd me cheerfully, and by Consequence, Faithfully, and Diligently" (159). Unlike Moll, who provides few details about the running of her plantation, Jack includes a long narrative about how he tames his Negro slaves. Instituting a system that combines terror and mercy, he wins the gratitude of slaves delivered from threatened punishment. He shows, in other words, an understanding of how effectively a covertly despotic government can work, and even becomes a model for others: "now the Plantation was famous for it; so that several other Planters began to do the same. . . . the Plantations in *Maryland*, were the better for this Undertaking, and they are to this Day less Cruel and Barbarous to their *Negroes*, than they are in *Barbados*, and *Jamaica*; and 'tis observ'd the *Negroes* are not in these Colonies so desperate, neither do they so often run away, or so often plot mischief against their Master, as they do in those"

(149). Jack even institutes his own version of Transportation, selling off any "sullen stupid Fellow" who resists his benevolent rule.

Given that Jack possesses all the necessary resources to set up a kind of alternate kingdom in America, it becomes imperative that he, like Moll and Jemy, reinhabit his British identity. These successful colonials must imagine no better ending to their labors in America than retirement to their "real" home in England. Having triumphed over the rigors of the New World, they can reenter the only polity that matters. In England, Moll and Jemy can live out their lives not only in model penitence, but also in genteel leisure; in England, Jack and his reclaimed wife not only reap the benefits of their American riches, but also move in such rarefied circles that, as the title page announces, Jack "resolves to dye a General." Meanwhile, their colonial possessions are to be managed for them by lesser mortals: Moll's mild-mannered (and incestuously conceived) son and Jack's permanently humbled Tutor, neither of whom poses any threat to the sovereign power of the metropole. Defoe's two American novels hold out the hope of financial and social regeneration to be achieved in the colonies, but assure readers that the best—and most politically threatening—settlers will always be homebound. As Defoe himself put it in a 1707 *Review* essay, "*England* is the true Center of all her own People."[54]

SMOLLETT AND COLONIAL CORRUPTIONS

Humphry Clinker articulates an indictment of British society more deeply felt and acerbic than any complaint voiced by the victimized Moll and Jack. From the cesspools of Bath to the chaos of London to the poverty of Scotland, Matthew Bramble and his family discover in their travels a nation suffering from the corrosive effects of institutional and systemic corruption. Even the country squirearchy, as represented by the Burdocks, the Bayards, and Lord Oxmington, spectacularly fails to provide the kind of hospitality and rationality so prized by traditionalists like Bramble. Given the parlous state of the kingdom, the sensible and sensitive Briton can only disengage and retreat . . . but not too far. While condemning widespread anarchy and degeneracy in Britain, *Humphry Clinker* emphatically rejects the solution proposed (albeit problematically) in Defoe's works; it abjures escape to the place where Moll and Jemy can "live as new People in a new World" (383) and where Jack prospers both materially and emotionally. Defoe might emit mixed signals about colonial settlement in the New World; for

Smollett, writing in 1771 during an alarming exodus from Scotland to the colonies, America represents a double danger: it siphons off manpower that could otherwise help build a strong post-Union Scotland, and it distributes wealth in the home country in a destructively egalitarian way. In *Humphry Clinker,* Smollett argues against emigration by showing how colonial adventuring has damaged the social and political health of the mother country and by depicting life in America as dangerously savage.

Lismahago, during his debate with Bramble about the Act of Union, asserts that England gained more than Scotland because Scotland provided a most valuable resource—an army of imperial workers: "They got an accession of above a million of useful subjects, constituting a never-failing nursery of seamen, soldiers, labourers and mechanics: a most valuable acquisition to a trading country, exposed to foreign wars, and obliged to maintain a number of settlements in all four quarters of the globe. In the course of seven years, during the last war, Scotland furnished the English army and navy with seventy thousand men, over and above those who migrated to their colonies, or mingled with them at home in the civil departments of life" (317). For once, Lismahago hardly exaggerates. Ned C. Landsman points out that while early attempts at establishing Scottish settlements in America failed, "the turning point in Scottish emigration was the Seven Years' War . . . which attracted large numbers of Scottish soldiers after mid-century. . . . Perhaps 40,000 Scots ventured to America during the next dozen years.[55] This enormous outflow created a depopulation deplored by contemporary witnesses. Samuel Johnson and James Boswell, traveling in Scotland in 1773, repeatedly encounter signs of escalating emigration, including a dance called "*America.* Each of the couples . . . successively whirls round in a circle, till all are in motion; and the dance seems intended to shew how emigration catches, till a whole neighbourhood is set afloat." Johnson, echoing Defoe's notion of England as center, laments that "all that go may be considered as subjects lost to the *British* crown; for a nation scattered in the boundless regions of *America* resembles rays diverging from a focus."[56] Like Johnson, who finds that "oppression might produce a wish for new habitations,"[57] Smollett ascribes this massive exodus at least in part to English punitive policies in the wake of the Jacobite uprisings of 1715 and 1745, policies that de-cultured Highlanders by disarming them and depriving them "of their ancient garb. . . . the government could not have taken a more effectual method to break their national spirit" (277).[58] Unlike Johnson, who fears that "nobody born in any other parts of the world will choose this country for his residence," and like Defoe, who claims that ". . . all the Poverty of *Scotland* . . . proceeds from a want of improving the Lands in *Scotland* to the Degree, they may and ought to be improv'd,"[59] Smollett's novel insists that proper economic incentives can indeed repopulate the Highlands: "Our people have a strange itch to colonize America, when the uncultivated parts of our own island might be settled to great advantage" (294). Bramble eagerly praises the superior quality of Scottish produce and the grace of Scottish women (160–61) and compares Scottish systems of justice, education, and social welfare favorably with those in England. This list of advantages, Smollett seems to argue, should convince Scots not to abandon their home for uncertain futures and dangerous confrontations in the colonies.

In other writings, Smollett pays tribute to American colonists, "who cultivate the country, are hardy, industrious, and generally substantial" and even asks an admirer in New Jersey to "commend me to all my Friends in America. I have endeavoured more than once to do the Colonies some service."[60] *Humphry Clinker,* however, takes up a hostile position as it participates in a polemical dialogue about the American colonies as refuge and opportunity. As Michael Zuckerman reminds us, promotional literature extolling America competed with negative images of the colonies: "chiaroscuro constructions, damning European darkness and blazoning American brilliance, were responses to equal but opposite condemnations of the new continent." *Humphry Clinker* joins the voices attempting to stanch the flow of useful manpower from Scotland to America. It also extends Smollett's condemnation, expressed in *Continuation of the History of England,* of those who seem to have lost their British rationality in the wake of military victories in America: "At this period [1761] the strength of Great Britain appeared in the zenith of its power and splendour. The people of England were seemingly transported beyond the limits of sober reason and reflection. . . . The spirit of revelry maddened through the land." Like other texts that Bruce McLeod labels "anti-empire," *Humphry Clinker* negotiates the impact of having an empire, especially when consumer culture kicks in and social divisions appear to wobble precariously.[61]

Matthew Bramble, in one of his many diatribes against the new social (dis)order, connects the collapse of traditional hierarchies with the agents of empire: "All these absurdities arise from the general tide of luxury, which hath overspread the nation, and swept away all, even the very dregs of the people. Every upstart of fortune, harnessed in the trappings of the mode, presents himself at Bath . . . Clerks and factors from the East Indies, loaded with the spoil of plundered provinces; planters, Negro-drivers, and hucksters, from our American plantations, enriched they know not how; agents, commissaries, and contractors, who have fattened in two successive wars, on the blood of the nation; usurers, brokers, and jobbers of every kind" (65). Of course, Bramble targets the whole phenomenon of commercialism with what Susan L. Jacobsen calls its attendant "plethora of political, social, religious, and moral corruptions,"[62] but significantly, most of the "dregs" he lists are those who participate in the imperial project. One of the few upstarts individualized in Bramble's narrative is a "negro-driver, from Jamaica, [who] pay[s] overnight, to be master of one of the rooms, sixty-five guineas for tea and coffee to the company, and leave[s] Bath next morning, in such obscurity, that not one of his guests had the slightest idea of his person" (87). Another is the ungrateful Paunceford, who makes a fortune abroad and turns his back on his early benefactor Serle (97–100). And of course Bramble's first antagonist at Bath is "a Creole gentleman," whose Negro servants are beaten by Bramble as punishment for their insolence as well as their "dreadful blasts" on the French horn, and who, despite being a colonel, "prudently declined any farther prosecution of the dispute" (60–61).[63] Each of these imperial profiteers represents an aspect of what ails Britain: extravagance, ingratitude, incivility, and cowardice.

Even those who have honorably served their nation in imperial wars are scarred by the engagement. In a coffeehouse in Bath, Bramble encounters old friends who bear the marks of their patriotic service: rear-admiral Balderick, "metamorphosed into an old man, with a wooden leg and a weatherbeaten face, which appeared the more ancient from his grey locks," and "what remained of colonel Cockril, who had lost the use of his limbs in making an American campaign" (84–85). The most egregious example of the human cost of empire is, of course, Lismahago, upon whose body are inscribed the mutilations inflicted by imperial adventuring and who epitomizes the forgotten veteran. Lismahago's plight elicits from the Bramble party sympathy for his troubles and anger at the government that has abandoned him: "our pity was warmed with indignation, when we learned, that in the course of two sanguinary wars, he had been wounded, maimed, mutilated, taken, and enslaved, without ever having attained a higher rank than that of lieutenant" (224).[64] Moreover, the home government, while exploiting the fruits of empire and those who fight to win them, remains deplorably ignorant of the new world that funds British prosperity (and extravagance). The Duke of N— —, after being tutored in Canadian geography by Captain— —, exclaims, "Egad! I'll go directly, and tell the king that Cape Breton is an island" (145). Not only does the duke mangle the names of the tribes that make up the League of the Iroquois, he facetiously parodies rituals crucial to forging alliances with American Indians: "Let 'em have plenty of blankets, and stinubus, and wampum; and your excellency won't fail to scour the kettle, and boil the chain, and bury the tree, and plant the hatchet—Ha, ha, ha!" (144–45). Like the East India Company director who "asked Clive whether 'Sir Roger Dowlat' [Siraj-ud-daula] was a baronet,[65] the Duke of N— — epitomizes the ignorance of the governing class at home.

The home country, as represented in *Humphry Clinker*, suffers from a range of ills brought about by imperial wealth, which is responsible for social chaos and political corruption. Colonial wars maim British soldiers, who are then abandoned by an ungrateful government. And the commercialism attending imperial success so disrupts traditional rural life that it has led to an amassing of lower classes in urban areas, where they *"all tread upon the kibes of one another:* actuated by the demons of profligacy and licentiousness, they are seen every where rambling, riding, rolling, rushing, jostling, mixing, bouncing, cracking in one vile ferment of stupidity and corruption" (119). So-called economic progress has dispossessed rural populations of home and employment and set them adrift. And the influx to metropolitan areas has led not only to a blurring of class markers, but also to rampant consumerism, greed, crime, and disease.

And yet, when Lismahago, finding that his half-pay cannot support him in Britain, contemplates returning to the colonies to "pass the rest of his days among his old friends the Miamis, and amuse himself in finishing the education of the son he had by his beloved Squinkinacoosta," Bramble thinks "it is very hard, that a gentleman who had served his country with honour, should be driven by necessity to spend his old age, among the refuse of mankind, in such a remote part of the world" (305–6). According to this text, whatever the corruptions and miseries of life in the mother country, they are preferable to the violent and barbaric world confronting the European who settles in North America. To deflect the impulse to emigrate, *Humphry Clinker* sets out a multiplicity of arguments that paradoxically articulate the danger and futility of the British mission in America while promoting British national pride.

Paul-Gabriel Boucé argues that "the ritual mutilations described by Lismahago are on the shady borderline between sadism and buffoonery"; Robert Hopkins believes that Lismahago "serves as a catharsis" because "his Thurberlike mythic reduction of Indian captivity converts English anxieties about Indian massacres to a ludicrous, demonic myth"; Joanne Lewis sees Lismahago as "belonging, at least in part, to the world of *commedia dell'arte*" and his captivity as a "scenario for *commedia*, the domestic violence reminiscent of Punch and Judy. The terms of Smollett's narrative transmute history to farce."[66] These characterizations of Lismahago's captivity fail to take into account, I believe, Smollett's evident deep knowledge of contemporary discourse about Amerindians and the congruence of Lismahago's story with reports about Europeans captured by Indians. They also fail to recognize that, while accurately transmitting some known practices of Indians, Smollett tilts the narrative toward the grotesque for propaganda purposes: the account of Lismahago in captivity addresses English anxieties about colonial rivalries and transculturation and concludes that the attempt to win the hearts and minds of Amerindians is inherently doomed.

Writers on American colonial history point out that in an ironical reversal of British fantasies about the conversion and assimilation of native populations, Amerindians were distressingly successful at converting colonizers to their way of life. James Axtell says that "most of the Indians who were educated by the English — some contemporaries thought *all* of them — returned to Indian society at the first opportunity. . . . On the other hand, large numbers of Englishmen had chosen to become Indians." J. Norman Heard prefaces his summary accounts of eighteenth- and nineteenth-century captivities by quoting a 1753 letter from Benjamin Franklin, in which Franklin recounts the recidivism of rescued captives: "tho' rescued by their Friends, and treated with all imaginable tenderness to prevail with them to stay among the English, yet in a short time, they become disgusted with our manner of life, and the care and pains that are necessary to support it, and take the first opportunity of escaping again into the Woods, from whence there is no reclaiming them."[67] Among those who chose the Indian way of life were captives as disparate as Mary Jamison, captured by Shawnees in 1758, who married a Delaware Indian and lived happily among them until her death at age seventy-five; David Boyd, captured by Delawares in 1756, who, when returned to white society by his adoptive Indian father, "had to be closely guarded for weeks before he relinquished his plan" to return to the tribe; and eight-year-old John McCullough, captured in 1756, who had to be forced to visit his white family. An exasperated Cadwallader Colden remarked in 1717, "The English had as much Difficulty to persuade the People, that had been taken Prisoners

by the French Indians, to leave the Indian manner of living, though no
People enjoy more Liberty, and live in greater Plenty, than the common
Inhabitants of new-York do."[68]

Even narratives about gruesome torture inflicted by Indians refer to
occasional kind treatment from captors, which leads, in turn, to a degree of adaptation: Robert Eastburn is fed chocolate because "I was
unwell, and could not eat their course food"; John Leeth is well tended
by his Delaware father; John Gyles's frostbite is carefully treated with
fir-balsam; and Thomas Morris is presented with, of all things, a volume
of Shakespeare. Pierre Esprit Radisson, when his adoptive family
dresses him in native garb, admits that "I could not but fall in love wth
myselfe, if not yt I had better instructions to shun the sin of pride."[69]
Some of Smollett's literary contemporaries write laudatory accounts of
life among Amerindians. Arthur Young's heroine Emmera lives se-
cluded from all but Indians who "adore" her and rescue her from a vil-
lainous European, while Henry Mackenzie's young hero Annesley,
echoing Behn's characterization of Indian culture, regrets leaving "the
perfect freedom subsisting in this rude and simple state of society . . .
where greatness cannot use oppression, nor wealth excite envy."[70] Lismahago himself, of course, leaves his "advantages and honours" in the
Badger tribe only "in consequence of being exchanged for the orator of
the community, who had been taken prisoner by the Indians that were
in alliance with the English" (229). Both historical and literary accounts, then, attest to a disturbing inversion: instead of "civilizing" the
native population, British immigrants in America manifest a tendency
to admire and assimilate into tribal culture.[71]

Moreover, and perhaps more gallingly, while Amerindians rejected
English attempts to convert them, they responded more favorably to
French blandishments. Thomas Morris, writing in 1764, admires the
French for winning natives' affections by intermarrying and "prohibiting the sale of spirituous liquors to Indians"; he contrasts this to the
"scandalous practices" of some English traders, who alienate them by
"imposing on the drunken Indian in trade, abusing his drunken wife,
daughter, or other female relation." Robert Rogers's play *Ponteach; or
the Savages of America* (1766) explicitly lauds French colonial customs
while excoriating the English as "false, deceitful, knavish insolent."
After an English victory, Ponteach laments the change in masters:

> The French are all subdued,
> But who are in their Stead become our Lords?
> A proud, imperious, churlish, haughty Band,

The French familiarized themselves with us,
Studied our Tongues, and Manners, wore our Dress,
Married our Daughters and our Sons their Maids,
Dealt honestly, and well supplied our Wants,
Used no one ill, and treated with Respect.[72]

Rogers's play articulates a phenomenon verified by historians. Gordon
M. Sayre, for example, notes that Catholic missionaries embraced martyrdom in a way impressive to Indians and alien to Protestants: "For
French Catholics, suffering for one's faith led naturally to death. . . .
The privations of the new environment were part of the holy suffferings
of his [the Jesuit's] mission. If his reception turned from hospitable to
hostile, the objective of captivity was not resistance and redemption,
but martyrdom."[73] Thus, a shared belief in brave deaths contributed to
the phenomenon so mortifying to British imperialists: the Catholic
French were succeeding where the Protestant English were failing.
Even the hostile voice of Smollett's own *British Magazine* concedes the
efficacy of French missionaries:

> The missionaries scattered among the Indian tribes were generally strong,
> hale, and active, patient of hunger, cold, and fatigue: all of them were, more-
> over, enthusiasts who courted danger, and gladly exposed themselves to all
> manner of afflictions. They attended the Indians in all their martial excur-
> sions, appeared always in the hottest part of the battle, baptizing the infidels,
> and comforting the converts in their last moments: they themselves were
> generally wounded, often killed, sometimes taken and tortured to death by
> the most hideous torments. The example of men acting in this manner, from
> a spirit of benevolence, could not fail to make deep impressions upon sensi-
> ble minds' and accordingly they soon acquired the veneration of the In-
> dians.[74]

Indeed, so intertwined were Indian and French cultures in some places,
that, according to Heard, one Eunice Williams, taken by the Iroquois
from Massachusetts to Canada in 1704, refused to relinquish her hybrid
identity: "The daughter of a steadfast Protestant minister had become
converted to Catholicism and learned to love her Indian masters."[75]

Confronted by the alarming and embarrassing spectacle of the wrong
sorts of transculturation, British writers embarked on a discourse of ra-
tionalization and recuperation. One useful strategy was to paint the
French as both cunning and savage, thereby explaining their ascendancy in the competition for Amerindian alliances. As early as 1704,
Defoe had accused the French of "stirring up the *Indians* to make Dep-

redations, and Insult our Plantations, and to that purpose have supply'd them with Fire-Arms, Ammunition, and especially *Rum,* for their Encouragement." In 1762, Peter Williamson similarly complains of the tactics of a French priest who assures Indians that the English killed the son of God, and "that if the *English,* were, all destroyed, the son of the Good-man, who is God, would come again, and banish all evil spirits from their lands."[76] Thus also, early in "The History of Canada," we get an account of Le Caron and his fellow Jesuits who, instead of "explaining and enforcing the divine and amiable doctrines of the Gospel," have "inflamed the animosities subsisting between the different nations of the Indians": "They have taught them the arts of fraud, and the refinements of cruelty . . . misrepresented the neighbouring subjects of Britain, as monsters of impiety and brutality . . . they have supported and extended their own influence among those ignorant creatures by craft and hypocrisy, false miracles, and all variety of Jesuitical imposture."[77] This comprehensive indictment of French perfidy not only explains French inroads among Indians, but can actually make a merit of British failures, since presumably, British missionaries have never resorted to such sordid practices.[78] "The History of Canada" contains much more in this vein, emphasizing the ignorance of the Indians and the cunning ambition of the Jesuits, as well as their fanatical desire for "the crown of martyrdom."[79] Even when the narrative praises the fortitude and perseverance of French missionaries, as in the account of Father Jogues's bravery under torture, it follows up with a reiteration of Catholic zeal for martyrdom, which of course undermines the priest's heroism. Cadwallader Colden provides an example of the barbarity of secular French power when he recounts the Comte de Frontenac's decision to burn an Indian prisoner according to native custom; Colden includes a description of the gruesome torture and execution "to shew on the one Hand, what Courage and Resolution, Virtue, the Love of Glory and the Love of one's Country can instill into Mens Minds, even where Knowledge of true Religion is wanting; and on the other Hand, how far a false Policy, under a corrupt Religion, can debase even great Minds."[80] The French, in these accounts, are even more barbaric than the Indians because they torture and kill in the full knowledge that they are committing atrocities. In the end, however, the problem lies with the Indians themselves, whose inherent incapacity foils any attempt to "civilize" them: "the American natives are extremely dull; their faculties circumscribed, their sentiments incapable of refinement; and they seem to be very ill provided with the power of imagination." Indeed, in a gesture toward European unity, the *British Magazine* concludes, "The truth is, neither France nor England could derive much honour from any connexion with such cruel and irreclaimable savages, whom no precepts could enlighten, and no example humanize."[81]

Humphry Clinker participates in and even exceeds the kind of logical gymnastics which claim that Indians cannot be converted at all, except by Europeans who bring their own brand of savagery to the task. At the same time that the text represents the appalling barbarity of Amerindians, it shows native culture responding with dignity and even intellectual sophistication to French missionary incursions. In a masterly restructuring of familiar materials, Smollett manages to both depict Catholic zeal and to trivialize it. In Lismahago's narrative, the Jesuits ignore the Miamis' peaceful attempt to dismiss them, "persist[ing] in saying mass, in preaching, baptizing, and squabbling with the conjurors . . . till they had thrown the whole community into confusion" (232). The exasperated Indians then try, condemn, and burn them at the stake, "where they died singing *Salve regina,* in a rapture of joy, for the crown of martyrdom which they had obtained" (232). By representing the disruptive effects of Jesuit interventions in a hitherto stable and contented native society, the narrative recasts missionary enthusiasm as petty (and stubborn) interference and thus makes English failure at conversion seem culturally respectful.[82]

In any case, the Indians in *Humphry Clinker* are too cynical to be converted. Like the dignified Chief Lontac in Bage's *Hermsprong,* and unlike the docile and easily manipulated tribe in *The Female American* (1767), Smollett's Indians confidently assert the superiority of their own forms of belief.[83] Their primitive tenets—"They . . . worship two contending principles; one the fountain of all Good, the other the source of all evil . . . pay adoration to a Supreme Being, who creates and sustains the universe" (231)—can more than hold their own against canting Catholicism. The natives scoff at the Jesuits' accounts of "miracles," of "mysteries and revelations, which they could neither explain nor authenticate"; they are horrified by a God who would not only inflict mortality on his only son, but allow him "to be insulted, flagellated, and even executed as a malefactor"; and as for the creed of transubstantiation, they consider it impious to pretend "to create God himself, to swallow, digest, revive, and multiply him *ad infinitum,* by the help of a little flour and water" (231). Interestingly, Smollett here projects on to the French an English experience of Indian cynicism regarding Christianity. John Oldmixon, writing in 1741, recounts questions addressed to the Reverend John Elliot in 1646: *"How there could be an Image of God, since it was forbidden in the Second Commandment?* This probably arose from Mr *Elliot's* saying Man was created after God's own Image. There is Simplicity in this, but more Reflection than would be found in many of our Peasants under a like Lecture."* In fact, these Indians reject Christianity *"for the* English, *that are* Christians, *will cheat the* Indians *of their Land . . . your Knowledge of Books does but make you the more cunning to cheat others, and so does more Harm than Good."* Finally, the Indians name two or three preachers in New York, *"who instead of preaching their pious Religion, taught them to drink."*[84] In a series of deft moves, Smollett re-writes such English/Protestant failures as French/Catholic ones; the French missionary project is represented in *Humphry Clinker* as a social evil undertaken by ridiculously fanatical men whose risible beliefs are appropriately interrogated and rejected by a suspicious native culture.

While he mocks the notion of French Catholic tenets taking root in native culture, Smollett also portrays the evil practices of that culture. The tortures inflicted on Lismahago and Murphy resemble descriptions in other captivity narratives: John Gyles writes that "sometimes an old shrivell'd Squaw will take up a Shovel of hot Embers and throw them into a Captive's Bosom"; Jean Lowry watches the agonies of a fellow captive: "first they Scalp'd him alive. . . . They heated their Daggers in the fire and pushed them into the fleshy parts of his Body"; Peter Williamson recounts that as prisoners are being burnt alive, "one of the villains with his scalping knife, ript open their bellies, took out their entrails, and burnt them before their eyes, whilst the others were cutting, piercing and tearing the flesh from their breasts, hands, arms and legs, with red hot irons, 'till they were dead." The *British Magazine* relates the suffering of Father Jogues: "Having tore off his nails with their teeth, they crushed all his fingers, and thrust a sword through his right hand . . . they tore off his nails, and bit off his two forefingers."[85] Lismahago, too, is dismembered and wounded, but he is subjected to even worse torments: "some of his teeth were drawn, or dug out with a crooked nail; splintered reeds had been thrust up his nostrils and other tender parts; and the calves of his legs had been blown up with mines of gunpowder dug in the flesh" (228). Given the wide availability of narratives describing actual episodes of excruciating torture, one has to look carefully at the particular details added in Smollett's fiction. These additions, I suggest, signify something more than a novelist's desire for effect, or for what Colley calls "the pornography of real or invented Indian violence";[86] they are part of Smollett's warning about the consequences of imperial adventuring. The splintered reeds *invade* Lismahago's body; not only his nostrils but "other tender parts" suffer penetration. If these "parts" refer to his penis and anus, the infliction of pain becomes sexualized, so that monstrous perversion is added to the already grotesque tortures devised by Indians, who also enact on the European body the invasion of their territories. Similarly, while Smollett's description of running the gauntlet evokes the experience of Father Jogues and his companion René Goupil who "were set upon by the women and children, who mangled them in such a manner, that there was not a spot on their bodies free of scar or wound," here again Smollett adds a sexual dimension rarely included in historical accounts: Murphy has been castrated by women while "passing through the different whigwams [*sic*] or villages of the Miamis."[87] In *Humphry Clinker,* the women's bloodlust supersedes the sachem's need for a son and heir, and their pleasure in inflicting sexual abuse overrides their desire for an able recruit for the tribe. The "crooked nail" and the "gunpowder dug in the flesh," represent more than the Indian desire to invade the European body. They are, in fact, artifacts of the industrial world brought to America by Europeans, tools provided to the natives by the colonizing culture, now turned against the imperial power in a fitting though appalling way. In a monstrous reenactment of European incursions into American territories, Indians use the invaders' weapons to penetrate and destroy them.

Lismahago, of course, survives his ordeal. His friend Murphy is not so lucky, perhaps because his Irish body is less sturdy than Lismahago's Scottish one. Murphy, "mangled by the women and children [and] rendered altogether unfit for the purposes of marriage" (228), undergoes further tortures until he is mercifully killed, heroically singing his death song. In his treatment of this particular ritual, Smollett once again both replicates and manipulates factual accounts, such as Colden's description of the Indian tortured and executed by de Frontenac: the young man dies at the stake, singing about his own courage and his memories of inflicting similar punishment on many Frenchmen.[88] The death song, in other words, asserts power, agency, and masculinity even under horrific circumstances. Smollett, in one economical move, manages to trivialize this crucial aspect of Indian culture at the same time that he demonstrates British pluck. Murphy, in the agonies of death, sings not of past military exploits nor of Christian salvation, but the *Drimmendoo,* Gaelic for "black cow with a white back" (403, n. 67). It is a last gesture of Rabelasian defiance and mockery, a parodic gesture of bravura, diminishing both French martyrs like Jean de Brébeuf and Indian warriors. Murphy's tormentors are also, of course, cannibals: like the trader in Williamson's narrative and Captain Robertson in Rutherfurd's *The Siege of Detroit,* Murphy becomes "a hearty meal" (228) for his captors. Cannibalism, while certainly not unheard of in tribal cultures, must have been unusual enough that Rutherfurd feels compelled to explain that "this shocking piece of barbarity is practiced only by some of the Indian nations to the northward, The Six Nations, who use their prisoners, while alive, much worse than they do, yet never eat human flesh, when *they* do, not for want of food, but as a religious ceremony, or rather from a superstitious idea that it makes them prosperous in war."[89] In *Humphry Clinker,* cannibalism is represented as simply another aspect of the Indians' exuberant, drunken pleasure in torturing their victims. Smollett's Indians, then, are not only as cruel as those described in nonfictional narratives, they are also sadists, sexual perverts, and casually heartless cannibals.[90]

This is no place for a civilized British man; it is fit for only those already tainted, like Mountain in *Master of Ballantrae* or the abandoned son of Effie Deans and George Staunton in Scott's *Heart of Midlothian.* Scott's narrative disposes of the inconvenient boy by shipping him off to America, where he "fled to the next tribe of wild Indians. He was never more heard of; and it may therefore be presumed that he lived and died after the manner of that savage people, with whom his previous habits had well fitted him to associate."[91] Yet Lismahago contentedly makes his home there, marrying Squinkinacoosta, producing a child by her, and succeeding his adoptive father as Sachem. Such an outcome is so emphatically *not* desirable that Smollett needs to make tribal life, even for survivors of horrific tortures, seem no healthy alternative to an admittedly diseased home country.[92] Having constructed a narrative that might be misconstrued as advocating reconciliation to a savage culture and a cannibalistic wife, Smollett provides a corrective accessible to the densest reader: he shows that Lismahago has joined a society tainted by its own version of feminized commodification. Just as the upstart London citizen's "wife and daughters appear in the richest stuff, bespangled with diamonds" (119), Amerindian society too contains women who consume *goods* as well as flesh.

When Tabitha interrogates Lismahago about Squinkinacoosta's wedding clothes, "whether she wore high-breasted stays or bodice, a robe of silk or velvet, and laces of Mechlin or minionette," whether she "used *rouge,* and had her hair dressed in the Parisian fashion," he replies that neither "the simplicity of their manners nor the commerce of their coun-

try would admit of those articles of luxury which are deemed magnifi-
cence in Europe" (229–30). Tabitha's persistent queries elicit the
information "that his princess had neither shoes, stockings, shift, nor
any kind of linen" (230). Squinkinacoosta, then, seems to represent a
primitive (and positive) alternative to the kind of European fashion that
requires Lydia to sit "above six hours under the hands of a hairdresser,
who stuffed [her] head with as much black wool as would have made
quilted petticoat" (125) and brings Tabitha to an Edinburgh ball
dressed "in a full suit of damask, so thick and heavy, that the sight of it
alone, at this season of the year, was sufficient to draw drops of sweat
from any man of ordinary imagination" (261; one is reminded of the
hyperbolically inappropriate attire of the English visitors in Suriname).
Juxtaposed to these excesses of female finery, the relative nakedness
of Squinkinacoosta might be seen as a virtue, especially in a text that,
according to David Weed, posits a robust masculinity that "resists infection from the femininity intertwined with England's commercial society."[93] A woman who can devise and execute tortures with the best of
her tribe, who "vied with the stoutest warrior in eating the flesh of the
sacrifice," and who can hold her liquor when others succumb to intoxi-
cation (229) must at least be free of the feminine vanity and desire for
ornament so distressing to eighteenth-century males. Indeed, Squinkinacoosta's lack of linen fits the picture of simplicity drawn by Jean de
Léry in 1578 and by Behn in 1688. Behn emphasizes the Amerindians'
modesty despite their nakedness, "so like our first Parents before the
Fall, it seems as if they had no Wishes' (*Oroonoko* 39).[94] Squinkinacoosta, however, is just as wedded to wedding finery as any English
miss; only the nature of the ornamentation differs. In place of stays,
lace, and rouge, she adorns herself with "bobbins of human bone—one
eye-lid was painted green, and the other yellow; the cheeks were blue,
the lips white, the teeth red. . . . a couple of gaudy parrot's feathers were
stuck through the division of the nostrils—there was a blue stone set in
the chins." Lismahago's bride bedecks herself with earrings, bracelets,
and necklaces, and "about her neck was hung the fresh scalp of a Mohawk warrior, whom her deceased lover had lately slain in battle—and
finally, she was anointed from head to foot with bear's grease, which
sent forth a most disagreeable odour" (230). Rather than representing
native simplicity as a counter to European female vanity, Squinkinacoosta demonstrates that Indian women too crave cosmetics and jewels
and scents, some of which are even more repellant than those adorning
Swift's Celia and Corinna. When M. A. Goldberg argues that Smollett
is posing the same kind of cultural relativism that the Scottish critics

and historians employed in examining and evaluating "the noble savage," thereby making an "analogy between the American Indians and the Scots," he misreads, I believe, this part of Lismahago's narrative. The grotesque accessories with which Squinkinacoosta adorns herself underline the text's conviction that bad as commercialism might be in Britain, life among the savages of America provides no real escape.[95]

In any case, the barbarians have already stormed the gate, not only in the persons of those "planters, Negro-drivers and hucksters, from our American plantations" (65), but also in the shape of products and practices that penetrate and pervert British life as they have Lismahago's body. Medicines from America turn out to be overpriced and useless, like the "Gengzeng" Bramble orders, "though I doubt much, whether that which comes from America is equally efficacious with what is brought from the East Indies" (667). Some newfangled medical practices, in fact, borrow the murderous habits of American Indians and must be energetically resisted by John Bull. When Squire Burdock is injured, the good apothecary Grieve employs traditional British methods like letting blood and applying poultices. The squire's snobbish wife and worthless son, however, insist on calling in a surgeon who "could not tell whether there was a fracture, until he should take off the scalp" (200). Unlike Lismahago at the hands of Indians, Burdock escapes a scalping, returning to consciousness just before the operation. Significantly, as he overpowers the surgeon's assistants, he asserts his national character, exclaiming, "in a bellowing tone, 'I ha'n't lived so long in Yorkshire to be trepanned by such vermin as you'" (200). Burdock the vigorous English squire reclaims control over his body, foiling the possibly homicidal intentions of his son ("signor Macaroni") and wife. The barbaric Indian practice of scalping may have invaded British shores, but "an old fox in the West Riding" (200) can and does protect himself from it.[96]

At the end of the novel, on the occasion of his marriage to Tabitha, Lismahago distributes gifts to his new family. Matthew Bramble gets "a fine deer's skin, and a Spanish fowling-piece"; Jery is given "a case of pistols curiously mounted with silver"; and Winifred Jenkins receives "An Indian purse, made of silk grass, containing twenty crown pieces." Tabitha herself becomes the proud possessor of "a fur cloak of American sables, valued at fourscore guineas" as well as a wedding ring, "a curious antique, set with rose diamonds [which] had been in the family two hundred years" (390). Except for the ring, a precious relic of a rich Celtic past, the gifts all represent colonial spoils: the guns are the detritus of a previous imperial presence in North America, whose technology of power has dwindled to the status of souvenirs, and Winifred's purse is an artifact of transculturation, the Amerindian receptacle that houses (or perhaps swallows) British coins. Tabitha's cloak is multivalent, since "an Indian wearing clothes made from marten (a species of weasel related to the sable) was clad in a commodity reserved for royalty in Europe. . . . Yet pelts were not fully clothes to the explorers' eyes, as they simply covered one's skin with another's and seemed more like raw materials than finished garments."[97] Where the guns might serve as a salutary *memento mori*, and the purse as a symbol of the financial cost of maintaining colonies, the bridal gift both disrupts the social hierarchies so dear to the text's heart *and* connects the Welshwoman Tabitha to the savage Squinkinacoosta. The produce and refuse of America penetrate even the hallowed grounds of Brambleton Hall, and Tabitha, like the actors in Dryden's *Indian Queen* decked out with American feathers sent by the narrator of *Oroonoko* (39)—indeed, like the nation itself—adorns herself with the sheddings of the colonial world. In *Humphry Clinker*, Smollett suggests that the American colonies have damaged the home country much more than they have benefited it: they have enriched the wrong kinds of Britons, thereby destabilizing social relations and endangering the national health, and, as Lismahago's captivity narrative demonstrates, they have mutilated the British body (and body politic, for emigration and transculturation can only jeopardize the wholeness of the state). In the end, America's contribution to Britain consists of trinkets and carcasses and a degraded culture.

Defoe and Smollett describe two different Americas. Defoe's New World offers safety, prosperity, and possibly moral regeneration to those who have the means and the will to profit from its opportunities; these fortunate felons overcome early missteps and achieve both financial and social respectability. The most successful colonists, however, feel the pull of Britain most strongly, for only at home can they attain and inhabit that most desirable of all identities: leisured gentry. Smollett's novel presses the claims of home even more urgently by construing the New World as a site of moral and physical danger, a place that produces social upstarts who will never be accepted by the real country gentry like the Bramble family and one that literally eats away at the British body. Where Defoe's texts seek to circumvent the danger represented by ambitious colonies by making home the object of desire, Smollett's novel insists that Britons should stay home for their own health and that of the nation. In both cases, imperial adventuring in America can never replicate the satisfactions inherent in identifying with the privileged family of Britons.

Entr'acte. Between Empires: Wollstonecraft's *Maria, or The Wrongs of Woman*

MORE THAN THE THIRTY YEARS BETWEEN THEIR COMPOSITION DI-vide Smollett's last novel and Mary Wollstonecraft's unfinished final work: gender, political ideologies, and two revolutions separate *Humphry Clinker* and *Maria, or The Wrongs of Woman* (written 1796, published posthumously in 1798). Whereas Smollett, in Byron Glassman's words, is "alarmed at the threat to established modes and institutions," Wollstonecraft, notes Gary Kelly, wants to "make the novel serve Revolutionary feminism by finding a form answerable to both her revolutionary purpose and an unrevolutionized readership."[1] From these disparate historical and ideological contexts, however, Smollett and Wollstonecraft generate interestingly similar indictments of the appalling effects of a new ideology of commercialism, and both comprehensively reject the New World as a desirable alternative to oppressive conditions prevailing in Britain. Both texts, in the end, propose retreats within the realm, so that the Brambles retire to quiet domesticity in Monmouthshire and Maria to an unspecified place "in the country" (151).[2]

Indeed, much as they excoriate the policies and practices of the nation, Smollett and Wollstonecraft exhibit a degree of patriotism, perhaps even xenophobia, about the world beyond Britain. Exposure to Continental Europe serves only to vitiate English character. Squire Burdock in *Humphry Clinker*, for example, "is . . . blessed with an only son, about two and twenty, just returned from Italy, a complete fiddler and dilettante; and he slips no opportunity of manifesting the most perfect contempt for his own father" (199). And when Bayard takes his wife to Rome as a measure of economy, he finds that she "was continually surrounded by a train of expensive loungers, under the denominations of language-masters, musicians, painters, and ciceroni." Snubbed by Roman aristocracy, she returns to England from "travels [which] had produced no effect upon her, but that of making her more expensive and fantastic than ever" (331). In *Maria*, France provides a "place of refuge" for Darnford's assailants and subsequently seems to destabilize his own fidelity to Maria (142, 152), while Lisbon, where her uncle goes "to seek the succour of a milder climate" (104), becomes instead the site of his lonely death. Moreover, like *Humphry Clinker, Maria* provides a set piece that can serve as propaganda against emigration to America, now an independent republic. Interestingly, in the tangled web of strategies and motivations that drive the texts' rejection of America, there also emerges a distinct preference for the second empire forming in the East.

One might imagine that the vindicator of the rights of men and women would argue, as does Bage's Hermsprong, that the United States offers equality and opportunity to those oppressed by the static hierarchies of Britain. Indeed, Wollstonecraft at one time had planned to settle in the new republic with Gilbert Imlay, who, in his novel *The Emigrants* (1793) compared "the happiness of the people who are forming an empire in this remote part of the world, with the vanity and distractions which the depravity of the European manners have made general on your side of the water."[3] By the time she composes *Maria*, however, Wollstonecraft's views on America seem to have undergone a thorough revision, and the nation is no more attractive than were the colonies in *Humphry Clinker. Maria* participates in the development of a new ideology about America: the text represents the United States not as a wilderness housing alien savages but as a model of crass commercialism and vulgar ostentation. Within the brief narrative about Darnford's sojourn in America, Wollstonecraft embeds a compressed but comprehensive critique of a thoroughly depraved culture.

Darnford, like Lismahago, travels to America on a military mission, not to fight the French over territories, but to subdue the rebel colonists, and his motivation is no more patriotic than Colonel Jack's—he turns to military service because he has dissipated his patrimony and has "no resource but to purchase a commission in a new-raised regiment, destined to subjugate America" (44). With no particular commitment to Britain's imperial agenda, he easily succumbs to a species of transculturation when he is captured by the Americans and becomes converted to republicanism by books and by his captor/host: "My political sentiments now underwent a total change; and dazzled by the hospitality of the Americans, I determined to take up my abode with freedom" (44). The romance, however, quickly fizzles, and, like Fanny Trollope a quarter century later, Darnford finds in the United States not freedom but puritanical manners combined with vulgar materialism and almost parodic attempts to perform gentility. Wollstonecraft's harsh depiction of a brutish America may stem, of course, from her continuing rage against Imlay's sexual betrayals; as Moira Ferguson and Janet Todd point out, "*The Wrongs of Woman* enabled her to vent her anger at Imlay's behaviour."[4] I suggest, however, that there are political as well as personal issues being played out in the text. In a move that establishes her credentials as a respectable patriot, Wollstonecraft exports to America those homegrown ideologies and behaviors she finds dangerous and degrading.

Darnford's narrative about America offers startling parallels to Bramble's representation of an England degenerating into boorish bourgeois culture. Speaking of the newly rich in Bath, Bramble complains, "Knowing no other criterion of greatness, but the ostentation of wealth, they discharge their affluence without taste or conduct" (66); of the elite classes in American towns, Darnford says, "The only pleasure wealth afforded, was to make an ostentatious display of it; for the cultivation of the fine arts, or literature, had not introduced into the first circles that polish of manners which renders the rich so essentially superior to the poor in Europe" (45).[5] Americans thus occupy a lower evolutionary rung than Europeans, much as women and racial others do in Thomson's *Seasons*. Moreover, Darnford's comment targets one of the fundamental ideologies of the new nation when he insists on the positive effects of the hierarchy of wealth and position obtaining in Britain.[6] Similarly, Darnford's narrative locates in America the kind of unregulated polity that Bramble finds at home, where "the wise patriots of London have taken it into their heads, that all regulation is inconsistent with liberty" (*HC* 154; one thinks again of Dryden's "moody, murmuring race"). Darnford in fact ascribes to Independence itself the degenerate practices he loathes: "an influx of vices had been let in by the Revolution, and the most rigid principles of religion shaken to the centre" (45). Darnford's language conflates America and France in an echo of the kind of paranoid pairing mockingly critiqued in *Hermsprong*. Most disturbing to both Bramble and Darnford is the conviction that commerce has ruined civic character: Bramble fumes that "all the people I see, are too much engrossed by schemes of interest or ambition to have any room left for sentiment or friendship" (154); Darnford, reversing Imlay's accusation that "while in England a principal object of the government has been that of the aggrandizement of commerce, every principle of the human heart seems to have been contaminated," concludes that the American national character reflects "a phenomenon in the history of the human mind—a head enthusiastically enterprising, with cold selfishness of heart" (45).[7] Industry, which Thomson identi-

fies and praises as a particularly British virtue, becomes in Wollstonecraft's text a vice that has gripped the inhabitants of the nation on the
other side of the Atlantic.

Darnford despises America because he cannot abide its worship of
commerce and commodity and longs for the more civilized, less materialistic Old World. What he conveniently elides from his dissection of
American values is that they came with British settlers, and that commerce and consumption were crucial to the survival of the British empire and to the home government. Colonial trade, as Smollett so clearly
demonstrates, enriched a whole new class in Britain and created a mutual interdependency between colonies and the mother country. Moreover, as historian T. H. Breen points out, colonial consumption of
British products led to a complex combination of identification and resistance, as reliance on British goods made the colonists more British:

> The road to Americanization ran through Anglicization . . . before these
> widely dispersed colonists could develop a sense of their own common iden-
> tity, they had first to be integrated fully into the British empire. Royal gov-
> ernment in colonial America was never large enough to effect Anglicization.
> Nor could force of arms have brought about this cultural redefinition. Such
> a vast shift in how Americans viewed the mother country and each other
> required a flood of consumer goods, little manufactured items that found
> their way into gentry homes as well as frontier cabins. According to anthro-
> pologist James Deetz, this transformation of everyday material culture
> "meant that on the eve of the American Revolution, Americans were more
> English than they had been in the past since the first years of the colonies."[8]

Constructing a consumer culture in America was, of course, always part
of the imperial project of the home country, as we have seen in Defoe's
disquisitions on what the colonies can do for Britain. At the same time,
the American qualities that Darnford inveighs against, ones that D. W.
Meinig characterizes as clichés circulating in Britain circa 1800 — "the
middle-class character of society and economy . . . the informality and
egalitarianism in manners, the assertive individualism and independence, the pervasive materialism and commercialism"[9] — equally define
an emerging and increasingly powerful sector of British society in the
eighteenth century. Indeed, Wollstonecraft's text participates in a strategy of displacement; Rozbicki suggests that "the derision directed
against the American nouveaux riches was to a large degree a function
of social change in Britain and of attempts by old elites to maintain the
cultural demarcation lines of their own authority in the face of the rising
commercial class."[10]

Interestingly, Wollstonecraft's views on commercialism seem to have shifted during the decade. In 1790, she endorses middle-class enterprise when she proposes, in *A Vindication of the Rights of Men*, that "the only security of property that nature authorizes and reason sanctions is, the right a man has to enjoy the acquisitions which his talent and industry have acquired," a sentiment that both Thomson and Defoe might share. By 1796, however, she passionately attacks the consequences of the same talent and industry; they lead, according to her *Letters Written during a Short Residence in Sweden, Norway, and Denmark*, to "mushroom fortunes . . . the men, indeed, seem of the species of the fungus, and the insolent vulgarity which a sudden influx of wealth usually produces in common minds, is here very conspicuous. . . . An ostentatious display of wealth without elegance, and a greedy enjoyment of pleasure without sentiment, embrutes them."[11] Wollstonecraft constructs, therefore, a narrative about America that replicates her own perception of Europe. Ironically, these criticisms about rampant materialism reflect the attitude of contemporary Europeans toward Britain itself. David S. Landes points out that "in the eighteenth century, Continental observers saw the English as great materialists," and quotes Voltaire, Andreas Riem, and the Comte de Mirabeau, all of whom disparage the greed and calculating commercialism of the British. He adds, "A hundred years later, the Americans became the new target of obloquy, the British now joining their erstwhile critics in scorning these *nouveaux riches*."[12] Alexis de Tocqueville makes a similar (but class-based) point when he talks about English contempt for American manners: "The English make game of the manners of the Americans; but it is singular that most of the writers who have drawn these ludicrous delineations belonged themselves to the middle classes in England, to whom the same delineations are exceedingly applicable; so that these pitiless censors furnish, for the most part, an example of the very thing they blame in the United States: they do not perceive that they are deriding themselves, to the great amusement of the aristocracy of their own country."[13] Wollstonecraft appears to be in the vanguard of more than the feminist movement; *Maria* positions itself as an early example of "othering" the boor within and transporting the nation of shopkeepers across the Atlantic.

Even the women in America are caricatures of their counterparts in Europe. Just as Squinkinacoosta parodies the ornamentation favored by European women, Darnford's female acquaintances exhibit all the worst qualities (vanity, coquetry, envy) of British women: they have "all the airs and ignorance of the ladies who give the tone to the circles

of the large trading towns in England. . . . All the frivolity which often
. . . renders the society of modest women so stupid in England, here
seemed to throw still more leaden fetters on their charms" (45). Women
in America display both prudery and vulgarity; they bore Darnford to
such an extent that "I could only keep myself awake in their company
by making downright love to them." American women are so "inferior
to our European charmers" that when he returns to London, "the
women of the town . . . appeared like angels to me" (45–46) — that is,
even prostitutes are preferable to American ladies.[14] This wholesale
condemnation of American women strikes a particularly jarring note in
a text in which, as Conger notes, "women bond together to combat
men's tyranny, transforming mutual sympathy into a redemptive sister-
hood."[15] In a text that strives to provide a community of and for women
so inclusive as to welcome gentry-class Maria, prostitute/thief Jemima,
washerwoman Peggy, and the haberdasher who shelters Maria, it is
shocking to find a whole nation of women excluded and despised without narrative commentary. Like the commercial man, the shallow
woman, "romantic and inconstant . . . vain and mean,"[16] seems to have
left Britain and taken up residence in America.

Darnford's disaffection from American society replicates but exceeds
that of bored and homesick British officers stationed in the colonies;
Barrow quotes a customs officer in Boston who writes home, "this is
the finest Country and Climate I ever saw, Yet I begin to grow sick of
the people."[17] Sickened by the vulgarity of men and vanity of women in
American towns, Darnford retires to the countryside, enacting a reprise
of Pope and Thomson's poetic solitude and Bramble's retreat to Wales,
but the pastoral and domestic idylls in those texts find no counterpart
in the untamed expanses of America. Where Imlay portrays an abundant and well-stocked natural wonderland — "The fertile and boundless
Savannas were covered with flocks of buffalo, elk, and deer, which appeared to wanton in the exuberance of their luxurious pastures"[18] —
Darnford discovers only suffocating boredom. He looks in vain for
"something better than [to] vegetate with the animals that made a very
considerable part of my household" (46), and, unlike Bramble in the
Scottish Highlands, finds no delight in wild landscapes. Indeed, the
very expansiveness of the country offers impediment to enjoyment:
"The eye wandered without an object to fix upon over immeasurable
plains . . . whilst eternal forests of small clustering trees, obstructed the
circulation of air, and embarrassed the path, without gratifying the eye
of taste" (46). Instead of finding refreshing solitude or congenial company in his retreat, Darnford, like Crusoe, reads a footprint as "a dread-

ful warning" of murderous Indians lurking nearby. America and its citizens, in *Maria,* are both empty and empty-headed, dangerous and dull, self-indulgent and self-aggrandizing. Darnford joyfully quits "the land of liberty and vulgar aristocracy, seated on her bags of dollars" (46).

Wollstonecraft's anti-emigration narrative refutes almost programmatically the claims advanced in Imlay's *Emigrants,* which specifically courts British subjects who face difficulties in the home country.[19] The heroine's father "was an eminent merchant in the city of London, part of whose family having been extravagant, ruined his fortune, and obliged him to seek an asylum in America"; Mrs. W— — invites her friend Laura to leave her unhappy domestic situation in Bristol and join "our little circle" in Pittsburgh, to "come to these Arcadian regions where there is room for millions, and where the stings of outrageous fortune cannot reach you"; Caroline's uncle, appealed to by a repentant servant who had previously betrayed him, promises the villain "passage to America . . . where as he would not have temptations to commit acts of wickedness, he might live to become a useful citizen."[20] Imlay's America, like Defoe's colonies, offers refuge and regeneration to financially, emotionally, or morally troubled Britons, turning them into prosperous, contented, and upright citizens. Darnford's narrative in *Maria* overturns every element of this idyllic portrait, representing America as a site of crass commercialism, vulgar manners, and landscapes that are paradoxically both too expansive and claustrophobic.

Even before the final break with Imlay, however, Wollstonecraft had shifted her focus from public to private issues and turned away from engagement with global affairs. As Gary Kelly says, by 1794 "her main interest . . . was in saving her revolutionary domesticity. She saw herself representing domesticity and the life of the imagination as Imlay became more immersed in 'business.'"[21] Indeed, in a series of letters to Imlay, Wollstonecraft deplores his increasing financial ambitions and his immersion in European commercial projects and berates his greed: "When you first entered into these plans, you bounded your views to the gaining of a thousand pounds. It was sufficient to have procured a farm in America, which would have been an independence. You find now that you did not know yourself, and that a certain situation in life is more necessary to you than you imagined."; from Scandinavia she writes to warn him that "you—yourself, are strangely altered, since you have entered deeply into commerce."[22] Ironically, it was Imlay's shift from seeking retirement in America to engaging in European business affairs that alienated him from Wollstonecraft and led to the sexual betrayals that traumatized her to the point of attempted suicide. In *Maria*, Wollstonecraft takes a complex revenge: Imlay, the European man of commerce, becomes reincarnated as a whole nation of vulgar businessmen.

The diatribe against America may also originate in Wollstonecraft's move toward what Susan Sniader Lanser has called "compensatory conservatism," a move already evident in her complicated rendering of class divisions in *A Vindication of the Rights of Woman*.[23] In *Maria*, a text she knew to be radically feminist as well as one that "also contains more general social comment, in its criticism of institutions such as hospitals and workhouses, and social evils such as the practice of impressments,"[24] Wollstonecraft may have strategically chosen to align herself with conservative criticism of America. During a period when "intellectual radicalism can be observed going underground," and given her own vulnerability to "social ostracism [and] public vilification,"[25] Wollstonecraft may well have chosen to take a conservative position on at least one contemporary controversy. Whether the unrelievedly hostile portrait of America is a revenge against Imlay or a way to temper the revolutionary feminism of *Maria*, the text certainly stands at the beginning of a centuries-long construction of the Ugly American, ostentatious, vulgar, materialistic, "the man who sits next to you on the transatlantic flight with endless stories about the size of his car, mispronouncing the names of European cities."[26] Less than two decades after the loss of the colonies, *Maria* is already assuring Britain that it has not lost much.

In any case, a better empire is in the offing. Unlike Defoe, who rejects the East because "the *Indian* Trade drains the whole of the Western World of their ready Money . . . and the *Indians* and *Chinese* are enrich'd in Trade at the Expence of all the Commerce of *Europe*,"[27] Wollstonecraft follows Smollett in hinting at the advantages of imperial activity in Asia. Although Smollett's text includes East Indian factors in its list of undesirables, it offers a tantalizing glimpse of the eastern empire. Touched by the highwayman Martin's gallantry and spirit, Matthew Bramble agrees to help him leave his life of crime. When Martin proposes retiring to the country, Bramble demurs, because the quiet ways of rural Britain would not suit Martin's "active and enterprising disposition—I would therefore advise you to try your fortune in the East Indies—I will give you a letter to a friend in London . . . for a commission in the company's service" (222). The rewards of service in India are demonstrated in the narrative of Captain Brown, who "had, from a spirit of idleness and dissipation, enlisted as a soldier in the service of the East-India company," where he had recommended himself to Clive and consequently "had honestly amassed above twelve thousand pounds," (303), which he intends to use to support his family back in Scotland. Contrast this to Lismahago's oppressive poverty, and we see that India is the part of the British empire that enriches worthy soldiers.[28] *Maria*, too, demonstrates the honest profitability of Indian service; Maria's uncle goes to India as a nobleman's confidential secretary, and "realize[s], by good luck, rather than management, a handsome fortune" (77), which he uses to support his nieces. It is worth noting that both texts emphasize (as does Scott's *Guy Mannering*) that these Indian fortunes are amassed without participating in the kind of corruption and exploitation that had tainted the reputation of so many returning nabobs and for which Warren Hastings was tried. Both texts claim that honest and even accidental fortunes can be acquired in India, that Britons can return from India with scalps and reputations intact, and that money accumulated from the East is put to good use in the home country. While America inflicts physical and mental bruising, while it leads to dangerous transculturation or disgusted disillusionment, India beckons the adventurous and industrious Briton to wealth and respectability. Both *Humphry Clinker* and *Maria* counsel turning away from the Wild West to witness the sun of the British Empire rise in the East.

3

Peripheral Visions: Robert Bage's *Hermsprong* and Elizabeth Hamilton's *Letters of a Hindoo Rajah*

> In short, we suffer'd 'em to survey us as they pleas'd, and we
> thought they wou'd never have done admiring us. . . . and all . . .
> ask'd, If we had Sense, and Wit? if we cou'd talk of affairs of Life,
> and War, as they cou'd do?
>
> —*Oroonoko*

> Throughout this dialogue I had been incommoded by the observa-
> tion of Secundra Dass. . . . our eyes were in each other's faces—you
> might say, in each other's bosoms; and those of the Indian troubled
> me with a certain changing brightness, as of comprehension.
>
> —*Master of Ballantrae*

AT ABOUT THE SAME TIME THAT MARY WOLLSTONECRAFT WAS PLAC-
ing America and India at the margins of her domestic drama, two of her
contemporaries produced texts that deployed the peripheries to critique
the metropole. Robert Bage's *Hermsprong; or Man as He Is Not* and Elizabeth Hamilton's *Translation of the Letters of a Hindoo Rajah* (both published in 1796) serve up scathing views of late eighteenth-century
British life, views modulated through the eyes of the colonized, in a
kind of inversion of what Homi Bhabha defines as the aim of colonial
discourse: "The objective of colonial discourse is to construe the colonized as a population of degenerate types on the basis of racial origin,
in order to justify conquest. . . . What is increased is the visibility of the
subject as an object of surveillance, tabulation, enumeration and, indeed, paranoia and fantasy."[1] Bage's self-styled "American savage" and
Hamilton's Hindu Rajah (as well as her Brahmin) travel to Britain to
discover a world in which church, state, and ruling elite collude to perpetuate inequities and iniquities. Scrutiny from the increasingly disillu-
sioned Zāārmilla and the stoutly righteous Hermsprong exposes the
home country's utter lack of moral authority to govern other cultures;

114

moreover, the critiques these outsiders articulate are frequently specifically comparative, so that British social practices are shown to be invidious in light of the superior customs of India and America.[2] The character of the imperial center, then, becomes the subject of scrutiny from the peripheries.

Bage and Hamilton approach their subjects from opposing ideological camps. Bage, living in Birmingham during the heyday of the Lunar Society, connected both professionally and personally with William Hutton (a victim of the counterrevolutionary Bastille Day riots of 1795), articulates a political radicalism that "leads [him] to be classified today with the 1790s Jacobin writers." Hamilton, raised in rural Scotland and subsequently a member of literary circles in both London and Edinburgh, produces a work explicitly anti-Jacobin, one "immediately recognized as a contribution to the increasingly polemical literary battles of the 1790s and early 1800s."[3] That satiric criticism of British society should come from both "left" and "right" is not in itself surprising; as John Dinwiddy and Gary Kelly point out, "the radicals seem to have thought that demystifying satire was a better way of striking at the monarchy than melodramatic violence," and anti-Jacobin novels, "in spite of their satire on ideas and characters of the English Jacobins . . . continued many of the themes of social criticism developed in English Jacobin fiction."[4] What *is* remarkable is that both Bage and Hamilton foreground colonized spokesmen (although, of course, Hermsprong's status as colonized subject is profoundly problematic), and that readers are invited not only to agree, but also to identify with representatives of the "inferior" culture.[5] In this chapter, I argue that these authors' ventriloquist engagement with imperial subjects modifies and complicates their ideological positions. Hamilton's Hindus expose the home country's lack of moral authority to govern other cultures even while her double-voiced text interrogates the seemingly superior standards of the Indian critics themselves, so that neither Britain nor Hindu India can claim moral ascendancy. Her text implies that the only hope for the imperium lies in a willingness to see itself through the eyes of cultural others, to respect and even emulate the virtues of those it aims to rule, and to thereby develop a hybridized imperial character. Bage's radical individualism, manifested in derogatory statements about British institutions as well as in his idealized descriptions of life in North America, is undercut by the hero's membership in the ruling elite of the home country but underscored by that hero's rejection of traditional aristocratic values.

Interestingly, although both texts have much to say about the rights and responsibilities of women in the metropole, neither constructs more progressive gender relations in the peripheries. Bage's text presents a series of victimized Englishwomen, some complicit in their miserable fates because of their timid conventionality. Caroline Campinet, despite her father Lord Grondale's multiple sadistic acts, cannot detach herself from the patriarchal system of authority; her maternal aunt Mrs. Merrick lives in lonely seclusion because "in her youth she had been deserted by her lover for a richer woman" (75), while her paternal aunt Mrs. Garnet cannot countenance even so mild a rebellion as clandestine correspondence with her niece, and fears incurring Grondale's displeasure if she attends his church. To these passive feminine characters, Bage opposes a couple of spirited women who either flout the patriarchal system or manipulate it to their own ends. Lord Grondale's mistress Mrs. Stone is a highly complex character who cannot be adequately considered within my current argument. She, like the housekeeper/mistress in *Maria,* craves the economic and social security of marriage, but her outspoken defense of Caroline demonstrates an independence and courage particularly noteworthy in a woman without social position or power. Maria Fluart is, of course, Bage's masterpiece, a heroine descended from Anna Howe and ancestress of Elizabeth Bennet, and in fact more refreshing and lovable than either. Miss Fluart is consistently intelligent, witty, ingenious, and devastatingly forthright—when it suits her purposes. Her sexual openness (as when she laughingly describes Grondale's gropings and his pornographic art collection), her verbal facility, and her unwavering loyalty to Caroline make her the female moral center of this book and more attractive than the male one. I cannot imagine a reader who would not applaud with awe and delight when, after tricking Lord Grondale into allowing Caroline's escape from his house, she responds to his dire threats by calmly "producing a pistol, and almost overturning his lordship as she passed" (302).[6]

Having created such a delightful product of the Old World, Bage, understandably, cannot produce a better model from the new, although in *Mount Henneth* he tells the story of Miss Melton, kidnapped and brought to a bawdy house, where she "asserted her claim to independency and freedom, (for she is an American) with great spirit and force of language."[7] Nowhere does *Hermsprong* provide a corrective for the portrait of frivolous American femininity that Wollstonecraft has painted in *Maria.* Indeed, the only American woman in the text participates entirely in the kind of patriarchal system that so much of the narrative assails: "Lodiquashow, the wife of Lontac, the best of squaws, the most obedient of wives, had never presumed to sit down in the presence of the Great Beaver, till she had brought him six children" (250). The tribal life has, as we shall see, much to teach Europeans, but emancipation of women is not one of them.

Similarly, Hamilton cannot find in Hindu culture a woman to match the ideal in *her* text: Lady Gray, who, with "an understanding enriched by the accumulations of Wisdom, a temper regulated by the precepts of Christianity, and a heart replete with tenderness," can nurse her invalid husband and educate her children while simultaneously managing "the affairs of her family, and the concerns of his estate" (299). Lady Gray embodies the standard against which the insipid Lady Ardent and the intellectual but repulsively masculine Miss Ardent (who lacks even the wit of the masculine Mrs. Selwyn in Frances Burney's *Evelina*) are judged and found wanting. To some extent, Hamilton extenuates the flaws of these inadequate women; both Zāārmilla and his English friend Dr. Severan, echoing Wollstonecraft, attribute women's deficiencies to faulty education and insufficient opportunity to live rationally in a culture that values women only for their looks and superficial charms. But Indian society offers no alternate, desirable paradigm of gender equality, perhaps because, as Rosemary Raza observes in the opening paragraphs of her book discussing British women writing on India, "Female infanticide, seclusion of women, the Hindu custom of prohibiting the remarriage of widows, and *ḋati* . . . were abuses which were considered to degrade India in the scale of civilization."[8] The unreconstructed sexist prince Māāndāāra, who has already returned one wife to her father because he was "disgusted with her peevishness, and still more, with the plainness of her countenance," dismisses the notion that women should be educated: "To what purpose should they have judgment or understanding? Were they not made subservient to the will of man? If they are docile, and reserved, with enough of judgment to teach them to adorn their persons, and wear their jewels with propriety, and never presuming to have a will of their own, follow implicitly the direction of their husband . . . it is all that can be wished for" (105).

Māāndāāra's contempt for women is even exceeded by that of the Brahmin Sheermaal, who extols "the institution of Brahma, by which creatures, incapable of acting with propriety for themselves, are effectually put out of the way of mischief, by being burned with the bodies of their husbands. . . . Laudable practice! By which the number of *old women* is so effectually diminished!" (129).[9] Given these articulations of gender ideology, one might wonder how Isobel Grundy can claim that

Hamilton constructs in India "a possibly less sexist culture, and a certainly less sexist male individual."[10] Grundy alludes, of course, to Zāārmilla, who participates in the Indian custom of arranged and early marriages (after praising "the innocent and playful prattle of the little Zamarcanda," he offers this young sister as wife to the misogynistic Māāndāāra), but also looks forward to a companionate marriage with Māāndāāra's sister (138) and later sincerely mourns her death: "She, who was the companion of my days, the friend of my heart, whose gentle manners, and prudent counsels, smoothed the rugged path of life, and gave value to every blessing" (146). In Zāārmilla, Hamilton embodies her ideas of (and hopes for) enlightened Hinduism, although it must be noted that Indian women, like the natives of America in *Hermsprong*, fail to provide an alternative to superficial and conventional British women.

In *Hindoo Rajah*, only the Scots have enlightened attitudes toward women. Sheermaal, after castigating the English system of educating women while commending homologous attitudes within English and Indian cultures—"in that country, as well as in this, all men allow that there is nothing so amiable in a woman as the *helplessness* of *mental imbecility*" (129)—turns disapprovingly to the unacceptable customs prevailing in Scotland, where mothers "employ themselves in the education of their children, in teaching their daughters the duties of domestic life, and instilling into their tender minds the principles of piety and virtue." Scottish coeducational day schools instill in girls an unsuitable "wish to excel . . . altogether incompatible with the preservation of ignorance"; they allow young women to develop ease in the company of the opposite sex; worst of all, this inappropriate education gives female minds "such an odious degree of firmness, as often enabled them to sustain, with dignity, the most bitter decrees of adverse fortune, and their bodies acquired such a repulsive degree of health, as rendered them equal to the discharge of every active duty." Fortunately, Sheermaal continues, the English system of education has so far encroached northwards that Scottish women, even the daughters of Highland chiefs, "will soon be as amiably frivolous, as engagingly ignorant, as weak in body, and in mind, as the pupil of the greatest Boarding School in London" (131). Hamilton's unsubtle rhetoric not only demonstrates the devastating cultural effects of "internal colonialism" but also argues that a nation that is in the process of destroying enlightened gender ideologies on its own island cannot pretend to reform sexist practices half a world away.[11]

Both Hamilton and Bage attack the quotidian habits of upper-class Britons, habits generally characterized as dissipated, extravagant, and frivolous. *Hermsprong*'s Miss Fluart describes the useless and self-destructive life of a London buck: "An animal which bounds over all fences. Breakfasts in London; dines at Newmarket; devotes six days and nights to the fields of sport, of hazard, and champagne; and having done all that he has to do, that is, lost his money, returns to town, to the arms of his fair Rosabella; dozes away forty-eight hours between love and compunction; awakes; damns all impertinent recollections; sends for an Israelite; signs, and is again a buck" (158). A similar catalogue of ill-spent hours describes the activities of Lord Grondale's houseguests, who rise at eleven to eat, drink, and gamble away the day "in a gentlemanlike manner" (258). Grondale himself suffers from gout and other "drinking diseases" (71). Hermsprong, in contrast, washes down his meals "with a quart or two of good spring water," much to the disgust of his landlord Mr. Tunny (100). His abstemiousness and simplicity lead Hermsprong to dread English social dinners, which he finds "melancholy" in their insipid conversation and gluttonous consumption: "Not content with this mass of amusement, you continue your beneficence to that unfortunate viscus, the stomach, under the name of dessert, till it almost faints under the obligation. No matter; spur it on with wine" (208). Zāārmilla, too, is shocked at the grossness of English appetites, deploring

> that custom of devouring the flesh of so many innocent, and unoffending animals, whose lives are daily sacrificed in order to procure a short-lived, and inelegant enjoyment, to the vitiated palates of these voluptuaries. The injustice done to these animals, is however, amply revenged, by the quantities of liquors, which it is the custom to swallow at the conclusion of their cruel feasts; and which, when taken in great quantities, seldom fails to pervert the senses, and reduce the reason to a temporary level with the victims of their gluttony. (170)

Other eighteenth-century writers take up this trope of appetitive excess among Britons abroad and at home. In *Hartley House, Calcutta: A Novel of the Days of Warren Hastings*, Phebe Gibbes describes the groaning tables and heavy drinking of English colonials, and Benjamin Franklin points to his own abstemious practices in contrast to his fellow workers at Watts's printing house in London. He himself "drank only water; the other workers . . . were great guzzlers of beer"; however, impressed by Franklin's superior strength, some of his English colleagues were moved to eschew beer at breakfast.[12]

Hamilton and Bage criticize not only the gluttony of English society, but also its general frivolity and extravagance. Zāārmilla and Sheermaal find the European passion for cards beyond comprehension, and their unfamiliarity posits an Indian society that remains untainted by the rage for gaming that saps the time and money of the masters in the home country. So alien is this pastime that Sheermaal speculates that card playing must be a religious rite—"And to this Poojah of idols, termed CARDS, do the major part of the people devote their time; sacrificing every enjoyment of life, as well as every domestic duty to the performance of this singular devotion" (114–15)—while the more knowledgeable Zāārmilla pities those "doomed to stifling in a crowded room, during the length of an evening, with no other employment, than that of turning over little bits of printed paper!" (224).[13] Although perhaps the most dangerous of English habits, gaming forms only a part of the national habit of extravagance. Dr. Severan, in his potted biography of Sir Caprice Ardent, describes the nobleman's feverish (and expensive) hobbies, which shift rapidly from racehorses to clothes to ruinous improvement of his estate (216–20). *Hermsprong* catalogues numbers of lives ruined by high living, from Mr. Jones, who is forced to sell his home, to Grondale's crony Mr. Lowram, who liquidates his estates and allocates half the proceeds to "a fund for gaming" (258). In stark contrast to Hermsprong, who prefers philanthropy to spending "all my money in accommodating myself" (166), upper-class Englishmen indulge their appetites to the point of bankruptcy; unlike Sheermaal and Zāārmilla, who both come to the rescue of indigent English families, the ruling class in *Hindoo Rajah* exhibit no charitable impulses.

Of course, Bage's American and Hamilton's Indians do not march in lockstep, and their differences point up the contrast between cultures of the first and second empires. Hermsprong speaks admiringly of native Americans' skill at hunting, which develops in them "intrepidity" (97), while Hamilton's Indians deplore foxhunting as a pointless activity that destroys farmlands (217, 293; they echo Pope's criticism). The Hindus see the preservation of game as an indulgence requiring "many volumes of their laws . . . to preserve these sacred birds from being injured by the unhallowed hands of any of the lower Cast" (116, 120).[14] For Hermsprong, hunting constitutes part of American vigor, as does traveling by foot; he "will walk you forty miles in a morning," marvels Tunney, and he shocks his friend Glen by walking to London for the "pleasure" of it (100, 166). His pedestrian feats echo those of John Davis, who undertakes on foot much of his travel in America and invokes classical and modern authors as models: "The foot-traveller need not be ashamed of his mode of journeying. To travel on foot, is to travel like *Plato* and *Pythagoras;* and to these examples may be added the not less illustrious ones of *Goldsmith* and *Rousseau.*"[15] Hermsprong tells Miss Campinet and Miss Fluart that in his youth, he "could almost run up a tree like a squirrel; almost catch an antelope; almost, like another Leander, have swam over a sea to a mistress" (253). In Europe, he feels fettered by inaction, much as Franklin in London "felt a want of bodily exercise I had been us'd to in America."[16] American energy, especially the physical skills acquired from Amerindians, contrasts favorably with British weakness: note that Grondale is crippled by gout and Sir Philip Chestrum "was feeble, small, and half animated" (201).[17] *Hindoo Rajah* does not pit English lassitude against Indian activity; on the contrary, Zāārmilla comments on how English people, "even of an exalted rank, occasionally walk: nor is it thought any degradation, to make use of their own legs" (211). Perhaps Hamilton participates in the general view of the Hindus as a gentle, weak people, although certainly the text's two travellers show no sign of the lethargy that Sophia Goldsborne in *Hartly House, Calcutta* ascribes to Hindus, who "have so little passion for vigorous exertions, that it is a favourite maxim with them, That it is better to sit than to walk, to lie down than to sit, to sleep than to wake, and that death is best of all."[18] Despite such local differences, however, Bage and Hamilton produce similar indictments of the morals and habits of upper-class English society, from the trivial dissipation of dancing — Zāārmilla expresses shock when he sees British officers "publicly degrading themselves by dancing for [Hastings's] amusement" (165), and Hermsprong calls dancing "frivolity and grimace" (254) — to their gluttony and selfish extravagance. The social habits of the ruling elite in Britain look empty and degenerate under the gaze of the American and the Indian.[19]

Isaac Kramnick has argued that "English radicalism sought to topple the social order of rank and privilege" and to "replace that society with a new liberal ideal, a society of achievement. . . . The bourgeoisie made themselves into a class through political and cultural struggle with a system in which they saw talent and merit achieve little."[20] Certainly in the class wars represented in *Hermsprong,* aristocrats and their followers are always the villains, tyrannizing the middle and lower classes, who are too often quiescent in the face of class oppression. The narrator Glen tells Hermsprong, "We English are not supposed to be deficient in freedom, but we don't kick lords. We have tolerably awful ideas of rank" (162). Part of Hermsprong's agenda and effect is to empower those who occupy subaltern positions and who fear the wrath of Grondale and his cronies: he rouses the long-suffering curate Woodcock to confront Dr. Blick, even though Blick then dismisses the curate "for taking the part of a young coxcomb against me; and telling me to my teeth, that I was wrong in argument, and rude in manner" (110); he emboldens Mrs. Garnet to attend church despite her fear of antagonizing Lord Grondale (170–71); and he rescues the passive Mr. Wigley from Grondale's trumped-up charge of debt. Indeed, Glen, hearing Hermsprong's exhortation to Mrs. Garnet, "felt myself raised, and exalted by it. I almost began to think myself a man" (171). Clearly, one of Hermsprong's missions is to teach English lower orders to assert their equality, a lesson he himself has learned from Amerindians; when Caroline Campinet asks where in the world "humility to a proud man . . . is not paid," he promptly replies, "among the Aborigines of America" (139).

Although Hermsprong does indeed empower his friends, we should also note that, to some extent at least, this seemingly hidebound English society is already in a state of protest against the privileges of rank. Glen, the bastard son of Squire Grooby and cottager Ellen Glen, may not kick lords, but neither does he abject himself to them. When Lord Grondale tries to intimidate him for daring to speak to Miss Campinet, he calmly replies, "I am happy in your contempt, my lord," and stands his ground while Grondale and Blick retreat (144–45). Later, Glen recounts to Hermsprong his attempt to intercede with Grondale on Mrs. Garnet's behalf: "I accosted him with all the exterior marks of respect; and with that appearance of humility which is required in this, and I believe most countries, from little persons to great ones" (161). Glen's language here reveals his contempt for class privilege and his self-conscious *performance* of ritualistic respect; not only does he drop the act when rudely rebuffed by Grondale, but goes so far as to chastise his lordship: "Before you became a lord, it would have been well to have learnt the manners of a gentleman" (162). Again, Grondale has no recourse except silence, retreat, and "a look that *ought* to have annihilated so insignificant an atom as myself" (162). Despite his wealth and rank, despite his passionate desire to bully his inferiors, Grondale remains helpless when baited by the "nobody" Glen.

One might say that Glen can defy Grondale because, although obscure, he is at least independent, having an annuity of eighty pounds from his father. But even those who directly depend on Grondale, his own servants, maintain a state of covert mutiny against his authority. The footman James, thwarted in his attempt to screen Caroline from her father's wrath, accepts his dismissal from service with defiant plain

speaking: "I never desire to come into it [Grondale's presence], to see
the best young lady in the world, used worse than a Negro. . . . and
curse me . . . if I will, whilst I have life and limb" (192). When James
subsequently seeks employment with Hermsprong, the American asks
Grondale for a reference and receives instead an insulting letter dictated by Grondale to his steward. Grondale is unaware that, in an act
of quiet subversion, the steward adds a postscript: "Having obeyed my
lord's orders, I hope you will not take it ill, for how could I do otherwise? But as to James Smith, he's an honest a fellow as ever broke
bread" (193). Samuel Grant's little act of defiance not only subverts his
master's authority, but also asserts the autonomous identity of the ser-
vant/subaltern, who can and does choose to speak in his own voice.
Lord Grondale, although he does not know it, is surrounded by rebel-
lious underlings. When he, like Richardson's Harlowes, confines his
daughter to her room, he wishes her and Miss Fluart kept ignorant of
Mrs. Stone's return; "The ladies did know it however; and indeed every
thing that passed in the house which they chose to hear, for so great is
the difference betwixt kindness and tyranny, that where Lord Grondale
had only servants, Miss Campinet had friends" (296). After Miss Fluart
has arranged Caroline's escape, Grondale learns that all his orders regarding Caroline's detention have been flouted: she has received letters
and visits from Hermsprong, who has been in collusion with "the butler, a respectable man, who had seen with equal shame and disgust, the
infamous treatment, for so he scrupled not to call it, to which his beloved young mistress had been subjected" (302).

When Hermsprong accuses English society of "servile compliance"
with authority (327), he fails to account for all the small ways the unem-
powered resist the domination of the ruling class. Although Hermsprong does indeed provoke some overt rebellion, there already exists a
web of opposition against aristocratic power, a kind of subterranean
anti-government cabal of servants and outsiders. Read this way, Bage's
text may in fact be *more* radical than it seems, in that it represents the
lower orders as already engaged in guerrilla warfare. Harry T. Dickinson, explaining the failure of British radicalism in the 1790s, points to
popular loyalty to government, a loyalty inculcated by a "vast array of
newspapers, periodicals, pamphlets, tracts, sermons, and broadsides."
He adds that such loyalist propaganda portrayed radicals as "dangerous
and ambitious demagogues, who were jealous of the governing
classes. . . . The only British who would be seduced by such Jacobin
radicals were the idle and the dissolute."[21] Bage asserts, in the characters of Gregory Glen, Mr. Woodcock, James Smith, Samuel Grant, and

the butler, that resistance to class tyranny emanates from thoughtful, principled, hard-working men who witness and are appalled by the dissolute and oppressive behavior of their masters. Unlike Gilbert Imlay, who represents British servants as tools in collusion with evil masters, Bage suggests that the lower orders in Britain surpass their "betters" in morality and combat tyrannical authority whenever possible.

Bage privileges the middle and lower orders because he rejects inequalities based on birth and subscribes to "a new liberal ideal, a society of achievement . . . in which social mobility was possible and the rightful reward for ingenious people of talent and hard work."[22] Hamilton, of course, espouses no such social fluidity. Indeed, in her "Preliminary Dissertation" to *Hindoo Rajah*, she credits the Hindu caste system with preventing the kind of status anxiety that bedevils Western civilization: "Thus those sources of disquiet, which have held most of the empires of the earth in a state of perpetual agitation, were unknown to the peaceful children of Brahma. The turbulence of ambition, the emulation of envy, and the murmurs of discontent, were equally unknown to a people, where each individual, following the occupation, and walking in the steps of his fathers, considered it as his primary duty to keep in the situation that he firmly believed to have been marked out for him by the hand of Providence" (60). Although she later concedes that "the struggle of contending interests . . . the strife of emulation, and restlessness of ambition" might conduce to "intellectual energy" and "genius" (65), she clearly does not advocate the kind of class struggle espoused by Jacobins. She too, however, extols the virtues of the lower classes in Britain, carefully excluding them from her Swiftian satire of British society. The Brahmin Sheermaal comments that "the higher Casts in that country . . . are deficient in hospitality! . . . in this country the spirit of hospitality is only to be found beneath a roof of thatch"; when he is "repulsed with the language of contempt" from the house of a squire, he finds "cordial welcome" in a peasant's hut (116). Moreover, this peasant has suffered the tyranny of the village Lord, who has bundled him off to India for daring to marry the object of the lord's lust. Like Grondale persecuting the Wigleys, this lord too oppresses those who thwart his sexual desires, and like the lower orders in *Hermsprong*, those in *Hindoo Rajah* demonstrate that domestic happiness resides outside the mansions of the privileged classes.

Gary Kelly writes that Sheermaal's view of the lower classes participates in an ideology "adapted from pre-Revolutionary Sentimental ruralism . . . a middle-class fantasy widely disseminated during the mid-1790s, depicting the common people as a diminutive version of the vir-

tuous middle class, both freed from ideological and cultural subjection
to the decadent and courtly upper class and protected against contamination by 'Jacobinism.'"[23] Hamilton, however, complicates this fantasy;
the lower classes in *Hindoo Rajah* are vulnerable to both upper-class decadence and Jacobin contamination. Like Sheermaal's peasant, Dr. Severan's landscaper friend is a victim of class-based power: he goes to
prison for debt because he dare not press for payment from *his* debtors,
who "are all people of fortune, whose favour would be forever lost, by
an untimely application for money" (238). The economic and class system collude to oppress this independent working man because the only
clients he can accrue belong to the class that treats him with contemptu-
ous carelessness. On the other hand, the young servant Timothy Trundle, having swallowed Jacobin views "that all men were equal, and the
poor had as good a right to property as the rich," is arrested for robbing
one of the very *philosophes* who corrupted his morals. As he is dragged
off to prison, Timothy exclaims, "Ah! That I had kept to my good
grandmother's wholesome doctrine of hell and damnation! . . . I should
not now be at the mercy of a false friend, who laughed me out of the
fear of God—and now leaves me to the mercy of the gallows!" (254–
55).[24]

Hamilton's social radicalism, in fact, mirrors that of Bage; both advocate independence and the work ethic. The most admirable characters
in *Hindoo Rajah* engage in the professions: Dr. Severan, the scientist; his
friend, the landscaper; and the family of Zāārmilla's friend, Mr. Denbeigh. Denbeigh's sisters have married worthy professionals: one is a
businessman who, like Bage's hardworking banker Sumelin, has, by industry and application, "obtained an ample share of the gifts of fortune"; the other is a busy physician. Denbeigh's brother "is a Professor
of the Art of Surgery" (287–88), and even Mr. Darnley, the country
squire who is to marry Emma Denbeigh, keeps busy with "the study of
Mineralogy and Botany" and has undertaken a course of "Agricultural
improvement" (293; compare this to the frivolous "improvements" of
Sir Caprice Ardent). Both Bage and Hamilton contrast upper-class
selfish frivolity with the sturdy good sense and respectability of the
working middle class, who remain, however, vulnerable to oppression
from above.

In her introduction to *Hermsprong*, Pamela Perkins echoes Gary Kelly's view that in Bage's novel "it is individual rather than institutional
or systemic change that sets the local world to rights, even though radi-

cal social change is discussed and applauded." Perkins bases her argument on the fact that "Bage turns Hermsprong's hearing into an
undignified rout for the villains, who despite believing themselves to
have the full weight of the aristocracy, the church, and the law behind
them, are unable even to bring their enemy to a full trial. Ultimately,
then, the satire is directed more against corrupt individuals than corrupt institutions." Mona Scheuermann, also emphasizing individual action, argues that the result of the hearing "was not inevitable. If Justice
Saxby had not been among the justices, if the junior justice who spoke
for Hermsprong had not done so, the outcome could well have been
different. The system does work, but the safety afforded by it is in fact
tenuous."[25] Despite their focus on individuals, however, both Bage and
Hamilton target what they perceive as corrupt institutions run by a corrupt class system: the church, the legal system, and the political establishment all come in for criticism, often in comparison to better
paradigms in North America and India.

   Hamilton wishes to expose the discrepancy between Christian doctrine and the actual behavior of European Christians. Her method consists of a fairly heavy-handed irony. Once he has read the English Bible
(glossed by his friend Captain Percy), Zāārmilla immediately assumes
that its percepts must dictate the "government, laws, and manners of
this highly favoured nation" (84). He believes that English clergymen
must be like Biblical heroes, "men who despite adventitious advantages
of rank and fortune, who regard no distinctions in their flock, but the
distinctions arising from internal worth, and intrinsic goodness; not
thirsting after worldly honours; nor given to luxury; strangers to avarice and pride. Having no bitterness against those who differ from them
in opinion, animosity, strife, or wrath, is never heard of among these
holy men" (86–87). Zāārmilla indignantly rejects Sheermaal's contention that in ten years' residence in Europe he never saw the Bible or
heard it spoken of, and confidently asserts that all European laws and
customs must be founded on the biblical directives "of Peace, Charity,
and Humility, and universal Benevolence. . . . The Mussulman fasts,
and the Hindoo performs Poojah, according to their respective laws,
and can we believe that the Christian alone treats with contempt the
authority of his God?" (140–41). Hamilton sustains this vein of sarcasm
when she has Zāārmilla ascribe Christians" blasphemy to "a consciousness of their own superior piety which they, doubtless, imagine, entitles
them to this degree of familiarity with their Maker" (162); in *Hermsprong* (103), the hypocritical cleric Blick defends swearing among mili-

tary men because "it supports a certain energy; and if soldiers and sailors were forbidden it, their courage would droop."

The Brahmin, of course, frankly despises those his patron Māāndaara labels "infidels, and impious eaters of blood" (101), specifically citing upper-class indifference to religious observance. He describes an English church service in which the priest is as dull as the audience is inattentive and finds that generally the higher classes ignore the Sunday Sabbath altogether, "except as a day particularly propitious for Travelling" (113).[26] Zāārmilla himself notes of upper-class churchgoers: "so successfully did they affect the concealment of their devotional sentiments, that no one would have suspected they had met together for any other purpose, but that of staring at each other's dress!"; he is shocked when his fashionable hostess ejects from her pew an elderly woman, "the humble child of poverty, and affliction" (206–7).[27] In *Hindoo Rajah*, as in *Hermsprong*, good clergymen do not advance within the church hierarchy; like Woodcock in Bage's text, Morton in Hamilton's fulfills clerical duties conscientiously, "never molested by the offer of what is called *preferment*, but . . . permitted to exercise his talents and virtues in a state of poverty, equal to that of the first teachers of Christianity" (177). In stark contrast to the English, Hindus pay extraordinary homage to their priests, who, Hamilton explains in her "Preliminary Dissertation," deserve respect because of their "peace, self-restraint, patience, rectitude, wisdom, and learning" (59). Moreover, she makes a point of censuring "those who take pleasure in pointing the shafts of sarcasm against the order of the Priesthood" (59) — people like her contemporary Jemima Kindersley, who "criticizes the Brahmins for their intellectual indolence and for keeping the masses of people in a state of ignorance."[28] In this dialogic text, however, the novel speaks back to the preface: Hamilton's Brahmin Sheermaal, although vindicated in his contempt for English culture, is an irascible and intolerant character whose hyperbolic diatribes against the English are unconvincing (even when accurate) until confirmed by the more-moderate Zāārmilla's observations. Sheermaal himself validates Kindersley's charge when he boasts that "it is doubtless from this wise example of our ancient Brahmins, that the priests of all religions have learned the art of concealing the simplicity of truth, under the dark and impenetrable cloud symbolical mystery, which none but they themselves can fully explain" (114). In a text that contrasts British indifference to Christian observances with Hindu reverence for established ritual, such self-professed priestcraft undermines the Brahmins' claim to virtuous authority.

And that authority is, in fact, challenged. Although "unwilling to speak with disrespect of a Bramin," Zāārmilla uses exceedingly harsh language about Sheermaal's prejudices, calling him false, foolish, ignorant, and malicious (139–40). In his resistance to Sheermaal, the Hindu Rajah resembles Bage's Hermsprong and Miss Fluart, who deny "implicit obedience" to clergy, professing reverence "for the character; little for the mere habit" (84, 298). Unlike Hamilton, Bage does not address the gap between Christian doctrine and actual practice, aiming his satire instead at the sycophantic contortions of Dr. Blick, who has so mastered the "agreeable art of assention" (74) that he can even summon divine history to support Lord Grondale's libertinism: invoking "how marriage and consuetinage existed together in patriarchal times, [he] proved that what was right then could not be wrong now; and that it was scarce possible that a lord should be wrong at any time" (155). Bage reserves his most withering contempt for the pre-revolutionary convent system in France, from which Hermsprong's father rescues his wife. In recounting this episode, Hermsprong speaks of "the diabolic policy that has dictated such cruel abstractions. . . . thank heaven, and common sense, nunneries are no more, or no more in estimation, at least, in France" (246).[29] According to Hermsprong, the long arm of Catholic oppression reaches even the English colonies; his father is urged to leave Philadelphia, warned that "Monsieur had the patronage of the convent; that the court had entered into his resentment, or rather that of the abbess; and that dark designs were forming against him" (247). Compared to the murderous practices of French Catholicism, the Church of England, even when represented by venal toadies like Dr. Blick, seems relatively harmless. This hostile view of the French and their religion, so important to Smollett's 1771 text, may seem anachronistic and gratuitous in 1796 when religion, at least temporarily, no longer defined differences between French and British imperialism. Bage's reasons, however, are strategic: attacking Catholic fanaticism allows him to articulate the radical principle of liberal secularism in the guise of a patriotic, anti-French narrative.

Significantly, it is French Catholicism that informs the only missionary impulse depicted in Bage's text. Hermsprong's mother, beset by guilt for having escaped from her convent, determines that "greater sins than hers might be expiated, by a conversion to Christianity of a few Nawdoessie females" (249). Her decision to proselytize produces one of the most comic episodes in the novel, as she fails first to convert the chief's wife, and then, even more spectacularly, Chief Lontac himself. Although the dignified Lontac refrains from contradicting her—"it is only for a native American to arrive at so high a degree of politeness, as to testify disapprobation, only by a respectful silence" (250) — he is finally goaded into countering with a narrative of his own about a parley between men and bears. When Hermsprong's mother exclaims that such a story is "preposterous . . . excessively absurd," Lontac calmly invokes the talking serpents and asses in *her* narrative and effectively puts her (and her religion) in her place by declaring, "I have not called your wonders absurd . . . I thought it more decent to believe" (251). Like the Miamis in *Humphry Clinker*, the Nawdoessie in *Hermsprong* cannot be converted, although they tolerate missionary overtures with patience.

Hamilton, too, somewhat surprisingly, seems to eschew missionary zeal. Despite his romantic idealization of Christian civilization, the Rajah never contemplates changing his religion. His desire to travel to Europe stems from an inquiring spirit rather than from religious conviction.[30] Like the British Orientalists studying Indian religions, he seeks to understand and appreciate the Other, not become one of them. He writes to Māāndāāra that "though it is necessary that every Hindoo should keep himself free from contamination, yet many holy men have found it possible to do so . . . even while they made their abode in the dwelling of the Mahommadans, and Christians" (99). Although there is no evidence that Zāārmilla, like Maharaja Madho Singh of Jaipur, travels across the black waters carrying Indian earth and silver jugs filled with water from the Ganges, he retains while in England Hindu customs such as solitary meals, and even manages to maintain Hindu rites: "At the first indication of the dawn of the morning, I went, as is my constant practice, to the river side, and, after the performance of the customary poojah, and having bathed in the refreshing stream, I strolled" (267). Not only does Hamilton preserve her hero's faith, she also explicitly praises Hinduism for its rejection of missionary ambitions and condemns Muslims for theirs. Recounting the Mughal invasion of India, she inveighs against the Muslim "fury of fanaticism. . . . Multitudes were sacrificed by the cruel hand of religious persecution . . . in the vain hope, that by destruction of a part, the remainder might be persuaded, or terrified into the profession of Mahommadenism" (68). Hinduism, by contrast, "Far from disturbing those who are of a different faith, by endeavours to convert them . . . does not even admit of proselytes to its own" (60).[31] The drive to convert, for Hamilton as for Bage, is a benighted one, originating in guilt or intolerance, conducted by illogic and violence, and ultimately ineffectual. Whether the European power occupies American tribal spaces or Indian palaces, these texts argue, it must respect and preserve native religions.

In the course of his initial burst of enthusiasm about English Christians, Zāārmilla writes: "The equality of human beings in the sight of God, being taught by their religion, it is a fundamental maxim of their policy, that no laws are binding, which do not obtain the consent of the people. All laws are therefore issued by the sanction of their representatives; every separate district, town, and community, choosing from among themselves, the persons most distinguished for *piety, wisdom, learning,* and *integrity,* impart to them the power of acting in the name of the whole" (85).[32] In fact, these two texts figure British society as anything *but* equal and just: although Bage's text focuses on the politics of revolution and Hamilton's on the politics of empire, both show that political institutions in the metropole are riddled with inequity and corruption, that power is exercised through violence and duplicitous machinations, and that the law is deployed to oppress the poor. Both participate in what David Punter finds in many eighteenth-century representations of the legal system: a "consistent discrediting of English legal mechanisms and institutions and concomitant speculation about other systems, whether they are located abroad or in internal subcultures."[33]

Sheermaal speaks of two instances of the absurd priorities of the British legal system. Witnessing a soldier being flogged for "purloining a few rupees from one of his officers," he concludes that "the morals of the people must be very pure, in whose eyes so small an offence can seem worthy of so great a punishment." Moments later, he is astonished to discover that the seducer of an officer's wife suffers no other consequence that to make a compensatory payment, a discovery that completely overturns his previous verdict: "Can virtue subsist among a people, who set a greater value upon a few pieces of silver, than upon their honour?" (104–5). Later, he is equally shocked when his peasant friend is brought to trial for accidentally killing game birds: "the cause in which they were then hearing evidence was instantly dismissed: it was, indeed, only concerning a man who was said to have beaten his wife almost to death: a trifling crime, in the eyes of these Magistrates, when compared to the murder of seven partridges!" (120). Zāārmilla's own encounter with the legal system produces a far more comprehensive and caustic judgment. Visiting a prison, he is horrified by conditions which recall to his mind the dungeons in which Muslims "confine their malefactors" (240). He laments that in these prisons "many thousands of the inhabitants of this land of freedom, are left to pine out a miserable existence, alike useless to themselves and to society" (242), an enunciation that might well be a prose redaction of Thomson's lines on the horrors of English jails, where "in the land of liberty . . . little tyrants raged,/ . . . /The free-born Briton to the dungeon chained/ . . . / And crushed out lives, by secret and barbarous ways,/That for their country would have toiled or bled" (*Winter*, 365–75). Both passages emphasize the bitter irony of potentially productive citizens of a free country being unjustly incarcerated under miserable conditions. Zāārmilla recoils from a system that punishes petty theft more severely than large-scale fraud and mingles brutal murderers with mere debtors; like Moll Flanders, he complains that such proximity, together with despair, turns the neophyte offender into a hardened, depraved criminal. Significantly, it is at this point in his sojourn that Zāārmilla concedes that the Brahmin's assessment of Britain was right and "implore[s] his pardon, for the incredulity with which I regarded his account of the conduct of Christians" (243).

Part of Hamilton's agenda is to validate the Warren Hastings/William Jones project to govern India by Indian laws. Like them, she holds "the view, of which Montesquieu had been the most famous exponent, that as the laws and customs were moulded by the environment and traditions of a particular society to fit its needs, it was unjustifiable to impose a different set of values produced by different circumstances."[34] If she depicts British laws as arbitrary, inequitable, and immoral, the argument for retaining indigenous laws gains strength. In a passage extolling the virtues of Warren Hastings, Zāārmilla particularly lauds the governor-general for restoring Hindu laws: "The pious Hindoo, no longer forced to submit to laws, that are repugnant to the spirit of his faith; no longer judged by the unhallowed ordinances of strangers, beholds with extatic [*sic*] gratitude, the holy Shaster rising" (163). He lauds the even-handed benevolence that extends this privilege even to Muslims, so that "the haughty Mussulman will receive, from Christian magnanimity, a degree of favour and protection, which the laws of his Prophet never taught him to bestow!" (164). Modern commentators have been more suspicious about the motives and effects of Hastings's act of cultural respect. David Musselwhite suggests that when the Regulating Act of 1773 tried to dilute the East India Company's authority by setting up a Supreme Court under Sir Impey Biggs, Hastings countered with a program to translate, study and establish Indian laws: "Thus it has been argued that British Oriental scholarship originated in the need to counterbalance the effects of the introduction into India of British judicial processes." Both C. A. Bayly and Ania Loomba point out that Hindu laws as established by the British were overtly elitist, consolidating a classist and patriarchal system. And Bernard S. Cohn describes the plan's unintended consequences: "After Jones announced his intention to provide Hindus with their own laws through the mediation of English judges assisted by court-appointed pundits, a peculiar kind of case law came into being . . . it is the chain of interpretations of precedents by English judges that became enshrined as Hindu law. . . . What had started with Warren Hastings and Sir William Jones as a search for the 'ancient Indian constitution' ended up with what they so much wanted to avoid—with English law as the law of India."[35]

None of these concerns disturbs Zāārmilla's celebration of Hastings's "benevolence, which has restored to our nation the invaluable privilege of being tried by our own laws" (164). Hamilton seems to be extolling, without reservation, this part of the Orientalist project. But a second look at Sheermaal's criticism of British laws complicates this reading and indicates that Hamilton was perhaps less than sanguine about the Brahminical system of justice. His indignation at the discrepancy between punishments doled out for petty pilfering and adultery seems to be humane and moral—after all, who can argue for property being more valuable than honor? But while the flogging remains repulsive, Sheermaal's horror is much compromised by what he believes should befall the adulterer: "the punishment of the aggressor . . . the sacrifice of his life, and the degradation of his family" (104). In other words, he proposes executing the seducer and punishing his family. To someone like Hamilton, educated in Scottish Enlightenment ideas, such draconian measures cannot have seemed appropriate or just. Again, the juxtaposition of wife beating and shooting partridges makes (and is meant to make) the English magistrate seem barbaric. Note, however, that Sheermaal, believing that the birds represent an English version of sacred cows, expects "to have heard the irrevocable mandate of immediate death; and knowing how vindictive the priests of all religions usually are toward those who have treated with contempt the objects of their superstitious veneration, I should have been well pleased to have compounded for his simple death, unattended by the tortures which I feared might be inflicted upon him" (121). If the consequences of establishing Hindu laws as promulgated by Brahmins leads to executing seducers and torturing those who accidentally commit sacrilege, then Indians are better off under British justice. Hamilton both distinguishes between and conflates the two judicial systems: she writes in favor of a Hindu legal system based on religion and morals rather than on the primacy of property; but she collapses the distinction when she exposes the arbitrary and intemperate punitive practices in both cultures. So while her conservatism sides with the theology-based, nonmaterialist perspective of the Brahmin, her Scottish Enlightenment perspective deplores the excessive zeal of that ideology.

Bage, like Hamilton, describes the inequities in English law, but in his text, as Perkins points out, upper-class attempts to manipulate the system usually founder. These failures, however, do not argue the stoutness of the British judicial system; rather, they demonstrate the power of wealth and reputation, even when attached to an unknown American. When Lord Grondale orders Mr. Corrow to find legal grounds to eject Hermsprong from the county, the lawyer finds himself in a quandary: "To press down to the earth, and under it, a poor man, is easy; it is the work of every day; but to make a man, with money in his purse, guilty of crimes he never committed requires a superior fund of knowledge of the more tortuous parts of the law, and superior intrepidity" (226).[36] When Sir Philip Chestrum brings spurious assault charges against him, Hermsprong is able to employ his banker Mr. Sumelin as "surety for peaceable demeanour" (240). When Hermsprong himself comes to Wigley's aid, he easily convinces the bailiff to release Wigley by giving the officer his word as well as "an acknowledgment of your humanity" (284; Hermsprong carefully distinguishes this "acknowledgment" from a bribe, but money certainly changes hands). While the egalitarian ideology of the novel foregrounds Hermsprong's innate virtues, his *essential* self, Bage also makes clear that the hero eludes Grondale's legal maneuvers because of his wealth and influence. Preparing to persecute Hermsprong as a French spy, Corrow frets about the difficulty of the task because "his reputation is actually rising in the county" (291); no doubt because of the philanthropic activities enabled by his wealth, he begins "to be considered as a man of property, as well as respectability" (306). Hermsprong has in fact joined the establishment, a position that protects him from legal malice. Perhaps the most visible evidence of his new status presents itself when Lord Grondale enters the courtroom with his "numerous suite," only to undergo "the mortification to see Hermsprong elegantly and rather richly drest . . . and accompanied by many gentlemen of genteel appearance" (308). Hermsprong astutely counters Lord Grondale with his own public performance of wealth and position. Just as Hamilton subtly undermines her critique of British law by pointing out the potential oppressiveness of a Brahminical framework, Bage problematizes his assault on the British system by showing how it works to his hero's advantage. Hermsprong's public persona is so potent that when Lord Grondale counts on the glorious uncertainty of the law to postpone dispossession by the antagonist who turns out to be the legitimate owner of his estate, Corrow and Blick cannot share his optimism; public opinion has shifted: "since the day of the sessions, [Hermsprong] had made the principal conversation of the county, and this conversation ran wholly in his favour" (318). Even before he provides legal proof of his claim, Hermsprong's wealth and connections dispose opinion in his favor. Punter observes that in the court scene, "Bage is on difficult ground. He has on the one hand to acquit him of the charges, while on the other maintaining his character as an instinctual radical."[37] Bage's strategy in negotiating this complex territory is to allow Hermsprong to preach equal justice while social and institutional biases work on his behalf.

If Bage softens his criticism of the English legal system by having his hero profit from its prejudices, he offers no such amelioration of his strident indictment of politics, as manifested both in long-established corruptions and in a new paranoia in the face of revolutionary movements. Lord Grondale's Parliamentary career serves as an example of corrupt expediency: his allegiance shifts from Opposition to Government and back, causing him to be "despised by both parties; but not so his boroughs," which eventually buy him a barony so that "Sir Henry Campinet was metamorphosed into Lord Grondale" (72). The new lord, in turn, presents lucrative livings to Dr. Blick, rewarding the clergyman's "activity and certain skilful manoeuvres, in a contested election . . . which trenched a little upon moral honesty" (108). Later Grondale persecutes his old friend because of "a contested election, in which Mr. Wigley had been active against a candidate supported by Lord Grondale" (285). Like Parson Adams in *Joseph Andrews* and Hawkins in William Godwin's *Caleb Williams*, Wigley is punished for exercising his rights as a British citizen.[38]

The feeble-minded Sir Philip Chestrum tries to turn Caroline Campinet against Hermsprong by declaiming, "what a rogue and rascal he is; and a French spy; and come to inveigle people to America" (279). Sir Philip's conflation of America and France may be dismissed as an instance of his general imbecility, but in fact, the conjunction becomes part of the legal case against Hermsprong: he is accused of being one of the "secret emissaries from France" who have fomented the miners' riot, and "has also counseled and advised sundry subjects of this his majesty's realm of England, to migrate to America, and hath promised pecuniary and recommendatory aid and assistance to enable them to do so" (309). The accusations reflect the view of alarmed conservatives, to whom the two revolutionary nations seemed aligned against beleaguered British values, just as they had been allied in America's Revolutionary War. Such anxieties were only exacerbated by harangues such as John Thelwall's lecture in April 1795, in which he warned that anti-revolutionary wars in Europe would cause starvation and asked from whom could Britain expect help: "from America, who, if she has one grain of justice or common sense, must love the cause of your enemy, and abhor your's? — America, who must regard every success you may happen to obtain, as a signal of alarm to her independence?"[39] America, home of *provocateurs* like Thomas Paine (Mr. Corrow's list of Hermsprong's crimes includes the fact that "he has read the Rights of Man" [289]), refuge to social radicals like Joseph Priestly and Thomas Cooper, seemed to conservative British thinkers no less menacing than the levelers and murderers across the Channel. So entrenched is the connection between Jacobin politics and emigration to America that Hermsprong himself makes a point of refuting the charge of seducing Wigley to migrate, asserting, "I have given him information only" (313).

Corrow feels some confidence in the campaign against Hermsprong because of the political climate in Britain. He concedes that urging emigration is not illegal, but "might, in the present temper of the times, be made something of"; similarly, Hermsprong's mild observation that the French constitution is not all bad and the British one not all good can be deployed against him because "the bench of justices will not bear such things now" (289). The treason trials of 1794 as well as royal proclamations and parliamentary acts had shown that the government would bear down hard on anyone perceived as dangerously radical; moreover, as Dickinson points out, loyal propaganda was far more widespread and effective than Jacobin publications.[40] Bage re-presents in his novel some of the tactics deployed against radicalism, from Dr. Blick's sermons in support of the July 1791 anti-Jacobin riots in Birmingham (164–65) to Mr. Saxby's insistence that Hermsprong fully disclose his identity to legal authorities. Referring to "these suspicious times," Saxby warns Hermsprong: "Every man incurring suspicion, who cannot, or who will not, give an explicit account of himself, is exposed to the animadversion of the magistrates. It is important to know your real name, that we may put in the proper track of inquiry. If you conceal it, or assume one not your own, you give, against yourself, a strong case of suspicion" (315–16). Saxby, of course, refers to the royal proclamation of May 21, 1792, that "called upon all loyal subjects to resist the radical attempts to subvert all regular government and . . . requested JPs and magistrates to make diligent enquiries" into suspected radical writers.[41] Perhaps responding to the suspicious times himself, Bage, in a series of careful moves, distances his hero from the French Revolution and the more extreme wing of English Jacobinism. Early in the text, Hermsprong tells the Sumelins, "All the malignant, as well as the better passions, are afloat in France; and malignant actions are the consequence" (90). At the hearing initiated by Grondale, it emerges that Hermsprong's politics are more loyalist than Jacobin; like the conservative pamphlets Dickinson cites, Hermsprong's speech to the rioting miners emphasizes the ease of their lives compared to the luxurious but stressful lives of the rich, and he insists that "there is no possible *equality of property* which can last a *day*. If you are capable of desiring it . . . you must wade through such scenes of guilt and horror to obtain it, as you would tremble to think of" (314). Having painted a Burkean picture of revolution, he goes even further down the patriotic path, striking down a rioter who has disparaged George III because "to revile your *King*, is to weaken the *concord* that ought to subsist betwixt him and all his *subjects*, and overthrow all civil order" (314). Hermsprong's exhortations to the miners sound remarkably similar to the propaganda aimed at poor people, propaganda that warned that once the property of the rich was attacked, the poor would lose all they had. Like conservative publications that argued that the privileged classes had their own troubles, "burdened with the cares of government and the responsibility of providing employment,"[42] Hermsprong speaks the language of propertied classes, and, fittingly, is immediately afterwards revealed as one of them. Furthermore, he confirms his participation in the privileges and practices of the elite when he inherits two fortunes, "and not liking the situation of things in France, I sold all I was able, and dispersed the money into different banks, principally in England, Italy, and America" (255). Republican sympathies, it seems, cannot be allowed to interfere with prudent investments, and Hermsprong, that American proponent of liberty and equality, not only deploys his money like a good bourgeois capitalist, but also belongs, by birth, to the aristocracy. His critique of the center emanates, then, from one who is firmly a part of its power elite.

If Bage's reconfiguration of his hero and his retreat into the rhetoric of conservatism seem cowardly, we should keep in mind that even Godwin toned down revolutionary language in the second edition of *Political Justice*, and that "by the time *Hermsprong* was published in 1796 the Directory ruled France, and Pitt's policy of repression had already sent several men to Botany Bay and driven others, such as Joseph Priestley, into exile. . . . The suspension of Habeas Corpus, the Treason Trials of 1793 and 1794, and the 'Two Acts' of 1795 had stifled English Jacobinism."[43] In this climate of patriotic fervor and suspicion, Bage seems courageous in continuing to compare America favorably to Britain.

Astutely, Bage praises America for possessing the very qualities — personal liberty and political tolerance — that conservatives like Burke identify as particularly British values. When Hermsprong, believing that he has lost Caroline, announces his intention to return to America, he complains of the rancorousness of British political discourse, contrasting it to the tolerant attitude of Americans: "To your polite hatred for opinion, generally they are strangers. I imagine they owe this to their diversity of religions which, accustoming them to see difference of opinion in a matter of the greatest importance, disposes them to tolerate it on all subjects, and even to believe it a condition of human nature. Their government too, embraces all sects, and persecutes none; and when there is no reward for persecution, and no merit attached to it, I suppose it possible for men to refrain from it" (328). Like Tocqueville, who admires the way "American clergy stand aloof from secular affairs . . . [and] know and respect the intellectual supremacy exercised by the majority,"[44] Hermsprong connects American democracy to its religious tolerance. We should note that Hermsprong speaks here about the new United States, not the tribal culture to which he had earlier attributed simplicity and a dignified respect for alien belief systems. Unlike Smollett, Bage depicts Native American culture as idyllic in its natural energy and civility; unlike Wollstonecraft, he represents the new nation as a haven of urbane inclusiveness in politics and religion. Hermsprong's vision of life in America is Utopian (as well as opulent): he will settle on his sixty thousand acres by the Potomac with "a society of friends within a two-mile ring; and I have imagined a mode of making it happy" even without his beloved Caroline's company (329). Although Hermsprong, like Moll, Jack, Lismahago, and Darnford, eventually chooses to settle in Britain, he remains an admirer of American culture.

Hamilton does not juxtapose good government in (non-British) India to the political corruptions and tyrannies in the home country. Indeed, if part of her agenda is "surreptitiously" to defend British colonial interests in India, she must demonstrate the inefficacy or malignity of indigenous rule.[45] And the text does indeed critique non-British rulers of India. Though Zāārmilla himself is a mild and enlightened prince, he appears to be the exception. He indignantly deplores the brutal rule of Bêâss Râye, that "pious Hindoo who had shed so many tears over the misfortunes of his country" when it groaned under Afghan control only to prove, once in power, to possess "a heart so *steeled* by avarice, as to be impervious to every sentiment of humanity" (146). Meeting Chait Singh, the Rajah of Benares, he finds him an ambitious upstart who is criminally ungrateful to his patron Warren Hastings: "the height of his elevation has made him giddy; he wishes to quit the staff which hitherto supported him" (154). He welcomes a visit from the rulers of Lolldong, only to find them obsessively and solipsistically berating the English for not having protected their villages from the Afghans; an exasperated Zāārmilla loses patience with them "when I found them obstinately persist in cherishing the feelings of selfish regret, for their own particular misfortune, while the miseries of thousands, who, on the same occasion, had lost their all, found no entrance into their hearts" (98).

Hamilton reserves her most bitter denunciation of native rule for the Mughal conquerors; her "Preliminary Dissertation" spells out, with Burkean intensity, the horrors visited on Hindus by Muslim masters who force Muslim laws on Hindu subjects, imposing crippling fines from "bigotted and venal judges"; who suppress Hindu commerce; and who, "in the effusions of their barbarous enthusiasm," demolish the ancient and beautiful temples and monuments of Hindu religion (68–69). Having enumerated the ravages of Muslim rule, Hamilton extols the virtues of British intervention and British government in a passage worth quoting at length because of its unproblematized comprehensiveness:

> In those provinces which . . . have fallen under the dominion of Great Britain, it is to be hoped that the long-suffering Hindoos have experienced a happy change. . . . in those provinces, the horrid modes of punishment, inflicted by the Mahommedans, have been abolished; the fetters, which restrained their commerce, have been taken off; the taxes are no longer collected by the arbitrary authority of a military chieftain, but are put upon a footing that at once secures revenue, and protects the subject from oppression. . . . That unrelenting persecution, which was deemed a duty by the ignorant bigotry of their Mussulman rulers, has, by the milder spirit of Christianity, been converted into the tenderest indulgence. Their ancient laws have been restored to them. . . . Agriculture has been encouraged by the most certain of all methods—the security of property; and all these advantages have been rendered doubly valuable, by the enjoyment of a blessing equal, if not superior, to every other—the Blessing of Peace, a blessing to which they had for ages been strangers. (70)[46]

The novel itself starkly contrasts Muslim India, which offers to the traveler's eye "ruined villages," to the "flourishing state of the country" under British rule, made possible by the peasant's confidence that his produce will not "be wrested from him by the open violence of the spoiler, or seized by the hard hand of rapacious avarice" (156–57). Hamilton's appreciation of the positive effect of British governance is congruent with that of some contemporaries who, unlike herself, had firsthand knowledge. Both William Hodges, traveling through India during the 1780s, and William Carey, arriving in Calcutta in 1793, attest to a degree of agricultural success in British Bengal, success that came about in part because of the end of military conflict and in part because of Cornwallis's experiments with a new system of tenantry.[47] Hamilton's praise for the fruits of Pax Britannia, as well as her disdain for most non-British powers in India, seems to confirm her role as apologist for colonial power.

Hindoo Rajah is particularly concerned to defend the British from charges of participation (or at least complicity) in the massacres of Afghans who survived the Rohilla war. In this, she follows the lead of her brother, who begins his history of the Rohillas with a strongly worded refutation of such accusations: "God forbid that *British troops* should ever be employed in acts of such detestable atrocity! . . . it may with confidence be affirmed, that, however high their sense of subordination, however ready at all times to obey the most perilous orders of their superior, had such a service been allotted to them, they would have turned from it with abhorrence!"[48] *Hindoo Rajah* figures British intervention as "the auspicious arms of the sons of mercy . . . [which] checked the fury of the Afgan Khans, who have so long oppressed our unhappy country" (78). In this text, genocidal attacks against the defeated Afghans come entirely from Hindus seeking revenge for years of tyrannical treatment rather than from British soldiers pressing their military advantage. Zāārmilla himself refuses to participate in sectarian and communal acts of vengeance, moved to forgiveness by seeing the Afghans flee in despair and terror: "While I contemplated their present calamity, the remembrance of their former tyranny passed into the bosom of oblivion" (79). As if to excuse, to some extent, this uncharacteristic ferocity of Hindus, Hamilton carefully describes the cruelty of Afghans even in defeat: Zāārmilla's messenger, carrying tidings of the war to Māāndāāra, is "seized and cut in pieces" by a band of brutal Afghans; yet another band kidnaps and starves Captain Percy, forcing him to "accompany their flight, in hopes that he might be the means of procuring them terms with the English" (81). Not only does the text exculpate the British from any blame in the Rohilla war, but it also demonstrates the manifest need for

British intervention and mediation among hostile groups of indigenous populations.

The British engagement with India may, in this text, have rescued the subcontinent from tyrannical invaders and internecine warfare, but it has also been responsible for some of the worst aspects of British national character, because maintaining empire requires developing and deploying technologies of power that dehumanize both sides of the colonial divide. The most repulsive example of the brutal practices of empire is, of course, institutionalized slavery, and Hamilton, like Behn, provides a moving description of its atrocities. (Interestingly, Bage's admiring depiction of America elides the presence of slavery in the land of liberty.) When Sheermaal visits a slave ship, he finds "some hundreds of the most wretched of the human race" cowering under "the savage looks of the white barbarians," and his wrath is compounded by the fact that this brutality is perpetrated "to procure a luxurious repast to the pampered appetites of these voluptuaries . . . to cultivate sugarcane." Sheermaal contrasts the abomination of imperial slavery to the benevolent, almost familial relationship between Indian masters and their slaves: the one "doomed to suffer all that cruelty, instigated by avarice, can inflict," the other having "bartered their liberty for protection" (111–12). However problematic the concept of a "benevolent" system of slavery might be, Hamilton, like other abolitionists of her time, excoriates the slave trade that supports imperial trade and profits. Furthermore, Sheermaal specifically connects British cruelty to European ideologies of race and color: "Had a ray of knowledge enlightened their understanding, through the tawny hue of the unlettered savage, they would have recognized the emanation of the creating Spirit" (111; again, of course, a modern reader notes Sheermaal's own prejudices). Desensitized to the humanity of slaves by the driving needs of the colonial economy, perpetuating an emerging ideology of color hierarchies, the servants of the empire become no better than the Mughals Hamilton attacks in her "Preliminary Dissertation."[49]

Slavery is only the most egregious example of the corrosive effects of empire. Hamilton also targets that species of intranational enslavement, the press-gang. As their ship approaches the coast of England, Zāārmilla is astonished to see among the sailors not joy at homecoming but "consternation, terror, and dismay!" (198), and he speculates that such terror can be inspired only by an infernal sea monster. That monster turns out to be a press-gang that conscripts thirty of the crew, leaving Zāārmilla to mourn the fate of "those brave fellows, whose useful labours have conduced to the enrichment, and prosperity of their country; who after an absence of twenty months, hoped to reap the reward of their toils, by returning to its bosom, [but who] were dragg'd reluctant victims to the infernal demon of power!" (199). The last phrase is crucial, for Hamilton is targeting *governmental* oppression, decreed by British naval authority and therefore even more repugnant than the entrepreneurial criminality of the kidnappers in *Oroonoko* and *Colonel Jack*. Daniel James Ennis explains that "the practice of pressing men from homeward-bound ships was actually preferred to the use of press-gangs on shore. The navy was virtually guaranteed to get an experienced seaman."[50] Making explicit what Pope had implied in *Windsor-Forest*, Hamilton shows that British state power is deployed to kidnap British citizens and force them into service, an oppression engendered by the need for imperial workers.

Hamilton also directs her scorn at another domestic abuse arising from the imperial project: the depredations of customhouse officers who "rifle, rob and plunder" ships coming from the colonies. Her caustic description of them recalls Swift's Yahoos, for "these savages bear so strong a resemblance to the English, that they might, at a slight view, be mistaken for the same; but, on a more accurate examination of their countenances, evident traces of their savage origin, may be easily traced" (200; interestingly, Hamilton's indignant disdain for these minions of empire brings her to a racial hierarchy of her own). Press-gangs and customs officers constitute part of the apparatus of the imperial state; they, like slave traders, enforce a coercive system required by global political and commercial ambitions.[51] The conflation of state and commerce is made visible when the ship Zaarmilla takes to England sails "in company with many floating fortresses of superior size, sent by the king of England, to protect the fleet of the Company" (188). Sheermaal's earlier voyage proceeds on board a warship, "a huge edifice, whose sides were clothed with thunder," palpably embodying British naval and imperial power (110). In *Hindoo Rajah*, Pope's prophecy in *Windsor-Forest* fulfills itself, as British trees leave their woods to "Bear *Britain*'s Thunder, and her Cross display,/To the bright Regions of the rising Day."

It becomes apparent that Hamilton's two agendas conflict: on the one hand, she deploys an enlightened and sensitive voice from the periphery to uncover the internal corruptions and the external abuses of an imperial power that has already vitiated the admirable culture it colonized north of its border, thereby demonstrating its unfitness to govern others; on the other hand, she insists that, given India's history of oppressive and quarrelsome regimes, British intervention on the Asian

subcontinent is a necessary and positive outcome and that British innovations in legal and administrative systems have been all to the good.
Given the collision of these two viewpoints on British rule in India, it is
difficult to locate a definitive or stable argument on imperialism in this
text. It is possible, however, to infer attitude from tone, so I want to
turn to two passages that may clarify Hamilton's complex and perplex-
ing position on British imperialism. Hamilton's characteristic ironic
mode in this text juxtaposes Zāārmilla's naïve belief in British virtues
to the manifest viciousness of some British practices. She deploys it
powerfully, for example, in Zāārmilla's passionate rejection of Sheermaal's account of the slave trade: "How could the lie-loving Bramin expect to be credited, when he asserts that Christians enter into the traffic
of blood! . . . invade the countries of the defenceless, and seizing, with
tiger-like ferocity, their unoffending children, bind them in the galling
chains of slavery, and devote them, as a cruel sacrifice, to the black
Goddess of affliction! . . . Ah! How little doth he know of the undeviat-
ing rectitude of the British Senate!" (141). The reader need not look to
Hamilton's own abolitionist beliefs to note how, in order to highlight
the criminality of this particular imperial practice, she counterpoises the
vicious realities of the slave trade with Zāārmilla's insistence that British Christians could not possibly engage in such inhumane behavior.
The clearly readable satire of this passage may help us understand
Hamilton's more implicit views on imperialism when we look back at
Zāārmilla's earlier paean to British colonial adventuring: "Benevolent
people of England! It is their desire, that all should be partakers of the
same blessings of liberty, which they themselves enjoy. It was doubtless
with this glorious view, that they sent forth colonies, to enlighten and
instruct, the vast regions of America. To disseminate the love of virtue
and freedom, they cultivated the trans-Atlantic isles: and to rescue *our*
nation from the hands of the oppressor, did this brave, and generous
people visit the shores of Hindostan!" (84)

If there exists a justification for engaging in imperial expansion that
produces such deleterious effects both at home and abroad, it lies in the
project to rescue and conserve a culture that is valuable in itself and for
what it can teach the West. Kate Teltscher argues that "for Hamilton,
Britain's role is the same in India and Europe: to protect traditional cultures against the dangerous innovations of both Islam and the French
Revolution." She echoes Nigel Leask's formulation that "Eliza Hamilton built her argument on an analogy between the Islamic conquest of

large parts of Hindu India and the impact of the French Revolution on Europe. In both cases it was the role of Britain, as the leading counter-revolutionary power, to redress the wrongs done to a traditional culture by newfangled ideas, whether based upon the Koran or the Rights of Man."[52] To preserve Indian culture, of course, the British have to learn about it, and the considerable body of scholarship on eighteenth-century Orientalism agrees that Hamilton and other admirers of William Jones's project strive to make India intelligible to Europe. In her "Preliminary Dissertation," Hamilton deplores British "ignorance, and apathetic indifference with regard to the affairs of the East" despite "elegant translations" as well as the exegeses produced "by the labours of men who have enjoyed the first rank in literary fame" (55–56). In the novel itself, Sheermaal rails against uninformed English citizens who do not know "whether the great city of Canouge was founded by a Hindoo or a Mussulman" (134), a gap that to him (and to Hamilton) compromises British claims to govern India. Among Sir Caprice Ardent's imbecilities is his conflation of India with China, and Hindu with Muslim (212; see the Duke of N— —'s ignorance of the Atlantic empire in *Humphry Clinker*), and the problematically intellectual Miss Ardent wins Zāārmilla's respect by being the first person to initiate a conversation on "the delightful subject of my dear native country" (226). The first requirement of imperial power is knowledge, and Hamilton enthusiastically sets out to disseminate it, not only in the background provided in the "Preliminary Dissertation," but also in the numerous references to Indian literature, mythology, history, and geography scattered throughout the text. As Perkins and Russell observe, "Hamilton was assembling and popularizing a mass of scholarship and literature which would perhaps not normally have found its way beyond a specialist audience" (31).[53]

Recent scholars, following Edward Said's lead, have tended to see Jones and his fellow Orientalists as a covert arm of imperialism, no less violent in their effects than press-gangs and naval armaments. The work of translation and interpretation has been characterized as both a kind of stealthy conquest and as a sop to guilty European consciences.[54] Hamilton herself, however divided she may be regarding the imperial project and about certain aspects of Hindu culture, commits herself unreservedly to bringing knowledge of India to Britain. Her dedication to Hastings specifies his role "AS THE DISTINGUISHED PATRON OF SHANSCRIT, AND PERSIAN LITERATURE" (54; John Drew affirms that "the new note of enthusiasm for things Indian had been sounded first by Warren Hastings when, as Governor-General of India, he introduced the translated *Bhagavad Gita* by saying that long after British domination in India had ceased to exist the Hindu scriptures would continue to be read").[55] Like an energetic and creative teacher of recalcitrant students, Hamilton finds multiple ways to interest her audience in the value of Indian culture: Sheermaal's and Zāārmilla's familiarity with the Bible might inspire some to aim for reciprocal knowledge of Indian religious writings; those with scientific inclinations might be attracted to "the astronomical apparatus still extant in the Tower of the Stars' in Benares, instruments whose functions were lost to memory until English scientists visited the site (154–55);[56] literary-minded patriots might be piqued by Zāārmilla's assertion that "the Mahhabaret was superior to the Iliad of Homer: or that Calidas was a dramatic Poet equal in excellence to Shakespeare" (227). In any case, Hamilton offers her text as a gateway to a fund of knowledge; not everyone can travel to India to experience and assimilate its culture, but all can read her book and gain *real,* valuable imperial wealth by asking the question Ania Loomba poses as essential to postcolonial studies: "What indigenous ideologies, practices and hierarchies existed alongside colonialism and interacted with it?"[57]

While Hamilton sets out a program to bring Indian culture to Britain, Bage describes how Hermsprong's parents bring European civilization with them to what they perceive as the cultural wasteland of the American Great Lakes. They settle into the wigwam built for them by the Nawdoessie with "our European servants, our books, our music, our instruments of drawing" (249), and Hermsprong receives, as far as possible, a European education in "languages, in mathematics, in I know not what. My father, always thinking of Europe, was desirous I should have a taste, at least, of the less useful, but more ornamental parts of knowledge"(252). Unlike Lismahago, Hermsprong's father insists upon his European identity and his European values even after ten years of living with the tribe and despite his admiration for their "virtues of friendship, hospitality and integrity" (252); his mother, as we have seen, retains her religion and even attempts to impose it on Native Americans. They bequeath their European culture to their son, who, much as he extols the simple pastimes of Amerindians, makes a distinction between them and himself because they are not literate, while "reading is . . . a part of my existence" (160). But if he embraces the literacy of Europeans and notes that Amerindians "fail in . . . intellectual pleasure" (211), Hermsprong has learned to doubt the absolute value granted to literacy by European culture. Comparing his solitary literary evenings with their social athletic ones, he weighs his "exquisite" pleasure against their "lively" ones, his "yawning lassitude" against their "salutary weariness"; he questions whether reading is always pleasurable or profitable, and wonders if European education does not make for superficiality (160). Later, in Paris, he suffers physically from the confined and shallow life of Europeans. Hermsprong longs for a Utopian world "in which all its members had the power, so to alternate the employments of the mind and body, that the operations of each might be enjoyment." Although he concedes that such a society cannot be found, "not even in America" (211), he clearly believes that the New World has more potential for offering it than does the tired world of Europe. So where Hamilton wants the British to know about the rich culture of the subcontinent they are about to rule in entirety, Bage reminds them of another continent's natural civilization that they have done so much to destroy. Either way, whether peripheral vision gazes at center from the vast historical and literary heritage of India or from the expansive spaces of America, Britain looks like a very tight little island indeed.

4

Rhetorical Manipulations: Walter Scott's *Guy Mannering* and *The Surgeon's Daughter*

*If there be any thing that seems Romantick, I beseech your Lordship to con-
sider, these countries do, in all things, so far differ from ours, that they produce unconceivable Wonders; at least, they appear so to us, because New and
Strange.*

— Dedication to Lord Maitland, *Oroonoko*

So that here would be Mr Alexander in the part of Dido, with a
curiosity inflamed to hear; and there would be the Master, like a
diabolical Æneas, full of matter the most pleasing in the world to
any youthful ear, such as battles, sea-disasters, flights, the forests of
the West, and (since his later voyage) the ancient cities of the Indies.
How cunningly these baits might be employed, and what an empire
might be so founded, little by little, in the mind of any boy, stood
obviously clear to me.

—*Master of Ballantrae*

IN THE PREFACE TO *THE SURGEON'S DAUGHTER*, ATTORNEY MR. FAIR-
scribe suggests to would-be novelist Chrystal Croftangry that he write
a tale about India rather than produce yet another narrative about that
worn-out yet still politically dangerous topic, the Highland Jacobites.
He assures Croftangry that he will find in India "as much shooting and
stabbing. . . . rogues. . . . adventurers. . . . great exploits" as ever available in the "wild Highlands." Croftangry pounces eagerly on the idea,
relishing the fact that India supplies ready-made heroes like Clive and
Cailliaud who are like "Homer's demigods," like "Spaniards among the
Mexicans." Moreover, he adds, India offers "the various religious cos-
tumes, habits and manners of the people of Hindostan—the patient
Hindoo, the warlike Rajapoot, the haughty Moslemah, the savage and
vindictive Malay—Glorious and unbounded subjects!" (155). Croftangry's list can be pointed to as a manifestation of the way British readers
could use demographic stereotypes to reassure themselves that India

146

could indeed be categorized and controlled, but it can also lead to a misunderstanding of Scott's own novelistic project. Robin Jared Lewis, for example, reads this passage as evidence of Scott's ignorant bias: "To accept . . . Sir Walter Scott's facile, prefabricated account of India's diverse races . . . was to gain a sense of security. One could always expect Hindus to be patient, Rajputs to be warlike, Muslims to be haughty."[1] Such an analysis of *The Surgeon's Daughter* conflates Walter Scott with one of his surrogate narrators, overlooking the always multivalent discourse of his novels. Consider, for example, the multiple plays on "unbounded subjects," which can refer ironically to colonized Indians bound to English masters, to characters or cultures that resist the very categories and boundaries constructed to contain them, or to the hybridity of the text itself. This kind of linguistic play, like the equation of heroism in Clive and conquistadors, constitutes encoded commentaries on imperialism, mediated through the naïve discourse of Croftangry. While Scott, with typical self-reflexive mockery, does indeed write into Croftangry's search for a topic some of his own cogitations about appropriate and publishable narratives, the preface represents, as Iain Gordon Brown has noted, "a classic instance of playful anonymity and convoluted suggestion."[2] Indeed, Scott anticipates (and invites) criticism of his own authorial hubris when, in answer to Croftangry's diffidence about undertaking an Indian tale despite knowing "nothing at all" about the place, he has Fairscribe respond with jovial dismissiveness, "Nonsense, my good friend. You will tell us about them all the better that you know nothing of what you are saying" (155).

Scott's irony regarding Croftangry's shallow understanding of India informs his project in both *The Surgeon's Daughter* (1827) and the earlier *Guy Mannering* (1815): his desire to uncover some of the ways in which stereotypes and simplifications about the subcontinent enter narratives in the home country and to link them to the strategies deployed by fiction makers. Together, the two novels represent imperial discourse as both engaging and manipulative; they set out a series of inversions and complications, demystifications and remystifications that challenge standard colonial narratives. In *Guy Mannering*, Scott constructs a cautionary tale about imperial fictions and maps onto it how novelistic practices intersect with that discourse; in *The Surgeon's Daughter*, he explores the consequences when the heated rhetoric of imperial conquest and romance overwhelms the subtleties he had coded in his earlier narrative about the British presence in India.

My argument inevitably depends on certain assumptions about Scott's engagement with contemporary politics and historiography. Recent scholarship has put to rest the notion that writers of the Romantic period ignore or withdraw from political or ideological debate, especially about Britain's global ambitions; indeed, the editors of two collections of essays devoted to the topic point out that, despite a self-proclaimed apolitical stance, "the Romantic period is a watershed in colonial history" and "British Romanticism itself—associated as it has been with the sublime, the exotic, and the 'primitive' . . . may be interpreted as a response to the collective experience, ideological requirements, and deforming effects of imperialism."[3] Scott's own political consciousness can scarcely be debated, although its nature, as Peter Garside has demonstrated, can be complex and sometimes opaque.[4] Scott's specific knowledge and understanding of imperial experiences in India has been amply outlined by Claire Lamont and Jane Millgate, as well as carefully debated by Iain Gordon Brown and Richard G. Jackson, who have examined possible sources of the information that went into writing *The Surgeon's Daughter*. Brown argues that, although Scott's knowledge of Indian geography and customs is secondhand and often wrong, he "was acutely aware of India" and "came to understand something of the pull of India and the magnet that it was and was to remain for Scots throughout the 19th century"; Jackson asserts that, in fact, Scott's knowledge, garnered in part from returned Indian veteran Colonel James Russell, was essentially accurate.[5] *Guy Mannering*, too, evokes from readers a degree of ambivalence (or even confusion) about its relation to history. James Reed finds that "though most of the action takes place towards the end of the American War of Independence, nothing in this novel relates to the broad movement of history," while Jane Millgate suggests that "for all the absence of public history there is an underlying emphasis on the workings of time." Graham McMaster says that "the novel is not a nostalgic account of Scott's boyhood but a parable of contemporary events," a point made more specific in Harry E. Shaw's argument that "Scott was no less the bard of the Napoleonic Wars in *Guy Mannering* and *The Antiquary* than he was in *Marmion*."[6] My own argument rests on a wholehearted agreement with David Hewitt's contention that "Scott is a thoroughly political writer,"[7] one who is aware not only of this critical moment in European history when Britain emerges both triumphant and shaken after the Napoleonic Wars, but also of how Britain's dominance in global politics will affect the way the nation will write itself in history. In the two novels I consider, Scott demonstrates that much of imperial rhetoric is dangerously fictional.[8]

One imperial fiction is, of course, the yarn that British colonists (at least those who survive tropical disease) all return to the homeland with vast fortunes acquired in India. So prevalent was this fiction that Phebe Gibbes's Sophia Goldsborne opens her narrative with an expressed desire to explode the myth of India as a "grave of thousands" and a "mine of exhaustless wealth."[9] Equally established was the "knowledge" that Indian wealth was often amassed through corruption and exploitation, and the figure of the returned nabob embodies much at the heart of Scott's narrative of the home-India trajectory. Debates about these returning nabobs enter into almost every form of discourse in the late eighteenth and early nineteenth centuries, from Burke's parliamentary speeches to Samuel Foote's play, and I have earlier pointed out how carefully Smollett and Wollstonecraft distinguish the good nabob from the venal one. In 1817, just two years after the publication of *Guy Mannering*, James Mill's history of India applauds the decision to replace Hastings with Cornwallis because the latter would not import to India a cadre of rapacious would-be nabobs: "Here there was no broken fortune to be mended! Here was no avarice to be gratified! Here was no beggarly, mushroom kindred to be provided for! No crew of hungry followers, gaping to be gorged!" Perhaps even more disturbing than shady sources of wealth was the fact that newly rich imperial workers caused fissures in the economic and social life of the metropole. As Tillman W. Nechtman notes, returning nabobs not only served as "suitable scapegoat[s]" for inflation at home, but also raised fears about political shifts: "The concern was that nabobs . . . would buy their way into the nation's political institutions and refashion them, upsetting the gains assured by Magna Carta, the Bill of Rights, and the Act of Settlement. Nabobs . . . had ruled as despots in South Asia, and they would expect to do the same once they sat in Parliament."[10]

Part of Scott's achievement in *Guy Mannering* lies in his questioning of the effects of empire without resorting to the easy deployment of the socially troubling or comically vulgar nabob. Despite his closing words about rebuilding the ruined Scottish castle Ellangowan with "a few bags of Sicca rupees" (354), Guy Mannering is no nabob of the sort who, according to Sir John Seeley, "were bringing back to England the plunder of the Mogul Empire, acquired no one knew how."[11] The evidence in the text makes clear that the bulk of his fortune is inherited from his uncle the London merchant: Mannering's letter to his friend Mervyn refers to "my uncle, Sir Paul Mannering, [who] left me sole heir and executor to his large fortune" (69), and Julia confirms this account when she tells Matilda that her father "despises commerce, (though, by the way, the best part of his property was made in that honourable profession by my great uncle)" (97). Mannering's behavior, too, contradicts the stereotype, for "though an East Indian, he was not partial to the ostentatious display of wealth" (102); in fact, nothing in the text connects Mannering with the kind of financial peculation targeted by Burke in his multiple speeches on Fox's East India Bill, the Nawab of Arcot's Debt, or the Impeachment of Warren Hastings.[12] Narrative commentary pointedly distinguishes Mannering from other India veterans after the colonel expresses surprise at the lawyer Pleydell's "candour and sound sense": "Were the learned advocate thinking on thee at this moment . . . might not he with equal reason wonder that from India, believed to be the seat of European violence and military oppression, had arrived an officer of distinction, open to compassionate and liberal feelings?" (210). Mannering, unlike the East India Company soldiers in *The Surgeon's Daughter*, has served in the regular army, perhaps augmented his uncle's commercial fortune a little, and has returned to take up his English inheritance to spend it, like Captain Brown in *Humphry Clinker*, quietly in Scotland. Nevertheless, there is widespread conviction in the homeland that Mannering's fortune must be colonial. Sheriff substitute Mac-Morlan calls him an Indian nabob (81), while Charles Hazlewood's parents promote a match with Julia Mannering because she is "of high family, with an Indian fortune" (108). The persistent conviction that Mannering must indeed have made his pile in India shows the power of imperial mythology; the notion of Indian wealth has taken such a powerful hold on the consciousness of the British public that both characters within narratives of returning colonials and those reading these stories firmly expect to encounter stereotypical nabobs.

The persistent and pernicious effects of a national desire to believe that untold wealth can be acquired in India are represented in *The Surgeon's Daughter* in the way Middlemas (the town as well as the character) attends to Tom Hillary when he returns to Scotland after a tour in India. Dressed in regimentals and flush with cash supplied by East India Company recruiters, Tom no longer inhabits his earlier identity as "a whipper-snapper of an attorney's apprentice, run away from Newcastle" (182). Instead, he accrues to himself the romance of imperial success:

> His merits were thought the higher, when it was understood he had served the Honourable East India Company—that wonderful company of merchants, who may indeed, with the strictest propriety, be termed princes. It

was about the middle of the eighteenth century, and the directors in Leaden-hall Street were silently laying the foundation of that immense empire, which afterwards rose like an exhalation, and now astonished Europe, as well as Asia, with its formidable extent, and stupendous strength. Britain had now begun to lend a wondering ear to the account of battles fought and cities won in the East; and was surprised by the return of individuals who had left their native country as adventurers, but now reappeared there sur-rounded by Oriental wealth and Oriental luxury, which dimmed even the splendor of the most wealthy of the British nobility. (201)

This passage nicely illustrates the multilayered narrative voice that re-quires careful parsing even while it carries the reader along its swift and exciting currents. By the "middle of the eighteenth century," the East India Company already stood accused, especially during the 1772 par-liamentary debates, of dishonorable practices and despicable behavior, and the Company headquarters in Leadenhall Street were already on the defensive against a government and population that sought, theoret-ically at least, to combine imperial power with humane rule by replacing the Company's venal troops with those loyal to the monarchy. As Perci-val Spear points out, "The difference in quality between the Company's Europeans and the King's troops continued right up to the time of Cornwallis, who frequently deplored the wretched quality of the Com-pany's Europeans."[13] Indeed, a few chapters later, the narrative voice combines bitter irony with explicit condemnation when it once again invokes "the Directors of the East Indian Company, [who] with that hardy and persevering policy which has raised to such a height the Brit-ish Empire in the East," have found a reliable way to recruit troops: because "the military service of the King was preferred, and that of the Company could only procure the worst recruits" (219), the Directors have devised a way to kidnap prospective soldiers in a kind of corporate replication of the military pressing condemned in *Colonel Jack, Maria,* and *Hindoo Rajah*. Scott thus reverses the public/private dichotomy in imperial service explored in *Hindoo Rajah* and articulated in Defoe's 1705 testimony to a Select Committee of the House of Lords; Defoe, like Pepys before him, avers that money constitutes "the Only Reason, why Our Seamen skulk, and hide Themselves from Public Service; since it can not be Expected The Sailors Should Covet to serv the Queen at 23s Per Month, when at The Same time, they can have 55s Per Month in The Service of the Merchant."[14] In Scott's (post-Hastings and post-Waterloo) text, military service for country is infinitely more honorable than engagement with the criminally greedy private Company. Thus, Croftangry's earlier characterization of the Directors can be read as either completely naïve or thoroughly satiric, a dichotomy the narrative reiterates when it tells us that the people of Middlemas heard Tom's stories of imperial grandeur "with different feelings, as their temperaments were saturnine or sanguine" (202). In either case, these passages make clear that responses to reports regarding Indian gold depend on the attitude and desire of the listener, who also needs to be alert to the way returning colonials can create fictions. Richard Middlemas's credulity, of course, originates less from naïveté than from greed and ambition, and the results for him are disastrous. The equation of Indian service with wealth, the narrative warns us, can be as destructive as it is often fictional.

But India provides the veterans in *Guy Mannering* with something at least as valuable as fortune: it conveys on them a public identity— visible, recognizable, narratable. Mannering tells Mervyn that his "military career in India" has given him "some satisfaction" (69), but the satisfactions seem to reside in the *effects* of that career once he has left it and returned to Britain. Of his official activities in India, Mannering mentions only the disjunction between the kind of hospitality expected of commanding officers and his own "habits of seclusion" (69). Note that Richard Middlemas profits from "that warm hospitality which distinguishes the British character in the East" (243), and Hamilton's Zāārmilla finds that the English in Calcutta "appeared to be no stranger to those laws of hospitality, of which our nation has long considered itself as the exclusive possessor" (164; he finds no comparable hospitality in the metropole). In fact, rather than satisfaction, what Mannering describes is a bleak life consisting of "battles, wounds, imprisonment, misfortunes of every description"; envying Mervyn's calm domestic life, he says, "*my* career has been one of difficulties, and doubts, and errors" (68–69). Once he returns to Britain, however, he reaps the benefits of that miserable career. At the Gordon's Arms at Kippletringan, his servant identifies him as "the famous Colonel Mannering, from the East Indies . . . [who] relieved Cuddiebum, and defended Chingalore, and defeated the great Mahratta chief" (66).[15] The effect of this announcement is instantaneous and electric: Deacon Bearcliff, "a man of great importance in the village" (60) confers on Mannering the celebrity status earned by a subject of newspaper reports; Mrs. Mac-Candlish, appalled that she has served him in the common room, bustles about to wait on this national hero; Mac-Morlan, a "man of intelligence and probity," unhesitatingly confides Godfrey Bertram's private affairs to "the well-known character of Colonel Manner" (72) and hopes "to attach to himself the patronage and countenance of a person of Mannering's wealth and consequence" (106). Later, the mourners at Margaret Bertram's funeral respectfully defer to his expertise and authority regarding Indian affairs, typically linking military and financial matters: "we have not done with your old friend Tippoo Saib yet . . . I am told, but you'll know for certain, that East Indian Stock is not rising" (215; in retrospect, we see that Scott himself is not yet done with Tipu Sultan, who turns up crucially in *The Surgeon's Daughter*). Even Dominie Sampson, normally as blissfully unaware of contemporary circumstances as he is knowledgeable about past events, learns to refer to his new patron as "the great Colonel Mannering from the Eastern Indies" (314). Mannering himself embraces this ready-made identity, defining himself as a returning colonial, whether self-deprecatingly—as when he thinks "an Indian must rub up his faculties a little, and put his mind in order, before he enters this sort of society" (226; he refers to his impending introduction to the great figures of the Scottish Enlightenment)—or pedantically, as when he lectures Lucy Bertram and Charles Hazelwood on "the peculiar notions and manners of a certain tribe of Indian" (159). India has conferred on this "proud, shy, reserved man" (200) a reputation and a public profile that precludes any need for explanation or judgment. He can simply occupy an identity fully constructed through report and narrative, and one independent of personal qualities.

But Mannering has taken to India a self already established and dignified by family and fortune; his "ancient" family boasts not only the rich merchant, but another uncle who is a bishop (69). Mannering's counterpart in *The Surgeon's Daughter* accrues no such simple respectability from his sojourn in India. Scott's account of Tresham/Witherington represents the intricate intersections of race, religion, politics, and empire. Unlike the solidly English and Oxford-educated Mannering, Tresham is an outcast and an exile, multiply othered by his Catholicism, his Jacobitism, and his illegitimate liaison with a Portuguese Jewess. A fugitive with "warrants out against him for treasonable practices" (239), he joins not the king's forces bringing justice and British administration to India but the Company whose corrupt practices require the intervention of His Majesty's government. For him, India provides both a refuge and an opportunity, a way to eradicate his past and forge a new identity, much as the American colonies offer new lives for Defoe's and Bage's characters. Unlike Mannering, Tresham does make his fortune as a servant of the East India Company, through military plunder and perhaps even civil corruption.[16] Returning to England, he remains connected to the Company, training its soldiers for the kind of service he himself had performed. Although the narrative emphasizes his probity and justice, it also implicates him in the unsavory domestic practices of the Company, since "he was never known to restore one recruit to his freedom from the service, however unfairly or even illegally his attestation might have been obtained" (220). In other words, Tresham's engagement with the East India Company has tied him permanently to its corrupt culture.

Moreover, Witherington, like Moll and Jemy, must live in constant dread of exposure; not all his military exploits in India suffice to overcome his "real" or past self: Catholic, Jacobite, rebel, seducer. His paranoia causes him to suppress his wife's anguish about their abandoned child and even to characterize her as delusional. Fearful that Adam Hartley may have overheard compromising words about their history, he tells the doctor that "she speaks sometimes about imaginary events which have never happened" (226). He makes it clear that none of his imperial exploits can save them from the danger of his Jacobite past and the disgrace of Richard's illegitimate birth: "think how much depends on this fatal secret—your rank and estimation in society—my honour interested that that estimation should remain uninjured. Zilia, the moment that the promulgation of such a secret gives prudes and scandal-mongers a right to treat you with scorn, will be fraught with unutterable misery, perhaps with bloodshed and death." (229–30). India has not and cannot offer Tresham the public reputation and acclamation so universally and unassailably conferred on Mannering. In effect, Scott works out in *The Surgeon's Daughter* the limits of a particular colonial narrative, one which imagines that military and financial success achieved in India can remake a compromised identity and bring it safely back to the homeland.

While a reconstructed self cannot be seamlessly reintegrated into British life, a whole range of traces of India are brought back by returning colonials. As Mannering and Bertram and Julia reestablish themselves in Britain, they bring with them conceptual and linguistic structures that refer back to the world left behind in India, allusions that signify assimilation or transculturation manifested in both casual verbal tics and more telling cultural attitudes. For example, when Guy Mannering figures the battle of wits between Pleydell and Sampson as a martial encounter, he oddly casts both sides as Indian: Dominie, he says, "was like a native Indian army . . . formidable by numerical strength and size of ordnance, but liable to be thrown into irreparable confusion by a movement to take them in the flank" (230), while Pleydell "was like the Mahratta cavalry; he assailed on all sides and presented no fair mark for artillery" (275). The metaphors, far from being arbitrary, reflect the realities of British military experience on the subcontinent. The first is an accurate rendering of Plassey, where Clive's small army defeated Siraj-ud-Daula's fifty thousand men "and a large train of massive, bullock-drawn cannon" because the Indians were "unnerved by the unfamiliar tactics of its adversaries"; the second might refer to Wellesley's difficulties against the cavalry of the Mahratha prince Jaswant Rao Holkar in 1805.[17] At another point, his daughter's uncharacteristically meek acquiescence to his plans puts him "in mind of the eternal salams of our black dependants in the East," an analogy that articulates his suspicion of and distaste for Oriental submissiveness. Yet a page later, Mannering thunderingly re-assumes his authority as "commandant . . . in my own family at least" (100–101), replicating in milder form the behavior of the father of Wollstonecraft's Maria: "In his family, to regain his lost consequence, he determined to keep up the same passive obedience, as in the vessels in which he had commanded" (*Maria* 75). Mannering has internalized his experiences in India to such an extent that they lie ready to hand as a way of interpreting and rerendering the world he occupies in Britain, but naturally, that interpretation is no more coherent or univocal than the experiences themselves have been.

Harry Bertram, too, although his time in India is brief, interprets and articulates his new circumstances by drawing on what he knew in India: his Wordsworthian meditation on the hills of Westmoreland includes an evocation of a "celebrated pass in Mysore country," reversing the process Nigel Leask describes as a particular process of Romantic imperialism: "Shrouding India in the melancholy, static idiom of the eighteenth-century culture of sensibility, it [the picturesque] thereby privileged the associative subjectivity of the (European) viewer over his or her (Indian) subject."[18] More significantly, Bertram ascribes to Indian memories his confused sense of recognition when he encounters Meg Merrilies in Cumberland: "Have I dreamed of such a figure? . . . or does this wild and singular looking woman recal to my recollection some of the strange figures I have seen in an Indian pagoda?" (123). It is as if Harry's memory itself has been remade in India, obliterating or obscuring his childhood in Scotland. Even phenomena less majestic or mysterious inevitably remind him of life in India. His admiration of the foxhunt at Liddesdale can be properly contextualized only by remem-

bering that he has "seen the princely sports of India, and ridden an ele-
phant a-hunting with the Nabob of Arcot" (135). We need to note here
that the text describes the Liddesdale hunt as conducted in such a way
as "would have shocked a member of the Pychely Hunt . . . without any
attention to the ordinary rules and decorums of the sport" (134–35); it
thus recalls the "unsportsmanlike" nature of the Nawab of Arcot's
hunts, which employed a mile-long net, into which animals were beaten
before being shot.[19] Bertram registers the un-English modes deployed
in both events, but his analogy is both unself-conscious and uncritical;
he construes neither hunt as "other" or evil, but is able to appreciate
the practices of the borderlands because of his knowledge of those of
the subcontinent. Even his internal and emotional states can be managed and altered through memories of his trials in India. Imprisoned at
Portanferry, feeling "a stronger disposition to melancholy than in my
life I ever experienced," he cheers himself by recalling worse misery in
India: "a Scottish jail shall not break . . . the spirits which have resisted
climate, and want, and penury, and disease, and imprisonment in a foreign land" (268). Bertram, like Mannering, inhabits a character solidly
forged by life in India. Indeed, his time there defines a self: asked by
Meg to identify himself, he replies, 'My name is Brown, mother, and I
come from the East Indies" (123), thus eliding not only his Scottish
childhood but also his Dutch youth. As for Julia Mannering, she cannot, of course, call on metaphors supplied by soldiering in the colonial
army, but her language too reverberates with memories of India, as
when she connects Mannering's inexplicable attachment to Dominie
Sampson to his preference for "a little mongrel cur" in India (156), or
informs Matilda that the gun used to defend Woodbourne against the
smugglers' attack is the kind "with which they shoot tygers, &c in the
East" (163). Indian public history invades even the ladylike English
hobby of drawing when she tells Matilda that she has "succeeded in
making a superb Hyder-Ally last night" (160). Perhaps even Sheermaal, who disdains the artistic ineptitude of British ladies because "not
one in five hundred is ever capable of copying from nature" (*Hindoo
Rajah*, 128), might approve of Julia's sketches. For all three former colonial residents, India retains currency and value, helping them define
themselves and make meaning of the world at "home." They consciously *and* intuitively see themselves as products of India, bringing
back to England and Scotland identities and viewpoints not available
to those who have not lived in the subcontinent.

These are not selves constructed in opposition or conscious superiority to the Otherness of India. Postcolonial critiques of imperial dis-

course have alerted us to the way in which colonized subjects can be deployed to construct a European subjectivity. Saree Makdisi, for example, pointing to the way in which Highlanders and Indians are aligned in James Mill's mind, says that "the two types are remarkable not so much in their similarities to each other, but in their radical difference from the third—equally constructed and invented—character-type he is invoking here by way of opposition: the cultivated, rational, honest, clean British Utilitarian whose apparent duty it was to stand as an example to Indians, Highlanders, and other Others of the 'proper way to be.'" Rajan, too, invokes the "classical relationship in which a dominant self defines a subjected other and then defines itself by the exclusion of that other."[20] But in Mannering, Bertram, and Julia, Scott posits an enriching of selfhood through assimilation rather than exclusion of the Other. He does not deploy the kind of binary oppositions outlined by Said: "The Oriental is irrational, depraved (fallen), child-like, 'different'; thus the European is rational, virtuous, mature, 'normal.'"[21] On the contrary, in *Guy Mannering*, Scott is at some pains to show how much of otherness, not defined negatively, informs ways of being and knowing in the homeland.

By 1827, Scott can no longer represent this kind of benign and productive hybridity. Unlike the returning colonials in *Guy Mannering*, the Indian veterans in *The Surgeon's Daughter* bring back the spoils and contagions of empire. General Witherington and his wife have acquired in India not new ways of seeing the world, but wealth, servants, commodities, and disease. When Zilia prepares herself to meet her long-lost son, she enacts a kind of Orientalized levee, reclining "on a heap of cushions, wrapped in a glittering drapery of gold and silver muslins, mingled with shawls, a luxury which was then a novelty in Europe" (229).[22] Witherington's Western body has suffered "a *coup de soleil* in India" (234), which leaves him liable to fits. These two are cautionary figures: Europeans whose exploitative relationship with India has brought them plunder but also pain.

It might be argued, then, that by 1827, Scott participates in the kind of imperial discourse that constructs India as the dangerous Other, an alien culture that contaminates and denatures British integrity and therefore must be purged. After all, the two villains of *The Surgeon's Daughter* have "gone native" in dress and allegiance and perhaps also in morality. Indeed, Mme. Montreville enters the narrative as a biracial cross-dresser, presenting a self that confuses and transgresses both nationality and gender: her riding habit and silk trousers resemble the costume of a "native chief," although her brow is "of European complexion" (249–50). She has aligned herself with Tipu Sultan in a pact that betrays both Britain and women, and Adam Hartley presciently cautions Menie Gray, "I doubt the propriety of your being under the charge of this unsexed woman, who can no longer be termed a European" (259). The terms that *are* employed to describe Mme. Montreville reflect the hybrid multiplicity of her identity: "the Queen of Sheba," "Semiramis," "Begum Mootee Mahu," "Amazon." Adela Montreville glories in her masculinity, defying Middlemas's feeble attempt to assert independence from her: "I am a woman, renegade, but one who wears a dagger, and despises alike thy strength and thy courage. I am a woman who has looked on more dying men than thou hast killed deer and antelopes. . . . Go where thou wilt, slave, thou shalt find thy mistress" (262). Richard Middlemas, too, displays a confusion of national and gender signs when he presents himself to Tipu Sultan as an Indian courtier, clothing his Western body "in a dress as magnificent in itself as it was remote from all European costume," and sporting both sword and eye makeup. Together, these two transculturated and adulterated Europeans represent transgressive boundary crossings that both titillate and repel, in what Rajan calls a "cluster of undesirabilities that continue to be illicitly desired. Enlightened civilizations must make these undesirabilities alien to themselves."[23]

I have no intention of arguing that Montreville and Middlemas are *not* examples of oriental contamination, nor do I claim that Scott rejects the discourse of moral infection. I would only point out that the contamination is multiple and complex. Montreville is no mere Scotch Miss seduced by Oriental mystique; she has de-nationalized herself by marrying "a Swiss officer in the French service" and by associating herself with his "parcel of desperate vagabonds, of every colour in the rainbow" (252). If, as Linda Colley has argued, Britain as a nation forged itself largely in opposition to French Catholicism,[24] then Montreville has become an Other long before she becomes the Begum. Hers is not a case of British identity being compromised by an encounter with India, but rather an instance of a confusion of identities finding a temporary and unstable home in multicultural India. Middlemas's fall into "nativeness" is equally complicated; it comes about as a result of his desire to *claim* an Englishness that is not his, from his insistence on being a Tresham rather than a Middlemas. Even as a boy in Scotland, ignoring the evidence of his mother's foreign origins and his father's Jacobitism, he insists on being identified as a "true-born Englishman . . . in right of my parents" (182). In Fort St. George in India, he resurrects this fiction, which leads to the duel during which he kills his colonel, thus being "obliged to fly from the British settlements" and enter the service of a native prince (245; one wonders if such would have been Bertram's fate if Mannering had been the one to fall in their duel).[25] Ironically, Middlemas turns into an Indianized Briton because of his stubborn refusal to acknowledge his biological hybridity.

In contrast, Hartley retains his Britishness in part by learning Indian modes of discourse; as if following the dictates of Sir William Jones (and Hamilton), Adam Hartley decides to "make the Oriental languages his study" in order to attend properly to his native patients. Even more importantly, he assimilates the system of civil intercourse practiced by Indians, and it is this "proper" transculturation that enables Hartley to rescue Menie Gray from the plots of Middlemas and Montreville. In a neat reversal of Saladin curing King Richard I in Scott's *Talisman* (1825), Hartley wins the Fakir Barak el Hadgi's gratitude and help not only by tending him during his illness, but also by "complying with . . . Mahomedan custom" (246) and developing an actual friendship with the fakir. (In a different kind of transculturation, the fakir also appreciates Hartley's sherbet, "which he preferred to his own, perhaps because a few glasses of rum or brandy were usually added to enrich the compound" [248].) Barak el Hadgi's faith in Hartley's mastery of Oriental codes of discourse is validated when Hartley skillfully deploys ritualized indirection while pleading Menie's case to the disguised Haidar Ali. So proficient does Hartley prove to be in wielding native tongue and custom that Haidar Ali is moved to exclaim, "Praised be God! He hath spoken like a Moullah" (275). If Middlemas and Montreville embody the evil consequences of going native, Hartley demonstrates the rewards of engaging appropriately with the custom of the country.[26]

Of course, India *does* seem to be a problematic space that enables hyper-romantic sensibilities and false narratives like those generated by Sophia Mannering and Mannering's subordinate Archer, not to mention the more straightforward deceptions of Tom Hillary. In India, Mannering casts himself as Othello and Brown/Bertram as Casio, with the "artful" Archer playing the provocative Iago; in India, Sophia deliberately plots a piece of sensational drama to enjoy its emotional effects (70–71); in India, Julia Mannering learns to love mystery and magic, in a version of what Katie Trumpener calls "the corruptions of the colonies" that must be purged before she can become a mature woman.[27]

Julia herself ascribes her fantasies to having been nurtured on Indian tales:

> You will call this romantic—but consider I was born in the land of talisman and spell, and in my childhood lulled by tales which you can only enjoy through the gauzy frippery of French translations. O Matilda, I wish you could have seen the dusky visages of my Indian attendants, bending impassive attention around the magic narrative, that flowed, half poetry, half prose, from the lips of the tale-teller. No wonder that European fiction sounds cold and meagre, after the wonderful effects which I have seen the romances of the East produce upon the hearers. (92)

I will return to this passage, but it is important to note here that although Julia dismisses the bloodless quality of European fiction, it is *that* fiction which her mother has read and replicated, *those* "romances [with] complicated intrigues" (95) that have disordered her imagination. Sophia Mannering's delusions are literary, like those of Charlotte Lennox's Arabella, of Eaton Stannard Barrett's Cherubina, and of Scott's own Waverley. If Julia indulges in romantic fantasies, perhaps it is because she "inherits all her [mother's] weakness" for European sentimental fiction rather than because she imbibes Indian stories. Similarly, Richard Middlemas's ambitions are first generated not by the Indian tales brought home by Tom Hillary, but by Nurse Jamieson's fantastic accounts of his ancestors, of his father "the grand gentleman . . . the diamonds [his mother] wore on her fingers, that could be compared to nothing but her own een . . . the arrival of his grandfather, and the awful man, armed with pistol, dirk, and claymore . . . the very Ogre of a fairy tale" (180). Like Julia, Richard learns romance from a mother-figure at home rather than from exotic tales told by Indian spinners.

Julia in fact comes by her self-proclaimed romantic tendencies from both parents. Mervyn twice connects father and daughter this way (88), and Julia herself says her father has "a tinge of romance in his disposition" (96–97). The reader need only glance at the opening chapters of *Guy Mannering* to see how romantically (and conventionally) Mannering the "youthful lover" (18) responds to nature and picturesque ruins. Nor does he outgrow this fanciful cast of mind; his reflections on seeing Ellangowan after seventeen years are reminiscent of passages from *Tintern Abbey* and *Childe Harold:* "The landscape was the same; but how changed the feelings, hopes, and views, of the spectator! Then, life and love were new, and all the prospect was gilded by their lays. And now, disappointed in affection, sated with fame, and what the world calls success, his mind goaded by bitter and repentant recollection, his best hope was to find a retirement in which he might nurse the melancholy that was to accompany him to his grave" (73). With parents like these, Julia Mannering hardly needs the influence of magical Eastern tales to develop a romantic imagination. Moreover, her fancies, like her mother's, belong firmly in a British literary tradition: she is the legitimate sister to two Lydias and a Marianne.

In fact, however, Julia Mannering seems to understand that her romantic rhetoric is largely performative and not her essential character. To Matilda she writes that, unlike her friend, she prefers the domestic to the sublime; she would "like to trim my little pinnace to a brisk breeze in some inland lake or tranquil bay," and is enamored of Brown because of "his good humour, lively conversation, and open gallantry" (161)—hardly Byronic qualities. Certainly, her playful flirtation with Pleydell, her mockery of the romantic impulses in her father, and her self-conscious theatricality regarding her own love affair ("Infatuated! A second time!" [305] she exclaims during the dramatic recognition scene) point to a heroine more at ease in domestic comedy than in romantic melodrama, a woman aware of the adolescent posturing she indulges in to entertain her friend. Just as he interrogates and problematizes facile conventions about India as the Dark Other against which European identity is constructed, Walter Scott also questions the notion that India is the source of heightened sensibility. He reminds us that romantic fancies can be homegrown phenomena, products of European dreams rather than Asian hallucinations.[28]

Graham Dawson says that stories of returning adventurers from India "provided writers like Scott (who had no personal experience of the subcontinent as a real geographical space) with a ready-made landscape of excitement and danger to test the wits and courage of British heroes." Patrick Brantlinger points out that "though he had never been to India, Sir Walter Scott tried his hand at an oriental novel in *The Surgeon's Daughter*." Both comments assume that Scott sees India only as a rhetorical opportunity and remains indifferent to its realities as location and culture. They also imply that he participates in what Sara Suleri calls "narratives of English India [which] are fraught with the idiom of dubiety, or a mode of cultural tale-telling that is neurotically conscious of its own self-censoring apparatus."[29] I am suggesting that in *Guy Mannering*, Scott attempts to head off the simplifying and overheated representations of imperial experience that provoke these postcolonial critiques. In *Guy Mannering*, India is neither a theoretical space nor a rhetorical opportunity, neither Burke's "Great Unknowable" nor

Jones's oriental text to be translated for Europeans.[30] India is a real place with real effects on people and history, effects that cannot be easily categorized or essentialized, and that need to be represented with all the complexity and inconsistency inherent in the native culture and the colonial enterprise. It is a space to which imperial settlers bring their own personal and cultural baggage (like Witherington's Jacobitism and Sophia's quixoticism), and from which they bring home narratives that inevitably interweave European imagination with Indian experience.

Guy Mannering has something to say about how essentializing representations of India are generated and circulated. Dawson points out that the effect of adventure stories depends on who is hearing them; for example, he says, the response in a "community, where soldiering would be a comparatively novel experience and the storyteller able to occupy the exotic identity of the wanderer returned, would differ markedly from that available in his regimental public, among comrades who had directly participated in those experiences with him."[31] We have noted how Colonel Jack takes advantage of the credulity of his Spanish captors when he enthralls them with tales of King Philip's gallantry in battles where "his Majesty had never been at all, and in some, where I had never been myself; but I found I talk'd to People who knew nothing of the Matter, and so any thing went down with them" (279). In *Guy Mannering*, narratives about the East are told to those who have no firsthand knowledge of the subject, for whom, as Bertram says, military adventurers occupy a particularly privileged position: "A retired old soldier is always a graceful and respected character . . . the most stupid veteran that ever faltered out the thrice-told tale of a siege and a battle, and a cock and a bottle, is listened to with sympathy and reverence" (111). Mannering, describing his bitter history in India, makes a point of contrasting his own life with that of Mervyn—"you, who have remained in the bosom of happiness . . . with content and a smooth current down the course of life" (68–69)—and Mervyn acknowledges the distinction, apologizing "for the pain I have given you, in forcing you to open wounds so festering" (87). In his commendable desire to spare his friend further pain, Mervyn unquestioningly swallows Mannering's version of events, and his own language about festering wounds echoes Mannering's characterization of himself as suffering for a very long time from "the catastrophe which has long embittered my life" (70).

But how long? Sophia dies eight months after the duel, and Mannering and Julia return to England shortly afterwards. If the cause of Mannering's melancholy brooding lies in his resentment and self-reproach regarding the Brown affair, then his Byronically blighted life has lasted about a year. Yet the impression he gives Mervyn and the reader is that he has borne the burden of unspeakable grief for years. Geographical distance has been retroped as temporal duration, the effect of which is to make Mannering a more interesting and pitiable character. The narrative recounting of the Indian adventure simply exists on its own terms and within its own emotional chronology. Shrewd, worldly Mervyn no more questions the details of Mannering's romantic self-presentation than schoolgirl Matilda investigates Julia's exciting narratives.

Although we never hear directly from Matilda Marchmont, to whose "faithful eye were addressed those formidable quires which issued forth from Mervyn Hall" (91), we know that she is a receptive and enthralled recipient of Julia's stories, whether about India or Scotland, about *looties* or smugglers. For her, Scotland may as well be India—exotic, exciting, foreign. Julia dutifully delivers what Matilda craves: adventure, suspense, battles, and love affairs. Profoundly aware of the effects of narrative, taking great pleasure in evoking the right mix of horror and sympathy, Julia becomes a gothic romancer. She benefits, of course, from actually inhabiting "romantic" locations, accruing to herself the kind of authority claimed by returning colonials and eliciting the same effect on credulous minds. When we look again at her description of those tales from "the land of talisman and spell," we note that she describes not the stories themselves, but their effects; it is the audience, those dusky Indian attendants, who are the focus of her gaze and her narrative. Like Meg Merrilies pronouncing her curse on the Bertrams, like Guy Mannering enacting a romantically tormented life, Julia deliberately heightens the drama in her own narratives to induce and replicate the "wonderful effects" she has witnessed in India.

As we have seen in the nurse's tale, which turns the "humble prose" of Middlemas's origins to the "boldest flights of poetry" (180), India is certainly not the only place that generates fictional narratives. Scott shows us the process of turning history into thrilling tale when he narrates the multiple versions of Harry Bertram's disappearance and of Mannering's role in that episode. At the Gordon's Arms, the landlady, the deacon, the precentor, and the postilion all offer competing versions of the story, in one of which Mannering is transformed from the "young English gentleman, who had just left the university of Oxford" (3) to "an ancient man, strangely habited. . . . His head, and his legs, and his arms, were bare, although it was winter time o' the year, and he had a grey beard three quarters lang" (64). The impulse to make an exciting event even more dramatic, the need to find coherent explanations for unsolved mysteries, the desire to populate a story with exotic characters flourish in a Scottish village as much as in an Indian cantonment. Time and distance allow a kind of flexibility that opens up space for narrative manipulations. As Mrs. Mac-Candlish says to Mannering about the incident, "There are mony idle clashes about the way and manner; for it's an auld story now, and every body tells it, as we were doing, their ain way by the ingle-side" (67).

Just as it is difficult to uncover the historical actuality behind multiple versions of a traumatic moment in Scotland, so is it hard to disentangle reality from myth in India. Witness the clash of interpretations Hartley encounters when he tries to ascertain the "truth" about Mme. Montreville and Middlemas. His friend Butler tells him that she betrayed her husband to Haidar Ali, while the military surgeon Esdale dismisses that charge as "a specimen of Madras gossip. The fact is, that she defended the place long after her husband fell." The same Esdale contradicts Major Mercer's accusation that Middlemas had mistreated English prisoners and is now Montreville's lover, asserting instead that "they were friends, Europeans in an Indian court, and therefore intimate; but I believe nothing more" (253–54). A reader would be perfectly justified in crediting Esdale's prosaic version of events, for the text tells us that not only had he been one of the prisoners Middlemas is purported to have brutalized, but also "was generally esteemed a rising man, calm, steady, and deliberate in forming his opinions" (253). But, in a dizzying turn, the next chapter of *The Surgeon's Daughter* belies Esdale's sensible and generous account, exposing the lovers and their plan to betray both political and personal allegiances. The most lurid fantasies about this repellant pair of traitors pale before the "reality" of their multiple plots to sell Menie Gray to Tipu Sultan, to betray Haidar Ali to the English, and to denounce each other for revenge and for self-preservation.

What is Walter Scott doing? Is he refuting his argument, implicit in *Guy Mannering* and in the early chapters of *The Surgeon's Daughter,* that India is no more exotic or theatrical than the homeland and that the hyperbolic narratives woven around Indian experiences are to be discounted by the careful reader? Is he participating in the kind of imperial discourse that Brantlinger characterizes as one that transfers "guilt for violence and rapacity from the home government or the British people as a whole to aggressive individuals acting at the periphery, and then from these individuals to the peoples they conquered"?[32] I suggest that Scott in *The Surgeon's Daughter* thematizes the effects of imperial practice and rhetoric when they are freed from the kind of checks he has proposed in *Guy Mannering;* he shows what happens to national character and national literature when audiences at home succumb to the fictions of empire. Richard Middlemas, robbed of the delusions of splendid ancestry that had been generated and nurtured by Nurse Jamieson, finds a ready substitute in the dazzling visions reported by Tom Hillary, and Tom's very hyperboles — "Not a stream did he mention but flowed over sands of gold, and not a palace that was inferior to those of the celebrated Fata Morgana" (203) — convince rather than caution, playing into his own desire. (Recall Colonel Jack's fantasy about "a stream of Golden Rivers in Mexico" [296]). Richard succumbs to the siren call of exotic narrative that MacKellar in *Master of Ballantrae* fears may seduce young Alexander Durrisdeer when he warns Henry that the Master will gain gradual ascendancy over Alexander through narrating exciting tales of empire. For Richard Middlemas, India supplies what is felt as lack and loss: "Ambition . . . was not lulled to sleep, though it was no longer nourished by the same hopes which had at first awakened it. The Indian Captain's oratory supplied the themes which had been at first derived from the legends of the nursery" (508). Once again, as with Sophia Mannering, European mythmaking resituates itself on Asian soil, and it is as if Waverley, rather than waking from romance to history, had simply replaced one set of fantasies with another. Such surrender to imperial fantasies constructs a new national identity: narrative produces character, which then generates overwrought texts, in a degenerate spiral of misdirected synergy. Richard Middlemas, trying to replicate his father's dream of constructing a reconstituted self in India, finds instead disgrace, disappointment, and the worst impulses of his own mind.

Unlike *Guy Mannering,* which offers a satisfying ending of retribution and restoration, *The Surgeon's Daughter* closes on a most dystopic note, belying Mr. Fairscribe's breezy assertion that India "is the true place for a Scot to thrive in" (155). Menie Gray and Adam Hartley do not marry; he dies of "a contagious distemper,"[33] and she returns to Middlemas a wealthy but dispirited spinster (her Indian fortune, fittingly, is one that Haidar Ali wrests from the European adventuress Montreville). Both Richard Middlemas and Adela Montreville die violently, the latter possibly by her own hand. The ambitions and fantasies that had brought these young people to India end in death or diminished life. Yet, as the text sardonically observes, ships from Europe continue to bring over "their usual cargo of boys longing to be commanders, and young women without any purpose of being married, but whom a pious duty to some . . . male relative, brought to India to keep his house, until they should find themselves unexpectedly in one of their own" (249).[34] Narratives about opportunities in India continue to flourish and to bring to the subcontinent the ignorant and the self-seeking, the unemployable and the unmarriageable. Inevitably, these undesirable colonials change the nature of the imperial experience, for the conquerors as well as for their victims. The rhetoric of empire comes to resemble the Mysore plain, where "rapine and war had suspended the labours of industry, and the rich vegetation of the soil had in a few years converted a fertile champaign country into an almost impenetrable thicket" (270). It becomes a rhetorical jungle through which truth can barely be discerned.[35] And finally, the renegade European, motivated by a combination of ambition and resentment, misled by tales of fame and fortune, his identity destabilized by uneasy hybridities, feverishly maneuvers himself under the "huge shapeless foot" of the beast he believed "awaited his occupancy" (284). In *Guy Mannering*, Walter Scott maps out some of the ways imperial experience can be productively brought home and cautions readers who might too easily credit tall imperial tales; in *The Surgeon's Daughter*, he figures for us, sometimes with ferocious humor, the inevitable darkening of the national character when imperial rhetoric stamps out the practice of suspicious reading.

Notes

INTRODUCTION

1. Robert Louis Stevenson, *The Master of Ballantrae, A Winter's Tale*, ed. Adrian Poole (London: Penguin, 1996), 192, 193. All subsequent references are to this edition. This motley crew and dramatic ending have elicited some misreadings. Alexander Clunas suggests that Mountain "is haunted and crazy because Secundra Dass has buried his master, after these men killed him," but the text makes clear that James's feigned death has been ascribed to mysterious natural causes. Jason Marc Harris, too, produces a confused reading of the ending when he places it "in India, where James, hoping to evade the hired murderers of his brother Henry by feigning death, plans to be resuscitated by his Indian servant Secundra." See Alexander B. Clunas, "'A Double Word': Writing and Justice in *The Master of Ballantrae*," *Studies in Scottish Literature* 28 (1993): 71, and Jason Marc Harris, "Robert Louis Stevenson: Folklore and Imperialism," *English Literature in Transition, 1880–1920* 4 (2003): 392. Clunas also conflates the diplomat Johnson with Governor Cadwallader Colden (or Clinton, as he is mistakenly named in the published version of the novel).

2. Robert Louis Stevenson, *The Letters of Robert Louis Stevenson*, 8 vols, ed. Bradford A. Booth and Ernest Mehew (New Haven, CT: Yale University Press, 1995), 6:105. Critics too have noted what Stevenson called "a decline into the fantastic" (297). Jenni Calder argues that *Master* "fails to communicate the ambience of eighteenth-century eastern America," but she also points to the propriety of setting the climax in the American wilderness, where the "landscape is disengaged, indifferent, even while it has colluded in violence. . . . The landscape does not aid interpretation; the frozen ground yields no clues." *Robert Louis Stevenson: A Life Study* (New York: Oxford University Press, 1980), 236; and "Figures in a Landscape: Scott, Stevenson, and Routes to the Past," in *Robert Louis Stevenson, Writer of Boundaries*, ed. Richard Ambrosini and Richard Dury (Madison: University of Wisconsin Press, 2006), 131–32. David Daiches locates the weakness not in America but in India when he declares that "if Stevenson had not sent the Master of Ballantrae to India and involved him with that preposterous puppet, Secundra Das . . . *The Master of Ballantrae* would have been Stevenson's first and only successful tragic novel." *Robert Louis Stevenson* (Norfolk, CT: New Directions, 1947), 76. Carol Mills agrees with Stevenson's depreciation when she states that "the work appears to disintegrate at the end" and ascribes the failure to a generic shift from romance to adventure, to "his gamble in violating the principle of unity of mood." "*The Master of Ballantrae:* An Experiment with Genre," in *Robert Louis Stevenson*, ed. Andrew Noble (London: Vision Press Ltd., 1983), 118, 131.

Douglas Gifford, on the other hand, praises "the final movement to a frozen wilderness, which worried Stevenson but does not worry the reader who has seen his instinctive skill in displacing both brothers from their humdrum or exotic backgrounds."

167

"Stevenson and Scottish Fiction: The Importance of *The Master of Ballantrae*," in *Stevenson and Victorian Scotland*, ed. Jenni Calder (Edinburgh: Edinburgh University Press, 1981), 85. Oliver S. Buckton detects a kind of self-reflexivity in the ending: "the *dénouement* also suggested his resistance to being 'boxed in' by narrative categories and generic conventions: even as he struggled to construct a coffin for *The Master of Ballantrae*, Stevenson recognized that his hero could not be contained." "Reanimating Stevenson's Corpus," in *Robert Louis Stevenson Reconsidered: New Perspectives*, ed. William B. Jones (Jefferson, NC: McFarland & Co., 2003), 56.

3. J. R. Hammond, *A Robert Louis Stevenson Companion: A Guide to the Novels, Essays and Short Stories* (London: Macmillan, 1984), 157.

4. *Letters*, 6:100. Scott Allen Nollen finds that setting the novel on three continents "enhances its adventurous qualities but also adds to its disjointed plot structure." *Robert Louis Stevenson: Life, Literature and the Silver Screen* (Jefferson, NC: McFarland & Co., 1994) 287.

5. Adrian Poole, in his introduction to the Penguin edition of the novel, points out that the Duries contribute nothing to empire, "But the natives on whose lands they intrude do insist on their place in the novel, and there is a savage narrative logic that brings together at the novel's climax the North American Indians and Secundra Dass. They represent the two extremes of native reaction to the incursion of colonialism: on the one hand, savage resistance, and on the other, slavish devotion" (xvi). Gerard Carruthers, in *Robert Louis Stevenson's Strange Case of Dr Jekyll and Mr Hyde, The Master of Ballantrae, and The Ebb-Tide* (Glasgow: Association for Scottish Literary Studies, 2004), points to the double historical sensibility of the text: "Even as *The Master of Ballantrae* is a historical novel dealing with the turbulent cultural events of eighteenth century Scotland, it also displays its late nineteenth century 'modernity'" (20).

6. Elwin Malcolm finds that "with the entrance of the Indian, Secundra Dass, the illusion becomes unconvincing, as by an intrusion of the incompatible." *The Strange Case of Robert Louis Stevenson* (New York: Russell & Russell, 1950), 230. I am arguing that incompatibility is in fact Stevenson's topic.

7. David Armitage, *The Ideological Origins of the British Empire* (Cambridge: Cambridge University Press, 2000), 2.

8. Lawrence James, *The Rise and Fall of the British Empire* (New York: St. Martin's Press, 1994), 194. Bruce P. Lenman, in "Aristocratic 'Country' Whiggery in Scotland and the American Revolution," invokes George Dempster, who resigned as a director of the East India Company "because of the depth of his hostility to the creation of a great British territorial empire in India, which he saw as likely in the long run to have the same corrosive effect on British government that the acquisition of an Asian empire once had on the Roman Republic." In *Scotland and America in the Age of Enlightenment*, ed. Richard B. Sher and Jeffrey R. Smitten (Edinburgh: Edinburgh University Press, 1990), 183.

9. Edward Said, *Culture and Imperialism* (New York: Vintage Books, 1994), 80.

10. For one account of *Oroonoko* as generative text, see Moira Ferguson, "*Oroonoko*: Birth of a Paradigm," in *Troping Oroonoko from Behn to Bandele*, ed. Susan B. Iwanisziw (Aldershot, UK: Ashgate Publishing Ltd., 2004), 1–15. Richard Frohock, in *Heroes of Empire: The British Imperial Protagonist in America, 1596–1764* (Newark: University of Delaware Press, 2004), points out that "scholars have presented *Oroonoko* . . . as a *terminus a quo* and viewed it as establishing lasting colonial paradigms" (53). Firdous Azim, in *The Colonial Rise of the Novel* (London: Routledge, 1993), situates *Oroonoko* as "the first

English novel" precisely because it "stands witness to and is part of the imperial project, as its initial admiration for its Black subject proves to be flirtatious and frivolous" (35, 45). Srinivas Aravamudan, in *Tropicopolitans: Colonialism and Agency, 1688–1804* (Durham, NC: Duke University Press, 1999) also insists that "a book on colonialism and eighteenth-century literature cannot begin without invoking Oroonoko" (29).

The idea for using Stevenson as a gateway came out of a series of conversations with Jane Millgate, who first alerted me to how comprehensively Stevenson rehearses eighteenth-century imperial motifs. As Millgate put it, "He accumulates them at enormous speed, one after the other in a deliberately outrageous fashion, not needing to pause, explain, or excuse because they are all just out there." I am delighted to acknowledge my debt to her. While revising this manuscript, I encountered Nigel Leask's "Scotland's Literature of Empire and Emigration, 1707–1918," *The Edinburgh History of Scottish Literature*, 3 vols., ed. Susan Manning (Edinburgh: Edinburgh University Press, 2007), 153–62, which also uses *Master of Ballantrae* "as a portal" (153) into consideration of Scotland and empire.

11. Laura Brown, *The Ends of Empire: Women and Ideology in Early Eighteenth-Century English Literature* (Ithaca, NY: Cornell University Press, 1993), 36.

12. Aphra Behn, *Oroonoko: or, The Royal Slave*, ed. Catherine Gallagher and Simon Stern (Boston: St. Martin's Press, 2000), 43. All subsequent references are to this edition.

13. Daniel Defoe, *The History and Remarkable Life of the Truly Honourable Col. Jacque, Commonly Call'd Col. Jack*, ed. Samuel Holt Monk (London: Oxford University Press, 1970), 279; Elizabeth Hamilton, *Translations of the Letters of a Hindoo Rajah*, ed. Pamela Perkins and Shannon Russell (Peterborough, Ontario: Broadview Press Ltd., 1999), 80; Walter Scott, *Chronicles of the Canongate*, ed. Claire Lamont (Edinburgh: Edinburgh University Press, 2000), 245. All subsequent references are to these editions.

James H. Merrell, describing the contest between Europeans and Amerindians for linguistic dominance, says, "The intruders did eventually win the war of words, but it was a long struggle, waged against stiff opposition. . . . Most early interpreters were colonists who mastered a native language, not Indians speaking English." James H. Merrell, "'The Customes of Our Countrey': Indians and Colonists in Early America," in *Strangers within the Realm: Cultural Margins of the First British Empire*, ed. Bernard Bailyn and Philip D. Morgan (Chapel Hill: University of North Carolina Press, 1991), 127, 129.

14. Robert Bage, *Hermsprong; or Man as He Is Not*, ed. Pamela Perkins (Peterborough, Ontario: Broadview Press Ltd., 2002), 252. All subsequent references are to this edition.

15. Homi K. Bhabha, *The Location of Culture* (London: Routledge, 1994), 86.

16. Laura J. Rosenthal, "*Oroonoko*: Reception, Ideology, Narrative Strategy," in *The Cambridge Companion to Aphra Behn*, ed. Derek Hughes and Janet Todd (Cambridge: Cambridge University Press, 2004), 153.

17. Daniel Defoe, *The Fortunes and Misfortunes of the Famous Moll Flanders*, ed. David Blewett (London: Penguin, 1989), 134. All subsequent references are to this edition.

18. Diane Simmons, *The Narcissism of Empire: Loss, Rage and Revenge in Thomas de Quincey, Robert Louis Stevenson, Arthur Conan Doyle, Rudyard Kipling and Isak Dinesen* (Brighton, UK: Sussex Academic Press, 2007), 1; John Kucich, *Imperial Masochism: British Fiction, Fantasy, and Social Class* (Princeton, NJ: Princeton University Press, 2007), 4, 26. Robert Markley's brilliant analysis of Dryden's *Amboyne* (1672) points out

that the play deploys the "theatrics of martyrdom as a strategy of self-definition." *The Far East and the English Imagination, 1660–1730* (Cambridge: Cambridge University Press, 2006), 151.

19. Robert Kiely, *Robert Louis Stevenson and the Fiction of Adventure* (Cambridge, MA: Harvard University Press, 1965), 198.

20. G. K. Chesterton, *Robert Louis Stevenson* (New York: Sheed and Ward, 1955), 113.

21. Joanna Lipking, "'Others', Slaves, and Colonists in *Oroonoko*," in *Cambridge Companion to Aphra Behn*, 183. In this struggle, she suggests, "Suriname might be viewed . . . as a developing colony at a very early stage" (182). Frohock echoes this analysis when he casts the conflict in terms of class: "Oroonoko's heroic orientation also makes him vulnerable to members of the lower class who have assumed positions of civic power in the American colonies. . . . the American colonial experience allows members of the criminal class to exercise real power and to position themselves, in a real sense, as the 'Lords,' and, 'Masters' of honor-bound men like Oroonoko" (62–63).

22. J. H. Elliott, *Empires of the Atlantic World: Britain and Spain in America, 1492–1830* (New Haven, CT: Yale University Press, 2006), 326–27; Nicholas B. Dirks, *The Scandal of Empire: India and the Creation of Imperial Britain* (Cambridge, MA: Belknap Press of Harvard University Press, 2006), 7.

23. Christopher Flynn, in *Americans in British Literature, 1770–1832: A Breed Apart* (Aldershot, UK: Ashgate Publishing Ltd., 2008), provides a thorough analysis of the ways in which English writers read post-Independence America. On the one hand, "America served as an imaginary space against which to measure English realities. . . . in part because it exhibited a functioning democracy in a time when many of the democratic elements of English political life were being challenged" (80); on the other hand, for writers such as Frances Trollope and Basil Hall, "gross table manners, religious primitivism, a degraded speech, and inclination to spit on the carpet, and constant drinking all defined the American as a civilized barbarian" (137).

24. Ralph Cohen's characterization of Thomson's Torrid Zone could apply to Behn's description of Suriname: "in these happy isles the people live without the corruptions brought by Christianity and the inhabitants of the temperate zone." *The Unfolding of The Seasons* (Baltimore: Johns Hopkins University Press, 1970), 136.

25. Laura Brown argues that "the political endpoint of Behn's narrative is nothing less than the reenactment of the most traumatic event of the revolution, the execution of Charles I" (55).

26. Joanna Lipking, "Confusing Matters: Searching the Backgrounds of *Oroonoko*," in *Aphra Behn Studies*, ed. Janet Todd (Cambridge: Cambridge University Press, 1996), 268.

27. Walter Scott, *Waverley*, ed. P. D. Garside (Edinburgh: Edinburgh University Press, 2007), 147.

28. Dirks, *Scandal of Empire*, 5.

29. Tzvetan Todorov, *The Conquest of America: The Question of the Other*, trans. Richard Howard (Norman: University of Oklahoma Press, 1999), 49–50.

30. Stephen Greenblatt, *Marvelous Possessions: The Wonder of the New World* (Chicago: University of Chicago Press, 1991), 11, 20, 66–68.

31. Markley, *Far East*, 3.

32. Bhabha, *Location of Culture*, 67, 83. Rajani Sudan, in *Fair Exotics: Xenophobic Subjects in English Literature, 1720–1850* (Philadelphia: University of Pennsylvania Press,

2002), brings together Greenblatt's articulation of wonder with Bhabha's theory of Othering: "The initial attraction of the foreign becomes frightening to the British subject, thus giving rise to the repudiation of the thing that provoked illicit or dangerous desire. . . . In early eighteenth-century Britain, a primary strategy of national self-definition was the xenophobic differentiation of self from nonwhite colonial others; the strategy was naturalized" (6–9). Bruce McLeod, in *The Geography of Empire in English Literature, 1580–1745* (Cambridge: Cambridge University Press, 1999), says, "As imperialism brings disparate groups into proximity with one another, strategies must be created to ensure that proximity does not slide into familiarity or transgression. Increasingly the question for empire was how to utilize yet keep segregated the Yahoos, savages, natives, and Hottentots that are supposedly British subjects" (217). Ros Ballaster's *Fabulous Orients: Fictions of the East in England, 1662–1785* (Oxford: Oxford University Press, 2005) connects differentiation to European readings of Oriental tales, readings that "enable a fruitful pose, especially for the British on the threshold of western empire in India, as dispassionate judge of fixed, indeed stagnating power relations" (5).

33. Suvir Kaul, *Poems of Nation, Anthems of Empire: English Verse in the Long Eighteenth Century* (Charlottesville: University Press of Virginia, 2000), 89.

34. Alan Sandison makes the perceptive point, "There is fine irony in Secundra Dass coming near to having the final passionate word . . . and that that word should be (pointing to Henry and MacKellar) 'all gallows-murderers.'" *Robert Louis Stevenson and the Appearance of Modernism: A Future Feeling* (Houndmills, UK: Macmillan Press Ltd., 1996), 308.

35. *New York Times Magazine*, January 16, 2005, 19.

36. T. M. Devine, *Scotland's Empire, 1600–1815* (London: Allen Lane, 2003); Douglas J. Hamilton, *Scotland, the Caribbean and the Atlantic World, 1750–1820* (Manchester, UK: Manchester University Press, 2005). It is not possible here to provide a bibliography of the large body of work dealing with Scotland and empire, but much of it will be cited throughout my study.

37. Eric Richards, "Scotland and the Uses of the Atlantic Empire,' in *Strangers within the Realm*, 68–69; Kenneth McNeil, *Scotland, Britain, Empire: Writing the Highlands, 1760–1860* (Columbus: Ohio State University Press, 2007), 10; Bruce P. Lenman, "Colonial Warfare and Imperial Identity,' in *Scotland and the Americas, 1600–1800* (Providence, RI: John Carter Brown Library, 1995), 77. Evan Gottlieb, *Feeling British: Sympathy and National Identity in Scottish and English Writing, 1707–1832* (Lewisburg, PA: Bucknell University Press, 2007), 46. Devine says that following failures to establish independent Scottish colonies, "penetration of the English empire by stealth after 1707 turned out to be much more effective and profitable" (xxvii). Armitage, speaking of the centrality of naval power to imperial dominance, adds that "competing English and Scottish maritime ideologies were either subsumed within, or survived alongside, comprehensively British conceptions throughout the course of these centuries" (102).

38. Mark Netzloff, "Writing Britain from the Margins: Scottish, Irish, and Welsh Projects for American Colonization," *Prose Studies* 25, no. 2 (August 2002): 2–3. Robert J. C. Young, *Colonial Desire: Hybridity in Theory, Culture and Race* (London: Routledge, 1995), 3. Netzloff argues that "even while colonialism provided the opportunity for the formation of diasporic British identities, the material circumstances of colonial expansion ensured that these colonies remained within the economic control of the English state and London-based companies" (20).

39. William Robertson, *The History of the Reign of the Emperor Charles V* (1792; repr., London: Routledge/Thoemmes Press, 1996), IV:319; Conrad Russell, "John Bull's Other Nations: The English Belief That They Are the Only Ones Here," *TLS* (March 12, 1993): 3.

40. Kathryn Tidrick, whose *Empire and the English Character* (London: I. B. Tauris & Co. Ltd., 1990) looks at myths that proliferated about English imperialists in Africa and India after 1840, uses the term *English* rather than *British* because "though Scots and Irish and even Welsh proliferated throughout the empire, the ideas by which they were consciously guided as imperialists were English in origin" (1).

41. Andrew Hook, *Scotland and America: A Study of Cultural Relations 1750–1835* (Glasgow: Blackie, 1975), 14, 48. Martha McLaren, *British India and British Scotland, 1780–1830: Career Building, Empire Building, and a Scottish School of Thought on Indian Governance* (Akron, OH: University of Akron Press, 2001), 2, 234.

42. Hamilton, *Scotland*, 3; Aaron Fogleman, "From Slaves, Convicts, and Servants to Free Passengers: The Transformation of Immigration in the Era of the American Revolution," *Journal of History* 85, no. 1 (June 1998): 46. See also Linda Colley, *Captives: Britain, Empire, and the World, 1600–1850* (New York: Random House, 2002): "Oliver Cromwell enslaved hundreds of defeated Scots in the 1650s, dispatching them . . . to the West Indies" (143).

43. Hamilton, *Scotland*, 2.

44. In Sydney Owenson's 1806 best seller *The Wild Irish Girl: A National Tale*, ed. Kathryn Kirkpatrick (Oxford: Oxford University Press, 1999), Father John deplores the fact that Ulster has become a "Scottish colony" in which Milesian heart has been supplanted by "prudential maxims of calculating interest," but concedes that Scottish Ireland is prosperous, a place where the worker "enjoys the fruits of his industry, and acquires a relish for the comforts and conveniencies of life" (198). This is diametrically opposed to the kind of conflation Felicity Nussbaum cites when she notes that "the Scots origin of 'Mungo' draws implicit connections between the barbarian internal to Great Britain, the Scotsman stuck in an early stage of primitivism, and the foreign 'savage.'" *The Limits of the Human: Fictions of Anomaly, Race and Gender in the Long Eighteenth Century* (Cambridge: Cambridge University Press, 2003), 8.

45. Hammond, *Stevenson Companion*, 160.

46. Manfred Malzah, "Voices of the Scottish Empire," in *Robert Louis Stevenson, Writer of Boundaries*, ed. Richard Ambrosini and Richard Dury (Madison: University of Wisconsin Press, 2006), 158. Ann C. Colley, in *Robert Louis Stevenson and the Colonial Imagination* (Aldershot, UK: Ashgate, 2004) expresses a similar view when she says Stevenson in the South Pacific was "in the odd position of thinking of himself both as a victim and as an intrusive colonial" (5). Kucich suggests that "masochistic fantasy enabled Stevenson to resolve on colonial ground ideological contradictions that were at the heart of his own class identity" (29) and that he "found the colonies a place to experiment with integrated magical/melancholic projects and perhaps to reclaim their moral authority from the imperial opportunists who both fascinated and troubled him" (76).

47. Penny Fielding, *Writing and Orality: Nationality, Culture, and Nineteenth-Century Scottish Fiction* (Oxford: Clarendon Press, 1996), 161.

48. Colley, *Robert Louis Stevenson*, 142.

49. Hamilton, *Translations*, 10. Their introduction lists the literary celebrities she counted in her circle; these included Walter Scott, James Hogg, Joanna Baillie, and Francis Jeffrey.

CHAPTER 1. GLOBAL NATIONALISMS

1. John Dennis, *The Critical Works of John Dennis*, 2 vols., ed. Edward Niles Hooker (Baltimore: Johns Hopkins University Press, 1943), 2:137; Samuel Johnson, *Lives of the English Poets*, 2 vols. (London: Oxford University Press, 1967), 2:359. Johnson concedes that the multiplicities of *The Seasons* makes order unattainable and perhaps irrelevant.

2. Martin C. Battestin, *The Providence of Wit: Aspects of Form in Augustan Literature and the Arts* (Oxford: Clarendon Press, 1974), 220; Maynard Mack, "On Reading Pope," *College English* 22, no. 2 (November 1960): 101; Janis A. Tomlinson, "Landscape into Allegory: J. M. W. Turner's *Frosty Morning* and James Thomson's *The Seasons*," *Studies in Romanticism* 29, no. 2 (Summer 1990): 193; Frans De Bruyn, "From Georgic Poetry to Statistics and Graphs: Eighteenth-Century Representation and the 'State' of British Society," *The Yale Journal of Criticism* 17, no. 1 (2004): 119. Earl R. Wasserman searches rather reluctantly for coherence in *Windsor-Forest*, saying that "we have no choice but to attempt to read it as an artistic unity." (*The Subtler Language: Critical Readings of Neoclassic and Romantic Poems* (Baltimore: Johns Hopkins University Press, 1959), 102.

3. Robert Crawford, *Devolving English Literature* (Oxford: Clarendon Press, 1992), 45–49. Ralph Cohen, on the other hand, finds the poem's appreciation of nature specifically English: "The fact that natural description could be considered a peculiarly English trait permitted even the 'nature' of the poem to be turned to nationalistic purposes." (*The Art of Discrimination: Thomson's Seasons and the Language of Criticism* (Berkeley: University of California Press, 1964), 419.

4. James Sambrook, *James Thomson, 1700–1748: A Life* (Oxford: Clarendon Press, 1991), 53; Crawford, 53.

5. Laura Brown, *Alexander Pope* (London: Basil Blackwell, 1985), 40; Christopher Hitt, "Ecocriticism and the Long Eighteenth Century," *College Literature* 31, no. 3 (Summer 2004): 132; Leopold Damrosch, Jr., *The Imaginative World of Alexander Pope* (Berkeley: University of California Press, 1987), 204; Dustin H. Griffin, *Alexander Pope: The Poet in the Poems* (Princeton, N.J: Princeton University Press, 1978), 77, 79; Wallace Jackson, *Vision and Revision in Alexander Pope* (Detroit, MI: Wayne State University Press, 1983), 32; Briraj Singh, "*Windsor Forest* as a Modern and Postmodern Poem," *Historical Reflections/Réflexions Historiques* 18, no. 3 (1992): 30. Ruben Quintero, too, argues that *Windsor-Forest* resists classification, having "acquired a protean aspect which may be more a product of a hermeneutic circle than of true generic intractability." (*Literate Culture: Pope's Rhetorical Art* (Newark: University of Delaware Press, 1992), 43. Roger Lund adds that "the metaphor of *Concordia discors*, and the matrix of allusions which serves to support it, have a significant bearing on how we interpret the details of the poem." ("The Eel of Science: Index Learning, Scriblerian Satire, and the Rise of Information Culture," *Eighteenth-Century Life* 22, no. 2 (1998): 29.

6. Susan J. Wolfson, "Introduction: Reading for Form," in *Reading for Form*, ed. Susan J. Wolfson and Marshall Brown (Seattle: University of Washington Press, 2006), 12. The collection includes J. Paul Hunter's "Formalism and History: Binarism and the Anglophone Couplet," which masterfully demonstrates the insistent complexity generated by the seeming closures of the couplet form: "Pope may well be the cleverest and most subtle employer of couplet ramifications, but he is far from the only poet to understand the couplet's structural abilities to invert, reverse, or complicate balance

and antithesis as manifestations of binary strategies and understanding of the world" (143).

7. Richard Bevis finds "considerable evidence that Pope became disgusted with the corruption of English life during the decade following the publication of 'Windsor Forest'" ("From Windsor Forest to Bartholomew Fair: The Education of an Imperialist," *English Studies in Canada* 17, no. 2 (June 1991): 155; Robin Grove says that after the "graceful" tribute to Denham in *Windsor-Forest,* "Pope was too good at his task. Almost immediately, the patrician manners of his couplet-form are brought to so high a degree of visibility that they simultaneously perfect and mock themselves, revealing how they too are open to contradiction, parody, reversal." ("Nature Methodiz'd," *The Critical Review* 26 (1984): 60, 63. Christine Gerrard, "Pope and the Patriots," in *Pope: New Contexts,* ed. David Fairer (New York: Harvester Wheatsheaf, 1990), 32. John Richardson's commentary combines Brown's critique with that of those who see *Windsor-Forest* as a relatively immature work: "The obscurities and ambiguities of the poem arise . . . less from a need to complicate, as with the later poems, than from a wish to avoid uncomfortable perceptions and a desire to manage unease." ("Alexander Pope's *Windsor Forest:* Its Context and Attitudes toward Slavery," *Eighteenth-Century Studies* 35, no. 1 (2001): 2.

8. Joseph Roach, in *Cities of the Dead: Circum-Atlantic Performance* (New York: Columbia University Press, 1996), provides a nuanced reading of the ways in which Pope engages with the politics of war and peace. He contextualizes Pope's position in the antiwar sentiment prevailing at the time of the poem's composition, saying that "Tories like Pope could point to a war weariness that had become a general malaise by 1710" (134).

The question of Pope's knowledge of and support for the slave trade has been helpfully debated by a number of critics. Richard Bevis believes that "Pope may not have known of the existence of the Assiento (slavery) clause of the Treaty" (151). Howard Erskine-Hill confidently asserts that "at the very historical moment when Britain proposed specifically to engage in the slave trade on an enlarged scale, Pope's idealistic poetic vision totally repudiates slavery." ("Pope and Slavery," in *Alexander Pope: World and Word,* ed. Howard Erskine-Hill. Proceedings of the British Academy, 91 Oxford: Oxford University Press, 1998: 36. Jonathan Pritchard argues that Pope was well aware of the slave trade, in part because his nephew John Rackett was part of it. ("Pope, John Rackett, and the Slave Trade," *SEL* 45 no. 3 (Summer 2005): 579–601). John Richardson attributes the poem's seeming complacency about slavery to Pope's attempt to retain the patronage of both Whigs and Tories: "The story of *Windsor Forest's* political position and its attitude towards slavery, then, is a story of conviction sacrificed to group allegiance, to friendship, and to self-interest" (12).

In a carefully argued discussion of Addison's objections to *Windsor-Forest,* Robert Cummings suggests that the poem's refusal to become political epic, its turn to aestheticism, its "recourse to mere poetry" raised Addison's ire. See "Addison's 'Inexpressible Chagrin' and Pope's Poem on the Peace," *Yearbook of English Studies* 18 (1988): 151. I am arguing that in fact *Windsor-Forest* is a political epic, but one that goes well beyond political factionalism in its interrogation of imperialism.

9. *The Poems of Alexander Pope,* ed. John Butt (London: Methuen, 1963). All references to Pope's poems are from this edition and cited with line number.

10. Robert M. Shmitz, *Pope's Windsor Forest, 1712: A Study of the Washington University Holograph,* Washington University Studies, Language and Literature, n.s. no. 21 (Saint

Louis, MO: Washington University, 1952), 19. A version of this line of thinking turns up in lines 241–44, which describe the healthful properties of English vegetation.

11. Alan Bewell, *Romanticism and Colonial Disease* (Baltimore: Johns Hopkins University Press, 1999) 19. His analysis of *Jane Eyre* shows how, in the moment when Rochester finds solace in the fresh wind from Europe, Brontë "produces one of the most powerful expressions in Victorian literature of an imperial ecological myth. Here liberty, purity, and health are expressed in a geographical symbolism of air and atmosphere" (287).

12. Sanford Budick reads these lines as a straightforward celebration of British power, so that Olympus yields to humbler mountains "just as the vainglorious mountains of ancients and idolaters are displaced by the holy mountains of *Paradise Lost*. The Stuart monarch assimilates the dislocated mythic substance of Pan and Pomona, Flora and Ceres." "Pope and the Hidden God," in *Critical Essays on Alexander Pope,* ed. Wallace Jackson and R. Paul Yoder (New York: G. K Hall, 1993), 144.

13. Daniel Defoe, *A Tour Thro' the whole Island of Great Britain.* 3 vols. (London: Strahan, 1724–27), 1:4.

14. *English Historical Documents, 1660–1714,* 13 vols., ed. Andrew Browning (New York: Oxford University Press, 1953) 8:836.

15. Griffin, *Alexander Pope,* 81; Pat Rogers, "*Windsor-Forest, Britannia* and River Poetry," *Studies in Philology* 77 (1980) 295. Kaul suggests that in the nationalistic poems he discusses, "the oceans made feasible a new internationalism, albeit one in which . . . crucial emblems and technologies of modernity radiate *outward* from the island center of Britain" (39). See also Singh: "the spirit of English enterprise can go abroad in the interests of trade and commerce with wholly gratifying results" (40).

16. Kaul, *Poems of Nation,* 89. And I am, of course, citing Stephen Greenblatt's *Marvelous Possessions: The Wonder of the New World* (Chicago: University of Chicago Press, 1991), especially pages 6, 14, 23, 56–58.

17. G. Wilson Knight, *Laureate of Peace: On the Genius of Alexander Pope* (London: Routledge and Kegan Paul, 1954), 22.

18. Wasserman, *Subtle Language,* 167; Hitt, "Ecocriticism" 132; Brown, *Alexander Pope,* 30–34; Helen Deutsch, *Resemblance & Disgrace: Alexander Pope and the Deformation of Culture* (Cambridge, MA: Harvard University Press, 1996), 55–56; David Morris, *Alexander Pope: The Genius of Sense* (Cambridge, MA: Harvard University Press, 1984), 118. See also Bevis, who refers to "the youthful enthusiasm for converting Windsor's oaks into imperial hulls" (159). Critics also point to Pope's allusion to the Stuarts as the precious burdens carried by royal oaks; see, for example, Wasserman, 110 and Clark Lawlor, "War, Peace and Sexual Politics in Alexander Pope's *Windsor-Forest,*" in *Guerres et paix: La Grande-Bretagne au XVIIIe siècle,* ed. Paul-Gabriel Boucé (Paris: Université de la Sorbonne Nouvelle, 1995), 257.

19. Daniel Defoe, *A Tour through the Whole Island of Great Britain,* ed. Pat Rogers (Harmondsworth, UK: Penguin, 1971), 153.

20. Markley, *Far East,* 4. Markley notes that Thomas Mun, in *A Discourse of Trade* (1621), "argues that cutting down trees for shipbuilding is good for employment, national wealth, and the defense of the realm" (46).

21. Robert Greenhalgh Albion, *Forests and Sea Power: The Timber Problem of the Royal Navy, 1652–1862* (Cambridge, MA: Harvard University Press, 1926), 109–18. He adds that the desire for agricultural land also prevented growth of forests: "for every enclosure made for the growth of oak, there were dozens intended for agriculture. These

latter involved the destruction of hedgerow oaks, and sometimes whole groves were grubbed up. Land once lost for timber purposes was seldom recovered" (119).

22. Jeremy Black, introduction to *The British Navy and the Use of Naval Power in the Eighteenth Century*, ed. Jeremy Black and Philip Woodfine (Atlantic Heights, NJ: Humanities Press International, 1989), 4; Oliver Warner, *The British Navy: A Concise History* (London: Thames and Hudson, 1975), 29–30. N. A. M. Rodger adds that "all European navies depended more or less on mast timber and naval stores imported from the Baltic." *The Command of the Ocean: A Naval History of Britain, 1649–1815* (New York: W.W. Norton & Co, 2004), 175.

23. Dustin Griffin, *Patriotism and Poetry in Eighteenth-Century Britain* (Cambridge: Cambridge University Press, 2002), 56–57.

24. There is a double irony, therefore, in Brown's contention that "The English navy, then, the agent of imperialism, is absent from the poem, replaced by the picturesque pastoral image of the oak" (30).

25. Rodger, *Command of the Ocean*, 178; Black, 10.

26. David Howarth, *British Navy, British Sea Power: How Britain Became Sovereign of the Seas* (New York: Carroll and Graf, 2003).

27. Rodger, *Command of the Ocean*, 166.

28. Edward Gregg quotes Queen Anne's dismissive comment on the Vigo engagement: "you know I never looked ye Sea fight as a victory, & I think what has bin said upon it, as ridiculous as any body can do." Of course, she was writing to Lady Marlborough, and may have wanted to counter the Tory depreciation of Blenheim; as Gregg says, "The queen had immediately perceived that Blenheim represented a turning-point . . . but the Tories were thunderstruck at the victory. They attempted to place it on equal footing with the capture of Gibraltar . . . under the command of the Tory admiral Sir George Rooke . . . the main thrust of their propaganda was to belittle the Marlborough's victory." *Queen Anne* (New Haven, CT: Yale University Press, 1980) 165, 190.

29. Howarth, *British Sea Power*, 244. He adds that British maritime power prevailed after the war only because French, Dutch, and Spanish fleets were more weakened. Bevis locates Pope's disillusionment with the navy later than I do, pointing to Dulness's epic yawn in *The Dunciad*, 4:617–18: "The puny imperial pretensions of Great Britain, deprived of the moral authority that alone could justify them, have been swallowed up by the image of a greater expansionist power, and the Navy that in 1713 seemed destined to carry light to the heathen sits yawning with them in the 'Universal Darkness'" (160). Note that the line immediately before the yawn calls attention to "Unfinish'd Treaties," so that Pope deplores the lack of diplomatic as well as military progress.

30. Kaul, *Poems of Nation*, 140.

31. Warner, *British Navy*, 48; Samuel Pepys, *The Diary of Samuel Pepys*, 11 vols., ed. Robert Latham and William Matthews (Berkeley: University of California Press, 1983), 8.394; *English Historical Documents* 832–33; Howarth, 251. Warner points out that desertion from the navy had a long tradition in England: "when Edward III was assembling the fleet with which he fought a sanguinary battle off Sluys . . . in June 1340, his officers met with much difficulty, particularly on the east coast of England. So much was this so that a long list was made of ships 'which would do nothing by the King's order', some then having 'stealthily left the Fleet, after receiving wages'" (12). England was not alone in its difficulty finding seamen; Lawrence James says that Louis IV's fleet suffered from a "permanent shortage of skilled sailors" in part because the revocation of the Edict of Nantes (protecting French Protestants) had sent many Atlantic seamen to

England. *The Rise and Fall of the British Empire* (New York: St. Martin's Press), 1994, 55.

32. John Chalker finds "an apparent naïveté in Pope's patriotism" in the lines referring to Gibraltar. *The English Georgic: A Study in the Development of a Form* (Baltimore: Johns Hopkins University Press, 1969), 79. Bevis agrees: "Not only is there no hint of disgust at the generic aggression, no sympathy with the 'defenceless' town . . . and no recognition of its right to peace and prosperity . . . there is instead a smug pride in the home team's lopsided victory" (153–54). Pope's revisions here support Bevis's argument, for the new lines replace a more individuated and more pathetic portrait in the 1712 manuscript: "The Young, the Old, one Instant makes our Prize,/And o'er their Captive Heads Britannia's Standard flies" (Schmitz, 24).

33. Pat Rogers, *The Symbolic Design of Windsor-Forest: Iconography, Pageant, and Prophecy in Pope's Early Work* (Newark: University of Delaware Press, 2004), 98.

34. It has, of course, been argued that Pope in fact celebrates naval power (whether military or commercial) as part of the Tory agenda. Rodger points out that the Tory government in 1710 pursued a "Blue-Water policy" (178), and Rogers says that 'an emphasis on naval, as opposed to military, force was a touchstone of Tory sentiment." ("John Philips, Pope, and the Political Georgic," *Modern Language Quarterly* 66, no. 4 (December 2005): 434. Pope's political ambivalence at this time has been discussed by Christine Gerrard, who says that Pope resisted Lyttleton's urgings to write a patriotic poem, and by J. A. Downie, who takes issue with the standard identification of Pope with Tories and Jacobites. Gerrard, "Pope and the Patriots," *Pope: New Contexts*, 25–43; Downie, "1688: Pope and the Rhetoric of Jacobitism," 9–24. John Richardson locates *Windsor-Forest* at the moment when Pope was moving away from Whig friends and toward Tory patronage (7–9).

35. Heather Jurgens, "*Windsor-Forest* and Augustan Stability," *Unisa English Studies* 2 (1967): 18; Quintero, *Literate Culture*, 62. This is, of course, at the heart of Brown's argument that "the displacement of the military and political into the pastoral makes an evocation of imperial oppression possible even in this celebration of the English nation" (38). See also Bevis: "Albion's armies . . . define the chase and the war as proximate acts compelling the same emotions from the same youths" (23); Budick says that the principle of displacement includes the "theme of violence sublimated. . . . Dangerous energies are only imprisoned and directed to higher ends" (140).

36. Damrosch, *Imaginative World*, 276.

37. Wasserman and Ronald Paulson both see an ambiguity even in the description of innocent victims. Wasserman points to the pikes that tyrannize the rivers (132), and Paulson argues that the resplendent appearance of the pheasant "make[s] him a symbol of pride and its consequent fall, of vanitas and pathetic loss." ("The Aesthetics of Georgic Renewal: Pope," in *Critical Essays on Alexander Pope*, ed. Wallace Jackson and R. Paul Yoder (New York: G. K. Hall, 1993) 124.

38. Beth Fowkes Tobin, in *Colonizing Nature: The Tropics in British Arts and Letters, 1760–1820* (Philadelphia: University of Pennsylvania Press, 2005), reads the hunting scenes quite differently; she finds that the poem "naturalizes these activities by stressing the seasonal aspect of hunting and implying that the hunter's activities, because they are in harmony with the seasons, are as natural as the farmer's" (39).

39. My reading finds congruence where John Chalker finds contrast:' 'The Norman hunt is inspired by passion and leads to the disintegration of order. The modern huntsman, in contrast, takes his place in a fruitful and prosperous scene" (78).

40. Thomson too compares man unfavorably to beasts of prey, which have at least the grace to hunt by night: "As if their conscious ravage shunned the light/Ashamed. Not so the steady tyrant, man" (*Autumn* 389–90). I am reminded by both hunting scenes of Tess Durbeyfield's meditation on hunters, "strangely accoutred, a blood-thirsty light in their eyes. . . . they ran amuck, and made it their purpose to destroy life—in this case harmless feathered creatures, brought into being by artificial means solely to gratify these propensities." (Thomas Hardy, *Tess of the D'Urbervilles*, ed. Scott Elledge (New York: Norton, 1991) 218.

41. See Morris: "both warfare and hunting are, for Pope, arts that are unworthy of England's potential for civilized improvement" (122); and Singh: "if the hunt is praised but also criticized, foreign wars are criticized but also praised" (35). Jackson rightly points out that "To hunt man with Nimrod, or nymph with Pan, or pheasant with swain, or France with England provides a variety of exercises that are all highly inter-changeable and compatible" (25). I extend their arguments by suggesting that even after actual military conflict is over, the very possession of imperial power serves to corrupt the character.

42. Wasserman, *Subtle Language*, 159. Cummings reads these lines as further evidence of Pope making aesthetic what was military and political: "The notion that France bleeds forever is made a triumph only of poetry and not of arms" (149).

43. Helen Cam, *England before Elizabeth* (New York: Harper & Row, 1960), 152, 177. Pope's reference to (and preference for) the negotiated Peace of Utrecht also looks forward to William Makepeace Thackeray's famous passage about Waterloo and its effect on the French:

> They pant for an opportunity of revenging their humiliation; and if a contest, ending in a victory on their part, should ensue, elating them in their turn, and leaving its cursed legacy of hatred and rage behind to us, there is no end to the so-called glory and shame, and to the alternations of successful and unsuccessful murder, in which two high-spirited nations might engage. Centuries hence, we Frenchmen and Englishmen might be boasting and killing each other still, carrying out bravely the Devil's code of honour. *Vanity Fair: A Novel Without a Hero*, ed. Geoffrey and Kathleen Tillotson (Boston: Houghton Mifflin, 1963) 314

Pat Rogers finds that "Pope contrives to make his tribute to Edward III perform more than a narrow referential function: it integrates the historical material with the local setting as well as connects the chivalric and military themes with the current war and the prestige of the current monarch." ("John Philips," 437. The connection is indeed there, but it may work against the celebration of the current war.

44. I am in partial agreement here with Wallace Jackson, who points out that "throughout his career, Pope appears particularly alert . . . to the forms of human aggression. In *Windsor-Forest* his notations on this subject arise from a reflective engagement with history and the pervasiveness of its ruling principle, 'blood'" (18). I don't believe, however, that the poem's "subject lends itself to the aphoristic reduction that passion has imperial ends to serve, and that man is saved from himself by assimilation into the larger stream of national dedication. So in this way are we returned to the permissible terms of blood-letting" (26). It seems to me that Pope shows how imperial passions, including bloodlust, come back to Britain with those who have served the empire.

45. Quintero, *Literate Culture*, 63.

46. Mack, pointing out the biblical analogy here, says, "Isaiah, in part, has in mind

the future humiliation of kings and people who have humiliated Israel; Pope, in part, the restoration of kings and peoples who have been plundered by Europeans" (103).

47. Shmidz, 40.

48. In *Selected Poetry and Prose of John Dryden*, ed. Earl Miner (New York: Random House, 1969), line 45.

49. Rogers, "*Windsor-Forest, Britannia* and River Poetry," 297. Paul Fussell similarly connects place and patriotism: "The castle was begun by William the Conqueror, and its very idea stimulates Pope to a flurry of loyal sentiments . . . as he traces the history of British chivalry from Edward III to Queen Anne." (*The Rhetorical World of Augustan Humanism: Ethics and Imagery from Swift to Burke* (Oxford: Clarendon Press, 1965), 207.

50. Rogers, "*Windsor-Forest*," 298. Virginia C. Kenny, *The Country-House Ethos in English Literature, 1688–1750: Themes of Personal Retreat and National Expansion* (New York: St. Martin's Press, 1984), 76.

51. Gregg, *Queen Anne*, 107. Gregg quotes a letter from Anne to Lady Marlborough in which the future queen openly expresses her contempt for her brother-in-law: "that Monster who from ye first moment of his coming has used us at that rate . . . Suppose I did submit & that the King could change his nature so much as to use me with humanety [*sic*] . . . how would that Dutch abortive laugh at me & please himself with having got ye better. . . . she can waite with patience for a SunShine day. . . . She hopes England will flourish againe" (89). Wasserman points out that after 1688, it was "possible for Tories to turn the tables, and, taking advantage of the traditional Whiggish hatred of the Normans, to attach to the Conqueror the same kind of tyranny they found in William III" (114).

52. Jonathan Swift, *Journal to Stella*, ed. Harold Williams, 2 vols. (Oxford: Clarendon Press, 1948), 1.328. John Robert Moore points out that "In 1706, in advocating a general policy of deforestation, an able writer urged that Windsor Forest should be spared because Queen Anne herself occasionally hunted there. Such a fact must have been familiar to Pope, but it would not have suited his purpose; in his poem the royal hunters were men of violence and usurpation." "Windsor Forest and William III," *Modern Language Notes* 66, no. 7 (November 1951): 453.

53. Powerful rhetoric perhaps connects Queen Anne with Pope. As Budick suggests, Pope "points to the magic circle of public poetry in which poet and monarch can only conjure jointly" (139). According to Budick, the poem enacts a fantasy: "Pope's image of a controlling, reigning sovereign, who oversees toilsome industry and far-flung commerce, who must carefully manage her nation's stores so that plenty can be preserved, and who harmonizes the forces of discord into a loud chord of 'Peace!' is not the image of an Eve home on her hill in Eden. . . . Windsor-Forest/England cannot be Eden" (144).

54. Gregg, *Queen Anne*, 367.

55. The language used by Edward Gregg replicates the Whig attitude toward the Treaty of Utrecht: on a single page of his biography of Queen Anne, he uses the phrases "at the expense of the allies," "this stark betrayal of the allies," "such gross betrayal of the allies" (335). Ian K. Steele offers another angle on "perfidious Albion." According to Steele, "The most complex and enduring European peace in the early eighteenth century, the Peace of Utrecht, began as a four-month truce agreed to in August 1712. English, French, and Spanish forces were to refrain from war between 12 August and 12 December 1712." Because prizes taken at sea were valid until news reached the warring parties on the other side of the Atlantic, letters announcing the truce with

Spain were sent slowly, so that England could inflict more damage to the Spanish colonial interests. "The perfidiousness that is rightly associated with the English government in these peace negotiations was . . . evident." *The English Atlantic, 1675–1740: An Exploration of Communication and Community* (New York: Oxford University Press, 1986), 195–96). Obviously, I take issue with Lawlor's contention that "The fundamental assumption of Pope's representation of war and peace in *Windsor-Forest* is that masculinity is stable and conducive to peace. . . . femininity is unstable and likely to result in war unless measures are taken to bring it under masculine control" (266).

56. Rogers, "River Poetry," 298. Vincent Caretta, in "Anne and Elizabeth: The Poet as Historian in *Windsor Forest*," connects the Lodona episode with the poem's identification of the two queens: "Straying beyond the permissible bounds of the Forest, just as England strayed from its original principles after Elizabeth's reign, Lodona-England becomes the victim of lust and irrational passion. . . . The Lodona episode then would be Pope's mythic representation of the evils that befell England when she transgressed beyond the bounds of the original Constitution restored under Gloriana." *Studies in English Literature, 1500–1900* 21, no. 3 (Summer 1981), 433. Knight suggests that in *Windsor-Forest*, "An Elizabethan royalism is captured" (327).

57. *Elizabeth I: Collected Works*, ed. Leah S. Marcus, Janel Mueller and Mary Beth Rose (Chicago: University of Chicago Press, 2000), 329.

58. George Lillo, *The London Merchant*, ed. William H. McBurney (Lincoln: University of Nebraska Press, 1965), I.i.44–48.

59. Interestingly, Wallace T. MacCaffrey makes a reverse analogy in *Elizabeth I: War and Politics, 1588–1603* (Princeton, N.J.: Princeton University Press, 1992), 7:

> Superficially England's position in the 1590s seemed comparable with that a century later—in the wake of the Glorious Revolution. In both eras she was part of a grand alliance that, in the 1590's as in the 1690's, aimed at checking the overweening ambitions of one great power and focused on a succession crisis. The maritime powers, England and the United Provinces, were partners, and England's enemies would seek to strike at her soft underbelly, Ireland. However, the analogy cannot be pressed further. The alliance of the 1690's was guided by the directing intelligence and the authority of William III. Elizabeth's England was little more than an auxiliary to her clamant partners.

Elsewhere, MacCaffrey points to Elizabeth's "cool conviction that there was no issue on which reasonable rulers could not reach accommodation. Surely all must see the obvious truth that nothing was more fruitless or destructive than war." (*Elizabeth I* (London: Edward Arnold, 1993), 182. She had, apparently, to contend for peace against Raleigh, who wrote: "If the late queen had believed her men of war as she did her scribes, we had in her time beaten the great empire in pieces, and made their kings kings of figs and oranges" (cited in Paul J. Hammer, *Elizabeth's Wars: War, Government, Society in Tudor England* (New York: Palgrave, 2003), 1. Like Elizabeth, says Gregg, Anne "was determined that nothing should prevent her kingdoms from enjoying the benefits of peace" (341).

60. John Barrell and Harriet Guest, "On the Use of Contradiction: Economics and Morality in the Eighteenth-Century Long Poem," in *The New Eighteenth Century*, ed. Felicity Nussbaum and Laura Brown (New York: Methuen, 1987) 136; Patricia Meyer Spacks, *The Varied God: A Critical Study of Thomson's The Seasons* (Berkeley: University of California Press, 1959), 174–75; Cohen, *The Art of Discrimination*, 129–30. See also Tomlinson, "Landscape into Allegory," 193 and Bruyn, "From Georgic Poetry to Sta-

tistics and Graphs," 119. Of course, Dr. Johnson had noted that "The great defect of the Seasons is want of method" but conceded that its multiplicities made order unattainable. *Lives of the English Poets,* 2 vols. (London: Oxford University Press, 1967), 2:359. Barrell, in an earlier study, points out that "whoever reads *The Seasons* must observe that it appears to be committed to two quite opposite views of history. On the one hand, the history of society has been one of decline, from an age of innocence to a period of luxury and strife; on the other, society has progressed . . . to a point of perfection." *English Literature in History, 1730–80: An Equal, Wide Survey* (New York: St. Martin's Press, 1983), 54.

61. Kaul, *Poems of Nation,* 144.

62. Ibid., 164.

63. Lennard J. Davis, *Resisting Novels: Ideology and Fiction* (New York: Methuen, 1987), 63.

64. Howard D. Weinbrot, in *Britannia's Issue: The Rise of British Literature from Dryden to Ossian* (Cambridge: Cambridge University Press, 1993) argues that British imperial ideology required commitment to trade: "natives . . . should not be destroyed or enslaved in the Spanish manner; instead, they should be turned into clothed middle-men who thereafter clothe their brothers and sisters in British garb" (258). Thomson's tactic clothes them in British identity as well as clothes. See also chapter 3 of Mary Louise Pratt's *Imperial Eyes: Travel Writing and Transculturation* (London: Routledge, 1992) for a sustained analysis of how descriptions of landscape and ethnography work together to "install a Eurocolonial discursive order whose territorial and visual forms of authority are those of the modern state" (65).

65. Jay Fliegelman, in *Prodigals and Pilgrims: The American Revolution against Patriarchal Authority, 1750-1800* (Cambridge: Cambridge University Press, 1982) reminds us that *The Seasons* was approvingly cited by both Benjamin Franklin and Tom Paine (42).

66. Margaret Ann Doody, in *The Daring Muse: Augustan Poetry Reconsidered* (Cambridge: Cambridge University Press, 1985), points out that "however disagreeable or embarrassing it may be both to people of other nations and to the British now . . . the poetry of the 'Augustan Age' is the poetry that arose during England's first great age of imperialism" (15).

67. Kathleen Wilson, *The Sense of the People: Politics, Culture and Imperialism in England, 1715–1785* (Cambridge: Cambridge University Press, 1998), 157.

68. Ibid., 152. See also Linda Colley, "Radical Patriotism in Eighteenth-Century England," in *Patriotism: The Making and Unmaking of British National Identity,* 3 vols., ed. Raphael Samuel (London: Routledge, 1989), 1:169–87, and P. J. Cain and A. G. Hopkins, "Gentlemanly Capitalism and British Expansion Overseas: The Old Colonial System, 1688–1850," *Economic History Review* 2nd ser., 39,4 (1986): 501–25. For a discussion of Thomson's own Opposition principles, see Philip Ronald Stormer, "Holding 'High Commerce with the Mighty Dead': Morality and Politics in James Thomson's *Winter,*" *English Language Notes* 29 (March 1992): 27–40.

69. Robert Bliss, *Revolution and Empire: English Politics and the American Colonies in the Seventeenth Century* (Manchester: Manchester University Press, 1990), 8–9.

70. Henry Grey Graham, *Scottish Men of Letters in the Eighteenth Century* (London: Adam and Charles Black, 1908), 300.

71. Ralph Cohen, in *The Unfolding of the Seasons* (Baltimore: Johns Hopkins University Press, 1970), wryly speculates that the uncivilized natives in the later passage, "if Thomson is not to contradict himself within ten lines, must refer to tribes other than the happy ones" (136).

72. Kaul notes that these lines, which enact the "entire allegory of the violence at the heart of trade," show the "attendant tensions and anxieties" of constructing a hymn to trade (158–59).

73. John More, *Strictures, Critical and Sentimental, on Thomson's Seasons; with Hints and Observations on Collateral Subjects* (London: Richardson and Urquart, 1777; facsimile, New York: Garland Publishing Co., 1970), 147–48.

74. Samuel Taylor Coleridge, *The Rhyme of the Ancient Mariner*, ed. Paul H. Fry (Boston: Bedford/St. Martin's, 1999), line 162 (1817 text). The best-known literary treatment of the siege of Cartagena and the subsequent disease that struck the forces is in Smollett's *Adventures of Roderick Random:* "The change of the atmosphere . . . conspired with the stench that surrounded us, the heat of the climate, our own constitutions impoverished by bad provision, and our despair, to introduce the bilious fever among us, which raged with such violence that three fourths of those whom it invaded, died in a deplorable manner; the colour of their skin, being by the extreme putrefaction of their juices, changed into that of soot." Ed. Paul-Gabriel Boucé (Oxford: Oxford University Press, 1981), 189–90.

75. Cohen points out that "In the torrid zone, at blaze of noon, the sun is itself oppressed . . . and elements are at war in a furious tropical storm." *Unfolding*, 131. Alan Dougald McKillop points out that in revising *Summer*, Thomson made the tropics less horrific, in accordance with "a better knowledge of geography, a quest for the earthly paradise, eagerness to point out the beneficent works of God in the creation, and propaganda for conquest and colonization." *The Background of Thomson's Seasons* (Hamden, CT: Archon Books, 1961), 148. While there are indeed descriptions of delights available in the torrid zone, the emphasis, it seems to me, remains on its barbarity.

76. Laura Brown, "Reading Race and Gender: Jonathan Swift," *Eighteenth-Century Studies* 23, no. 4 (Summer 1990): 436–39; Nussbaum, *Limits of the Human*, 11. Nussbaum adds, "For the monogenists, differences in pigmentation or physical features might then be ascribed to geography, migration, mutation, climate, diet, and cultural customs instead of descrete moments of creation. . . . In the more secular polygenetic account, inequalities and distinctions were explained by multiple creations having taken place in two or three places on one single historical occasion " (11–12). Sambrook, in the note to the lines quoted, says that "The influence of climate and other natural causes upon the national character and history of nations was a favourite topic for popular historians of the period" (247).

77. Anne McClintock, *Imperial Leather: Race, Gender and Sexuality in the Colonial Context* (New York: Routledge, 1995), 6–7. She extends this notion when she adds, "Through the rituals of domesticity, increasingly global and more often than not violent, animals, women and colonized peoples were wrested from their putatively 'natural' yet, ironically, 'unreasonable' state of 'savagery' and inducted through the domestic progress narrative into a hierarchical relation to white men" (35). Felicity Nussbaum, in *Torrid Zones: Maternity, Sexuality, and Empire in Eighteenth-Century English Narratives* (Baltimore: Johns Hopkins University Press, 1995) says that "the territory inhabited and penetrated by the colonist is figured as woman" (3). Balachandra Rajan makes a similar point: "The feminization of the land in America, allegedly empty and awaiting the masculine imprint, could be contrasted with the feminine civilization of a populous Orient. . . . The New World's proximity to innocence (and also to savagery) could be set against a sophistication in Asia perceived as verging on decadence." *Under Western Eyes: India from Milton to Macaulay* (Durham, NC: Duke University Press, 1999), 18. See also

Christopher Flynn, "Nationalism, Commerce, and Imperial Anxiety in Defoe's Later Works," *Rocky Mountain Review* (Fall 2000). Defoe is concerned to "represent the Other in terms that rendered it familiar yet inferior, and as such colonizable and possesable" (11).

78. See Nussbaum's analysis of Hogarth's *Marriage à la Mode:* "The geography of defect and race here intertwine with corrupt femininity and masculinity in England to domesticate and creolize them. The remarkable and regular conjunction of these categories of racial and gendered subjects complicate Englsih perceptions of the defective within and without the country" (16).

79. Nussbaum points out that "since the color of complexion was an index to virtue by the eighteenth century . . . a black Imoinda could not easily represent a decorous and heroic femininity on stage." *Limits of the Human,* 158. Spacks argues that 'the praise of English womanhood . . . seems a somewhat purposeless exercise in convention" (*Varied God,* 47), but in fact the description strengthens the link between beauty and color.

80. See Helen Carr and Peter Hulme in *Europe and Its Others: Proceedings of the Essex Conference on the Sociology of Literature, July 1984,* ed. Francis Barker, Peter Hulme, Margaret Iversen, and Diana Loxley (Colchester, UK: University of Essex, 1985). Carr, in "Woman/Indian: 'The American' and His Others," says "Woman is the European man's primary Other. . . . So the first effect of transferal is to naturalize the desire for, and legitimize the right to, possession" (49). Hulme, in "Polytropic Man: Tropes of Sexuality and Mobility in Early Colonial Discourse," talks about how this fantasy may be disrupted by natives: "even if you have the Virgin queen bringing fruitfulness to a barbarous yet virgin chaos through the surrogates of her male courtiers, the cosiness of this colonial romance is inevitably disturbed by the unfortunate presence of the other parties who were there beforehand and who could only be seen as, at best, recalcitrant fathers or brothers holding back the love-match" (18).

The staying power of this fantasy of imperialism is remarkable. In 1940, the British Library of Information issued a pamphlet designed to reassure those might question British policy regarding former colonies subsumed into the Commonwealth. *What Is British Imperialism?* explains that these territories are "not, from an economic point of view sufficiently advanced or sufficiently stable to support the grave responsibilities of self-government" or to deal with "dangerous political conditions or complex race problems" (4). Echoing the earlier ideology of empire as guardian, the pamphlet adds that "the British Commonwealth and its Allies are fighting to preserve the rich and promising growth of free communities against a violent resurgence of the crudest and most inhumane kind of imperialism led by Nazi Germany" (5).

81. Cohen, *Unfolding,* 166. Cain and Hopkins trace the way capitalist imperialism united otherwise antagonistic gentry and industrialists: "The pressures of class conflict often forced industrialists to come to terms with gentlemanly capitalism to create a broad front of propertied interests. Given their indirect relationship with the productive process, and their paternalist relations with their own more fragmented and less class-conscious workforce, gentlemanly capitalists could present themselves more easily as 'natural' leaders, while also benefiting from developments in which industrial capitalism was the most visible agent of change" (508).

82. For a different take on Thomson's peasants, see Tobin: "Thomson's depiction of rural England's husbandry and agriculture shares with Pope's the elision of the direct agricultural producer" (52).

83. Robin W. Winks, introduction to *British Imperialism: Gold, God, and Glory,* ed.

Robin W. Winks (New York: Holt, Rinehart and Winston, 1963), 3. The volume includes an excerpt from Elie Halévy, *A History of the English People in the Nineteenth Century* (1961), which reiterates this point: the British annexed colonies because they believed "that tropical conditions did not admit of the spontaneous development of great independent civilizations" (55). David Armitage, too, makes the point that "Thomson's Britannia . . . ruled an empire of difference, defined by its oppositions, where men would defend women, freemen would not be slaves, liberty would defeat tyranny, and the empire of the seas would outlive, outfight and outprosper military monarchies with territorial dominions" (173).

84. DeBruyn, "From Georgic Poetry," 116. Other critics who juxtapose the two poems include Battestin, Griffin, Kaul, and Crawford.

85. Damrosch, *Imaginative World,* 281.

86. Griffin, *Alexander Pope,* 77.

87. Sambrook, *James Thomson,* 74. Lawrence James, alluding to the episode of Captain Jenkins's ear during one such confrontation, says that by 1739, "the mercantile interest clamoured for war" (59). Defoe's *Colonel Jack,* discussed in the following chapter, represents at some length Spanish response to illicit trade.

88. Kathleen Wilson, "Empire, Trade and Popular Politics in Mid-Hanoverian Britain: The Case of Admiral Vernon," *Past and Present* 121 (November 1988): 79.

CHAPTER 2. FAMILIAL IDENTIFICATIONS

1. Tobias Smollett, *The Letters of Tobias Smollett,* ed. Lewis M. Knapp (Oxford: Clarendon Press, 1970), xxii.

2. Daniel Defoe, *The Letters of Daniel Defoe,* ed. George Harris Healey (Oxford: Clarendon Press, 1955), 344.

3. Defoe, *Letters,* 278. On the other hand, he writes with approval of Scots' celerity in taking advantage of opportunities made available by the Union: "as the Union open'd the Door to the *Scots* in our *American* Colonies, the *Glasgow* Merchants presently fell in with the Opportunity. . . . they send near fifty Sail of Ships every year" *A Tour Thro' the Whole Island,* 3:85–86.

4. *A Tour Thro' the Whole Island,* 3.viii, 5. Paula R. Backscheider finds that Defoe became less patient with Scots as he extended his stay: "He found the Scots stubborn, irrational, violent, refractory, susceptible to rumor, and fickle. . . . he tirelessly exhorted Scots to give up their foolish prejudices and join together to build a new Scotland." *Daniel Defoe, His Life* (Baltimore: Johns Hopkins University Press, 1989), 251.

5. Smollett, *Letters,* 33.

6. Daniel Defoe, *Defoe's Review,* 22 vols, ed. Arthur Wellesley Secord (New York: Columbia University Press, 1938), I:136. Defoe's writings have frequently been characterized as imperial propaganda: Aparna Dharwadker finds that Defoe "argues endlessly for colonial expansion." "Nation, Race, and the Ideology of Commerce in Defoe," *The Eighteenth Century* 39, no. 1 (1998): 64, and Bruce McLeod says Defoe "was up to his neck in colonial schemes for the Americas. . . . [his] eye is intrinsically colonial." *The Geography of Empire in English Literature,* 177, 200. J. A. Downie connects Defoe's colonial and commercial agendas: "The character of Defoe's imperialist vision is mundane rather than ideological. His fiercely practical mind was stimulated by the increased opportunities for trade which empire offered rather than by a visionary scheme of British

hegemony." "Defoe, Imperialism, and the Travel Books Reconsidered," *Critical Essays on Daniel Defoe*, ed. Roger D. Lund (New York: G. K. Hall and Co., 1997), 85.

7. Daniel Defoe, *Atlas Maritimus and Commercialis* (London: James and John Knapton, 1728), 328.

8. *A Tour Thro' the Whole Island*, 3.140, 147. Amit Yahav-Brown is one of many critics who note this consistent pattern of return: Defoe's heroes "invariably gravitate back to England throughout their lives, even though they make most of their money outside their native country." "At Home in England, or Projecting Liberal Citizenship in *Moll Flanders*," *Novel* 35, no. 1 (Fall 2001): 25.

9. Azim, *Colonial Rise of the Novel*, 85; Lucette Desvignes notes "avec amusement qu'elle a choisi la vieille Angleterre pour le terme d'une vie dont la plénitude a ses racines dans le Nouveau Monde." "Vues de la terre promise: les visages de l'Amérique dans *Moll Flanders* et dans l'*Histoire de Manon Lescaut*," *Transactions of the Fourth International Congress on the Enlightenment*, ed. Teodore Besterman (Oxford: Voltaire Foundation, 1976), 551; Rita di Giuseppe suggests that "it is perhaps the final irony that she should choose to go back to an England rife with repression when many subjects of the crown were in either self-imposed or enforced exile." "The Ghost in the Machine: *Moll Flanders* and the Body Politic," *Quaderni di Lingue e Letteratura* 18 (1993): 326. See also Tony Dunn, "Moll Flanders: Body and Capital," *Q/W/E/R/T/Y* 7 (October 1997): 61, and Brett C. McInelly, "Exile or Opportunity?: The Plight of the Transported Felon in Daniel Defoe's *Moll Flanders* and *Colonel Jack*," *Genre* 22 (2001): 213. Yahav-Brown advances the interesting thesis that "when Defoe brings Moll back to England, he underscores the significance of the rights-bearing status of political membership for anyone born under English jurisdiction" (37).

10. David Leon Higdon, "The Chronology of *Moll Flanders*," *English Studies* 56 (1975): 318.

11. Lincoln B. Faller, *Crime and Defoe: A New Kind of Writing* (Cambridge: Cambridge University Press, 1993), 168; Yahav-Brown, "At Home in England," 33. But see John Richetti, who argues in *Defoe's Narratives: Situations and Structures* (Oxford: Clarendon Press, 1975) that events in Moll's childhood are not represented as traumatic but "are as much illustrations of her independence and somehow instinctive sense of strong isolation as they are examples of social determinism" (98).

12. Walter Scott uses a similar plot device in *The Heart of Midlothian;* Effie's fugitive son boards a ship to avoid legal authorities, but the ship-master, "inured by his evil trade to every species of treachery . . . secured the person of the fugitive, and having transported him to America, sold him as a slave, or indentured servant, to a Virginia planter" Ed. David Hewett and Alison Lumsden (Edinburgh: Edinburgh University Press, 2004), 467. Both episodes reenact the kidnapping of Oroonoko by the duplicitous English captain.

13. Lou Caton, "Doing the Right Thing with *Moll Flanders*: A 'Reasonable' Difference between the Picara and the Penitent," *CLA Journal* 40, no. 4 (June 1997): 514–15. Beth Swan echoes Caton's reading: Moll's "optimism reflects Defoe's belief in transportation as a means of allowing felons the opportunity to break the pattern of crime and make a new life for themselves within society rather than in conflict with it." "Moll Flanders: The Felon as Lawyer," *Eighteenth-Century Fiction* 11, no. 1 (October 1998): 45.

14. A. Roger Ekirch, *Bound for America: The Transportation of British Convicts to the Colonies, 1718–1775* (Oxford: Clarendon Press, 1987), 158. Peter Wilson Coldham says that

"the majority [of convicts] were fated to remain tied to a form of serfdom which distinguished them little from bonded slaves." *Emigrants in Chains: A Social History of Forced Emigration to the Americas, 1607-1776* (Phoenix Mill, UK: Alan Sutton Publishing Ltd., 1992), 1.

15. Richard Hakluyt, *Divers Voyages Touching the Discoverie of America* (Ann Arbor, MI: University Microfilms Inc., 1966; facsimile of 1582 edition), 1–2. Paula R. Backscheider quotes a 1704–1705 judgment from a justice of the peace: "they are lewd idle fellows, and it is fitting the country should be clear'd of them. They are strong able body'd men and may do good service either in her Majesty's Plantations or army" (485). Coldham cites a contrary view: a 1606 letter from Francis Bacon to Villiers argues that criminals were not fit to populate a new colony (45).

16. Ekirch, *Bound for America*, 16, 3. John O'Brien argues that when the Jacobites of 1715 were banished to America, "the interests of both sides were served; the Jacobites avoided the gallows, and the government avoided having to put the rebels on trial for treason, which might have raised public sympathy." "Union Jack: Amnesia and the Law in Daniel Defoe's *Colonel Jack,*" *Eighteenth-Century Studies* 32, no. 1 (1998): 72.

17. 4 Geo I, Cap. XI, reproduced in Coldham, Appendix III, 165. Coldham adds that the act also forced reluctant colonies to accept convicts: "The evil consequences in the overseas territories were not, from now on, to be weighed heavily against the obvious advantages to the mother country" (61). Ekirch, too, concludes that "transportation was intended to serve British, not colonial needs. Despite Parliament's reference in the Transportation Act to America's want of servants, clearly judges, juries, and high crown officials never gave genuine consideration to labour shortages in banishing men and women to America" (45). Both *Moll Flanders* and *Colonel Jack* are set before the Transportation Act, so felons in these texts are *granted* transportation; after the act, transportation itself became a sentence.

18. *English Historical Documents, American Colonial Documents to 1776,* ed. Merrill Jensen (New York: Oxford University Press, 1955), 489. Alan Taylor points out that "planters readily resorted to the whip, convinced that only fear and pain could motivate servants. . . . Until their terms expired, the servants were fundamentally property rather than people." *American Colonies* (Harmondsworth, UK: Penguin, 2001) 143. Alan Atkinson's research indicates that for the first two decades of transportation, convicts were treated like indentured servants, but as their numbers increased, they were more likely to be treated like slaves: "the process of degradation can be traced back to the 1718 Act. An Englishman valued the right of consent, shaped as it was, in principle, to his condition in life. The 1718 Act had separated the right of consent from the business of transportation" "The Free-Born Englishman Transported: Convict Rights as a Measure of Eighteenth-Century Empire," *Past and Present* 144 (August 1994): 101, 103–4. See also George E. Boulukos, "Daniel Defoe's *Colonel Jack,* Grateful Slaves, and Racial Difference," *ELH* 68 (2001). Boulukos argues that, in 1722, the term *slave* was not exclusive to African laborers and that *Colonel Jack* narrativizes an emerging sense of racial status (615–16). Richard Dunn notes that white servants in America "resented cultivating tobacco and cotton in the hot sun and either idled or tried to escape," which led to increased importation of African slaves. "Servants and Slaves: The Recruitment and Employment of Labor," *Colonial British America: Essays in the New History of the Early Modern Era,* ed. Jack P. Greene and J. R. Pole (Baltimore: Johns Hopkins University Press, 1984), 166.

Of course, convicts of means could circumvent the degrading and dangerous fate described by Aaron S. Fogelman: "After sentencing, British authorities marched groups of convicts through the streets in chains to the ships. Because they made the long voyage to America below deck in cramped quarters, their death rate was high (about 14 per cent)." "From Slaves, Convicts, and Servants to Free Passengers," 56. Coldham cites the notorious thief Jenny Diver as an example of a transported convict who drew on illicit earnings to ease her passage to the New World; moneyed convicts like Jenny (and Moll) could "ride in cheerful consort with the contractor in his carriage to the ship, take up their quarters in a private cabin, spend the voyage in sociable indolence, and spend only as much time at the port of landing as it took to arrange their freedom and passage onwards" (128). See also Ekirch on special treatment for "well-to-do transports" (102).

19. Abbot Emerson Smith, *Colonists in Bondage: White Servitude and Convict Labor in America, 1607–1776* (Chapel Hill: University of North Carolina Press, 1947), 233.

20. Moll thus circumvents the provision in Article XII of the Habeas Corpus Act of 1679, which specifically excludes rights of convicts and indentured servants: "nothing in this Act shall extend to give benefit to any person who shall by contract in writing agree with any merchant or owner of any plantation, or any other person whatsoever, to be transported to any parts beyond seas, and receive earnest upon such agreement, although that afterwards such person shall renounce such contract." *English Historical Documents, 1660–1714,* 95.

21. David S. Lovejoy, "Virginia's Charter and Bacon's Rebellion, 1675–1676," *Anglo-American Political Relations, 1675–1775,* ed. Alison Gilbert Olsen and Richard Maxwell Brown (New Brunswick, NJ: Rutgers University Press, 1972), 33. David W. Galenson says that by the 1660s, more than half of arrivals in Maryland "failed to become landowners, and none of these former servants acquired great wealth." *The Cambridge Economic History of the United States,* vol. 1, *The Colonial Era,* ed. Stanley L. Engerman and Robert E. Gallman (Cambridge: Cambridge University Press, 1996), 188.

The situation did not improve later in the seventeenth century. David Alan Williams tells us, "By 1692 King William's War had thoroughly disrupted the tobacco trade and closed European markets. . . . In some years no tobacco ships at all appeared in the upper reaches of the Potomac, tobacco rotted on the wharfs and in warehouses, and colonists were reduced to growing cotton and weaving their own linsey-woolsey." "Anglo-American Virginia Politics, 1690–1735," *Anglo-American Relations,* 81. Richard S. Dunn believes that the phenomenon of continuing lower-class emigration can be explained by the failure to find work in port cities: "Only such a pattern can explain why English laborers flocked in great numbers to Virginia and Barbados at a time when disease, mortality rates, and agricultural working conditions were so disadvantageous to newcomers" (162).

22. McInelly, "Exile or Opportunity," 211. Since transportation was no longer voluntary by the time Defoe composed these two texts, the propaganda in favor of transportation must be directed to the British public, who might have had some reservations about the wholesale export of criminals to America. My own reading is more congruent with that of Richetti, who connects Moll and Jack's success in America to their highly developed sense of individuality (141, 165). One sign of Moll's and Jack's separateness from other convicts and servants can be seen in their blithe dismissal of their peers. Moll's silence regarding her fellow convicts has been noted by Desvignes: "Pas un mot sur les autres malheureux qui faisaint partie du même convoie . . . Moll évite le contact

de ses compagnes de misère" (547). Note that Jack disposes of Captain Jack's career in one paragraph and never refers to the fate of "the other *Englishman,* who was my fellow Deserter" in Scotland (118).

23. Jack's plaint sounds remarkably like that of William Byrd, who wrote in 1690: "wee are here att the end of the World . . . and Europe may bee turned topsy turvy ere wee can hear, a Word of itt." Qtd. in Ned C. Landsman, *From Colonials to Provincials: American Thought and Culture, 1680–1760* (Ithaca, NY: Cornell University Press, 1997), 9. Patrick Brady calls *Moll Flanders'*s America an "anti-Paradise": "the characters continue to think of the New World alternative as a prison, an exile, from which they yearn to escape and return to the familiar reality of Europe." "Unknown Spaces, Far Frontier: The New World as Anti-Paradise from *Moll Flanders* to *Riders in the Chariot,*" *Proceedings of the 12th Congress of the International Comparative Literature Association,* ed. Roger Bauer, Douwe Fokkema and Michael DeGraat (Munich: Inducium Verlag, 1990), 57.

24. Jack enacts what Pepys suggests was the wish of many unpaid English sailors: "it is certain, that as it now is, the seamen of England in my conscience would, if they could, go over [and] serve the King of France or Holland rather than us" (*Diary,* 8:291).

25. Benedick Anderson refers to the "new political entities that sprang up in the Western hemisphere between 1776 and 1838" as "historically the first such states to emerge on the world stage" *Imagined Communities: Reflections on the Origin and Spread of Nationalism,* rev. ed. (London: Verso, 1991), 46. E. J. Hobsbawm asserts that "in its modern and basically political sense the concept *nation* is historically very young." *Nations and Nationalism Since 1780: Programme, Myth, Reality,* 2nd ed. (Cambridge: Cambridge University Press, 1992), 18. Linda Colley's influential consideration of the much earlier rise of British national identity begins by positing that "they came to define themselves as a single people not because of any political or cultural consensus at home, but rather in reaction to the Other beyond their shores." *Britons: Forging the Nation 1707–1837* (New Haven, CT: Yale University Press, 1992), 6. Similarly, the opening pages of Colley's *Captives: Britain, Empire, and the World, 1600–1850* (New York: Anchor Books, 2002) connects Britain's small size with its imperial ambitions: "The physical smallness of these islands encouraged the rich, powerful and ambitious of England, Wales, Scotland and Ireland to filter into just one extraordinarily large metropolis, London. . . . the different elites of these islands developed, from very early on, a shared avidity for imperial investments, ideas and adventures" (11).

26. N. A. M. Rodger suggests that to the French, "It seemed a good moment to advance the cause of James VIII, with few troops in Scotland, and many people less than fully committed to the Union or to Queen Anne's government." He attributes the mission's failure to the Comte de Forbin's "carelessness verging on frivolity" (173). Edward Gregg cites similar reasons for both the attempt and the failure, saying that "anti-union feeling was more important than traditional loyalty to the house of Stuart in paving the way for James Francis Edward Stuart" (261); he adds that British and Dutch intelligence had advance knowledge of the mission.

27. Ellen Pollak, "*Moll Flanders,* Incest, and the Structure of Exchange," *The Eighteenth Century* 30, no. 1 (1989): 9–10; Carl R. Lovitt, "Defoe's 'Almost Invisible Hand': Narrative Logic as a Structuring Principle in *Moll Flanders,*" *Eighteenth-Century Fiction* 6, no. 1 (October 1993): 6. Anne Louise Kibbie objects to Pollak's conflation of patriarchy and capitalism as Moll's antagonists: "the event must be understood within a proto-capitalist discourse rather than as an exception or alternative to it." "Monstrous Generation: The Birth of Capital in Defoe's *Moll Flanders* and *Roxana,*" *PMLA* 110, no.

5 (October 1995), 1024. Both Blewett and Faller suggest that Moll's earlier marriage to Robin prefigures "the appalling irony of her marriage to her own brother." David Blewett, *Defoe's Art of Fiction: Robinson Crusoe, Moll Flanders, and Roxana* (Toronto: University of Toronto Press, 1979), 61; Faller, 119.

28. Richetti, "The Family, Sex, and Marriage in Defoe's *Moll Flanders* and *Roxana*," *Studies in the Literary Imagination* 15, no. 2 (1982): 28. Jay Fliegelman, discussing the plot of Jean-François Marmontel's *The Bad Mother* (1766), finds in it an example of a more conventional rendition of the family romance set in America: "Thus do son, wife, and mother-in-law become the nucleus of a new family whose members have essentially chosen to live with one another. Significantly, the home of this rehabilitated family is America. There one may marry for love; there the son who is denied a fortune may earn it by the sweat of his brow; and there the prodigal parent must come and repent." *Prodigals and Pilgrims*, 53.

29. I cannot agree with Melissa J. Ganz's assertion, "It is fitting, of course, that Moll reasserts her identity as Jemy's wife in America—a land so rich in symbolism as a site for broken ties and new beginnings. In America, Defoe imagines a new union and new life for Moll, signaling his dissatisfaction—indeed break—with English marriage law." "*Moll Flanders* and English Marriage Law," *Eighteenth-Century Fiction* 17, no. 2 (January 2005): 182. Bernard Gensane's reading destabilizes the whole notion of marriage as legal and spiritual tie: "Le mariage n'est pas un état mais une 'circonstance' produite par d'autres 'circonstances.'" "Robinson et Moll: Deux corps dans le monde," *Le Corps dans tous ses états*, ed. Marie-Claire Renyer (Bordeaux: Université de Bordeaux, 1995), 157.

30. Michael F. Suarez, "The Shortest Way to Heaven? Moll Flanders' Repentance Reconsidered," in *1650–1850: Ideas, Aesthetics, and Inquiries in the Early Modern Era*, ed. Kevin Cope (New York: AMS Press, 1997), 3–28. Sallie Minter Strange argues for Moll's repentance: "Newgate is the place to which Moll is led in sorrow, a hell of circumstance and soul, and from which she is released in joy to the New World which becomes alternatively a kind of heaven." Strange believes that "Moll's lies in the New World are told to protect her husband and her son." "Moll Flanders: A Good Calvinist," *South Central Bulletin* 36 (Winter 1976: 154. But the similar rationale proposed by the mother undermines the notion of Moll as altruistic liar. Moll's own linking of material comfort and virtue is echoed by M. A. Goldberg, who asserts that "only in the colonies, with improved socio-economic circumstances, can virtue and principles emerge for Moll." "*Moll Flanders*: Christian Allegory in a Hobbesian Mode," *University Review* 3, no. 3 (1967): 276. For another reading of this episode, see Thomas Grant Olsen, "Reading and Righting in *Moll Flanders*," *Studies in English Literature* 41, no. 3 (Summer 2001): 478: "the secret of incest threatens the narrative if it is kept a secret, but it also threatens the narrative if it is told, because what traditionally drives narrative is the conventional family structure of heterosexuality, marriage, and reproduction, and these narratives of structure are jeopardized when incest is present."

31. Of course, those who ascribe Moll's criminality to greed rather than need have a point. See, for example, Samuel J. Rogal's assessment that "by any standard, Moll enjoyed periods of prosperity far beyond . . . her most ambitious needs." "The Profit and Loss of Moll Flanders," *Studies in the Novel* 5 (1973): 101. See also Robert Alter, who points to Moll's drive to accumulate wealth beyond necessity. "A Bourgeois Picaroon," in *Twentieth-Century Interpretations of Moll Flanders: A Collection of Critical Essays*, ed. Robert C. Elliott (Englewood Cliffs, NJ: Prentice-Hall, 1970), 63–77.

32. Tony Dunn notes that Moll divulges her name once she falls within the legal system, "impelled to make visible a hitherto submerged connection between the law and her self-definition. She wills her anonymity into legal identity" (63). Richetti points to Newgate's "power to suppress and transform the self." (*Defoe's Narratives*, 134), although unlike Dunn, he argues for Moll's rediscovered sense of personal power. John Rietz attributes Moll's transformation in Newgate to "the reappearance of masculine authority" in the person of Jemy "Criminal Ms-Representation: Moll Flanders and Female Criminal Biography," *Studies in the Novel* 23, no. 2 (Summer 1991):b 189). To some extent, Moll's self-castigation in response to Jemy's danger replays the repentance of Adam and Eve in *Paradise Lost* when they move from mutual to self-recrimination.

33. Women servants were not much in demand, in part because they lacked the strength for plantation work. Of the 96,000 indentured emigrants between 1607 and 1699, only 20 percent were women. For details on these numbers, see Richard Dunn, "Servants and Slaves" 159; Gregory Dunston, *Moll Flanders: An Analysis of an Eighteenth-Century Criminal Biography* (Chichester, UK: Barry Rose Publishers, 1997), 219; Fogelman, "From Slaves, Convicts," 44.

34. Defoe's pitying contempt for Jacobites is well known. For example, on October 8, 1706, a *Review* essay asks, "What an unhappy wretched Sort of People are those, we call *Jacobites?* . . . a Confusion of Nations form'd in their own Imaginations, centred upon a meer nothing" (3:485). Sensible Scots, he asserts, particularly resent Stuart pretensions because they remember Stuart tyranny, and know that the Act of Union will protect them from Stuart claims: "This Advantage therefore will immediately accrue by the Union, that the great Question about the Succession is answer'd at once; the Son of King *James*, if so he shall be call'd, is effectually fore-clos'd, and the Voice of the whole Kingdom of *Scotland* joins with us in this secluding and universal Negative, *We will not have this Man to reign over us*" (3:487).

35. William Makepeace Thackeray, *The History of Henry Esmond*, ed. John Sutherland and Michael Greenfield (Harmondsworth, UK: Penguin, 1970), 498–513.

36. Smith reports that during the spring and summer of 1716, 639 Jacobites were transported, of which 150 were sent to Virginia. Apparently, they retained their sense of rights as British citizens: "No sooner had they arrived in Virginia and Maryland than they petitioned the governor, protesting against their servitude, and quoting the Habeas Corpus Act to prove even their deportation illegal" (199).

37. William H. McBurney, "Colonel Jacque: Defoe's Definition of the Complete English Gentleman," *Studies in English Literature, 1500–1900* 2, no. 3 (Summer 1962): 335.

38. John J. McCusker and Russell R. Menard, *The Economy of British America, 1607–1789* (Chapel Hill: University of North Carolina Press, 1985), 46, 48. David W. Galenson points out that "from a very early date, many governments at the level of both the colony and the local community recognized that the colonial economy was simply not subject to their oversight and control." *Cambridge Economic History*, 1:152). Richard S. Dunn adds that "down into the 1670s . . . English colonization everywhere in America had been pervaded by a spirit of *laissez-faire*." "Imperial Pressures on Massachusetts and Jamaica, 1675–1700," *Anglo-American Political Relations*, 53.

39. *American Colonial Documents to 1776*, 247; vol. 9 of *English Historical Documents*, 12 vols., Gen. Ed. David C. Douglas. The Naval Stores Act of 1704 emphasizes the asymmetric relationship between colonies and home when it reminds that "her Majesty's colonies and plantations in America were at first settled, and are still maintained and

protected, as a great expense of the treasure of this kingdom, with a design to render them as useful as may be to England" *English Historical Documents, 1660–1714,* 545.

40. Tobias Smollett, *Continuation of the Complete History of England* (London: Richard Baldwin, 1763), 4:4–5.

41. *English Historical Documents to 1776,* 371. Thomas C. Barrow too cites Shirley and other concerned British officials in North America. He quotes a 1739 letter from the lieutenant governor of New York as well as a 1752 letter from New York's Governor Clinton, who laments that "it is not easy to imagine to what an enormous hight [*sic*] this transgression of the Laws of Trade goes on in North America." "The Old Colonial System from an English Point of View," *Anglo-American Political Relations,* 129.

42. James Abercromby, *Magna Charta for America: James Abercromby's "An Examination of the Acts of Parliament Relative To the Trade and the Government of our American Colonies" (1752) and "De Jure et Gubernatione Coloniarum, or an Inquiry into the Nature, and the Rights of Colonies, Ancient, and Modern" (1774),* ed. Jack P. Greene, Charles F. Mullett, and Edward C. Papenfuse, Jr. (Philadelphia: American Philosophical Society, 1986), 205.

43. Armstrong connects Jack's sociopathic behavior to the moral chaos prevailing after the Civil War: "Paradoxically, the personal ambition which makes Jack careless of his fellow human beings is what binds him to them and to his historical moment, for it proves that he is the offspring of that careless and divided society in the first place, even as he perpetuates its history of conflict and betrayal" (111). For a contrary view, see Virginia Ogden Birdsall, who finds that Defoe's characters, unlike those of Richardson, Fielding, and Smollett, are not developed "against the background of a social scene whose values define them and whose challenges absorb them" (*Defoe's Perpetual Seekers: A Study of the Major Fiction* (Lewisburg, PA: Bucknell University Press, 1985) 18.

44. Faller, *Crime and Defoe,* 185; Hans H. Andersen, "The Paradox of Trade and Morality in Defoe," *Modern Philology* 39, no. 1 (August 1941): 39. Faller also points out that Jack "fall[s] foul of the legal systems of all three of the great European powers" (171) through his Jacobitism, dueling, and contraband trade.

45. Interestingly, Defoe expresses some sympathy for the Spanish point of view on illegal trading: "The *Spaniards* likewise have bid fair to put an End to a very pernicious Trade (to them) carried on clandestinely upon this Coast . . . by Sloops lying off and on upon the Coast, and Canoes coming off to them in the Night; where the *Spaniards* generally brought their Money, and carried the Goods on shore clandestinely, and so disposed of them to their own great Advantage" (*Atlas,* 305).

46. Ironically, as Barrow points out, British officials in the American colonies lacked authority because "not only did the rigidity of the instructions provided for them deprive them of some of the maneuverability—flexibility—so essential to political success, but more seriously they were never given full control of that most basic of political weapons—the power of patronage" (132).

47. John J. McCusker says that in the seventeenth century, "Mercantilism's infatuation with expanding overseas trade was reinforced by an important corollary. The promotion of one's own merchants diminished the power of foreign merchants. . . . The world of the mercantilist was a 'zero-sum' world, a world in which trade and bullion were fixed in amount. It was a predatory world. Our gains were our enemies' losses." "British Mercantilist Policies and the American Colonies," *Cambridge Economic History,* 339).

48. See Srinivas Aravamudan on *Captain Singleton:* "Casuistical reasoning on Wil-

liam's part convinces Bob that religious *conversion* and economic *exchange* are conceptual equivalents. Trading freight of sin and shiploads of goods for ready money and a clear conscience, the partners in crime become gentlemen merchants." *Tropicopolitans: Colonialism and Agency, 1688–1804,* 94.

49. Michael J. Rozbicki, "The Curse of Provincialism: Negative Perceptions of Colonial American Plantation Gentry," *Journal of Southern History* 63, no. 4 (November 1997): 727. Ronald Paulson, in "Emulative Consumption and Literacy: The Harlot, Moll Flanders, and Mrs. Slipslop," reminds us that "part of Defoe's context was the fact that emulative spending, the indulgence in fashionable consumption, was coming to be regarded by many as advantageous to the British economy." *The Consumption of Culture, 1600–1800: Image, Object, Text,* ed. Ann Bermingham (New York: Routledge, 1995), 388. Michael Shinagel, in *Daniel Defoe and Middle-Class Gentility* (Cambridge, MA: Harvard University Press, 1968), points out that "Moll is prouder of outfitting James like a very fine gentleman than she is of outfitting herself; her pleasure in gentility is now in large part the vicarious pleasure of knowing she is securely married to a true gentleman at last" (159). But true gentility still resides in England; as Peter Huhn argues, "through a combination of work and luck they amass a fortune in America and return to England as respectable and wealthy gentleman planters, by which they have finally achieved social inclusion." "The Precarious Autopoiesis of Modern Selves: Daniel Defoe's *Moll Flanders* and Virginia Woolf's *The Waves,*" *European Journal of English Studies* 5, no. 3 (2001): 339.

50. James Axtell, *The European and the Indian: Essays in the Ethnohistory of Colonial North America* (New York: Oxford University Press, 1981), 53.

51. As early as 1698, Sir Josiah Child was complaining that New England was not a profitable colony because the region "produces generally the same we have here, viz. Corn and Cattle" (qtd. in Galenson, *Cambridge Economic History,* 201).

52. McCusker and Menard point to the "changed dimensions of colonial overseas trade" during the eighteenth century: "The natural extension of the coastwise commerce . . . developed eventually into a network of intercolonial trades that stretched from Newfoundland to Barbados—and beyond." Moreover, "British American trade came to be controlled by merchants resident in Colonial ports. . . . They started to compete directly in the business that merchants in the mother country traditionally thought of as entirely their own. . . . By the 1770s West Indians were importing a variety of manufactured goods from the continental colonies. . . . The implications of this trade for the economic development of the colonists on the Continent were immense" (78–80; 288–89).

53. Abercromby, *Magna Carta for America,* 82; *Atlas,* 99. Christopher Flynn suggests that Defoe "addresses his imperial anxieties with written attempts to define America as bound to Britain by economic interests and legal decisions." "Nationalism, Commerce, and Imperial Anxiety in Defoe's Later Works," 14. See also David Armitage's discussion of Josiah Child, Charles Davenant, and William Wood: all three argued that "the flourishing colonies encouraged manufactures, shipping and employment at home, to the advantage of England. However, this could only be sustained by firm regulation of the colonies, under the terms of the Navigation Acts." *Ideological Origins,* 167.

54. Defoe, *Review,* 4.402.

55. Ned C. Landsman, "Immigration and Settlement," introduction to *Scotland and the Americas, 1600–1800,* by Michael Fry (Providence, RI: John Carter Brown Library, 1995), 16. Linda Colley too estimates 40,000 Scots as well as 55,000 Protestant Irish

and 30,000 English and Welsh went to America between 1760 and 1776 (*Captives*, 200). T. M. Devine echoes Landsman's research on chronology, but raises the number of Scottish emigrants to 45,000 between 1763 and 1775. He adds that "for the first time the exodus to the Americas became a truly national phenomenon drawing from all classes of society and most regions of the country" (108). Alan Taylor calculates that "Scots emigration soared to 145,000 between 1707 and 1775," outnumbering by far English settlers in the colonies. *American Colonies*, 294, 316. For a detailed analysis of numbers, distribution, and motivations of emigrants, see David Dobson, *Scottish Emigration to Colonial America, 1607–1785* (Athens: University of Georgia Press, 1994).

Eric Richards calls Scottish emigration to America "a variant of their penetration of England" but finds "key differences: for instance, the transatlantic migrations were more concentrated and caused a fear of wholesale population loss in Scotland" (91). In fact, according to Dobson, "By the early 1770s the British government was becoming so concerned by the level of emigration from the Highlands that it at times discouraged or hindered it" (155). Even earlier in the century, alarmists like James Abercromby and Thomas Pownall went so far as to question the legality of emigration. See Peter N. Miller, *Defining the Common Good: Empire, Religion and Philosophy in Eighteenth-Century Britain* (Cambridge: Cambridge University Press, 1994), 197, 205.

56. *Johnson's Journey to the Western Islands of Scotland and Boswell's Journal of a Tour to the Hebrides with Samuel Johnson, LL.D.*, ed. R. W. Chapman (London: Oxford University Press, 1970), 346, 119. Taylor alludes to the alarm of "imperial officials" during the 1770s: "elite observers . . . saw no profit to the mother country in the loss of British laborers and tenants into the woods of America" (441). Johnson's lamentation finds a contemporary resonance in Prime Minister Gordon Brown's comment during an interview with *Time* magazine: "All the songs of Scotland are sad songs. . . . They're songs about people who will never see each other again because they've gone to America," April 28, 2008, p. 37.

57. *Journey*, 85.

58. See Dobson, *Scottish Immigration*, 154: "the Highlanders, clearly wishing to maintain their traditional culture and society, preferred to emigrate to the New World rather than be assimilated into the culture and society of Lowland Scotland." Elaine Jordan cites a correspondent in *The Military Register* who characterizes Scottish emigrants as "*all old soldiers* . . . obliged to contemplate transporting themselves into a new and precarious existence in the woods and wilds of North America." "The Management of Scott's Novels," *Europe and Its Others: Proceedings of the Essex Conference on the Sociology of Literature, July 1984*, 2 vols., ed. Francis Barker, Peter Hulme, Margaret Iversen, and Diana Loxley (Colchester: University of Essex, 1985), 2:149.

59. *Journey*, 87; *Review*, 4.187.

60. Smollett, *Continuation of the Complete History*, 1:220; *Letters*, 114.

61. Michael Zuckerman, "Identity in British America: Unease in Eden," *Colonial Identity in the Atlantic World, 1500–1800*, ed. Nicholas Canny and Anthony Pagden (Princeton, NJ: Princeton University Press, 1987), 123; *Continuation*, 4:223; McLeod, *Geography of Empire in English Literature, 1580–1745*, 30. This assessment is echoed by Robert Giddings, who argues that *Humphry Clinker* is "a portrait of a society at a particular stage of development, as the nation slowly changed from supporting itself . . . into a country which fed its population and provided for its luxuries by overseas trade." "Matthew Bramble's Bath: Smollett and the West Indian Connection," *Smollett: Author of the First Distinction*, ed. Alan Bold (London: Vision Press, 1982) 49. See also Sharon

Harrow's *Adventures in Domesticity Gender and Colonial Adulteration in Eighteenth-Century British Literature* (New York: AMS Press, 2004). Harrow's "governing theme" is that "eighteenth-century British literature figured colonial otherness as a force that would underwrite financial stability as it undermined social hierarchy" (2–3).

62. Susan L. Jacobsen, "'The Tinsel of the Times': Smollett's Argument against Conspicuous Consumption in *Humphry Clinker*," *Eighteenth-Century Fiction* 9, no. 1 (October 1996): 72. David M. Weed associates commercialism with debilitating feminization: "England's social body incorporates the ill effects of commercialism into its public institutions and civic and social life, and . . . it produces effeminate men who participate in an epidemic spread of luxury, bodily waste, consumption, and 'cannibalism.'" "Sentimentalism, Misogyny and Medicine in *Humphry Clinker*," *SEL* 37, no. 3 (Summer 1997): 615. John Dwyer suggests that Scots were particularly disturbed by the new economic order: "Luxury, Scottish writers believed, was spreading. . . . alongside the commercialization of Great Britain, as wealth began to find itself in the hands of 'nabobs' and 'contractors' who, it was argued, had neither the training nor the temper of mind to use it properly." *Virtuous Discourse: Sensibility and Community in Late Eighteenth-Century Scotland* (Edinburgh: John Donald Publishers Ltd., 1987), 97.

63. Richard Ligon, writing in 1653, describes the music of Caribbean Negroes: "the drum all men know, has but one tone; and therefore variety of tunes have little to do in this music" (qtd. in the Bedford *Oroonoko*, 361).

64. Jonathan Swift, in Book III of *Gulliver's Travels*, also makes reference to ungrateful governments: those who have provided the best service to princes and states "all appeared with dejected Looks and in the meanest Habit; most of them telling me they died in Poverty and Disgrace, and the rest on a Scaffold or a Gibbet." *The Writings of Jonathan Swift*, ed. Robert A. Greenberg and William Bowman Piper (New York: W. W. Norton, 1973), 172. The prematurely aged Balderick may prefigure Admiral Baldwin in Jane Austen's *Persuasion*, characterized by Sir Walter Eliot as "the most deplorable looking personage you can imagine, his face the colour of mahogany, rough and rugged to the last degree, all lines and wrinkles, nine grey hairs of a side, and nothing but a dab of powder at top." *The Novels of Jane Austen*, 5 vols., ed. R. W. Chapman (London: Oxford University Press, 1933), V:20.

65. P. J. Marshall, *Problems of Empire: Britain and India, 1757–1813* (London: George Allen and Unwin Ltd., 1968), 26. Colley points out that Britons at home evinced very little interest in colonial conditions, including captivity by Indians, until midcentury: "once troops from Britain and their families began crossing the Atlantic in substantial numbers, after the outbreak of the Seven Years War in 1756, the metropolitan market for tales of Indian captivity, as for other information about North America, would skyrocket. With large numbers of their own kind now flooding over to America . . . this vast territory and all its complex dangers came to seem to Britons at home infinitely more real and absorbing" (161).

Nancy Armstrong and Leonard Tennenhouse have offered a fascinating account of the literary effects of the new interest in captivity narratives. In "The American Origins of the English Novel, *American Literary History* 4, no. 3 (Autumn 1992): 386–410, they argue that captivity narratives developed precisely those attributes most commonly associated with the rise of the English novel: epistolarity, individualism, middle-class domesticity, and the feminized consciousness.

66. Paul-Gabriel Boucé, *The Novels of Tobias Smollett* (London: Longman, 1976), 240; Robert Hopkins, "The Function of Grotesque in *Humphry Clinker*," *Huntington Library*

Quarterly 32 (1969): 173–74; Joanne Lewis, "Death and the Comic Marriage: Lismahago in Harlequin Skeleton," *Studies in Eighteenth-Century Culture* 18 (1988): 406, 411. In a similar vein, Kenneth Simpson, commenting on Smollett's coarse humor, says, "an account of atrocities perpetrated upon the lieughtenant and his companion by the American Indians, is a sequence which is certainly offered as ironic comment on the vogue of the travel adventure." *The Protean Scot: The Crisis of Identity in Eighteenth-Century Scottish Literature* (Aberdeen: Aberdeen University Press, 1980, 16. John Richetti takes a more complex view: "Comprised of literary and documentary materials that encompass the contradictory areas of Cervantic caricature, the horrors of North American captivity narrative, and the inequities of advancement in the eighteenth-century British army, Lismahago points to his own complicated status as a character simultaneously comic and deeply serious, both grotesque and engagingly pathetic in his pride and considerable intelligence." *The English Novel in History, 1700–1780* (London: Routledge, 1999), 186. Evan Gottlieb, in *Feeling British*, carefully differentiates between narrative viewpoints when he says that "although the Scottish half-pay lieutenant is made partially sympathetic by his subsequent narrative of his capture and wounding by Native Americans, he continues to be viewed primarily as a figure of fun by Jery" (90).

67. James Axtell, *The European and the Indian*; J. Norman Heard, *White into Red: A Study of the Assimilation of White Persons Captured by Indians* (Metuchen, NJ: Scarecrow Press, 1973), 10. Bruce McLeod echoes Franklin: "New England leaders worried over the European captives who refused to return to 'civilized' society, since Indian life appeared attractive to some in contrast to the discipline and drudgery of life for the majority of English colonists" (152).

68. Heard, *White into Red*, 25–30, 65, 130; Cadwallader Colden, *The History of the Five Indian Nations of Canada, which are dependent on the Province of New York, and are a barrier between the English and the French in that part of the World* (New York: Allerton Book Co., 1904), 263. Colley says that so many British soldiers had been assimilated into tribal culture that a rescued or ransomed soldier could face court-martial "unless he could somehow prove that he really had been forced to cross the culture line against his will." *Captives*, 196.

69. Robert Eastburn, *A Faithful Narrative, The Garland Library of Narratives of North American Indian Captives*, 111 vols., ed. Wilcomb E. Washburn (New York: Garland Publishing Inc., 1978), 8:10; Ewell Jeffries, *A Short Biography of John Leeth, with an Account of His Life among the Indians*, ed. Reuben Gold Thwaites (1831; repr., New York: Benjamin Blom, Inc., 1972), 27; John Gyles, *The Memoirs of Odd Adventures, Strange Deliverances, &c. in the Captivity of John Gyles, Esq.; Commander of the Garrison on St. George's River* (Boston: S. Kneeland and T. Green, 1736), 17; Thomas Morris, *Journal of Captain Thomas Morris* (Ann Arbor, MI: University Microfilms, Inc., 1966; rpt. from Captain Thomas Morris, *Miscellanies in Prose and Verse* [London: James Ridgeway, 1791]), 12; Pierre Esprit Radisson, *Voyages of Peter Esprit Radisson, Being an Account of His Travels and Experiences among the North American Indians, from 1652–1684*, ed. Gideon D. Scull (1885; repr., New York: Burt Franklin, 1967), 34.

70. Arthur Young, *The Adventures of Emmera, or The Fair American. Exemplifying the Peculiar Advantages of Society and Retirement*, 2 vols. (1773; repr., New York: Garland Publishing Inc., 1974), 1:221, 2:80; Henry Mackenzie, *The Man of the World*, 2 vols. (New York: Garland Publishing Inc., 1974), 2:182–83.

71. Charlotte Sussman's subtle analysis of Lismahago's story argues that in *Humphry*

Clinker, "the problem of how to assimilate, or acculturate, other cultures . . . is redacted into a problem of oral consumption"; not only is the English body poisoned by imported food, but Indian ritualistic cannibalism is seen as "evidence of a tribe's ability to retain its social coherence in the face of a colonizing invasion. . . . the colonial encounter violates Europe, rather than the New World." "Lismahago's Captivity: Transculturation in *Humphry Clinker,*" *ELH* 61, no. 3 (1994): 598, 600–601. For another reading of European anxieties and captivity narratives, see Helen Carr, "Woman/Indian: 'The American' and His Others," 2:52. "the Indians are the ones in at any rate potential sexual possession, and the narrative can enact and resolve the colonists' deep fears of being dominated and mastered by the Indian, of having their identity and power as European men destroyed."

72. Morris, *Journal,* 26–27; Robert Rogers, *Ponteach; or the Savages of America,* in *Representative Plays by American Dramatists,* ed. Montrose J. Moses (New York: E. P. Dutton & Co., 1918), 143.

73. Gordon M. Sayre, *Les Sauvages Américains: Representations of Native Americans in French and English Colonial Literature* (Chapel Hill: University of North Carolina Press, 1997), 22, 260. James H. Merrill notes that "tribes beyond the frontier were for the most part indifferent to the Christian message as translated by the English, in part because English clergymen, unlike Jesuits operating in New France, rarely visited Indian territory. . . . Jesuits, with a tolerance for native ways, a gift for languages, and a religion rich in symbol and ritual, enjoyed considerable success. English Protestants, on the other hand, usually lacked the delicate touch needed to convert distant Indians" (147–48).

74. "The History of Canada," *British Magazine,* June 1760: 351. The failure of English missionaries would be particularly painful for those who, like John Eliot of Massachusetts, saw "in the conversion experiences of the Indians themselves a model for the spiritual renewal of a colony struggling to cope with both the internal strife of ecclesiastical conflict and the anxiety over England's uncertain future in the wake of the Restoration. . . . missionary work not only seemed to exempt itself from the bitter debates within English Protestantism. It also offered the English a way of imagining themselves as a Protestant nation united against Roman Catholicism." Thomas Scanlan, *Colonial Writing and the New World, 1583–1671: Allegories of Desire* (Cambridge: Cambridge University Press, 1999), 155, 159.

75. Heard, *White into Red,* 20. Peter Hulme, in *Colonial Encounters: Europe and the Native Caribbean, 1492–1797* (London: Methuen, 1986) talks about the suspicious hybridity of Britons who served as interpreters: "they had to be so steeped in Algonquin culture that their very identity as Englishmen, and therefore their political reliability, became suspect. They became, as it were, cultural half-breeds, inhabiting that dangerous no-man's land between identifiable cultural positions" (142).

76. *Defoe's Review,* 1:136; Peter Williamson, introduction to *French and Indian Cruelty: Exemplified in the Life and Various Vicissitudes of Fortune of Peter Williamson,* by Michael Fry (1762; repr., Bristol: Thoemmes Press, 1996), 45. The French, says Williamson, 'were sent to dispossess us in that part of the world, [are] indefatigable in their duty, and continually contriving, and using all manner of ways and means to win the *Indians* to their interest" (8). Eastburn complains of the French Governor of Quebec that "even in Times of *Peace,* he gives the *Indians* great Encouragement to *Murder* and *Captivate* the poor Inhabitants on our Frontiers" (38). William Fleming's Delaware captors tell his wife *"That the French were better off than the English, for they had a great many Old Men among*

them that could forgive all their Sins, and these Men had often assured the Indians it was no Sin to destroy Hereticks, and all the English were such." William and Elizabeth Fleming, *A Narrative of the Sufferings and Surprizing Deliverance of William and Elizabeth Fleming, The Garland Library*, 8:16). John Gyles, on the other hand, encounters a good Franciscan priest who has told Indians "that excepting their errors in Religion, the English were a better people than themselves," and that God will punish those who hurt the English (19).

77. *British Magazine*, April 1760: 198.

78. In his "Address to the British Colonists in North America" (1777), Edmund Burke, sounding remarkably like Thomson, spells out this notion of British restraint regarding Indians: "born in a civilized country, formed to gentle manners, trained in a merciful religion. . . . We rather wished to have joined you in bringing gradually that unhappy part of mankind into civility, order, piety and virtuous discipline, than to have confirmed their evil habits, and increased their natural ferocity, by fleshing them in the slaughter of you, whom our wiser and better ancestors had sent into the wilderness, with the express view of introducing, along with our holy religion, its humane and charitable manners." *The Portable Edmund Burke*, ed. Isaac Kramnick (Harmondsworth, UK: Penguin, 1999), 278.

79. *British Magazine*, May 1760: 132.

80. Colden, *History*, 169–70.

81. *British Magazine*, June 1760: 352; March 1761: 153. Francis Jennings works out the murderous implications of such an attitude: "their mode of existence and cast of mind were such as to make them incapable of civilization and therefore of full humanity . . . the savage creatures of the wilderness, being unable to adapt to any environment other than the wild, stubbornly and viciously resisted God or fate, and thereby incurred their suicidal extermination" (15). T. H. Breen points to another result of Indian resistance to European culture. Unlike imported slaves, they were not part of the labor system in the colonies and therefore of no practical use to the settlers; once the fur trade collapsed, "the Indians, now dependent upon European commerce, had little to offer in exchange for guns and cloth, kettles and knives. Under these conditions, Indians were easily exploited, abused, and cheated out of whatever they still possessed." "Creative Adaptation, People and Cultures," *Colonial British America: Essays in the New History of the Early Modern Era*, ed. Jack P. Greene and J. R. Pole (Baltimore: Johns Hopkins University Press, 1984), 214. James H. Merrell sums up these lethal results with elegant economy: "in the end it proved easier to kill Indians than convert them, easier to make them speak English than to make them listen to a sermon, easier to get them into a courtroom than into a church, easier to bring them to acknowledge the English King than the English God" (152).

82. Axtell points out that stoicism "served the Jesuits well in Indian country. Personal courage, especially in the face of death, was appreciated in Europe, but from the American natives it drew special respect . . . The Iroquois were even more impressed when Father Jogues, his hands mutilated by torture during his previous captivity, returned to the Mohawks in 1646 to pursue the cause of peace and Christ" (*Invasion*, 86). Sayre takes a less admiring approach when describing the execution in 1649 of Jean de Brebeuf, who "complied with the custom of singing the *chanson de mort* by substituting a sermon . . . by substituting his proselytizing sermon for the *chanson de mort*, Brebeuf subverted the customs of torture, for his heroic forbearance did not enhance the power of those who conquered him when he patronizingly claimed to suffer for their lost souls" (299–300).

83. Anonymous, *The Female American; or, the Adventures of Unca Winkfield*, ed. Michelle Burnham (Peterborough, Canada: Broadview Press Ltd., 2001). The narrator glosses over the fact that she manipulates the native tribe's belief system in order to promulgate Christianity: after exploiting their worship of the sun-god in order to achieve authority, she tells them that such worship is sacrilegious; at the end of the text, she and her clergyman husband, in an unacknowledged parody of imperial practice, determine "to collect all the gold treasure there, to blow up the subterraneous passage, and the statue, that the Indians might never be tempted to their former idolatry" (154).

84. John Oldmixon, *The British Empire in America. Containing the History of the Discovery, Settlement, Progress and State of the British Colonies on the Continent and Islands of America.* 2 vols. (1741; repr., New York: Augustus M. Kelly, 1969), 1:91, 98–99, 277.

85. Gyles, *Memoirs of Odd Adventures*, 7; Jean Lowry, *A Journal of the Captivity of Jean Lowry and Her Children, The Garland Library*, 8:6; Williamson, *French and Indian Cruelty*, 19; *British Magazine*, September 1760:538. The tortures described in captivity narratives hardly exceed those suffered by Robert François Damiens after his attempt on Louis XV in 1757. Charles Dickens offers a literary rendering of them in *A Tale of Two Cities*: "his right hand, armed with the knife, will be burnt off before his face; . . . into wounds which will be made in his arms, his breast, and his leg, there will be poured boiling oil, melted lead, hot resin, wax, and sulphur; finally . . . he will be torn limb from limb by four strong horses." (Oxford: Oxford University Press, 1988), 205.

86. Colley, *Captives*, 177.

87. *British Magazine*, September 1760: 538. Radisson's story does include castration—"They cut off yor stones and the women play wth them as wth balles" (54)—but the victims are emphatically not, as Murphy is, destined to become "the spouse of a beautiful squaw" (228). Heard tells us that David Boyd "had to run the gauntlet, which amusement, for the Indians, consisted in running a prescribed limit between two lines made up of vindictive squaws and young savage rogues armed with sticks, stones, or whatever suited their purpose best" (60). There are, however, benign versions of the gauntlet recounted in some captivity narratives. Robert Eastburn, captured in 1756, speaks of being pelted with nothing worse than dirt and gravel. Richard VanDerBeers, *Held Captive by Indians: Selected Narratives, 1642–1836* (Knoxville: University of Tennessee Press, 1994), 162. James Smith, captured in 1755, reports: "They [squaws] all laid violent hold of me, and I for some time opposed them with all my might, which occasioned loud laughter by the multitude that were on the bank of the river. At length one of the squaws made out to speak a little English . . . and said, 'no hurt you.' On this I gave myself up their ladyships, who were as good as their word; for though they plunged me under water and washed and rubbed me severely, yet I could not say they hurt me much" (qtd. in Axtell, *European*, 186). Splinters figure in Heard's description of the gruesome scalping and execution of an Englishwoman in 1756: "they laid burning splinters of wood, here and there, upon her body" (67), but in her case, though the splinters inflict terrible pain, they do not penetrate her body. Describing the progressive luridness of captivity narratives, VanDerBeers writes:

> The infusion of melodrama and sensibility into the narratives, appropriately ornamented and stylistically embellished, capitalized on what became an increasingly profitable market for properly "literary" narratives of Indian captivity in the later eighteenth and early nineteenth centuries. . . . the earlier propagandist impulse deliberately played up Indian horrors and outrages, but more to solicit strong anti-Indian sentiments than to evoke pity and terror for the captive himself. It was but a short, almost inevitable step from narrative excesses for the pur-

pose of propaganda to excesses in the interest of sensation and titillation, from promoting hatred to eliciting horror, from inspiring patriotism to encouraging sales, from chauvinism to commercialism. (xxxviii)

88. Colden, *History*, 171. See Mackenzie's *Man of the World*, in which the dying Indian captives sing "the glory of their former victories, and the pleasure they had received from the death of their foes; concluding always with the hopes of revenge from the surviving warriors of their nation" (2:177).

89. [Jehu Hay], *The Siege of Detroit in 1763: The Journal of Pontiac's Conspiracy and John Rutherford's Narrative of a Captivity*, ed. Milo Milton Quaye (Chicago: Lakeside Press, 1958), 229. Richard White, in *The Middle Ground: Indians, Empires, and Republics in the Great Lakes Region, 1650–1815* (Cambridge: Cambridge University Press, 1991) describes the horrifying method the Senecas took to demoralize their Miami enemies during the Iroquois wars of the mid-seventeenth century: "Every night as the Senecas traveled home, they killed and ate a Miami child. And every morning they took a small child, thrust a stick through its head and sat it up on the path with its face toward the Miami town they had left. Behind the Senecas came the pursing Miamis, and at every Seneca campsite, brokenhearted parents recognized their child" (4–5). Interestingly, Smollett omits one of the most gruesome details included in some captivity narratives. Both Gyles (12) and Radisson (53) refer to the practice of forcing captives to eat parts of their own bodies. The omission underscores Sussman's argument about "the threat of the literal disappearance of European culture into the belly of America" (602).

Todorov postulates that characterizing natives as savages provides a rationale for enslaving them: "We can say that this line of argument unites four descriptive propositions as to the Indians' nature to a postulate that is also a moral imperative. These propositions: the Indians have a slave's nature; they practice cannibalism; they make human sacrifices; they are ignorant of the Christian religion" (154). Greenblatt, referring to Columbus's letter proposing trading slaves for beasts, echoes Todorov's analysis: "those Indians identified as cannibals will be hunted down, seized torn from their lands and their culture, loaded onto ships still stinking of the animals for whom they are being exchanged, and sent into slavery" (72).

90. Robert Crawford rightly connects Smollett's depiction of Amerindian atrocities with his desire to advance English appreciation of Scotland: "the English tended to view Scottish society as primitive in comparison with their own, but the Scotland to be presented by these Welsh visitors appears all the more refined by contrast with the account of Amerindian 'simplicity of . . . manners', where fingers are sawn off with rusty knives and eyes are scooped out to be replaced with burning coals" (70).

91. Walter Scott, *The Heart of Midlothian*, 467.

92. Gottlieb is exactly right when he suggests that advancing the notion of post-Union family unity "means revisiting two 'primitive' social formations that the novel initially rejects as un-British: the North American Indians whose tribal values force Lismahago to marry their chieftain's daughter, and the Highlanders whose clan system facilitates a form of belonging that is both attractive and worrying to Bramble" (97).

93. Weed, "Sentimentalism." 615. Nussbaum quotes a 1764 letter from Elizabeth Montagu to Elizabeth Carter in which Montagu inverts the contrast between European finery and Amerindian simplicity. Describing women getting ready for a Masquerade, she says, "A friseur is employ'd three hours in a morning to make a young Lady look like a virgin Hottentot or Squaw, all art ends in giving them the ferocious air of uncomb'd savages." *Limits of the Human*, 141.

94. Scanlan describes Léry's appreciation of native simplicity: "Léry asserts that the shamelessness with which the Indians display their bodies is more easily defended than the 'sumptuous display' in dress exhibited by many Europeans" (47).

95. M. A. Goldberg, *Smollett and the Scottish School: Studies in Eighteenth-Century Thought* (Albuquerque: University of New Mexico Press, 1959), 165–67. Williamson finds that Indians 'are very proud, and take great delight in wearing trinkets" (21), and Mary Rowlandson writes disapprovingly of the squaw Wettimore: "a severe and proud Dame she was, bestowing every day in dressing herself neat as much time as any of the Gentry of the land: powdering her hair, and painting her face, going with Neck-laces, with Jewels in her ears, and Bracelets upon her hands." *The Sovereignty and Goodness of God. Together with the Faithfulness of His Promises Displayed. Being a Narrative of the Captivity and Restoration of Mrs. Mary Rowlandson, and Related Documents*, ed. Neal Salisbury (Boston: Bedford/St. Martin's 1997), 97.

96. Lismahago bears the monstrous scars of his encounter with hostile Indians in Ticonderoga, who "rifled him, broke his scull with the blow of a tomahawk, and left him for dead . . . so that the scull was left naked in several places, but these he covered with patches" (224). Axtell notes that "contrary to popular belief, scalping was not necessarily a fatal operation; the historical record is full of survivors." *European* 34–35. Perhaps the most comic version is Williamson's story of the Irishman who was too drunk to realize he had been scalped (72). Rutherfurd carefully explains that "the scalp is not, as is commonly believed, the whole skin of the head, but is only uppermost part of the crown" (241).

97. Sayre, *Les Sauvages Américains*, 154.

ENTR'ACTE

1. Byron Glassman, "Religious Attitudes in the World of *Humphry Clinker*," *Brigham Young University Studies* 6 (1965): 65; Gary Kelly, *Revolutionary Feminism: The Mind and Career of Mary Wollstonecraft* (New York: St. Martin's Press, 1992), 206.

2. Claudia Johnson, in *Equivocal Beings: Politics, Gender, and Sentimentality in the 1790s: Wollstonecraft, Radcliffe, Burney, Austen* (Chicago: University of Chicago Press, 1995), says that Maria and Jemima must "retreat from the insurmountable corruption of men and of the masculine public sphere" (69). Syndy McMillen Conger similarly notes the private, ahistorical aspect of the text's conclusion, but adds that change is in the wind: for the protagonists, "the old regime with its hierarchies, petty monarchs, and moss-covered opinions, is permanently over, even if the men in charge of their society . . . have not yet noticed." *Mary Wollstonecraft and the Language of Sensibility* (Madison, NJ: Fairleigh Dickinson University Press, 1994), 178. S. D. Harasym's Derridean/Lacanian reading (one wishes it had not consistently called Darnford Danford and Jemima Jessica) posits an inevitable deferral of resolution in Wollstonecraft's fiction: "the novels take on a fatalistic tone, caught within the phallogocentric discourse of their time and, furthermore, Wollstonecraft's ideology is bound within the patriarchal prison-house of language. Perhaps it is this failure to envision an alternative system which fissures and finally deconstructs Wollstonecraft's utopian hopes and leads to her inability to finish *Maria, or the Wrongs of Woman?*" "Ideology and Self: A Theoretical Discussion of the 'Self' in Mary Wollstonecraft's Fiction," *English Studies in Canada* 12, no. 2 (June 1986): 170.

3. Gilbert Imlay, *The Emigrants*, ed. W. M. Verhoeven and Amanda Gilroy (Harmondsworth, UK: Penguin, 1998), 212.

4. Moira Ferguson and Janet Todd, *Mary Wollstonecraft* (Boston: Twayne, 1984), 104. Claudia Johnson suggests that "a pained rendering of Wollstonecraft's experience with Imlay, the Darnford/Maria episodes finally judge male culture to be so corrupt as to make effective reciprocity between the sexes impossible" (65). Flynn speculates that Wollstonecraft may have at least collaborated on the composition of *The Emigrants*, and notes that "it is a product of the radical circle in London in which both she and Imlay traveled" (55).

5. Traveling through the colonies in 1759–60, Andrew Burnaby already detects and articulates a much more nuanced civilization than Darnford's generalizations imply. He finds Virginians inclined to "acts of extravagance, ostentation, and a disregard of economy," while Pennsylvanians "are a frugal and industrious people: not remarkably courteous and hospitable." In Massachusetts he finds that the 100-year long presence of Harvard College "has produced a very good effect. The arts are undeniably forwarder in Massachusetts Bay than either in Pennsylvania or New York." *Burnaby's Travels Through North America*, intro. Rufus Rockwell Wilson (1798; repr., New York: A. Wessels Company, 1904, 55, 96, 139). John Davis, too, in his four and half years in the United States, finds both spurious pretensions to gentility (as in the planter Mr. H — — and his Pope-spouting wife) and genuine grace, as in the establishment of Mr. Drayton, who may live in a log cabin, "but his table was sumptuous, and an elegance of manners presided at it that might have vied with the highest circles of polished *Europe*." Introduction to *Travels of Four Years and a Half in the United States of America during 1798, 1799, 1800, 1801, and 1802*, by A. J. Morrison (New York: Henry Holt and Company, 1909), 52–57, 82.

6. In 1827, Fanny Trollope makes the same assessment of American backwardness, imputing their lack of polish to an education that dismisses classical literature, the English canon, and even modern European greats like Rousseau and Voltaire, who now "seem known more as naughty words, than as great names." *Domestic Manners of the Americans*, ed. Pamela Neville-Sington (London: Penguin, 1997), 243. Trollope also connects Americans' truncated education to their love of wealth, and adds, "when the money-getting begins, leisure ceases, and all of lore which can be acquired afterwards, is picked up from novels, magazines, and newspapers" (255).

7. Imlay, *Emigrants*, 214. American obsession with money is one of Trollope's constant themes, and she asserts that "this sordid object, for ever before their eyes, must inevitably produce a sordid tone of mind, and, worse still, it produces a seared and blunted conscience on all questions of probity" (235). Nancy E. Johnson, in "'Seated on her Bags of Dollars': Representations of America in the English Jacobin Novel," *The Dalhousie Review* 82, no. 3 (Spring 2002) finds that Darnford is more realistic about America than is Hermsprong: "Darnford casts the young nation as a site of broken promises and lost opportunities, a scene of excessive poverty and wealth, and a place of shallow gestures toward cultivation" (432).

8. T. H. Breen, "An Empire of Goods: The Anglicization of Colonial America, 1690–1776," *Journal of British Studies* 25, no. 4 (1986): 497. Jack P. Greene and J. R. Pole echo this viewpoint when they argue that the elite in the new world embarked on a process of replicating social practices of the old world and took "pride in the extent to which their societies were becoming increasingly Anglicized." "Reconstructing British-American Colonial History: An Introduction," *Colonial British America: Essays in the New*

History of the Early Modern Era, ed. Jack P. Greene and J. R. Pole (Baltimore: Johns Hopkins University Press, 1984), 15.

9. D. W. Meinig, *The Shaping of America: A Geographical Perspective on 500 Years of History,* 2 vols. (New Haven, CT: Yale University Press, 1986), I.440.

10. Rozbicki, 750.

11. Mary Wollstonecraft, *A Vindication of the Rights of Men* (Amherst, NY: Prometheus Books, 1996) 40; *Letters Written during a Short Residence in Sweden, Norway, and Denmark,* ed. Carol H. Poston (Lincoln: University of Nebraska Press, 1976), 186–87.

12. David S. Landes, *The Wealth and Poverty of Nations* (New York: W. W. Norton, 1998), 235.

13. Alexis de Tocqueville, *Democracy in America,* ed. Andrew Hacker, trans. Henry Reeve, rev. Francis Bowen (New York: Washington Square Press, 1964), 254–55.

14. Trollope, who writes scathingly of the dress, intellect, and manners of American women, does provide an excuse: because domestic servants are hard to find and keep in America, women "cannot have leisure for any great development of the mind; it is, in fact out of the question; and, remembering this, it is more surprising that some among them should be very pleasing, than that none should be highly instructed" (49). De Tocqueville, on the other hand, praises the education and freedom of thought evinced by American women, professing himself "frequently surprised, and almost frightened, at the singular address and happy boldness with which young women in America manage to manage their thoughts and their language" (237).

15. Conger, *Mary Wollstonecraft,* 161. See also Susan Sniader Lanser's cogent argument about Wollstonecraft's desire to transcend class in order to form a communal female voice: "*The Wrongs of Woman* struggles to deconstruct the ideology that attaches women more firmly to men of their class than to one another across class boundaries." *Fictions of Authority: Women Writers and Narrative Voice* (Ithaca, NY: Cornell University Press, 1992) 231.

16. Mary Wollstonecraft, *A Vindication of the Rights of Woman,* ed. Carol H. Poston (New York: W. W. Norton, 1988), 75.

17. Barrow, "Old Colonial System," 132.

18. Imlay, *Emigrants,* 204.

19. The editors' introduction to *The Emigrants* notes that the novel was "clearly directed toward a British audience. . . . there is no evidence that the novel was read in America, and it was first published there in a facsimile edition in 1964" (xxxi).

20. Imlay, *Emigrants,* 5, 43, 127.

21. Kelly, *Revolutionary Feminism,* 171.

22. Mary Wollstonecraft, *Collected Letters of Mary Wollstonecraft,* ed. Ralph M. Wardle (Ithaca, NY: Cornell University Press, 1979), 279; *Letters Written during a Short Residence,* 187. Imlay for a time was involved in complex conspiracies to effect a French and American alliance against Spanish territories in America. When that plan collapsed, he engaged in various business dealings in France and England. Nancy Johnson rightly asserts that "America was for Wollstonecraft less a symbol of liberty and more a sign of economic opportunism that corrupted, rather than enhanced, the self" ("Seated," 434).

23. In "Befriending the Body: Female Intimacies as Class Acts," *Eighteenth-Century Studies* 32, no. 2 (Winter 1998–99), Lanser traces the ways in which Sapphic women in the eighteenth-century deployed class conservatism as a way to "strengthen the divide between the virtuous body and the immoral one. . . . It is . . . not surprising that some

gentry sapphists re-asserted their standing through words and deeds that affirmed the *status quo*" (189–90). For example, Lanser notes the antirevolutionary stance of Eleanor Butler and Sarah Ponsonby, who "enact the conservatism of their class at its extreme" (191).

24. Harriet Devine Jump, *Mary Wollstonecraft: Writer* (New York: Harvester/Wheatsheaf, 1994), 131.

25. Marilyn Butler, "Introductory Essay," in *Burke, Paine, Godwin, and the Revolution Controversy,* ed. Marilyn Butler (Cambridge: Cambridge University Press, 1984), 11; Kelly, *Revolutionary Feminism,* 196. Verhoeven and Gilroy point out that during the 1790s, journals such as *British Critic* and *Gentlemen's Magazine* printed many articles against emigration schemes (xvii).

26. Gerard Baker, "A Callow Cowboy Stumbles at a Cultural Divide," *Financial Times,* (May 30, 2002, 13. Baker, writing on George W. Bush's trip to Europe, says that "Europeans . . . simply find Mr. Bush irredeemably uncouth, a walking, talking version of every American cliché they love to hate."

27. Defoe, *Atlas,* 220.

28. Both John P. Zomchick and Frederick M. Keener see Martin's emigration as a way to dismiss a problematic figure, and both note that Brown is produced as a corrective paradigm. Keener says, "All Lismahago's disabilities Brown has addressed in his own career and overcome." "Transitions in *Humphry Clinker,*" *Studies in Eighteenth-Century Culture* 16 (1986): 160. Zomchick argues that "Bramble, by giving Martin his ticket to a possible fortune, also risks creating his hated mushroom nabob," so the text needs to introduce the successful but virtuous East Indian veteran. "Social Class, Character, and Narrative Strategy in *Humphry Clinker,*" *Eighteenth-Century Life* 10, no. 3 (October 1986): 181. Michael Warner points out that "England's movement into America was in most ways parallel with its movement into India," with the same administrators and investors engaged in both hemispheres: "Clive, before his death in 1774, was slated to quell American unrest following the Boston Tea Party; Cornwallis compensated for the loss of America by consolidating Bengal." "What's Colonial about Colonial America?," in *Possible Pasts: Becoming Colonial in Early America,* ed. Robert Blair St. George (Ithaca, NY: Cornell University Press, 2000), 61.

CHAPTER 3. PERIPHERAL VISIONS

1. Homi Bhabha, "The Other Question: Difference, Discrimination and the Discourse of Colonialism," *Literature, Politics and Theory: Papers from the Essex Conference, 1974–84,* ed. Francis Barker, Peter Hulme, Margaret Iverson, and Diana Loxley (London: Methuen, 1986), 154–56. Hamilton anticipates the effect Lisa Lowe attributes to Vasant A. Shahane's 1975 anthology of Indian writings on E. M. Forster: "it poses the notion of a native point of view over and against the ruling British perspective that traditionally considered India a colorful backdrop to the central British drama, and Indians as peripheral objects to be colonized and scrutinized rather than as possessing a point of view themselves." *Critical Terrains: French and British Orientalisms* (Ithaca, NY: Cornell University Press, 1991), 103.

2. Claire Grogan, in "Crossing Genre, Gender and Race in Elizabeth Hamilton's *Translation of the Letters of a Hindoo Rajah,*" *Studies in the Novel* 34, no. 1 (Spring 2002); makes the point that "the reader [of *Hindoo Rajah*] is persuaded . . . that Britain and the

Westerner rather than the East and Easterner require improvement and reform" (25). Ketake Kusheri Dyson suggests that "A relative lack of arrogance went with the political insecurity of the British in India in the latter part of the eighteenth century. . . . The 'wisdom of the East' and the 'noble savage' became sticks with which to chastise European civilizations." *A Various Universe: A Study of the Journals and Memoirs of British Men and Women in the Indian Subcontinent, 1765–1856* (Delhi: Oxford University Press, 1978), 19). Discussing William Hickey's *Memoirs* (1749–1809), Dyson finds Hickey "paints an unforgettable picture of British society in both London and Calcutta. He depicts it as frivolous, unscrupulous, immersed in fashion, addicted to heavy eating, hard drinking, gambling, and dueling" (154). David Cannadine, opposing Said on constructions of "otherness," argues that the British empire was "concerned with . . . the 'construction of affinities" on the presumption that society on the periphery was the same as, or even on occasions superior to, society in the metropolis." *Ornamentalism: How the British Saw Their Empire* (Oxford: Oxford University Press, 2001), xix.

3. Pamela Perkins, introduction to *Hermsprong*, 23; Pamela Perkins and Shannon Russell, introduction to *Hindoo Rajah*, 13.

4. John Dinwiddy, "Conceptions of Revolution in the English Radicalism of the 1790s," in *The Transformation of Political Culture: England and Germany in the Late Eighteenth Century*, ed. Eckhart Hellmuth (Oxford: Oxford University Press, 1990), 549; Gary Kelly, *English Fiction of the Romantic Period, 1789–1830* (London: Longman, 1989), 60.

5. I cannot agree with Kate Teltscher's argument that the reader of *Hindoo Rajah* can "still . . . condescend to the ignorant foreigner . . . as an *unwitting* critic, the Indian cannot lay claim to any substantial moral authority over the society criticized." *India Inscribed: European and British Writing on India, 1600–1800* (Delhi: Oxford University Press, 1995), 142). Although Zāārmilla's initial enthusiasm regarding English society may be naïve, his subsequent critiques (for example, of the legal system or salon society) are clear-eyed disparagements. He is, I suggest, an example of what Srinivas Aravamudan calls "a tropicopolitan" who "challenge[s] the developing privilege of Enlightenment cosmopolitans" (6).

6. Obviously, I diverge from the assessments of Gary Kelly and Pamela Perkins on Bage's women. Kelly says that, although Bage believes in the equality of women, "he seems to have been incapable of making any of his female characters, apart from the secondary ones, as interesting and vivacious as an Elizabeth Inchbald or a Mary Wollstonecraft." *The English Jacobin Novel, 1780–1805* (Oxford: Clarendon Press, 1976), 41. Perkins finds that the effect of Miss Fluart's iconoclasm is attenuated by Miss Campinet's conventionality: "As long as the main heroine does and says what she ought and patiently rebukes her witty friend's excesses in a properly ladylike manner, the wit of the secondary heroine is contained and to a certain extent neutralized." "Playfulness of the Pen: Bage and the Politics of Comedy," *Journal of Narrative Technique* 26, no. 1 (Winter 1996): 39–40. To me, Miss Fluart is anything but secondary; in every sense except within a conventional marriage plot, she is the heroine of *Hermsprong*, one whose independence is held up as a model for less courageous women.

7. Bage, *Mount Henneth*. 2 vols. (1782; repr., New York: Garland, 1979), 75.

8. Rosemary Raza, *In Their Own Words: British Women Writers and India, 1740–1857* (Oxford: Oxford University Press, 2006), xii. In their attitudes toward women's education, both Hamilton and Bage reflect Wollstonecraft's views. Hermsprong even cites *A Vindication of the Rights of Woman*, which, he says, "affirms that the mode of their educa-

tion turns the energies of their minds on trifles" (213). Critics agree that Hamilton's position is both feminist and conservative: Kelly, for example, distinguishes her from Wollstonecraft and Hays because hers is a domestic and religious feminism. *Women, Writing, and Revolution, 1790–1827* (Oxford: Clarendon Press, 1993), 142–43. Perkins and Russell add, "while the radical Wollstonecraft frames the question in terms of future improvement of society, the conservative Hamilton suggests that improved education for women will return society to a happier past and that in providing that education, society will be true to the religious principles it already claims to embrace" (17).

9. Eliza Fay's acerbic comment on sati equates European and Indian attitudes: "this practice is entirely a political scheme intended to insure the care and good offices of wives to their husbands, who have not failed in most countries to invent a sufficient number of rules to render the weaker sex totally subservient to their authority." *Original Letters from India (1779–1815)*, ed. E. M. Forster (N.Y.: Harcourt, Brace, and Co., 1925), 214. W. T. Moncrieff's comic play *The Cataract of the Ganges; or, The Rajah's Daughter: A Grand Romantic Drama, In Two Acts* (London: Cumberland, 1823), includes a parodic Crusoe figure whose take on sati makes a distinction between the two cultures: "in my country when a man dies, he does get rid of his wife for some time at all events — but here a poor devil of a husband no sooner pops into the other world, than his wife jumps out of the frying pan into the fire, and follows him" (I.ii.p.11).

10. Isobel Grundy, "'The barbarous character we give them': White Women Travellers Report on Other Races," *Studies in Eighteenth-Century Culture* 22 (1992): 83. Felicity Nussbaum finds that in *Hindoo Rajah* "no woman, Eastern or Western, is truly the equal of man . . . Hamilton's novel berates women of both nations instead of exploiting the radical potential for uniting their cause." *Torrid Zones: Maternity, Sexuality, and Empire in Eighteenth-Century English Narratives*, 171–2. In his diatribe against Hindu culture, Alexander Fraser Tytler asserts: "The influence of female society on the morals of all nations has been acknowledged to be very beneficial; but as if to deprive the natives of every means of improvement, the shasters teach them to despise their women, and to keep them in a state of continued subjection and degradation. To this cause may be ascribed much of the criminality which we find among all ranks." *Considerations on the Political State of India*, 2 vols. (London: Perry and Col, 1815), 1:236–37.

11. Michael Hechter, in *Internal Colonialism: The Celtic Fringe in British National Development, 1536–1966* (Berkeley: University of California Press, 1975), shows that one result of Union was the coercive Anglicization of Scottish education and language as part of the imperial project: "As the civil service expanded, particularly in the colonization and administration of India, English education was a definite advantage in enabling a candidate to pass the examination procedure" (116).

12. Phebe Gibbes, *Hartly House, Calcutta: A Novel of the Days of Warren Hastings*, ed. John McFarlane (1789; repr., Calcutta: Thacker, Spink, & Co., 1908), 130; Benjamin Franklin, *The Autobiography of Benjamin Franklin and Selections from His Other Writings*, ed. Henry Steele Commager (New York: The Modern Library, 1950), 52–53. Although Hermsprong ascribes many of his healthy habits to his upbringing among Amerindians, he concedes that "there are improvident characters among them; and the number is not diminished by your rum bottles" (210). He does not, however, comment on his own father "having distributed presents of rum and tobacco" among the Nawdoessie tribe (249).

13. A personal note: I remember adult relatives in Calcutta spending whole days

playing "Twenty-Nine," a version of bridge popular in all parts of Indian society. Of course, as far as I know, no bets were involved.

14. Dyson points to the disparity in attitudes toward killing animals; to European travelers in India, "'sport' was unobjectionable, even when it meant the destruction of rare animals and birds simply for the sake of collecting stuffed specimens, while a goat-sacrifice or a sheep-sacrifice, where the flesh was eaten afterwards, was felt to be a disgusting and barbarous ceremony" (74). Hamilton herself shares Indians' (and Pope's and Thomson's) distaste for hunting. Praising the good squire Mr. Darnley, old Mr. Denbeigh says, "The sufferings of a poor timorous animal, harassed by fatigue, and tortured by the agonizing sensations of excessive fear, were not necessary for his amusement" (298).

15. Davis, 63.

16. Franklin recounts that the English are deeply impressed by his strength and his swimming prowess (52, 56–57). Jay Fliegelman, describing the importance of Lockean pedagogy to the revolutionary movement in American, says that "it was stoical—urging physical hardiness as well as rational self-sufficiency." *Prodigals and Pilgrims*, 14.

17. In Bage's *Mount Henneth*, the hero encounters a group of wounded Hessian mercenaries returning from America. A German soldier tells him, "If . . . you can make the Americans cut their own throats, you may succeed in retaining your sovereignty; for as to yourselves, and we Germans to help you, you really cut so few per annum, that you must call in the assistance of the next generation. The misfortune is, they breed as fast as you" (295). In both novels, Bage contrasts American energy with British weakness.

18. Gibbes, *Hartley House*, 141. See also Frances Burney's *A Busy Day*, (1800), in which the heroine assures her sister that "the Native Gentoos are the mildest and gentlest of human beings." Ed. Tara Ghoshal Wallace (New Brunswick, NJ: Rutgers University Press, 1984), 1:493–94. V. G. Kiernan believes that "experience of Bengal in particular led to its inhabitants being considered extraordinarily spiritless and docile." (*The Lords of Human Kind: Black Man, Yellow Man, and White Man in an Age of Empire* (Boston: Little, Brown and Co., 1969), 33. Eliza Fay, with characteristic acidity, says, "notwithstanding their apparent gentleness and timidity, the Hindoos will meet death with intrepid firmness—they are also invincibly obstinate, and will *die* rather than concede a point" (217; her formulation recalls to mind Smollett's Jesuit missionaries). Tytler dismisses the myth of the gentle Hindu and cites instead a plethora of crimes and delinquencies in Bengal, among them "a general depravity of manners, and the want of all religious and moral principle among the Brahmins and the lower orders of the natives" (204–5). It should give us pause that Tytler writes this in a manual for Englishmen setting out to serve the empire, young men "sent to the enjoyment of wealth and power *while they are yet boys*" (xiii; his italics).

19. Kenneth Ballhatchet points out that just as the British were horrified by Indian customs such as child marriage and polygamy, "Indians . . . were often shocked by European manners, not only in eating, drinking and personal hygiene but in the indecorous behaviour of ladies baring their shoulders and even dancing on social occasions." *Race, Sex and Class under the Raj: Imperial Attitudes and Policies and Their Critics, 1793–1905* (New York: St. Martin's Press, 1980), 5. Dyson adds that to the British, Hinduism seemed primitive and pagan, while to Hindus, the British, "with their drunken parties and mixed dancing . . . seemed a people who had no code to live by" (69–70). Both Perkins and Mona Scheuerman note that American characters "slash through the corruptions of European society" and expose "the degeneracy of the European concepts

of civilization and pleasure." Perkins, "Playfulness of the Pen," 33; Scheuerman, *Social Protest in the Eighteenth-Century English Novel* (Columbus: Ohio State University Press, 1985), 208.

20. Kramnick, *Republicanism*, 4, 27. Kelly points out that "Bage's friends were merchants and industrialists, and they were being hurt by a war waged, so it seemed, solely by the aristocratic oligarchy who held the reins of power." *The English Jacobin Novel, 1780–1805*, 31. Marilyn Butler makes a similar point when she posits that Bage and his circle were "opposed to the American War: not merely for the effect it might have on their immediate business interests, but because Ministerial policy towards the colonists was an interference from the centre with the liberty of the middle-class subject." *Jane Austen and the War of Ideas* (Oxford: Clarendon Press, 1975), 76.

21. Harry T. Dickinson, "Popular Loyalism in Britain in the 1790s," in *The Transformation of Political Culture*, 506, 512. See also Richard Slotkin, who traces the shift in European attitudes toward American individualism after the French Revolution: "The postrevolutionary European writer could hardly help despairing of the Enlightenment's dream and deserting it for Burkean conservatism, Napoleonic despotism, or Romantic irrationalism." *Regeneration through Violence: The Mythology of the American Frontier, 1600–1860* (Norman: University of Oklahoma Press, 1973), 345.

22. Kramnick, *Republicanism*, 4.

23. Gary Kelly, *Women, Writing and Revolution*, 137. Teltscher too points out that Sheermaal's accounts "depict a morally depraved, irreligious land, with virtue surviving only in the cottages of the poor and remote regions of Scotland" (140).

24. Timothy Trundle's crime and justification mirror an event in the household of David Mallet, Thomson's countryman and friend in London. Henry Grey Graham recounts: "Consternation, it is said, arose one day when the man-servant ran off with the silverplate. When caught the fellow impudently told his master that he (Mr. Mallet) was alone to blame for the theft, because his infidel talk had taken away his belief in a future judgment" (280–81). Although Graham takes the anecdote from Thomas Davies's 1818 biography of Garrick, it is possible that some version of it may have reached Hamilton through her circle of Scottish intellectual friends.

25. Gary Kelly, *English Fiction*, 28; Perkins, introduction, 45; Scheuermann, *Social Protest*, 218. Nancy E. Johnson is more positive about the institution itself, although she rightly connects legal power to the power of property: "The legal system rises to the occasion and acknowledges truth when expressed by a man endowed with individual rights (and plenty of property)." *The English Jacobin Novel on Rights, Property and the Law: Critiquing the Contract* (Houndmills, UK: Palgrave/Macmillan, 2004), 99.

26. In Jane Austen's *Persuasion*, Anne Elliot remains uneasy about her cousin Mr. Elliot's past because "she saw there had been bad habits; Sunday-travelling had been a common thing." *The Novels of Jane Austen*, V:161. The Jacobin John Thelwall believes that Americans are overly religious because "Sunday travelling makes a man a prophaner." *The Politics of English Jacobinism: Writings of John Thelwall*, ed. Gregory Claeys (University Park: Pennsylvania State University Press, 1995), 55.

27. In *Hermsprong*, Grondale's mistress does not attend church, "not for want of piety; but because she could not sit with ease in any seat but Lady Grondale's; and his lordship had not yet invited her thither in a way she could perfectly approve" (163). Hermsprong himself, despite his rejection of class privilege and organized religion, acquires a pew as a consequence of buying property in the neighborhood.

28. Dyson, *Various Universe*, 24. Dean Mahomet's glowing account (1794) of Indian

culture concedes that Brahmins "considerably benefit from their [the common people's] credulity." *The Travels of Dean Mahomet: An Eighteenth-Century Journey through India,* ed. Michael H. Fisher (Berkeley: University of California Press, 1997), 53.

29. English anti-Catholicism, particularly regarding monastic life, is, of course, a common literary trope at this time. Matthew Lewis's *The Monk* (1796) relies on anticonventual feeling to achieve its gothic effects, and Charles Maturin's *Melmoth the Wanderer* (1820) depicts the horrors of forced monasticism.

30. Although there are of course documented journeys to Europe undertaken by Indians in the eighteenth century, Harihar Das notes the rarity of such travels: "that the contemplative Indian should fare forth from his long seclusion is interesting historically and still more psychologically . . . to cross the *Kalapanee* [black water] was considered by orthodox Indians to be a defilement." "The Early Indian Visitors to England," *Calcutta Review* 13 (October 1924): 83.

31. In *Mount Henneth*, Foston finds that when he tries to preach Christianity in India, "I was heard with a holy horror, but nothing invidious or abusive was retorted upon me" (205). Perkins and Russell point out that "like many Western Europeans of her day, Hamilton was vehemently anti-Muslim." ("Introduction," 24). She also, of course, ascribed to the conservative theory of Indian society held by Edmund Burke, William Jones, and William Robertson, who did not want to interfere with Indian religions; see, for example, George D. Bearce, *British Attitudes toward India, 1784–1813* (London: George Allen and Unwin Ltd., 1968), 61. In 1767, even before Jones began his project to preserve Indian culture, John Z. Howell "criticized all his predecessors' views that the Hindus were 'a race of stupid and gross idolaters.' Most of the more recent accounts of the Hindus, he argued, were by those of the 'Romish communion,' who had a vested interest in denigrating Hindus, as they wanted to convert them to Catholicism. Howell stigmatized Roman Catholic tenets as more idolatrous than those of the Hindus." Bernard S. Cohn, *Colonialism and Its Forms of Knowledge: The British in India* (Princeton, NJ: Princeton University Press, 1996), 25. Hamilton's viewpoint opposes designs such as Charles Grant's 1792 missionary project in India, of which Homi Bhabha says, "What is suggested is a process of reform through which Christian doctrines might collude with divisive caste practices to prevent dangerous political alliances. Inadvertently, Grant produces a knowledge of Christianity as a form of social control which conflicts with the enunciatory assumptions that authorize his discourse." *The Location of Culture* (London: Routledge, 1994), 87.

32. Munshī Ismāʿil, visiting England in 1772–73, talks of the political system in equally glowing terms: "The peasantry . . . do not suffer from the oppression and blows of the landholder. According to the King's law every man is himself free, but without power over others. A balanced connection has become established whereby the King fears the ministers, the landholders the peasantry, and the populace the law. Through the interposition of this moderating chain of behaviour each man is accountable, and none causes pain or injury." Simon Digby, "An Eighteenth Century Narrative of a Journey from Bengal to England: Munshī Ismāʿil's *New History*," in *Urdu and Muslim South Asia: Studies in Honour of Ralph Russell,* ed. Christopher Shackle (London: School of Oriental and African Studies, University of London, 1989), 59.

33. David Punter, "Fictional Representation of the Law in the Eighteenth Century," *Eighteenth-Century Fiction* 16, no. 1 (Autumn 1982): 47.

34. Marshall, *Problems of Empire,* 61.

35. David Musselwhite, "Trial of Warren Hastings," *Literature, Politics and Theory,*

83. C. A. Bayly says that the Hindu laws were based on "textual and high caste interpretations. . . . European influences and the British concern for stability helped consolidate the desire of Indian elites for hierarchy and control." *Indian Society and the Making of the British Empire, The New Cambridge History of India*, 4 vols., ed. Gordon Johnson (Cambridge: Cambridge University Press, 1988), 2:76. According to Ania Loomba, "Pundits became the spokesmen for a vast and heterogeneous Hindu population, and facilitated the replacement of multiple local non-scriptural laws and procedures by a standardized, inflexible 'brahminical' (and more patriarchal) version of Hinduism, which received ideological sanction by Oriental scholarship." *Colonialism/Postcolonialism* (London: Routledge, 1998), 167–68. Cohn 74–75.

36. Grondale's charge to Corrow reminds one of Lady Booby employing lawyer Scout to eject Joseph Andrews and Fanny from her parish; Scout assures her of success, because "the laws of this land are not so vulgar to permit a mean fellow to contend with one of your ladyship's fortune." Henry Fielding, *Joseph Andrews*, ed. Martin C. Battestin (Boston: Houghton Mifflin Co., 1961), 243.

37. Punter, "Fictional Representation," 66.

38. In one of his many provocative letters to Grondale, Hermsprong writes that Wigley is being persecuted "for virtue; for to support the freedom of elections, is surely a political virtue, in every creed but the creed of courtiers" (290). Smollett targets the same kind of political corruption when George Prankley rebuffs his old friend Tom Eastgate's request for patronage because "he had promised the living to another man, who had a vote in the county, where he proposed to offer himself a candidate at the next general election" (103). Dinwiddy states that few English radicals "were more than parliamentary reformers" and even the London Corresponding Society "could justifiably point out that their immediate and overt political objectives fell within the bounds of constitutional reform" (539, 542). Bage's text outlines the corruptions which justified these reform movements.

39. Thelwall, *Politics*, 157. Kramnick suggests that "in the late eighteenth century, America embodies the inversion of social order, the shattering of the great chain of being, the violation of political and social principles that for centuries had appeared God-given" (292). J. R. Jones, in *Britain and the World, 1649–1815* (Sussex, UK: Harvester Press, 1980), writes similarly of the political climate in summer 1792: "Events in France opened everyone's eyes to a possibility that very few had previously appreciated, namely that all existing political, social and religious institutions, forms and values could be totally destroyed: political action and violence could be used to impose a new order" (242).

40. Dickinson says, "Selections from Burke were published in provincial newspapers and, in the intense Burke/Paine controversy, the publication of conservative tracts far outnumbered those on the radical side" (526–27). Andrew McCann, in *Cultural Politics in the 1790s: Literature, Radicalism and the Public Sphere* (Harmondsworth, UK: Macmillan, 1999), looks at how "a climate of political unease and military conflict enabled orators like Edmund Burke and the slew of conservative pamphleteers . . . to address with confidence a national community steeled against the Jacobin menace" (2). David Simpson argues that the conservatives were so successful because British political tradition rejected theoretical discourse: "The radicals of the 1790s inherited the disadvantages of a nationalist tradition already firmly set against system and theory. . . . The opponents of French Revolution and English reform thus inherited the discursive high ground in their dismissal of theory as inappropriate to an authentically British aesthetic

or political practice." *Romanticism, Nationalism, and the Revolt against Theory* (Chicago: University of Chicago Press, 1993), 52–53.

41. Dickinson, "Popular Loyalism," 516. He adds that the proclamation led to 150 meetings of magistrates across the country. C. A. Bayly points to "the sharp perception of danger among the ruling class, threatened as they felt themselves to be by the dissolution of social order at home and a fearsome military and ideological challenge abroad." *Imperial Meridian: The British Empire and the World, 1780–1830* (London: Longman, 1989), 100.

42. Dickinson, "Popular Loyalism," 508. Kramnick adds that although governmental authority eroded over the last half of the eighteenth century, it kept its power over the working classes: "There was one exception, however, to the government's inability or lack of desire to preserve traditional public restraints on merchants, landlords, and manufacturers: at no time did public authority retreat from its traditional controls on workers. Workers, for example, were still restrained by the force of public authority from combining in associations" (105). Paul Keen, in *The Crisis of Literature in the 1790s: Print Culture and the Public Sphere* (Cambridge: Cambridge University Press, 1999) examines the particular effect of establishment views on literature: "The excesses generated by the French Revolution, on the one hand, and by the information revolution on the other, converged into an antagonism towards those new readerships who, critics argued, could not be trusted to resist the inflammatory effects of seditious writing or the vagaries of literary fashion" (8).

43. Kelly, *English Jacobin Novel*, 58. The Treason Act defined as treason criticism of the government of the king, and the Seditious Meetings Act, aimed at the London Correspondence Society, set up serious roadblocks for meetings of more than fifty people. Dinwiddy says, "After the Terror and the Thermidorean reaction . . . the view of revolution as a basically benign, consensual, linear process obviously became hard to sustain. In his 1796 edition [of *Political Justice*], Godwin put a strong emphasis on the *costs* of revolution, on its tendency to replace one tyranny by another, and on its capacity for interrupting rather than advancing the course of improvement" (548).

44. de Tocqueville, 138–39. The Reverend Andrew Burnaby observes of Pennsylvania: "As to religion, there is none properly established; but Protestants of all denominations, Papists, Jews, and all other sects whatsoever, are universally tolerated" (95).

45. Nussbaum, *Torrid Zones*, 171. Nussbaum echoes Gary Kelly's contention that Hamilton's novel and her brother Charles's history of the Rohilla wars both aim "to justify British intervention in India." *Women, Writing, and Revolution*, 129. These characterizations would place Hamilton's work in what Cannadine calls one mode of imperial discourse: "that the native regimes and hierarchies were backward, inefficient, despotic, and corrupt, and had to be overthrown and reconstructed according to the more advanced model of Western society and politics." However, these scholars' analyses also dismantle Cannadine's dichotomy and place *Hindoo Rajah* in Cannadine's second mode: "that they were traditional and organic, an authentic world of ordered, harmonious, time-hallowed social relations of the kind that the Industrial Revolution was threatening (or destroying) in Britain" (12). Hamilton, in other words, propounds both versions of Indian government and culture.

46. Historians and literary critics have commented on how heavily imperial expansion in India depended on this sort of liberational discourse. Keen, for example, suggests that guilt about conquest "could be overshadowed by an alternative stress on the importance of introducing liberty into an area that had been enslaved by centuries of

less enlightened conquerors" (225); Nigel Leask points to the general consensus that "maintained that British power sought to liberate Hindus from the Islamic yoke of the Mughal empire." *British Romantic Writers and the East: Anxieties of Empire* (Cambridge: Cambridge University Press, 1992), 72; Ros Ballaster traces a shift "from an earlier identification with the Mughal dynasty as a model for an advanced and civilized culture. . . . Mughal government was reconceived as a predatory regime exploitative of a gentle and submissive 'native' population, the latter requiring the assistance of European powers such as Britain to liberate it from the yoke of Islamic absolutism." *Fabulous Orients: Fictions of the East in England, 1662–1785* (Oxford: Oxford University Press, 2005), 160. Kernan says that not only did the British feel that they had rescued Hindus, but also "a conviction was fixed in the British mind, unshakable in later days, that India without British rule must fall prey to anarchy and invasion" (33). Interestingly, Sir John Malcolm, Governor of Madras from 1827 to 1830, strongly argues against expansion of British power in India: "considering, as I do from all my experience, that it is our policy to maintain as long as we can all native states now existing . . . I do think that every measure should be adopted that is calculated to avert what I should consider as one of the greatest calamities, in a political point of view, that could rise to our empire, — the whole of India becoming subject to our direct rule." *The Government of India* (London: John Murray, 1833), 159.

47. Hodges "was eager to point out that the people were doing well in the areas under British management. He found Bengal 'highly flourishing in tillage of every kind'" (Dyson, 137). Tobin suggests that Hodges's portraits were ideologically motivated: "functioning as a defense of Hastings's government, *Travels in India* sought to portray British colonialism in India in a positive light" (142). George Smith, in *The Life of William Carey, D.D.: Shoemaker and Missionary, Professor of Sanskrit, Bengali, and Marathi in the college of Fort William, Calcutta* (London: John Murray, 1885), points out that Cary went "to the one province which was almost entirely British . . . the British peace, in Bengal at least, had allowed abundant crops" (67). Bearce describes the *zamindari* land/ rent system Cornwallis (Governor-General from 1786 to 1793) devised as one that mirrored English practice, and adds that the system failed quickly, causing more economic misery for the peasants (45). Martha McLaren points out "a surprising similarity between Indian land tenure at this time and Scotland's traditional land tenure system." *British India and British Scotland, 1780–1830*, 201. See Dr. Johnson's defense of Scottish Tacksmen against "men not defective in judgment or general experience, who consider the Tacksman as a useless burden of the ground, as a drone who lives upon the product of an estate . . . and who impoverishes at once the landlord and the tenant" (*Journey*, 78).

48. Charles Hamilton, *An Historical Relation of the Origin, Progress, and final Dissolution of the Rohilla Afgans in the Northern Provinces of Hindostan* (London: G. Kearsley, 1787), xiv. His account is confirmed by Dean Mahomet, who describes the victory and praises the gallantry of the British soldiers (89). Contrast Charles Hamilton's view with Pope's reference to sailors eager to kill on order.

49. Nussbaum notes that "'Complexion' in this period serves to isolate and exclude the human from the subhuman, the beautiful from the ugly, and the metropole from the periphery." "Women and Race: 'a different complexion,'" In *Women and Literature in Britain, 1700–1800*, ed. Vivien Jones (Cambridge: Cambridge University Press, 2000), 84. To eighteenth-century English men and women, Indians were conflated with Africans as "Black," though many contemporary writers saw differences which led, per-

haps, to a more complicated racism. Jemima Kinderslay, while she disliked the dark skin of Indians, thought Indian women had such fine features "that if they were set off by a fine red and white complexion they would be incomparable" (qtd. in Dyson 93). Gibbes's heroine speculates that the people of Bengal must be southern Persians because everyone is "black," but with "long hair and regular features" unlike the inhabitants of Guinea (27).

50. Daniel James Ennis, *Enter the Press-Gang: Naval Impressment in Eighteenth-Century British Literature* (Newark: University of Delaware Press, 2002), 67. Ennis describes the elaborate maneuvers of sailors who wanted to avoid being kidnapped. In 1795, an East India Company ship arrived at the Thames estuary; twenty-seven crew members had disembarked earlier, getting to the borders of London by back routes, then boarding coaches, firing their weapons, to make "the three-mile dash from the town of Poplar to the safe haven of the City of London, at which point they surrendered their arms at the East India House and collected their wages" (25). Jeremy Black says that "the Press, resort to which was necessary even in years of peace, represented one of the most formidable impositions of the eighteenth-century monarchy on its subjects" (21). Potential soldiers were also vulnerable. Michael H. Fisher, in the introduction to Dean Mahomet's *Travels*, says, "London newspapers reported that the Court of Directors [of the East India Company] illegally arranged for European men to be kidnapped and forcibly impressed into its armies" (15). My next chapter deals with Scott's treatment of this phenomenon in *The Surgeon's Daughter*.

51. Keen writes of eighteenth-century concerns that "the dynamics of empire would exacerbate the morally enfeebling effects of commerce. . . . These worries were aggravated by concerns about the aberrant nature of imperial commerce. . . . The worst . . . elements of British society were rising to the surface" (225). Marshall argues that at this time, the earlier congruence of anti-slavery and anti-imperial rhetoric collapses: "In the 1790s . . . the paths began to diverge. British rule in India seemed to be an outlet for the qualities coming to be most admired in the upper classes, high professional skill and benevolence; slavery embodied old and discredited values." "'A Free though Conquering People': Britain and Asia in the Eighteenth Century," An Inaugural Lecture in the Rhodes Chair of Imperial History, Delivered at King's College, London, Thursday March 5, 1981, 19.

52. Teltscher, *India Inscribed*, 139; Leask, *British Romantic Writers*, 101.

53. See Claire Grogan's nuanced reading, which posits that the novel belongs in the category of oriental study rather than oriental fable. Grogan argues that Hamilton's complex gender position requires a revision of the terms associated with Orientalism itself.

54. Said charges Jones with aiming "to subdue the infinite variety of the Orient . . . to domesticate the Orient and turn it into a province of European learning." *Orientalism* (New York: Vintage Books, 1979), 77–78. Bernard S. Cohn, too, calls the researches of the Orientalists "a European project, the end being to construct a history of the relationship between India and the West, to classify and locate their civilizations on an evaluative scale of progress and decay. . . . To appear legitimate in the eyes of the Indians, the British thought they had to demonstrate an interest in those Indians and institutions that were the carriers of the traditions" (46). Balachandra Rajan advances a somewhat milder assessment, suggesting that Jones's desire to reinstate Indian customs was "an important part of his troubled justification of the right of the British to govern India." *Under Western Eyes: India from Milton to Macaulay*, 87. Kelly and Keen focus on

the obfuscating nature of Orientalist scholarship: Kelly argues that "Charles Hamilton's translating and editing colonize Oriental texts while appearing to preserve and disseminate them, subsuming them in an Orientalist imperial project designed to supersede the culture, society, and state that produced them" (131) is in fact imperial appropriation; Keen says, "Like Hamilton's, Jones's argument moves from a compensatory insistence on the importance of perfecting colonial government to a triumphant emphasis on the study of literature as an end in itself which wholly erases the violent origins of colonial domination which made this possible" (220). Teltscher agrees: "These representations tend to obscure the violence and disruption of colonial intervention and make British authority in India appear natural and unproblematic" (9).

Those who see the Orientalist project in a more positive light blame later developments for distorting the scholarly aims of Jones and his disciples. Bayly points to a generational shift: "The rediscovery of classical Indian languages and translation of modern texts was initiated by the savants of the Enlightenment, but its 'practical' purpose was soon emphasized. The men of Wellesley's generation, young civil servants, could only be released from dependence on Indians by command of their language" (150). Suresh Chandra Ghosh detects an earlier tension: "Sir William Jones and the 'Asiatic Society' in their work were acting against the general trend of British society in Bengal . . . the forces released by the Industrial Revolution and religious revival— were not as favourable to a continued growth of administration and enthusiasm for Indian culture." *The Social Condition of the British Community in Bengal, 1757–1800* (Leiden: E. J. Brill, 1970), 169. Raymond Schwab's magisterial and indispensable book *The Oriental Renaissance: Europe's Rediscovery of India and the East, 1680–1880*, trans. Gene Patterson-Black and Victor Reinking, foreword by Edward Said (New York: Columbia University Press, 1984) ascribes Romantics' special attraction to India to "the fact that it posed, in its totality, the great question of the Different" (6). Schwab does not deny the imperial uses of scholarship, but praises the "extraordinary undertaking" of Hastings and Jones, reserving his scorn for nineteenth-century interventions: "It was England's great disgrace to be too self-seeking in India to avoid violent reactions . . . in order to protect those who followed Jones from certain of those who followed Hastings, the scholars were obliged to struggle against conspiracies of narrow-mindedness" (43).

55. John Drew, *India and the Romantic Imagination* (Delhi: Oxford University Press, 1987), 81.

56. Dean Mahomet refers to "some European Gentlemen, led hither by the love of science and antiquity, [who] discovered a great many astronomical instruments, of a large size, admirably well contrived, though injured by the hand of time. It was supposed they might have been constructed some centuries ago, under the direction of the great Akbar, the fond votary of science" (79). In fact, an observatory in Benares was one of the Jantar Mantars built by Maharaja Sawai Jai Singh in the middle of the eighteenth century.

57. Loomba, *Colonialism*, 17. Gauri Viswanathan writes about the eventual (and ironic) distortion of the Orientalist project; in the nineteenth century, she says, "while Englishmen of all ages could enjoy and appreciate exotic tales, romantic narrative, adventure stories, and mythological literature for their charm and even derive instruction from them, their colonial subjects were believed incapable of doing so because they lacked prior mental and moral cultivation required for literature—especially their own—to have any instructive value for them." *Masks of Conquest: Literary Study and British Rule in India* (New York: Columbia University Press, 1989), 5.

CHAPTER 4. RHETORICAL MANIPULATIONS

1. Robin Jared Lewis, "The Literature of the Raj," *Asia and Western Fiction*, ed. Robin W. Winks and James R. Rush (Honolulu: University of Hawaii Press, 1990), 55. Homi Bhabha, in his discussion of colonial discourse, says "the stereotype, which is its major discursive strategy, is a form of knowledge and identification that vacillates between what is always 'in place', already known, and something that must be anxiously repeated . . . as if the essential duplicity of the Asiatic or bestial licence of the African that needs no proof, can never really, in discourse, be proved." *Location of Culture*, 66. Kate Teltscher provides an example of this kind of reflexive categorizing when she quotes from the Belgian traveler Balthazar Solvyns's characterization of kinds of Hindus: "The *Brahman* has a mild and pious air; the *Kuttery* is haughty and bold in appearance; cunning and mercantile caution is marked on the countenance of the *Byce*" (130).

2. Iain Gordon Brown, "Griffins, Nabobs and a Seasoning of Curry Powder: Walter Scott and the Indian Theme in Life and Literature," in *The Tiger and the Thistle: Tipu Sultan and the Scots in India, 1760–1800*, ed. Anne Buddle, Pauline Rohtagi, and Iain Gordon Brown (Edinburgh: National Gallery of Scotland, 1999), 71. Claire Lamont, too, sees the complications in Croftangry's preface: "At the outset of an imperial narrative, we find expressions of doubt. It was common in the eighteenth century, as later, to regard the extension of British power in India as unparalleled. Scott does not subscribe to that view, using the problematic comparison of the Spanish conquest of Mexico. . . . Scott was typical of many British people of his day in not criticising his country's imperial endeavour as such, but being alert to the anxieties it engendered" ("Scott and Eighteenth-Century Imperialism: India and the Scottish Highlands," in *Configuring Romanticism*, ed. Theo d'haen, Peter Liebragfe, and Wim Tigges (Amsterdam: Rodopi, 2003), 39–40.

3. *Romanticism and Colonialism: Writing Empire, 1700–1830*, ed. Tim Fulford and Peter J. Kitson (Cambridge: Cambridge University Press, 1998), 3; *Romanticism, Race, and Imperial Culture, 1780–1834*, eds. Alan Richardson and Sonja Hofkosh (Bloomington: Indiana University Press, 1996), 5. Yoon Sun Lee contextualizes her fascinating study of Scott's *Antiquary* in his visit to the field of Waterloo; see *Nationalism and Irony: Burke, Scott, Carlyle* (New York: Oxford University Press, 2004). These and other recent work redress Nigel Leask's lament that "Romantic Studies . . . in Britain have been slow to address the imperial components of the culture." *British Romantic Writers and the East*, 11.

4. Peter Garside, "Scott, the Eighteenth Century and the New Man of Sentiment," *Anglia: Zeitschrift fur Englische Philologie*, Band 103 (1985): 73–76.

5. Lamont, "Historical Note on 'The Surgeon's Daughter,'" *Chronicles*, 449–55; Millgate, introduction, *Guy Mannering*, ed. P. D. Garside (London: Penguin, 2003), xvi-xviii; Brown 71–72; Jackson, "Introducing Guy Mannering," manuscript essay.

6. James Reed, *Sir Walter Scott: Landscape and Locality* (London: Athlone Press, 1980), 69; Jane Millgate, *Walter Scott: The Making of the Novelist* (Toronto: University of Toronto Press, 1984), 68; Graham McMaster, *Scott and Society* (Cambridge: Cambridge University Press, 1981) 159; Harry E. Shaw, *The Forms of Historical Fiction: Sir Walter Scott and His Successors* (Ithaca, N.Y.: Cornell University Press, 1983), 73. Ian Duncan echoes Millgate's assessment when he says that *Guy Mannering* does not address public history but that "history is troped in terms of place or setting." *Modern Romance and*

Transformations of the Novel: The Gothic, Scott, Dickens (Cambridge: Cambridge University Press, 1992), 111. John Lauber's contention that "the reader is hardly conscious of 'history' at all" in *Guy Mannering* represents a contrary view. *Sir Walter Scott* (Boston: Twayne, 1989), 49.

7. David Hewitt, "Scott's Art and Politics," in *Sir Walter Scott: The Long Forgotten Melody* (London: Vision, 1983), 63.

8. Molly Youngkin's "'Into the woof, a little Thibet wool': Orientalism and representing 'reality' in Walter Scott's *The Surgeon's Daughter*," *Scottish Studies Review* 3, no. 1 (Spring 2002), points to the limits of postcolonial theory in addressing Scott's complexities: "narrative strategies, such as those used by Scott in *The Surgeon's Daughter* to create a fantastical plot, might more fully illuminate the connections between modes of representation, especially those of genre, the resulting representations of the relationship between coloniser and colonised, and the degree to which cultural authority is claimed in those representations" (51).

9. Gibbes, *Hartley House*, 1.

10. James Mill, *The History of British India*, 6 vols. (London: Baldwick, Craddock and Joy, 1826), 4:469; Tillman W. Nechtman, "A Jewel in the Crown? Indian Wealth in Domestic Britain in the Late Eighteenth Century," *Eighteenth-Century Studies* 41, no. 1 (2007): 72. Nechtman echoes points raised by Balachandra Rajan and Renu Juneja. Rajan says that "the influx of nabobs built on the ruin of India created stresses in the English social fabric. . . . Class conflicts and Enlightenment ideology combined at this point to create a brief interval in which the equity of empire could be questioned" (81). Juneja, discussing literary representations of nabobs, finds that "the eighteenth-century literary response to the nabob is rather complicated in that the moral outrage is linked with social outrage; we might even argue that it is sustained by social outrage, and that if the nabobs had not violated social hierarchies on their return their acquisition of wealth might have escaped overt criticism and literary satire." *Journal of Commonwealth Literature* 27 (1992): 187. See also Dirks's characterization of Burke's rhetoric, which provided "as frightening an account of the class mobility afforded by the imperial connection as any broadsheet rant or Haymarket skit about nabobs" (80).

11. J. R. Seeley, *The Expansion of England: Two Courses of Lectures* (London: Macmillan, 1931), 288. Seeley adds that there were fears that "the English character could be corrupted" by association with Hindus and these corrupt returning colonials would in turn taint the English political system itself. Mannering, of course, craves retirement rather than engagement in British political life. Henry Mackenzie's *Man of the World* also invokes the good colonial in Mr. Rawlinson, who "was sent to the East Indies, and returned . . . with some thousand pounds, and a good conscience, to his native country" (I.269). Bage, on the other hand, constructs both a derogatory portrait returning nabob in the despicable Mr. Birimport in *Man as He Is* and a positive one in Mr. Foston, who "went out a writer in the service of the East India Company, but was a lieutenant under Col. Clive, when the chapter of accidents, and the exercise of all the virtues of humanity, gave him possession of a fortune" *Mount Henneth*, 1:34).

12. See *The Writings and Speeches of Edmund Burke*, gen. ed. Paul Langford; vol. 5, *India: Madras and Bengal 1774–1785*, ed. P. J. Marshall and William B. Todd (Oxford: Clarendon Press, 1981). Burke deplores "the deep silent flow of this steady stream of wealth" from India to Europe, and rails against "the avaricious youth who rule and exploit the colonies in the service of the East India Company" (492, 402). For recent treatments of the clash between Burke and Hastings, see Nicole Reynolds, "Phebe Gib-

bes, Edmund Burke, and the Trials of Empire," *Eighteenth-Century Fiction* 20, no. 2 (Winter 2007–8): 151–76 and Julie Murray, "Company Rules: Burke, Hastings, and the Specter of the Modern Liberal State," *Eighteenth-Century Studies* 41, no. 1 (2007): 55–69. Speaking of Burke's rhetorical performance as prosecutor, Reynolds argues that "appealing to his audience's sense of aristocratic entitlement, Burke established himself as defender of those privileges across cultures" (161). Murray points to the unstable paradox of Burke's position: while he constitutes himself as enemy of the East India Company because of "the dreadful totality of the corporate body," he also must contend with his "well-known fondness for the community—and by extension the social and political order—that he believes corporate structures produce" (64).

In working out the sources of Mannering's income and the nature of his service in India, I am indebted to Peter Garside, who suggests that "Scott is making a conscious effort to disassociate his elder hero from this stereotype" (personal correspondence). Nigel Leask, in his overview "Scotland's Literature of Empire and Emigration, 1707–1918," agrees that "Scott's *Guy Mannering* . . . represents a significant revision of this Nabob stereotype" (161), but he remains convinced that Mannering's fortune is made in India; his "Indian wealth now props up the shaky neo-feudal order of Scotland-within-Britain against the destabilising forces of 'democratic' social aspiration" (161).

13. Percival Spear, *The Nabobs: A Study of the Social Life of the English in Eighteenth-Century India* (Gloucester, MA: Peter Smith, 1971), 29. Martha McLaren refers to John Malcolm's conviction that "the company army would never be really effective until incentives were provided for good service" (36).

14. Defoe, *Letters*, 74.

15. T. M. Devine talks about how Indian military engagement could create celebrities: "The first to catch the imagination was the successful storming of the capital of Tipu Sultan [1799]. . . . His overthrow, spearheaded by the 73rd and 74th Highlanders, under the command of the Scottish General David Baird, had a powerful impact at home" (357). Making Tipu Sultan a character in *The Surgeon's Daughter* allows Scott to remind his readers of this Scottish triumph in imperial engagement.

16. Lawrence James details sources and amounts of colonial accumulation of wealth: for example, Mir Jafir of Bengal gave Clive and other English officials up to £234,000 (129–31).

17. James, *Rise and Fall*, 128, 133. Garside, in "Meg Merrilies and India," in *Scott in Carnival: Selected Papers from the Fourth International Scott Conference, Edinburgh 1991*, ed. J. H. Alexander and David Hewitt (Aberdeen: Association for Scottish Literary Studies, 1993), also notes Mannering's tendency to use Indian analogies for Scottish experiences. He adds that "Surviving letters between Scott and [Sir John] Malcolm, who had returned from India at an age not dissimilar to Mannering's and was engaged in writing his *History of Persia*, indicate a mutual enthusiasm for cross-cultural comparisons involving Scottish history and the East" (164).

18. Nigel Leask, *Curiosity and the Aesthetics of Travel Writing, 1770–1840: "From an Antique Land"* (Oxford: Oxford University Press, 2002), 175. Elsewhere, Leask discusses John Leyden (a friend of Scott), whose "perceptions of India are marked by constant comparisons with his native Scotland, for example, revealing a Border shepherd's disdain for the urbanised Englishman, Leyden lavished "a mountaineer's . . . approbation" upon the "frank, open, and bold demeanor" of the Tamil natives, which he contrasted with the "mean and cringing aspect of all the native Hindoos"; Leask also points to Leyden's poetry, "in which Indian landscapes often figure as palimpsests for his native

hills." ("Towards an Anglo-Indian poetry? The colonial muse in the writings of John Leyden, Thomas Medwin and Charles D'Oyly," in *Writing India, 1757–1990: The Literature of British India*, ed. Bart Moore-Gilbert (Manchester, UK: Manchester University Press, 1996) 59–60.

19. Spear, *The Nabobs*, 90.

20. Saree Makdisi, *Romantic Imperialism: Universal Empire and the Culture of Modernity* (Cambridge: Cambridge University Press, 1998), 114–15; Rajan, 3.

21. Said, *Orientalism*, 40.

22. The Indian shawl is something of significance in this tale. As Lamont astutely points out in her introduction to the Penguin edition of the *Chronicles*, Croftangry's narrative is distorted (and degraded) when his audience of women becomes distracted by "a disquisition upon shawls" (*Surgeon's Daughter* 287): "the masculine story of the British in India yields only death and defeat; and when recounted in Britain is feminised into a matter of shawls and exotic horrors." Introduction, *Chronicles of the Canongate*, ed. Claire Lamont (London: Penguin, 2003), xxvi. Rivalry over an Indian shawl provokes the catastrophe in Scott's *St. Ronan's Well* (1824). See my "Walter Scott and Feminine Discourse: The Case of *St. Ronan's Well*," *The Journal of Narrative Technique* 19, no. 2 (Spring 1989): 233–47.

23. Rajan, *Under Western Eyes*, 91.

24. Linda Colley, *Britons: Forging the Nation 1707–1837*. See especially the introduction and chapter 1.

25. Richard Middlemas's criminal and treasonous move recalls Elizabeth Fay's account of one Captain Ayres, who enlisted in the East India Company after a career of highway robbery in England, only to continue committing robberies in India until he deserted British forces to join Haidar Ali's service (125).

26. Elizabeth Fay, imprisoned by Haidar Ali's forces, is counseled to "address a *tender* memorial to Hyder Ali, whose general character for gallantry, would not admit of his refusing any request made by a *fair* lady" (127). Fay is ultimately released through the mediation of a Mr. Isaac, which leads her to write an encomium on Jews (160).

Claire Lamont finds that in *The Surgeon's Daughter*, Scott is "pessimistic about crossing boundaries," denying to Richard Middlemas the kind of narrative indulgence he has extended to Edward Waverley: "There was both Hanoverian and Jacobite in Scott: the boundary between the two was for him imaginatively crossable, whereas the boundary between British Christian and Indian Muslim was not." "Scott and Eighteenth-Century Imperialism," 44. In Hartley's carefully calibrated transculturation, however, Scott depicts an acceptable, even laudable (and life-saving) mode of crossing. For another view of Scott on transculturation, see Robert Crawford: "*Waverley* matters most as a multicultural novel. If it has a 'target', then that target is mainly the oppressive prejudice represented by Colonel Talbot. His speech condemning those whose barbaric speech he considers little better than that of 'the negroes in Jamaica' hints at the way in which cultural and linguistic issues raised by the book are universal ones" (130).

27. Katie Trumpener, *Bardic Nationalism: The Romantic Novel and the British Empire* (Princeton, NJ: Princeton University Press, 1997), 187–88.

28. Ros Ballaster describes her project as one that "demonstrates the ways in which the East came to be understood as a (sometimes *the*) source of story, a territory of fable and narrative. The Orient is a place to be turned into story as well as a place where story originates and where story has political and material effect" (17). Schwab says

that in the Romantic period, "India was something that the Occident began to seek again. Next to the influence of adventure, and overtaking it, was the influence of an inexhaustible fairy-tale Orient" (347). Ian Duncan argues that "for the rational and civilized British, alienated from a magical reality, the work of imagination can be grounded only on individual desire; this is the essence of Scott's critique of romantic poetics. Its power is that of a black-magical solipsism, binding the self and others in a destructive fabric of erotic illusion. India is 'an area of darkness'. Scott falls back on the conventions of anti-romance to articulate the fears that attend the magic narrative of the realization of desire (*Modern Romance*, 124). I read *Guy Mannering* as a text that posits that the "area of darkness" encompasses British space as much as Indian territory.

29. Graham Dawson, *Soldier Heroes: British Adventure, Empire and the Imagining of Masculinities* (London: Routledge, 1994), 60; Patrick Brantlinger, *Rule of Darkness: British Literature and Imperialism, 1830–1914* (Ithaca, NY: Cornell University Press, 1988), 24; Sara Suleri, *The Rhetoric of English India* (Chicago: University of Chicago Press, 1992), 3–5.

30. Michael J. Franklin, "Accessing India: Orientalism, Anti-'Indianism' and the Rhetoric of Jones and Burke," in *Romanticism and Colonialism*, 56.

31. Dawson, *Soldier Heroes*, 13.

32. Brantlinger, *Rule of Darkness*, 81. Suleri argues that "the Indian subcontinent is not merely a geographic space upon which colonial rapacities have been enacted, but is furthermore that imaginative construction through which rapaciousness can worship its own misdeed" (4–5).

33. Bewell notes that after the cholera epidemic of 1817, all of the subcontinent was seen as infected and infectious: "Contact with India always had its dangers, but now they were magnified tenfold" (244).

34. The stereotype of women heading East to find husbands causes Gibbes's heroine to determine not to marry in India (8). Thackeray, of course, draws on this risible type when he narrates, in *Vanity Fair*, the ongoing attempts of Glorvina O'Dowd to snare a husband in India.

35. Scott's articulation of the ravages of exploitative colonialism recalls, of course, the most intense passages of Burke's speeches on British misrule in India. Interestingly, as Regina Janes has pointed out, Burke deploys Haidar Ali as the figure of a necessary scourge against corrupt colonials: "But however much Burke expresses vindictive rage and revels in the justice of disaster, the instrument of disastrous justice was gone [the speech in question—on the Nawab of Arcot—was delivered in 1785, three years after Haidar Ali's death]. One more external restraint had collapsed, and the vehemence of Burke's imagery erupts from the certainty that there was nothing to be done." ("In Florid Impotence He Spoke: Edmund Burke and the Nawab of Arcot," *Studies in Eighteenth-Century Culture* 16 (1986): 102–3. Catherine Jones invokes the same Burkean passage in her summary of the plot of *The Surgeon's Daughter*, which she says "ends in a vision of apocalyptic destruction that links the trauma experienced by the individual characters to a wider public history: recent and continuing anxieties of empire." (*Literary Memory: Scott's Waverley Novels and the Psychology of Narrative* (Lewisburg, PA: Bucknell University Press, 2003), 149.

Works Cited

Abercromby, James. *Magna Charta for America: James Abercromby's "An Examination of the Acts of Parliament Relative To the Trade and the Government of our American Colonies" (1752) and "De Jure et Gubernatione Coloniarum, or an Inquiry into the Nature, and the Rights of Colonies, Ancient, and Modern" (1774).* Edited by Jack P. Greene, Charles F. Mullett, and Edward C. Papenfuse, Jr. Philadelphia: American Philosophical Society, 1986.

Albion, Robert Greenhalgh. *Forests and Sea Power: The Timber Problem of the Royal Navy, 1652–1862.* Cambridge, MA: Harvard University Press, 1926.

Alter, Robert. "A Bourgeois Picaroon." In *Twentieth-Century Interpretations of Moll Flanders: A Collection of Critical Essays,* edited by Robert C. Elliott, 63–77. Englewood Cliffs, NJ: Prentice-Hall, 1970.

Andersen, Hans H. "The Paradox of Trade and Morality in Defoe." *Modern Philology* 39, no. 1 (August 1941): 23–46.

Anderson, Benedick. *Imagined Communities: Reflections on the Origin and Spread of Nationalism.* rev. ed. London: Verso, 1991.

Anonymous. *The Female American; or, the Adventures of Unca Winkfield.* Edited by Michelle Burnham. Peterborough, Canada: Broadview Press Ltd., 2001.

Aravamudan, Srinivas. *Tropicopolitans: Colonialism and Agency, 1688–1804.* Durham, NC: Duke University Press, 1999.

Armitage, David. *The Ideological Origins of the British Empire.* Cambridge: Cambridge University Press, 2000.

Armstrong, Nancy and Leonard Tennenhouse. "The American Origins of the English Novel." *American Literary History* 4, no. 3 (Autumn 1992): 386–410.

Atkinson, Alan. "The Free-Born Englishman Transported: Convict Rights as a Measure of Eighteenth-Century Empire." *Past and Present* 144 (August 1994): 88–115.

Austen, Jane. *The Novels of Jane Austen.* 5 vols. Edited by R. W. Chapman. London: Oxford University Press, 1933.

Axtell, James. *The European and the Indian: Essays in the Ethnohistory of Colonial North America.* New York: Oxford University Press, 1981.

Azim, Firdous. *The Colonial Rise of the Novel.* London: Routledge, 1993.

Backscheider, Paula. *Daniel Defoe, His Life.* Baltimore: Johns Hopkins Press, 1989.

Baker, Gerard. "A Callow Cowboy Stumbles at a Cultural Divide." *The Financial Times,* May 30, 2002, 13.

Bage, Robert. *Hermsprong; or Man as He Is Not.* Edited by Pamela Perkins. Peterborough, Ontario: Broadview Press Ltd., 2002.

————. *Mount Henneth.* 2 vols. 1782. Reprint, New York: Garland Publishing Co., 1979.

Ballhatchet, Kenneth. *Race, Sex and Class under the Raj: Imperial Attitudes and Policies and Their Critics, 1793–1905.* New York: St. Martin's Press, 1980.

Ballaster, Ros. *Fabulous Orients: Fictions of the East in England, 1662–1785.* Oxford: Oxford University Press, 2005.

Barrell, John. *English Literature in History, 1730–80: An Equal, Wide Survey.* New York: St. Martin's Press, 1983.

Barrell, John, and Harriet Guest. "On the Use of Contradiction: Economics and Morality in the Eighteenth-Century Long Poem." In *The New Eighteenth Century.* edited by Felicity Nussbaum and Laura Brown, 121–43. New York: Methuen, 1987.

Barrow, Thomas C. "The Old Colonial System from an English Point of View." In *Anglo-American Political Relations, 1675–1775,* edited by Alison Gilbert Olsen and Richard Maxwell Brown. New Brunswick, NJ: Rutgers University Press, 1972.

Battestin, Martin C. *The Providence of Wit: Aspects of Form in Augustan Literature and the Arts.* Oxford: Clarendon Press, 1974.

Bayly, C. A. *Imperial Meridian: The British Empire and the World, 1780–1830.* London: Longman, 1989.

————. *Indian Society and the Making of the British Empire. The New Cambridge History of India.* 4 vols. Edited by Gordon Johnson. Cambridge: Cambridge University Press, 1988.

Bearce, George D. *British Attitudes toward India, 1784–1813.* London: George Allen and Unwin Ltd, 1968.

Behn, Aphra. *Oroonoko: or, The Royal Slave.* Edited by Catherine Gallagher and Simon Stern. Boston: St. Martin's Press, 2000.

Bevis, Richard. "From Windsor Forest to Barholomew Fair: The Education of an Imperialist." *English Studies in Canada* 17, no. 2 (June 1991): 151–61.

Bewell, Alan. *Romanticism and Colonial Disease.* Baltimore: Johns Hopkins University Press, 1999.

Bhabha, Homi K. *The Location of Culture.* London: Routledge, 1994.

————. "The Other Question: Difference, Discrimination and the Discourse of Colonialism." In *Literature, Politics and Theory: Papers from the Essex Conference, 1974–84,* edited by Francis Barker, Peter Hulme, Margaret Iverson, and Diana Loxley, 148–72. London: Methuen, 1986.

Birdsall, Virginia Ogden. *Defoe's Perpetual Seekers: A Study of the Major Fiction.* Lewisburg, PA: Bucknell University Press, 1985.

Black, Jeremy. Introduction. In *The British Navy and the Use of Naval Power in the Eighteenth Century,* edited by Jeremy Black and Philip Woodfine. Atlantic Heights, NJ: Humanities Press International, 1989.

Blewett, David. *Defoe's Art of Fiction: Robinson Crusoe, Moll Flanders, and Roxana.* Toronto: University of Toronto Press, 1979.

Bliss, Robert. *Revolution and Empire: English Politics and the American Colonies in the Seventeenth Century.* Manchester, UK: Manchester University Press, 1990.

Boucé, Paul-Gabriel. *The Novels of Tobias Smollett.* London: Longman, 1976.

Bouloukos, George E. "Daniel Defoe's *Colonel Jack*, Grateful Slaves, and Racial Difference." *ELH* 68 (2001): 615–31.

Brady, Patrick. "Unknown Spaces, Far Frontier: The New World as Anti-Paradise from *Moll Flanders* to *Riders in the Chariot.*" *Proceedings of the 12th Congress of the International Comparative Literature Association*. Edited by Roger Bauer, Douwe Fokkema and Michael De Graat Munich: Iudicium Verlag, 1990.

Brantlinger, Patrick. *Rule of Darkness: British Literature and Imperialism, 1830–1914.* Ithaca, NY: Cornell University Press, 1988.

Breen, T. H. "Creative Adaptation, People and Cultures." In *Colonial British America: Essays in the New History of the Early Modern Era*, edited by Jack P. Greene and J. R. Pole, 195–232. Baltimore: Johns Hopkins University Press, 1984.

———. "An Empire of Goods: The Anglicization of Colonial America, 1690–1776." *Journal of British Studies* 25, no. 4 (1986): 467–99.

British Library of Information. *What Is British Imperialism?* 1940.

Brown, Iain Gordon. "Griffins, Nabobs and a Seasoning of Curry Powder: Walter Scott and the Indian Theme in Life and Literature." In *The Tiger and the Thistle: Tipu Sultan and the Scots in India, 1760–1800*, edited by Anne Buddle, Pauline Rohtagi, and Iain Gordon Brown. Edinburgh: National Gallery of Scotland, 1999.

Brown, Laura. *Alexander Pope.* London: Basil Blackwell, 1985.

———. *The Ends of Empire: Women and Ideology in Early Eighteenth-Century English Literature.* Ithaca, NY: Cornell University Press, 1993.

———. "Reading Race and Gender: Jonathan Swift." *Eighteenth-Century Studies* 23, no. 4 (Summer 1990): 425–43.

Buckton, Oliver S. "Reanimating Stevenson's Corpus." In *Robert Louis Stevenson Reconsidered: New Perspectives*, edited by William B. Jones, 37–67. Jefferson, NC: McFarland & Co., 2003.

Budick, Sanford. "Pope and the Hidden God." In *Critical Essays on Alexander Pope*, edited by Wallace Jackson and R. Paul Yoder. New York: G. K. Hall, 1993.

Burke, Edmund. *The Portable Edmund Burke.* Edited by Isaac Kramnick. Harmondsworth, UK: Penguin, 1999.

———. *The Writings and Speeches of Edmund Burke.* Edited by Paul Langford. Vol. 5, *India, Madras and Bengal 1774–1785.* Edited by P. J. Marshall and William B. Todd. Oxford: Clarendon Press, 1981.

Burnaby, Andrew. *Burnaby's Travels Through North America.* Introduction by Rufus Rockwell Wilson. 1798, Reprint, New York: A. Wessels Co., 1904.

Burney, Frances. *A Busy Day; or An Arrival from India.* Edited by Tara Ghoshal Wallace. New Brunswick, NJ: Rutgers University Press, 1984.

Butler, Marilyn. "Introductory Essay." In *Burke, Paine, Godwin, and the Revolution Controversy*, edited by Marilyn Butler. Cambridge: Cambridge University Press, 1984.

———. *Jane Austen and the War of Ideas.* Oxford: Clarendon Press, 1975.

Cain, P. J. and A. G. Hopkins. "Gentlemanly Capitalism and British Expansion Overseas: The Old Colonial System, 1688–1850." *Economic History Review.* 2nd ser. 39, 4 (1986): 501–25.

Calder, Jenni. "Figures in a Landscape: Scott, Stevenson, and Routes to the Past." In

Robert Louis Stevenson, Writer of Boundaries, edited by Richard Ambrosini and Richard Dury, 121–32. Madison: University of Wisconsin Press, 2006.

———. *Robert Louis Stevenson: A Life Study*. New York: Oxford University Press, 1980.

Cam, Helen. *England before Elizabeth*. New York: Harper & Row, 1960.

Cannadine, David. *Ornamentalism: How the British Saw Their Empire*. Oxford: Oxford University Press, 2001.

Caretta, Vincent. "Anne and Elizabeth: The Poet as Historian in *Windsor-Forest*," *Studies in English Literature, 1500–1900* 21, no. 3 (Summer 1981): 425–37.

Carr, Helen. "Woman/Indian: 'The American' and His Others." *Europe and Its Others: Proceedings of the Essex Conference on the Sociology of Literature, July 1984*, edited by Francis Barker, Peter Hulme, Margaret Iversen, and Diana Loxley, 2:46–60. Colchester, UK: University of Essex, 1985.

Carruthers, Gerard. *Robert Louis Stevenson's Strange Case of Dr Jekyll and Mr Hyde, The Master of Ballantrae, and The Ebb-Tide*. Glasgow: Association for Scottish Literary Studies, 2004.

Caton, Lou. "Doing the Right Thing with *Moll Flanders:* A 'Reasonable' Difference between the Picara and the Penitent." *CLA Journal* 40, no. 4 (June 1997): 508–16.

Chalker, John. *The English Georgic: A Study in the Development of a Form*. Baltimore: Johns Hopkins University Press, 1969.

Chesterton, G. K. *Robert Louis Stevenson*. New York: Sheed and Ward, 1955.

Clunas, Alexander B. "'A Double Word': Writing and Justice in *The Master of Ballantrae*." *Studies in Scottish Literature* 28 (1993): 55–74.

Cohen, Ralph. *The Art of Discrimination: Thomson's Seasons and the Language of Criticism*. Berkeley: University of California Press, 1964.

———. *The Unfolding of The Seasons*. Baltimore: Johns Hopkins University Press, 1970.

Cohn, Bernard S. *Colonialism and Its Forms of Knowledge: The British in India*. Princeton, NJ: Princeton University Press, 1996.

Colden, Cadwallader. *The History of the Five Indian Nations of Canada, which are dependent on the Province of New York, and are a barrier between the English and the French in that part of the World*. New York: Allerton Book Co., 1904.

Coldham, Peter Wilson. *Emigrants in Chains: A Social History of Forced Emigration to the Americas, 1607–1776*. Phoenix Mill, UK: Alan Sutton Publishing Ltd., 1992.

Coleridge, Samuel Taylor. *The Rhyme of the Ancient Mariner*. Edited by Paul H. Fry. Boston: Bedford/St. Martin's, 1999.

Colley, Ann C. *Robert Louis Stevenson and the Colonial Imagination*. Aldershot, UK: Ashgate, 2004.

Colley, Linda. *Britons: Forging the Nation 1707–1837*. New Haven, CT: Yale University Press, 1992.

———. *Captives: Britain, Empire, and the World, 1600–1850*. New York: Random House, 2002.

———. "Radical Patriotism in Eighteenth-Century England." In *Patriotism: The Making and Unmaking of British National Identity*. 3 vols. Edited by Raphael Samuel, 1.169–87. London: Routledge, 1989.

Conger, Syndy McMillen. *Mary Wollstonecraft and the Language of Sensibility*. Rutherford, NJ: Fairleigh Dickinson University Press, 1994.

Crawford, Robert. *Devolving English Literature*. Oxford: Clarendon Press, 1992.

Cummings, Robert. "Addison's 'Inexpressible Chagrin' and Pope's Poem on the Peace." *Yearbook of English Studies* 18 (1988): 143–58.

Daiches, David. *Robert Louis Stevenson*. Norfolk, CT: New Directions, 1947.

Damrosch, Leopold Jr. *The Imaginative World of Alexander Pope*. Berkeley: University of California Press, 1987.

Das, Harihar. "The Early Indian Visitors to England." *Calcutta Review* 13 (October 1924): 83–114.

Davis, John. *Travels of Four Years and a Half in the United States of America during 1798, 1799, 1800, 1801, and 1802*. Introduction by A. J. Morrison. New York: Henry Holt and Co., 1909.

Davis, Lennard J. *Resisting Novels: Ideology and Fiction*. New York: Methuen, 1987.

Dawson, Graham. *Soldier Heroes: British Adventure, Empire and the Imagining of Masculinities*. London: Routledge, 1994.

De Bruyn, Frans. "From Georgic Poetry to Statistics and Graphs: Eighteenth-Century Representation and the 'State' of British Society." *The Yale Journal of Criticism* 17, no. 1 (2004): 107–39.

Defoe, Daniel. *Atlas Maritimus and Commercialis*. London: James and John Knapton, 1728.

———. *Defoe's Review*. 22 vols. Edited by Arthur Wellesley Secord. New York: Columbia University Press, 1938.

———. *The Fortunes and Misfortunes of the Famous Moll Flanders*. Edited by David Blewett. London: Penguin, 1989.

———. *The History and Remarkable Life of the Truly Honourable Col. Jacque, Commonly Call'd Col. Jack*. Edited by Samuel Holt Monk. London: Oxford University Press, 1970.

———. *The Letters of Daniel Defoe*. Edited by George Harris Healey. Oxford: Clarendon Press, 1955.

———. *A Tour Thro' the whole Island of Great Britain*. 3 vols. London: Strahan, 1724–1727.

———. *A Tour through the Whole Island of Great Britain*. Edited by Pat Rogers. Hammondworth, UK: Penguin, 1971.

Dennis, John. *The Critical Works of John Dennis*. 2 vols. Edited by Edward Niles Hooker. Baltimore: Johns Hopkins University Press, 1943.

Desvignes, Lucette. "Vues de la terre promise: les visages de l'Amérique dans *Moll Flanders* et dans l'*Histoire de Manon Lescaut*." In *Transactions of the Fourth International Congress on the Enlightenment*. Edited by Teodore Besterman, 543–57. Oxford: Voltaire Foundation, 1976.

de Tocqueville, Alexis. *Democracy in America*. Edited by Andrew Hacker, trans. Henry Reeve, rev. Francis Bowen. New York: Washington Square Press, 1964.

Deutsch, Helen. *Resemblance & Disgrace: Alexander Pope and the Deformation of Culture*. Cambridge, MA: Harvard University Press, 1984.

Devine, T. M. *Scotland's Empire, 1600–1815*. London: Allen Lane, 2003.

Dharwadker, Aparna. "Nation, Race, and the Ideology of Commerce in Defoe." *The Eighteenth Century* 39, no. 1 (1998): 63–84.

Dickens, Charles. *A Tale of Two Cities*. Edited by Andrew Sanders (Oxford: Oxford University Press, 1988.

Dickinson, Harry T. "Popular Loyalism in Britain in the 1790s." In *The Transformation of Political Culture: England and Germany in the Late Eighteenth Century*, edited by Eckhart Hellmuth, 503–33. Oxford: Oxford University Press, 1990.

Digby, Simon. "An Eighteenth Century Narrative of a Journey from Bengal to England: Munshi Ismā'il's *New History*." In *Urdu and Muslim South Asia: Studies in Honour of Ralph Russell*, edited by Christopher Shackle. 49–65. London: School of Oriental and African Studies, University of London, 1989.

di Giuseppe, Rita. "The Ghost in the Machine: *Moll Flanders* and the Body Politic." *Quaderni di Lingue e Letterature* 18 (1993): 311–26.

Dinwiddy, John. "Conceptions of Revolution in the English Radicalism of the 1790s.' In *The Transformation of Political Culture: England and Germany in the Late Eighteenth Century*, edited by Eckhart Hellmuth, 535–60. Oxford: Oxford University Press, 1990.

Dirks, Nicholas B. *The Scandal of Empire: India and the Creation of Imperial Britain*. Cambridge, MA: Belknap Press of Harvard University Press, 2006.

Dobson, David. *Scottish Emigration to Colonial America, 1607–1785*. Athens: University of Georgia Press, 1994.

Doody, Margaret. *The Daring Muse: Augustan Poetry Reconsidered*. Cambridge: Cambridge University Press, 1985.

Downie, J. A. "1688: Pope and the Rhetoric of Jacobitism." In *Pope: New Contexts*, edited by David Fairer, 9–24. New York: Harvester Wheatsheaf, 1990.

———. "Defoe, Imperialism, and the Travel Books Reconsidered." In *Critical Essays on Daniel Defoe*, edited by Roger D. Lund, 78–96. New York: G. K. Hall and Co., 1997.

Drew, John. *India and the Romantic Imagination*. Delhi: Oxford University Press, 1987.

Dryden, John. *Selected Poetry and Prose of John Dryden*. Edited by Earl Miner. New York: Random House, 1969.

Duncan, Ian. *Modern Romance and Transformations of the Novel: The Gothic, Scott, Dickens*. Cambridge: Cambridge University Press, 1992.

Dunn, Richard S. "Imperial Pressures on Massachusetts and Jamaica, 1675–1700." *Anglo-American Political Relations, 1675–1775*, edited by Alison Gilbert Olsen and Richard Maxwell Brown, 52–75. New Brunswick, NJ: Rutgers University Press, 1972.

———. "Servants and Slaves: The Recruitment and Employment of Labor." In *Colonial British America: Essays in the New History of the Early Modern Era*, edited by Jack P. Greene and J. R. Pole, 157–94. Baltimore: Johns Hopkins University Press, 1984.

Dunn, Tony. "Moll Flanders: Body and Capital." *Q/W/E/R/T/Y* 7 (October 1997): 59–67.

Dunston, Gregory. *Moll Flanders: An Analysis of an Eighteenth-Century Criminal Biography*. Chichester, UK: Barry Rose Publishers, 1997.

Dwyer, John. *Virtuous Discourse: Sensibility and Community in Late Eighteenth-Century Scotland*. Edinburgh: John Donald Publishers Ltd, 1987.

Dyson, Katake Kusheri. *A Various Universe: A Study of the Journals and Memoirs of British Men and Women in the Indian Subcontinent, 1765–1856*. Delhi: Oxford University Press, 1978.

Eastburn, Robert. *A Faithful Narrative. The Garland Library of Narratives of North American Indian Captives.* 111 vols. Edited by Wilcomb E. Washburn. New York: Garland Publishing Inc., 1978.

Ekirch, Roger A. *Bound for America: The Transportation of British Convicts to the Colonies, 1718–1775.* Oxford: Clarendon Press, 1987.

Elizabeth I. *Elizabeth I: Collected Works.* Edited by Leah S. Marcus, Janel Mueller, and Mary Beth Rose. Chicago: University of Chicago Press, 2000.

Elliott, J. H. *Empires of the Atlantic World: Britain and Spain in America, 1492–1830.* New Haven, CT: Yale University Press, 2006.

English Historical Documents, 1660–1714. 13 vols. Edited by Andrew Browning. New York: Oxford University Press, 1953.

English Historical Documents: American Colonial Documents to 1776. Edited by Merrill Jensen. New York: Oxford University Press, 1955.

Ennis, Daniel James. *Enter the Press-Gang: Naval Impressment in Eighteenth-Century British Literature.* Newark: University of Delaware Press, 2002.

Erskine-Hill, Howard. "Pope and Slavery."In *Alexander Pope: World and Word.* Edited by Howard Erskine-Hill. 27–53. Proceedings of the British Academy 91. Oxford: Oxford University Press, 1998.

Faller, Lincoln B. *Crime and Defoe: A New Kind of Writing.* Cambridge: Cambridge University Press, 1993.

Fay, Eliza. *Original Letters from India (1779–1815).* Edited by E. M. Forster. New York: Harcourt, Brace, and Co., 1925.

Ferguson, Craig. Interview. *The New York Times Magazine,* January 16, 2005, 19.

Ferguson, Moira. "*Oroonoko:* Birth of a Paradigm." In *Troping Oroonoko from Behn to Bandele,* edited by Susan B. Iwanisziw, 1–15. Aldershot, UK: Ashgate Publishing Ltd., 2004.

Ferguson, Moira, and Janet Todd. *Mary Wollstonecraft.* Boston: Twayne, 1984.

Fielding, Henry. *Joseph Andrews.* Edited by Martin C. Battestin. Boston: Houghton Mifflin Co., 1961.

Fielding, Penny. *Writing and Orality: Nationality, Culture, and Nineteenth-Century Scottish Fiction.* Oxford: Clarendon Press, 1996.

Fleming, William, and Elizabeth. *A Narrative of the Sufferings and Surprizing Deliverance of William and Elizabeth Fleming. The Garland Library of Narratives of North American Indian Captives.* 111 vols. Edited by Wilcomb E. Washburn. New York: Garland Publishing Inc., 1978.

Fliegelman, Jay. *Prodigals and Pilgrims: The American Revolution against Patriarchal Authority, 1750–1800.* Cambridge: Cambridge University Press, 1982.

Flynn, Christopher. *Americans in British Literature, 1770–1832: A Breed Apart.* Aldershot, UK: Ashgate Publishing Ltd., 2008.

———. "Nationalism, Commerce, and Imperial Anxiety in Defoe's Later Works.' *Rocky Mountain Review* (Fall 2000): 11–24.

Fogelman, Aaron S. "From Slaves, Convicts, and Servants to Free Passengers: The Transformation of Immigration in the Era of the American Revolution." *Journal of History* 85, no. 1 (June 1998): 43–76.

Franklin, Benjamin. *The Autobiography of Benjamin Franklin and Selections from His Other Writings.* Edited by Henry Steele Commager. New York: The Modern Library, 1950.

Franklin, Michael J. "Accessing India: Orientalism, 'Anti-Indianism' and the Rhetoric of Jones and Burke." In *Romanticism and Colonialism: Writing Empire, 1700–1830,* edited by Tim Fulford and Peter J. Kitson, 48–66. Cambridge: Cambridge University Press, 1998.

Frohock, Richard. *Heroes of Empire: The British Imperial Protagonist in America, 1596–1764.* Newark: University of Delaware Press, 2004.

Fussell, Paul. *The Rhetorical World of Augustan Humanism: Ethics and Imagery from Swift to Burke.* Oxford: Clarendon Press, 1965.

Galenson, David W. *The Cambridge Economic History of the United States.* Vol. 1, *The Colonial Era.* Edited by Stanley L. Engerman and Robert E. Gallman, 135–207. Cambridge: Cambridge University Press, 1996.

Ganz, Melissa J. "*Moll Flanders* and English Marriage Law." *Eighteenth-Century Fiction* 17, no. 2 (January 2005): 157–82.

Garside, Peter. "Meg Merrilies and India." In *Scott in Carnival: Selected Papers from the Fourth International Scott Conference, Edinburgh 1991,* edited by J. H. Alexander and David Hewitt, 154–71. Aberdeen: Association for Scottish Literary Studies, 1993.

———. "Scott, the Eighteenth Century and the New Man of Sentiment." *Anglia: Zeitschrift fur Englische Philologie,* Band 103 (1985): 71–89.

Gensane, Bernard. "Robinson et Moll: Deux corps dans le monde." In *Le Corps dans tous ses états,* edited by Marie-Claire Renyer, 155–69. Bordeaux: Université de Bordeaux, 1995.

Gerrard, Christine. "Pope and the Patriots." In *Pope: New Contexts,* edited by David Fairer, 25–43. New York: Harvester Wheatsheaf, 1990.

Ghosh, Suresh Chandra. *The Social Condition of the British Community in Bengal, 1757–1800.* Leiden, The Netherlands: E. J. Brill, 1970.

Gibbes, Phebe. *Hartly House, Calcutta: A Novel of the Days of Warren Hastings.* 1789. Reprint, Calcutta: Thacker, Spink, & Co., 1908.

Giddings, Robert. "Matthew Bramble's Bath: Smollett and the West Indian Connection." In *Smollett: Author of the First Distinction,* Edited by Alan Bold. 47–63. London: Vision Press, 1982.

Gifford, Douglas. "Stevenson and Scottish Fiction: The Importance of *The Master of Ballantrae.*" In *Stevenson and Victorian Scotland,* edited by Jenni Calder. 62–87. Edinburgh: Edinburgh University Press, 1981.

Glassman, Byron. "Religious Attitudes in the World of *Humphry Clinker.*" *Brigham Young University Studies* 6 (1965): 65–72.

Goldberg, M. A. "*Moll Flanders:* Christian Allegory in a Hobbesian Mode." *University Review* 3, no. 3. (1967): 267–78.

———. *Smollett and the Scottish School: Studies in Eighteenth-Century Thought.* Albuquerque: University of New Mexico Press, 1959.

Gottlieb, Evan. *Feeling British: Sympathy and National Identity in Scottish and English Writing, 1707–1832.* Lewisburg, PA: Bucknell University Press, 2007.

Graham, Henry Grey. *Scottish Men of Letters in the Eighteenth Century.* London: Adam and Charles Black, 1908.

Greenblatt, Stephen. *Marvelous Possessions: The Wonder of the New World.* Chicago: University of Chicago Press, 1991.

Greene, Jack P. and J. R. Pole. "Reconstructing British-American Colonial History: An Introduction." In *Essays in the New History of the Early Modern Era,* edited by Jack P. Greene and J. R. Pole, 1–17. Baltimore: Johns Hopkins University Press, 1984.

Gregg, Edward. *Queen Anne.* New Haven, CT: Yale University Press, 1980.

Griffin, Dustin H. *Alexander Pope: The Poet in the Poems.* Princeton, NJ: Princeton University Press, 1978.

———. *Patriotism and Poetry in Eighteenth-Century Britain.* Cambridge: Cambridge University Press, 2002.

Grogan, Claire. "Crossing Genre, Gender and Race in Elizabeth Hamilton's *Translation of the Letters of a Hindoo Rajah.*" *Studies in the Novel* 34, no. 1 (Spring 2002): 21–44.

Grove, Robin. "Nature Methodiz'd." *The Critical Review* 26 (1984): 52–68.

Grundy, Isobel. "'The barbarous character we give them': White Women Travellers Report on Other Races." *Studies in Eighteenth-Century Culture* 22 (1992): 73–86.

Gyles, John. *The Memoirs of Odd Adventures, Strange Deliverances, &c in the Captivity of John Gyles, Esq.; Commander of the Garrison on St. George's River.* Boston: S. Kneeland and T. Green, 1736.

Hakluyt, Richard. *Divers Voyages Touching the Discoverie of America.* Ann Arbor, MI: University Microfilms Inc., 1966. A facsimile of 1582 edition.

Hamilton, Charles. *An Historical Relation of the Origin, Progress, and final Dissolution of the Rohilla Afgans in the Northern Provinces of Hindostan.* London: G. Kearsley, 1787.

Hamilton, Douglas J. *Scotland, the Caribbean and the Atlantic World, 1750–1820.* Manchester, UK: Manchester University Press, 2005.

Hamilton, Elizabeth. *Translations of the Letters of a Hindoo Rajah.* Edited by Pamela Perkins and Shannon Russell. Peterborough, Canada: Broadview Press Ltd., 1999.

Hammer, Paul J. *Elizabeth's Wars: War, Government, Society in Tudor England.* New York: Palgrave, 2003.

Hammond, J. R. *A Robert Louis Stevenson Companion: A Guide to the Novels, Essays and Short Stories.* London: Macmillan, 1984.

Harasym, S. D. "Ideology and Self: A Theoretical Discussion of the 'Self' in Mary Wollstonecraft's Fiction." *English Studies in Canada* 12, no. 2 (June 1986): 163–77.

Hardy, Thomas. *Tess of the D'Urbervilles.* Edited by Scott Elledge. New York: W.W. Norton, 1991.

Harris, Jason Marc. "Robert Louis Stevenson: Folklore and Imperialism." *English Literature in Transition, 1880–1920* 4 (2003): 382–99.

Harrow, Sharon. *Adventures in Domesticity: Gender and Colonial Adulteration in Eighteenth-Century British Literature.* New York: AMS Press, 2004.

Hay, Jehu. *The siege of Detroit in 1763: The Journal of Pontiac's Conspiracy and John Ruthergurd's Narrative of a Captivity.* Chicago: Lakeside Press, 1958.

Heard, J. Norman. *White into Red: A Study of the Assimilation of White Persons Captured by Indians.* Metuchen, NJ: Scarecrow Press, 1973.

Hechter, Michael. *Internal Colonialism: The Celtic Fringe in British National Development, 1536–1966.* Berkeley: University of California Press, 1975.

Hewitt, David. "Scott's Art and Politics." In *Sir Walter Scott: The Long Forgotten Melody*, edited by Alan Bold, 43–64. London: Vision, 1983.

Higdon, David Leon. "The Chronology of *Moll Flanders.*" *English Studies* 56 (1975): 316–19.

Hitt, Christopher. "Ecocriticism and the Long Eighteenth Century." *College Literature* 31, no. 3 (Summer 2004): 123–47.

Hobsbawm, E. J. *Nations and Nationalism since 1780: Programme, Myth, Reality.* 2nd ed. Cambridge: Cambridge University Press, 1992.

Hook, Andrew. *Scotland and America: A Study of Cultural Relations, 1750–1835.* Glasgow: Blackie, 1975.

Hopkins, Robert. "The Function of Grotesque in *Humphry Clinker.*" *Huntington Library Quarterly* 32 (1969): 163–77.

Howarth, David. *British Sea Power: How Britain Became Sovereign of the Seas.* New York: Carroll and Graf, 2003.

Huhn, Peter. "The Precarious Autopoiesis of Modern Selves: Daniel Defoe's *Moll Flanders* and Virginia Woolf's *The Waves.*" *European Journal of English Studies* 5, no. 3 (2001): 335–48.

Hulme, Peter. *Colonial Encounters: Europe and the Native Caribbean, 1492–1797.* London: Methuen, 1986.

———. "Polytropic Man: Tropes of Sexuality and Mobility in Early Colonial Discourse." In *Europe and Its Others: Proceedings of the Essex Conference on the Sociology of Literature, July 1984.* 2 vols. Edited by Francis Barker, Peter Hulme, Margaret Iversen, and Diana Loxley, 2:17–32. Colchester, UK: University of Essex, 1985.

Imlay, Gilbert. *The Emigrants.* Edited by W. M. Verhoeven and Amanda Gilroy. Harmondsworth, UK: Penguin, 1998.

Jackson, Richard G. "Introducing Guy Mannering." Manuscript essay.

Jackson, Wallace. *Vision and Revision in Alexander Pope.* Detroit, MI: Wayne State University Press, 1983.

Jacobsen, Susan L. " 'The Tinsel of the Times': Smollett's Argument against Conspicuous Consumption in *Humphry Clinker.*" *Eighteenth-Century Fiction* 9, no. 1 (October 1996): 71–88.

James, Lawrence. *The Rise and Fall of the British Empire.* New York: St. Martin's Press, 1994.

Janes, Regina. "In Florid Impotence He Spoke: Edmund Burke and the Nawab of Arcot." *Studies in Eighteenth-Century Culture* 16 (1986): 91–105.

Jeffries, Ewell. *A Short Biography of John Leeth, with an Account of His Life among the Indians.* Edited by Reuben Gold Thwaites. 1831. Reprint, New York: Benjamin Blom, Inc., 1972.

Jennings, Francis. *The Invasion of America: Indians, Colonialism, and the Cant of Conquest.* Chapel Hill: University of North Carolina Press, 1975.

Johnson, Claudia. *Equivocal Beings: Politics, Gender, and Sentimentality in the 1790s. Wollstonecraft, Radcliffe, Burney, Austen.* Chicago: University of Chicago Press, 1995.

Johnson, Nancy E. *The English Jacobin Novel on Rights, Property and the Law: Critiquing the Contract.* Houndmills, UK: Palgrave/Macmillan, 2004.

———. "'Seated on her Bags of Dollars': Representations of America in the English Jacobin Novel." *The Dalhousie Review* 82, no. 3 (Spring 2002): 423–39.

Johnson, Samuel. *Lives of the English Poets.* 2 vols. London: Oxford University Press, 1967.

Johnson, Samuel, and James Boswell. *Johnson's Journey to the Western Islands of Scotland and Boswell's Journal of a Tour to the Hebrides with Samuel Johnson, LL.D.* Edited by R. W. Chapman. London: Oxford University Press, 1970.

Jones, Catherine. *Literary Memory: Scott's Waverley Novels and the Psychology of Narrative.* Lewisburg, PA: Bucknell University Press, 2003.

Jones, J. R. *Britain and the World, 1649–1815.* Sussex, UK: Harvester Press, 1980.

Jordan, Elaine. "The Management of Scott's Novels." In *Europe and Its Others: Proceedings of the Essex Conference on the Sociology of Literature, July 1984.* Edited by Francis Barker, Peter Hulme, Margaret Iversen, and Diana Loxley, 2:146–61. Colchester, UK: University of Essex, 1985.

Jump, Harriet Devine. *Mary Wollstonecraft: Writer.* New York: Harvester/Wheatsheaf, 1994.

Juneja, Renu. "The Native and the Nabob: Representations of the Indian Experience in Eighteenth-Century English Literature." *Journal of Commonwealth Literature* 27 (1992): 183–98.

Jurgens, Heather. "*Windsor-Forest* and Augustan Stability." *Unisa English Studies* 2 (1967): 15–22.

Kaul, Suvir. *Poems of Nation, Anthems of Empire: English Verse in the Long Eighteenth Century.* Charlottesville: University Press of Virginia, 2000.

Keen, Paul. *The Crisis of Literature in the 1790s: Print Culture and the Public Sphere.* Cambridge: Cambridge University Press, 1999.

Keener, Frederick M. "Transitions in *Humphry Clinker.*" *Studies in Eighteenth-Century Culture* 16 (1986): 149–63.

Kelly, Gary. *English Fiction of the Romantic Period, 1789–1830.* London: Longman, 1989.

———. *The English Jacobin Novel, 1780–1805.* Oxford: Clarendon Press, 1976.

———. *Revolutionary Feminism: The Mind and Career of Mary Wollstonecraft.* New York: St. Martin's Press, 1992.

———. *Women, Writing, and Revolution, 1790–1827.* Oxford: Clarendon Press, 1993.

Kenny, Virginia C. *The Country-House Ethos in English Literature, 1688–1750: Themes of Personal Retreat and National Expansion.* New York: St. Martin's Press, 1984.

Kibbie, Anne Louise. "Monstrous Generation: The Birth of Capital in Defoe's *Moll Flanders* and *Roxana.*" *PMLA* 110, no. 5 (October 1995): 1023–34.

Kiely, Robert. *Robert Louis Stevenson and the Fiction of Adventure.* Cambridge, MA: Harvard University Press, 1965.

Kiernan, V. G. *The Lords of Human Kind: Black Man, Yellow Man, and White Man in an Age of Empire.* Boston: Little, Brown and Co., 1969.

Knight, G. Wilson. *Laureate of Peace: On the Genius of Alexander Pope.* London: Routledge and Kegan Paul, 1954.

Kramnick, Isaac. *Republicanism and Bourgeois Radicalism: Political Ideology in Late Eighteenth-Century England and America.* Ithaca, NY: Cornell University Press, 1990.

Kucich, John. *Imperial Masochism: British Fiction, Fantasy, and Social Class.* Princeton, NJ: Princeton University Press, 2007.

Lamont, Claire. Introduction. In *Chronicles of the Canongate,* by Walter Scott. Edited by Claire Lamont. London: Penguin, 2003.

———. "Scott and Eighteenth-Century Imperialism: India and the Scottish Highlands." In *Configuring Romanticism,* Edited by Theo d'haen, Peter Liebragfe, Wim Tigges, 33–50. Amsterdam: Rodopi, 2003.

Landes, David S. *The Wealth and Poverty of Nations.* New York: W. W. Norton, 1998.

Landsman, Ned C. *From Colonials to Provincials: American Thought and Culture, 1680–1760.* Ithaca, NY: Cornell University Press, 1997.

———. "Immigration and Settlement." In *Scotland and the Americas, 1600–1800.* Introduction by Michael Fry, 15–26. Providence, RI: John Carter Brown Library, 1995.

Lanser, Susan Sniader. "Befriending the Body: Female Intimacies as Class Acts." *Eighteenth-Century Studies* 32, no. .2 (Winter 1998–99): 179–99.

———. *Fictions of Authority: Women Writers and Narrative Voice.* Ithaca, NY: Cornell University Press, 1992.

Lauber, John. *Sir Walter Scott.* Boston: Twayne, 1989.

Lawlor, Clark. "War, Peace and Sexual Politics in Alexander Pope's *Windsor-Forest.*" In *Guerres et paix: La Grande-Bretagne au XVIIIe siècle,* edited by Paul-Gabriel Boucé. Paris: Université de la Sorbonne Nouvelle, 1995.

Leask, Nigel. *Curiosity and the Aesthetics of Travel Writing, 1770–1840: "From an Antique Land."* Oxford: Oxford University Press, 2002.

———. *British Romantic Writers and the East: Anxieties of Empire.* Cambridge: Cambridge University Press, 1992.

———. "Scotland's Literature of Empire and Emigration, 1707–1918." In *The Edinburgh History of Scottish Literature,* edited by Susan Manning *et al.* 3 vols. 2:153–62. Edinburgh: Edinburgh University Press, 2007.

———. "Towards an Anglo-Indian poetry? The colonial muse in the writings of John Leyden, Thomas Medwin and Charles D'Oyly." In *Writing India, 1757–1990: The Literature of British India,* edited by Bart Moor-Gilbert, 52–85. Manchester, UK: Manchester University Press, 1996.

Lee, Yoon Sun. *Nationalism and Irony: Burke, Scott, Carlyle.* New York: Oxford University Press, 2004.

Lenman, Bruce P. "Aristocratic 'Country' Whiggery in Scotland and the American Revolution." In *Scotland and America in the Age of Enlightenment,* edited by Richard B. Sher and Jeffrey R. Smitten, 180–92. Edinburgh: Edinburgh University Press, 1990.

———. "Colonial Warfare and Imperial Identity." In *Scotland and the Americas, 1600–1800.* 77–88. Providence, RI: John Carter Brown Library, 1995.

Lewis, Joanne. "Death and the Comic Marriage: Lismahago in Harlequin Skeleton." *Studies in Eighteenth-Century Culture* 18 (1988): 405–17.

Lewis, Robin Jared. "The Literature of the Raj." *Asia and Western Fiction,* Edited by Robin W. Winks and James R. Rush, 53–70. Honolulu: University of Hawaii Press, 1990.

Lillo, George. *The London Merchant.* Edited by William H. McBurney. Lincoln: University of Nebraska Press, 1965.

Lipking, Joanna. "Confusing Matters: Searching the Backgrounds of *Oroonoko*." In *Aphra Behn Studies*, edited by Janet Todd. Cambridge: Cambridge University Press, 1996. 259–81.

———— "'Others,' Slaves, and Colonists in *Oroonoko*." In *The Cambridge Companion to Aphra Behn*, edited by Derek Hughes and Janet Todd, 166–87. Cambridge: Cambridge University Press, 2004.

Loomba, Ania. *Colonialism/Postcolonialism*. London: Routledge, 1998.

Lovejoy, David S. "Virginia's Charter and Bacon's Rebellion, 1675–1676." In *Anglo-American Political Relations, 1675–1775*, edited by Alison Gilbert Olsen and Richard Maxwell Brown, 31–51. New Brunswick, NJ: Rutgers University Press, 1972.

Lovitt, Carl R. 'Defoe's 'Almost Invisible Hand': Narrative Logic as a Structuring Principle in *Moll Flanders*." *Eighteenth-Century Fiction* 6, no. 1 (October 1993): 1–28.

Lowe, Lisa. *Critical Terrains: French and British Orientalisms*. Ithaca, NY: Cornell University Press, 1991.

Lowry, Jean. *A Journal of the Captivity of Jean Lowry and Her Children. The Garland Library of Narratives of North American Indian Captives*. Edited by Wilcomb E. Washburn. 1760. Reprint, New York: Garland Publishing Inc., 1978.

Lund, Roger. "The Eel of Science: Index Learning, Scriblerian Satire, and the Rise of Information Culture." *Eighteenth-Century Life* 22, no. 2 (1998): 18–42.

MacCaffrey, Wallace T. *Elizabeth I*. London: Edward Arnold, 1993.

————. *Elizabeth I: War and Politics, 1588–1603*. Princeton, NJ: Princeton University Press, 1992.

Mack, Maynard. "On Reading Pope." *College English* 22, no. 2 (November 1960): 99–107.

Mackenzie, Henry. *The Man of the World*. 2 vols. New York: Garland Publishing Inc., 1974.

Mahomet, Dean. *The Travels of Dean Mahomet: An Eighteenth-Century Journey through India*. Edited by Michael H. Fisher. Berkeley: University of California Press, 1997.

Malcolm, Elwin. *The Strange Case of Robert Louis Stevenson*. New York: Russell & Russell, 1950.

Malcolm, Sir John. *The Government of India*. London: John Murray, 1833.

Makdisi, Saree. *Romantic Imperialism: Universal Empire and the Culture of Modernity*. Cambridge: Cambridge University Press, 1998.

Malzah, Manfred. "Voices of the Scottish Empire." In *Robert Louis Stevenson, Writer of Boundaries*, edited by Richard Ambrosini and Richard Dury. Madison: University of Wisconsin Press, 2006.

Markley, Robert. *The Far East and the English Imagination, 1660–1730*. Cambridge: Cambridge University Press, 2006.

Marshall, P. J. "'A Free though Conquering People': Britain and Asia in the Eighteenth Century." An Inaugural Lecture in the Rhodes Chair of Imperial History. Delivered at King's College, London. Thursday March 5, 1981.

————. *Problems of Empire: Britain and India, 1757–1813*. London: George Allen and Unwin Ltd., 1968.

McBurney, William H. "Colonel Jacque: Defoe's Definition of the Complete English Gentleman." *Studies in English Literature, 1500–1900* 2, no. 3 (Summer 1962): 321–36.

McCann, Andrew. *Cultural Politics in the 1790s: Literature, Radicalism and the Public Sphere.* Harmondsworth, UK: Macmillan, 1999.

McClintock, Anne. *Imperial Leather: Race, Gender and Sexuality in the Colonial Contest.* New York: Routledge, 1995.

McCusker, John J. "British Mercantilist Policies and the American Colonies." In *Cambridge Economic History of the United States.* 3 vols. Vol. 1, *The Colonial Era.* Edited by Stanley L. Engerman and Robert E. Gallman, 337–62. Cambridge: Cambridge University Press, 1996.

McCusker, John J., and Russell R. Menard. *The Economy of British America, 1607–1789.* Chapel Hill: University of North Carolina Press, 1985.

McInelly, Brett C. "Exile or Opportunity? The Plight of the Transported Felon in Daniel Defoe's *Moll Flanders* and *Colonel Jack.*" *Genre* 22 (2001): 210–17.

McKillop, Alan Dougald. *The Background of Thomson's Seasons.* Hamden, CT: Archon Books, 1961.

McLaren, Martha. *British India and British Scotland, 1780–1830: Career Building, Empire Building, and a Scottish School of Thought on Indian Governance.* Akron, OH: University of Akron Press, 2001.

McLeod, Bruce. *The Geography of Empire in English Literature, 1580–1745.* Cambridge: Cambridge University Press, 1999.

McMaster, Graham. *Scott and Society.* Cambridge: Cambridge University Press, 1981.

McNeil, Kenneth. *Scotland, Britain, Empire: Writing the Highlands, 1760–1860.* Columbus: Ohio State University Press, 2007.

Meinig, D. W. *The Shaping of America: A Geographical Perspective on 500 Years of History.* 2 vols. New Haven, CT: Yale University Press, 1986.

Merrell, James H. " 'The Customes of Our Countrey': Indians and Colonists in Early America." In *Strangers within the Realm: Cultural Margins of the First British Empire,* edited by Bernard Bailyn and Philip D. Morgan, 117–56. Chapel Hill: University of North Carolina Press, 1991.

Mill, James. *The History of British India.* 6 vols. London: Baldwick, Craddock and Joy, 1826.

Miller, Peter N. *Defining the Common Good: Empire, Religion and Philosophy in Eighteenth-Century Britain.* Cambridge: Cambridge University Press, 1994.

Millgate, Jane. Introduction. *Guy Mannering.* Edited by P. D. Garside. London: Penguin, 2003.

———. *Walter Scott: The Making of the Novelist.* Toronto: University of Toronto Press, 1984.

Mills, Carol. "*The Master of Ballantrae:* An Experiment with Genre." In *Robert Louis Stevenson,* edited by Andrew Noble, 118–33. London: Vision Press, 1983.

Moore, John Robert. "Windsor Forest and William III." *Modern Language Notes,* 66, no. 7 (November 1951): 451–54.

More, John. *Strictures, Critical and Sentimental, on Thomson's Seasons; with Hints and Observations on Collateral Subjects.* New York: Garland Publishing Co., 1970. A facsimile of the first edition. London: Richardson and Urquart, 1777.

Morris, David. *Alexander Pope: The Genius of Sense.* Cambridge, MA: Harvard University Press, 1984.

Morris, Thomas. *Journal of Captain Thomas Morris*. Ann Arbor, MI: University Microfilms, Inc., 1966. Reprinted from Captain Thomas Morris, *Miscellanies in Prose and Verse*. London: James Ridgeway, 1791.

Murray, Julie. "Company Rules: Burke, Hastings, and the Specter of the Modern Liberal State." *Eighteenth-Century Studies* 41, no. 1 (2007): 55–69.

Musselwhite, David. "Trial of Warren Hastings." In *Literature, Politics and Theory: Papers from the Essex Conference 1976–84*, edited by Francis Barker, Peter Hulme, Margaret Iversen, and Diana Loxley, 77–103. London: Methuen, 1986.

Nechtman, Tillman W. "A Jewel in the Crown? Indian Wealth in Domestic Britain in the Late Eighteenth Century." *Eighteenth-Century Studies* 41, no. 1 (2007): 71–86.

Netzloff, Mark. "Writing Britain from the Margins: Scottish, Irish, and Welsh Projects for American Colonization." *Prose Studies* 25, no. 2 (August 2002): 1–24.

Nollen, Scott Allen. *Robert Louis Stevenson: Life, Literature and the Silver Screen*. Jefferson, NC: McFarland & Co., 1994.

Nussbaum, Felicity. *The Limits of the Human: Fictions of Anomaly, Race and Gender in the Long Eighteenth Century*. Cambridge: Cambridge University Press, 2003.

———. *Torrid Zones: Maternity, Sexuality, and Empire in Eighteenth-Century English Narratives*. Baltimore: Johns Hopkins University Press, 1995.

———. "Women and Race: 'a different complexion.'" In *Women and Literature in Britain, 1700–1800*, edited by Vivien Jones, 69–88. Cambridge: Cambridge University Press, 2000.

O'Brien, John. "Union Jack: Amnesia and the Law in Daniel Defoe's *Colonel Jack*.'; *Eighteenth-Century Studies* 32, no. 1 (1998): 65–82.

Oldmixon, John. *The First British Empire in America. Containing the History of the Discovery, Settlement, Progress and State of the British Colonies on the Continent and Islands of America*. 2 vols. 1741. Reprint, New York: Augustus M. Kelly, 1969.

Olsen, Thomas Grant. "Reading and Righting in *Moll Flanders*." *SEL* 41, no. 3 (Summer 2001): 467–81.

Owenson, Sydney. *The Wild Irish Girl: A National Tale*. Edited by Kathryn Kirkpatrick. Oxford: Oxford University Press, 1999.

Paulson, Ronald. "The Aesthetics of Georgic Renewal: Pope." In *Critical Essays on Alexander Pope*, edited by Wallace Jackson and R. Paul Yoder, 115–37. New York: G. K. Hall, 1993.

———. "Emulative Consumption and Literacy: The Harlot, Moll Flanders, and Mrs. Slipslop." In *The Consumption of Culture, 1600–1800: Image, Object, Text*, Edited by Ann Bermingham, 383–400. New York: Routledge, 1995.

Pepys, Samuel. *The Diary of Samuel Pepys*. 11 vols. Edited by Robert Latham and William Matthews. Berkeley: University of California Press, 1983.

Perkins, Pamela. "Playfulness of the Pen: Bage and the Politics of Comedy." *Journal of Narrative Technique* 26, no. 1 (Winter 1996): 30–47.

Pollak, Ellen. "*Moll Flanders*, Incest, and the Structure of Exchange." *The Eighteenth Century* 30, no. 1 (1989): 3–21.

Pope, Alexander. *The Poems of Alexander Pope*. Edited by John Butt. London: Methuen, 1963.

Pratt, Mary Louise. *Imperial Eyes: Travel Writing and Transculturation*. London: Routledge, 1992.

Pritchard, Jonathan. "Pope, John Rackett, and the Slave Trade." *SEL* 45, no. 3 (Summer 2005): 579–601.

Punter, David. "Fictional Representation of the Law in the Eighteenth Century." *Eighteenth-Century Fiction* 16, no. 1 (Autumn 1982): 47–74.

Quintero, Ruben. *Literate Culture: Pope's Rhetorical Art*. Newark: University of Delaware Press, 1992.

Radisson, Pierre Esprit. *Voyages of Peter Esprit Radisson, Being an Account of His Travels and Experiences among the North American Indians, from 1652–1684*. Edited by Gideon D. Scull. 1885. Reprint, New York: Burt Franklin, 1967. Rpt of 1885 ed.

Rajan, Balachandra. *Under Western Eyes: India from Milton to Macaulay*. Durham, NC: Duke University Press, 1999.

Raza, Rosemary. *In Their Own Words: British Women Writers and India, 1740–1857*. Oxford: Oxford University Press, 2006.

Reading for Form. Edited by Susan Wolfson and Marshall Brown. Seattle: University of Washington Press, 2006.

Reed, James. *Sir Walter Scott: Landscape and Locality*. London: Athlone Press, 1980.

Reynolds, Nicole. "Phebe Gibbes, Edmund Burke, and the Trials of Empire." *Eighteenth-Century Fiction* 20, no. 2 (Winter 2007–2008): 151–76.

Richards, Eric. "Scotland and the Uses of the Atlantic Empire. *Strangers within the Realm: Cultural Margins of the First British Empire*," edited by Bernard Bailyn and Philip D. Morgan, 67–114. Chapel Hill: University of North Carolina Press, 1991.

Richardson, John. "Alexander Pope's *Windsor Forest*: Its Context and Attitudes toward Slavery." *Eighteenth-Century Studies* 35, no. 1 (2001): 1–17.

Richetti, John. *Defoe's Narratives: Situations and Structures*. Oxford: Clarendon Press, 1975.

———. *The English Novel in History, 1700–1780*. London: Routledge, 1999.

———. "The Family, Sex, and Marriage in Defoe's *Moll Flanders* and *Roxana*." *Studies in the Literary Imagination* 15, no. 2 (1982): 19–35.

Rietz, John. "Criminal Ms-Representation: Moll Flanders and Female Criminal Biography." *Studies in the Novel* 23, no. 2 (Summer 1991): 183–95.

Roach, Joseph. *Cities of the Dead: Circum-Atlantic Performance*. New York: Columbia University Press, 1996.

Robertson, William. *The History of the Reign of the Emperor Charles V*. 1792. Reprint, London: Routledge/Thoemmes Press, 1996.

Rodger, N. A. M. *The Command of the Ocean: A Naval History of Britain, 1649–1815*. New York: W. W. Norton & Co., 2004.

Rogal, Samuel J. "The Profit and Loss of Moll Flanders." *Studies in the Novel* 5 (1973): 98–103.

Rogers, Pat. "John Philips, Pope, and the Political Georgic." *Modern Language Quarterly* 66, no. 4 (December 2005): 411–42.

———. *The Symbolic Design of Windsor-Forest: Iconography, Pageant, and Prophecy in Pope's Early Work*. Newark: University of Delaware Press, 2004.

————. "*Windsor-Forest, Britannia* and River Poetry." *Studies in Philology* 77 (1980): 283–99.

Rogers, Robert. *Ponteach; or the Savages of America. Representative Plays by American Dramatists.* Edited by Montrose J. Moses. New York: E. P. Dutton & Co., 1918.

Romanticism and Colonialism: Writing Empire, 1700–1830. Edited by Tim Fulford and Peter J. Kitson. Cambridge: Cambridge University Press, 1998.

Romanticism, Race, and Imperial Culture, 1780–1834. Edited by Alan Richardson and Sonja Hofkosh. Bloomington: Indiana University Press, 1996.

Rosenthal, Laura J. "*Oroonoko:* Reception, Ideology, Narrative Strategy." In *The Cambridge Companion to Aphra Behn,* edited by Derek Hughes and Janet Todd, 151–65. Cambridge: Cambridge University Press, 2004.

Rowlandson, Mary. *The Sovereignty and Goodness of God. Together with the Faithfulness of His Promises Displayed. Being a Narrative of the Captivity and Restoration of Mrs. Mary Rowlandson, and Related Documents.* Edited by Neal Salisbury. Boston: Bedford/St. Martin's, 1997.

Rozbicki, Michael J. "The Curse of Provincialism: Negative Perceptions of Colonial American Plantation Gentry." *Journal of Southern History* 63, no. 4 (November 1997): 727–52.

Russell, Conrad. "John Bull's Other Nations: The English Belief that They Are the Only Ones Here." *TLS* (March 12, 1993).

Said, Edward. *Culture and Imperialism.* New York: Vintage Books, 1994.

————. *Orientalism.* New York: Vintage Books, 1979.

Sambrook, James. *James Thomson, 1700–1748: A Life.* Oxford: Clarendon Press, 1991.

Sandison, Alan. *Robert Louis Stevenson and the Appearance of Modernism: A Future Feeling.* Houndmills, UK: Macmillan Press Ltd, 1996.

Sayre, Gordon. *Les Sauvages Américains: Representations of Native Americans in French and English Colonial Literature.* Chapel Hill: University of North Carolina Press, 1997.

Scanlan, Thomas. *Colonial Writing and the New World, 1583–1671: Allegories of Desire.* Cambridge: Cambridge University Press, 1999.

Scheuerman, Mona. *Social Protest in the Eighteenth-Century English Novel.* Columbus: Ohio State University Press, 1985.

Schwab, Raymond. *The Oriental Renaissance: Europe's Rediscovery of India and the East, 1680–1880.* Trans. Gene Patterson-Black and Victor Reinking. Foreward by Edward Said. New York: Columbia University Press, 1984.

Scott, Walter. *Chronicles of the Canongate.* Edited by Claire Lamont. Edinburgh: Edinburgh University Press, 2000.

————. *Guy Mannering.* Edited by P. D. Garside. Edinburgh: Edinburgh University Press, 2007.

————. *The Heart of Midlothian.* Edited by David Hewitt and Alison Lumsden. Edinburgh: Edinburgh University Press, 2004.

————. *Waverley.* Edited by Peter Garside. Edinburgh: Edinburgh University Press, 2007.

Seeley, J. R. *The Expansion of England: Two Courses of Lectures.* London: Macmillan, 1931.

Shaw, Harry E. *The Forms of Historical Fiction: Sir Walter Scott and His Successors.* Ithaca, NY: Cornell University Press, 1983.

Shinagel, Michael. *Daniel Defoe and Middle-Class Gentility.* Cambridge, NY: Harvard University Press, 1968.

Shmitz, Robert M. *Pope's Windsor Forest, 1712: A Study of the Washington University Holograph.* Washington University Studies, Language and Literature, n.s., no. 21. Saint Louis, MO: Washington University, 1952.

Simmons, Diane. *The Narcissism of Empire: Loss, Rage and Revenge in Thomas de Quincey, Robert Louis Stevenson, Arthur Conan Doyle, Rudyard Kipling and Isak Dinesen.* Brighton, UK: Sussex Academic Press, 2007.

Simpson, David. *Romanticism, Nationalism, and the Revolt against Theory.* Chicago: University of Chicago Press, 1993.

Simpson, Kenneth. *The Protean Scot: The Crisis of Identity in Eighteenth-Century Scottish Literature.* Aberdeen: Aberdeen University Press, 1988.

Singh, Briraj. "*Windsor Forest* as a Modern and Postmodern Poem." *Historical Reflections/ Réflexions Historiques* 18, no. 3 (1992): 29–44.

Slotkin, Richard. *Regeneration through Violence: The Mythology of the American Frontier, 1600–1860.* Norman: University of Oklahoma Press, 1973.

Smith, Abbot Emerson. *Colonists in Bondage: White Servitude and Convict Labor in America, 1607–1776.* Chapel Hill: University of North Carolina Press, 1947.

Smith, George. *The Life of William Carey, D.D.: Shoemaker and Missionary, Professor of Sanskrit, Bengali, and Marathi in the college of Fort William, Calcutta.* London: John Murray, 1885.

Smollett, Tobias. *The Adventures of Roderick Random.* Edited by Paul-Gabriel Boucé. Oxford: Oxford University Press, 1981.

———. *Continuation of the Complete History of England.* 4 vols. London: Richard Baldwin, 1763.

———. *The Expedition of Humphry Clinter.* Edited by Angus Ross. London: Penguin, 1967.

———. *The Letters of Tobias Smollett.* Edited by Lewis M. Knapp. Oxford: Clarendon Press, 1970.

Spacks, Patricia Meyer. *The Varied God: A Critical Study of Thomson's The Seasons.* Berkeley: University of California Press, 1959.

Spear, Percival. *The Nabobs: A Study of the Social Life of the English in Eighteenth-Century India.* Gloucester, MA: Peter Smith, 1971.

Spivak, Gayatri Chakravorti. *In Other Worlds: Essays in Cultural Politics.* London: Routledge, 1987.

Steele, Ian K. *The English Atlantic, 1675–1740: An Exploration of Communication and Community.* New York: Oxford University Press, 1986.

Stevenson, Robert Louis. *The Letters of Robert Louis Stevenson.* 8 vols. Edited by Bradford A. Booth and Ernest Mehew. New Haven, CT: Yale University Press, 1995.

———. *The Master of Ballantrae, a Winter's Tale.* Edited by Adrian Poole. London: Penguin, 1996.

Stormer, Philip Ronald. "Holding 'High Commerce with the Mighty Dead': Morality and Politics in James Thomson's *Winter.*" *English Language Notes* 29 (March 1992): 27–40.

Strange, Sallie Minter. "Moll Flanders: A Good Calvinist." *South Central Bulletin* 36 (Winter 1976): 152–54.

Suarez, Michael F. "The Shortest Way to Heaven? Moll Flanders' Repentance Reconsidered." In *1650–1850: Ideas, Aesthetics, and Inquiries in the Early Modern Era*, edited by Kevin Cope, 3–28. New York: AMS Press, 1997.

Sudan, Rajani. *Fair Exotics: Xenophobic Subjects in English Literature, 1720–1850*. Philadelphia: University of Pennsylvania Press, 2002.

Suleri, Sara. *The Rhetoric of English India*. Chicago: University of Chicago Press, 1992.

Sussman, Charlotte. "Lismahago's Captivity: Transculturation in *Humphry Clinker*," *ELH* 61, no. 3 (1994): 597–618.

Swan, Beth. "Moll Flanders: The Felon as Lawyer." *Eighteenth-Century Fiction* 11, no. 1 (October 1998): 33–48.

Swift, Jonathan. *Journal to Stella*. 2 vols. Edited by Harold Williams. Oxford: Clarendon Press, 1948.

———. *The Writings of Jonathan Swift*. Edited by Robert A. Greenberg and William Bowman Piper. New York: W. W. Norton, 1973.

Taylor, Alan. *American Colonies*. Harmondsworth, UK: Penguin, 2001.

Teltscher, Kate. *India Inscribed: European and British Writing on India, 1600–1800*. Delhi: Oxford University Press, 1995.

Thackeray, William Makepeace. *The History of Henry Esmond*. Edited by John Sutherland and Michael Greenfield. Harmondsworth, UK: Penguin, 1970.

———. *Vanity Fair: A Novel without a Hero*. Edited by Geoffrey and Kathleen Tillotson. Boston: Houghton Mifflin, 1963.

Thelwall, John. *The Politics of English Jacobinism: Writings of John Thelwall*. Edited by Gregory Claeys. University Park: Pennsylvania State University Press, 1995.

Thomson, James. *The Seasons and The Castle of Indolence*. Edited by James Sambrook. Oxford: Clarendon Press, 1972.

Tidrick, Kathryn. *Empire and the English Character*. London: I. B. Tauris & Co. Ltd, 1990.

Tobin, Beth Fowkes. *Colonizing Nature: The Tropics in British Arts and Letters, 1760–1820*. Philadelphia: University of Pennsylvania Press, 2005.

Todorov, Tzvetan. *The Conquest of America: The Question of the Other*. Translated by Richard Howard. Norman: University of Oklahoma Press, 1999.

Tomlinson, Janis A. "Landscape into Allegory: J. M. W. Turner's *Frosty Morning* and James Thomson's *The Seasons*." *Studies in Romanticism* 29, no. 2 (Summer 1990): 181–96.

Trollope, Fanny. *Domestic Manners of the Americans*. Edited by Pamela Neville-Sington. London: Penguin, 1997.

Trumpener, Katie. *Bardic Nationalism: The Romantic Novel and the British Empire*. Princeton, NJ: Princeton University Press, 1997.

Tytler, Alexander Fraser. *Considerations on the Political State of India*. 2 vols. London: Perry and Co., 1815.

VanDerBeers, Richard. *Held Captive by Indians: Selected Narratives, 1642–1836*. Knoxville: University of Tennessee Press, 1994.

Viswanathan, Gauri. *Masks of Conquest: Literary Study and British Rule in India*. New York: Columbia University Press, 1989.

Wallace, Tara Ghoshal. "Walter Scott and Feminine Discourse: The Case of *St. Ronan's Well.*" *The Journal of Narrative Technique* 19, no. 2 (Spring 1989): 233–47.

Warner, Michael. "What's Colonial about Colonial America?" In *Possible Pasts: Becoming Colonial in Early America,* edited by Robert Blair St. George, 49–70. Ithaca: Cornell University Press, 2000.

Warner, Oliver. *The British Navy: A Concise History.* Thames and Hudson, 1975.

Wasserman, Earl R. *The Subtler Language: Critical Readings of Neoclassic and Romantic Poems.* Baltimore: Johns Hopkins Press, 1959.

Weed, David M. "Sentimentalism, Misogyny and Medicine in *Humphry Clinker.*" *SEL* 37, no. 3 (Summer 1997): 615–36.

Weinbrot, Howard D. *Britannia's Issue: The Rise of British Literature from Dryden to Ossian.* Cambridge: Cambridge University Press, 1993.

White, Richard. *The Middle Ground: Indians, Empires, and Republics in the Great Lakes Region, 1650–1815.* Cambridge: Cambridge University Press, 1991.

Williams, David Alan. "Anglo-American Virginia Politics, 1690–1735." In *Anglo-American Political Relations, 1675–1775,* edited by Alison Gilbert Olson and Richard Maxwell Brown. New Brunswick, NJ: Rutgers University Press, 1970.

Williamson, Peter. *French and Indian Cruelty: Exemplified in the Life and Various Vicissitudes of Fortune of Peter Williamson.* Introduction by Michael Fry. 1762. Reprint, Briston, UK: Thoemmes Press, 1996.

Wilson, Kathleen. "Empire, Trade and Popular Politics in Mid-Hanoverian Britain: The Case of Admiral Vernon." *Past and Present* 121 (November 1988): 74–109.

Wilson, Kathleen. *The Sense of the People: Politics, Culture and Imperialism in England, 1715–1785.* Cambridge: Cambridge University Press, 1998.

Winks, Robin W. Introduction. *British Imperialism: Gold, God, and Glory.* Edited by Robin W. Winks. New York: Holt, Rinehart and Winston, 1963.

Wollstonecraft, Mary. *A Vindication of the Rights of Men.* Amherst, NY: Prometheus Books, 1996.

———. *A Vindication of the Rights of Woman.* Edited by Carol H. Poston. New York: W. W. Norton, 1988.

———. *Collected Letters of Mary Wollstonecraft.* Edited by Ralph M. Wardle. Ithaca, NY: Cornell University Press, 1979.

———. *Letters Written during a Short Residence in Sweden, Norway, and Denmark.* Edited by Carol H. Poston. Lincoln: University of Nebraska Press, 1976.

———. *Maria, or The Wrongs of Woman.* Introduction by Moira Ferguson. New York: W. W. Norton Co., 1975.

Yahav-Brown, Amit. "At Home in England, or Projecting Liberal Citizenship in *Moll Flanders.*" *Novel* 35, no. 1 (Fall 2001): 24–45.

Young, Arthur. *The Adventures of Emmera, or The Fair American. Exemplifying the Peculiar Advantages of Society and Retirement.* 2 vols. 1773. Reprint, New York: Garland Publishing Inc., 1974.

Young, Robert J. C. *Colonial Desire: Hybridity in Theory, Culture, and Race.* London: Routledge, 1995.

Youngkin, Molly. "'Into the woof, a little Thibet wool': Orientalism and representing 'reality' in Walter Scott's *The Surgeon's Daughter.*' *Scottish Studies Review* 3, no. 1 (Spring 2002): 33–57.

Zomchick, John P. "Social Class, Character, and Narrative Strategy in *Humphry Clinker.*" *Eighteenth-Century Life* 10, no. 3 (October 1986): 172–85.

Zuckerman, Michael. "Identity in British America: Unease in Eden." In *Colonial Identity in the Atlantic World, 1500–1800,* edited by Nicholas Canny and Anthony Pagden, 13–42. Princeton: Princeton University Press, 1987.

Index